A FOREIGN POLICY OF FREEDOM

'PEACE, COMMERCE, AND HONEST FRIENDSHIP'

RON PAUL

Foundation for Rational Economics and Education Inc.

Paul, Ron, 1935——
        A foreign policy of freedom.

ISBN-13: 978-0-912453-00-2
ISBN-10: 0-912453-00-1

Cover Design: Kathy White, The Mises Institute
Typesetting: M&M Graphics and Advertising

Printed in the United States of America.

FREE
P.O. Box 1776
Lake Jackson, Texas 77566
www.FREE-NEFL.com

CONTENTS

FOREWORD

by Llewellyn H. Rockwell, Jr.

Ron Paul has always believed that foreign and domestic policy should be conducted according to the same principles. Government should be restrained from intervening at home or abroad because its actions fail to achieve their stated aims, create more harm than good, shrink the liberty of the people, and violate rights.

Does that proposition seem radical? Outlandish or farflung? Once you hear it stated, it makes perfect sense that there is no sharp distinction between the principles of domestic and foreign policy. They are part of the same analytical fabric. What would be inconsistent would be to favor activist government at home but restraint abroad, or the reverse: restraint at home and activism abroad. Government unleashed behaves in its own interests, and will not restrict itself in any area of life. It must be curbed in all areas of life lest freedom suffer.

If you recognize the line of thinking in this set of beliefs, it might be because you have read the Federalist Papers, the writings of Thomas Jefferson or George Washington or James Madison, or examined the philosophical origins of the American Revolution. Or you might have followed the debates that took place in the presidential election of 1800, in which this view emerged triumphant. Or perhaps you read the writings of the free traders prior to the Civil War, or the opponents of the War on Spain, or those who warned of entering World War I.

Or perhaps you have read the speeches and books against FDR's New Deal: the same group warned of the devastating consequences of World War II. Or maybe, in more recent history, you understood the

i

animating principles behind the Republican takeover of Congress in 1994: a generation had turned away from all forms of foreign and domestic "nation building."

Not only does this Paulian view have a precedent in American history; it sums up the very core of what is distinctive about the American contribution to political ideas. The proposition was and is that people are better able to manage their lives than government can manage them. Under conditions of liberty, the result is prosperity and orderly civilization. Under government control, the result is relative poverty and unpredictable chaos. The proof is in the news every day.

How unusual, how incredibly strange, that Ron Paul, who has stood for these principles his entire public life, is criticized by some as a radical, outside the mainstream, and influenced by experimental ideas that are marginal at best. And why is he treated this way? Because he takes the ideas of Washington and Jefferson seriously, just as seriously as he takes the idea of freedom itself, and he does so in times when faith in Leviathan remains the dominant political ideology.

Ideology is such a powerful force that it has propped up policy inconsistency for more than a century. The left has a massive agenda for the state at home, and yet complains bitterly, with shock and dismay, that the same tools are used to start wars and build imperial structures abroad. The right claims to want to restrain government at home (at least in some ways) while whooping it up for war and global reconstruction abroad.

It doesn't take a game-theory genius to predict how this conflict works itself out in the long run. The left and the right agree to disagree on intellectual grounds but otherwise engage in a dangerous quid pro quo. They turn a blind eye to the government they don't like so long as they get the government they do like.

It's one thing for the left to grudgingly support international intervention. It makes some sense for a group that believes that government is omniscient enough to bring about fairness, justice, and equality at home to do the same for people abroad. In fact, I've never been able to make much sense out of left-wing antiwar activism, simply because it cuts so much against the idea of socialism, which itself can be summed up as perpetual war on the liberty and property of the people.

What strikes me as ridiculous is the right-wing view that government is incompetent and dangerous domestically—at least in economic and social affairs—but has some sort of Midas Touch internationally such that it can bring freedom, democracy, and justice to any land its troops deign to invade. Not that the right wing is principled enough to pursue its domestic views, but I'm speaking here of its campaign rhetoric and higher-level critique of government that you find in their periodicals and books. The precise critique of government that they offer for the welfare state and regulatory measures—they are expensive, counterproductive, hobble human energies—applies many times over to international interventions.

But the right always seems to have an excuse for its inconsistency. In the early fifties, many on the right said that the usual principle of nonintervention had to give way to the fight against communism because this was a uniquely evil threat facing the world. We have to put up with a "totalitarian bureaucracy" within our shores (words used by W.F. Buckley) for the duration in order to beat back the great threat abroad. And so Leviathan grew and grew, and never more than under Republican presidents. Then one day, communism went away, the regimes having collapsed from self-imposed deprivation and ideological change.

A few years went by after 1990 when the right was inching toward a Paulian consistency. Then 9/11 happened, and the great excuse for Leviathan again entered the picture. Never mind that, as Congressman Paul pointed out, the crime of 9/11 was motivated by retribution against ten years of killer U.S. sanctions against Iraq, U.S. troops on Muslim holy lands, and U.S. subsidies for Palestinian occupation. No, the American right bought into the same farce that led them to support the Cold War: Islamic fanaticism is a unique evil unlike anything we've ever seen, so we have to put up with Leviathan (again!) for the duration.

Well, Ron Paul didn't buy into it. He is unique in this respect, and this is especially notable since he has been under pressure from his own party and at a time when his party has ruled the executive, judicial, and legislative branches. He stuck by his principles, and not merely as a pious gesture. His critique of the post 9/11 warfare state has been spot on in speech after speech. He foresaw the failure of the U.S. invasion of Afghanistan. He never believed the nonsense about how U.S. bombs would transform Iraq into a modern democracy. He never went along with the propaganda lies about weapons of mass destruction. Nowadays, we often hear politicians say that they have changed their minds on the Iraq War and that if they had known then what they know now, they never would have gone along. Well, hindsight is child's play in politics. What takes guts and insight is the ability to spot a hoax even as it is being perpetrated. In any case, they have no excuse for not knowing: Ron Paul told them!

The freedom to trade internationally is an essential principle. It means that consumers should not be penalized for buying from anyone, or selling to anyone, regardless of the residence. Nor should domestic suppliers be granted anything like a monopoly or subsidized treatment. Nor should trade be used as a weapon in the form of sanctions. Ron Paul has upheld these principles as well, which makes him an old-fashioned liberal in the manner of Cobden and Bright and the American Southern tradition. He has also rejected the mistake of many free traders who believe that a military arm is necessary to back the invisible hand of the marketplace. For Ron Paul, freedom is all of a piece.

Ron Paul's singular voice on foreign affairs has done so much to keep the flame of a consistent liberty burning in times when it might otherwise have been extinguished. He has drawn public attention to the ideas of the Founders. He has alerted people to the dangers of empire. He has linked domestic and foreign affairs through libertarian analytics, even when others have been bamboozled by the lies or too intimidated to contradict them. He has told the truth, always. For this, every American, every citizen of the world, is deeply in his debt. In fact, I'm willing to predict that a hundred years from now and more, when all the current office holders are all but forgotten, Ron Paul's name will be remembered as a bright light in dark times.

We can't but be deeply grateful that Ron Paul's prophetic words have been collected in this book. May it be widely distributed. May its lessons be absorbed by this and future generations. May this treatise stand as an example of how to fight for what is right even when everyone else is silent. May it always be regarded as proof that there were men of courage alive in the first decade of the third millennium. May public and intellectual opinion someday rise to its level of intellectual sophistication and moral valor.

INTRODUCTION

A Personal Note

My involvement in politics came about due to an earlier interest in economics, which began in the 1960s after reading Friedrich Hayek's classic, *The Road to Serfdom*. This led me to study Austrian economics, especially the writings of Ludwig von Mises, which provided the best explanation of how central banking and government intervention in the market economy cause so much suffering. The Austrians explained, with great clarity, how inflation and the business cycle undermine the middle class and injure the poor. Armed with this knowledge, I became convinced that America was on the wrong track. The breakdown of the Bretton Woods pseudo-gold standard in August 1971 only confirmed the predictions of the Austrian economists. Alarmed, I made the decision to run for Congress in 1974—although I entertained little hope of winning. I felt it important to express myself concerning economic issues, particularly monetary policy.

Although I lost that race, by chance it positioned me to win a special election one year later. During four terms in Congress between 1976 and 1984, I served on the Banking committee and spent a lot of time dealing with monetary issues. During the early 1980s I served on the Gold Commission. This was the era of stagflation, and there was serious concern and confusion among politicians and economists regarding our economic future.

My overriding concern was the protection of individual liberty, private property, and free markets. Although I focused primarily on economic policy during this first tour in Congress, as time passed it became clear to me that economic policy (especially deficit financing) and monetary policy were closely interrelated with foreign policy and war. Today, I'm equally concerned with both our flawed foreign policy and our bad economic policies.

During the Reagan years I began to realize how special interests, with bipartisan support, drive our policy of foreign intervention. We sent troops to Lebanon and Granada; financial aid to Nicaragua; weapons to Iran and Iraq; military assistance to Osama bin Laden and Saddam Hussein; and bombed Libya—all for reasons other than American national security. These events motivated me to speak out more frequently on foreign affairs, and vote (often by myself) to make that point that we should follow the Constitution and the Founding Fathers by staying out of the affairs of foreign nations—especially when our meddling has nothing to do with national security interests.

It's obvious that foreign intervention cannot be separated from economic concerns about deficits, inflation, and taxes. Currently we see a trend toward world government, globalism, managed trade, and an institutionalized world financial system based on purely fiat money. This system is controlled by the industrial-banking-political elite.

This move toward political globalization, in contrast to free markets, free trade and commodity money, has ushered in an era that challenges national sovereignty and traditional borders.

The New World Order, under the banner of free trade, permits sanctions, tariffs, and privileges for politically connected special interests. Needless to say, I see great danger in this trend—danger to liberty, sovereignty, prosperity, and peace.

This book is a collection of statements I have made over the past 30 years dealing with foreign policy from the date I was first elected to Congress in 1976. Though I wrote and spoke less about foreign policy during my 12-year hiatus from Congress (1985-1997), I remained interested and continued to study carefully the case for noninterventionism. I did however, make public statements in opposition to the Persian Gulf War in 1991, and I consider today's war in Iraq a continuation of that conflict.

In various places throughout the book I have inserted current thoughts and insights into my reprinted speeches and articles.

"The means of defense against foreign danger historically have become the instruments of tyranny at home." —James Madison

CHAPTER 1

Upon the death of the Chinese dictator, I made this statement, which may be more hawkish than I would be today, but we certainly have moral authority to state our position without violating the independence of others.

September 15, 1976
THE DEATH OF MAO TSE-TUNG
HON. RON PAUL of TEXAS
IN THE HOUSE OF REPRESENTATIVES

Mr. Speaker, for many years now there has been virtual censorship in America about the true facts regarding oppression in Communist China. We are seeing this once again in the press coverage of the death of Mao Tse-tung. He is portrayed as a great leader and a shrewd politician—which indeed he was—but this completely overlooks the monstrous tyranny he exercised over the Chinese people.

There is no doubt that China is a very different place today than it was in 1949, but to equate change with progress would be a serious error. We simply cannot judge Mao Tse-tung outside a moral context. We cannot praise him for bringing industrial development to China while ignoring the millions of Chinese who were put to death for opposing communism and

1

the millions more who live, but in abject slavery.

It is true that Chinese values are different from those in America and the West, but it is foolish to believe that the Chinese people do not have the same yearning for freedom that we have. This fact is confirmed by the untold thousands who have risked their lives to escape Communist totalitarianism for the liberty of Hong Kong.

We are asked to be "realists" and overlook such unpleasantries because we need the support of Communist China as a balance to the growing military power of the Soviet Union. This is a foolish and shortsighted policy that simply repeats America's past error of treating all of our enemies' enemies as our friends. This policy has probably done more to destroy our credibility as a champion of freedom in the world than any other thing.

Americans pride themselves for having broken with the balance-of-power politics of Europe and establishing a foreign policy that not only upholds American interests, but is moral as well. This is a tradition which is as old as the country itself and which survives today, in spite of Henry Kissinger's efforts to destroy it.

It is unfortunate that our foreign policy has been so mismanaged that the American people now seem to equate a moral foreign policy with an interventionist foreign policy. The two are not at all synonymous. A condemnation of Communist tyranny ought not to imply the threat of U.S. intervention. Nor should it imply support for every petty dictatorship in the world that pays lip service to anticommunism.

America must remain forthright in a universal opposition to tyranny. This is why we must recognize Mao Tse-tung for what he was: perhaps the most oppressive dictator who ever lived. We should not be afraid to say so and we should make it clear to his successor that so long as the Chinese people remain slaves, they can expect no support from the United States. ■

"I hope our wisdom will grow with our power, and teach us that the less we use our power the greater it will be."—Thomas Jefferson

CHAPTER 2

The ongoing crackdown in Poland, and our funding of the oppressors, is yet again the focus here.

August 22, 1980
WORKERS OF THE WORLD, UNITE
HON. RON PAUL of TEXAS
IN THE HOUSE OF REPRESENTATIVES

Mr. Speaker, the striking factory and dock workers—whose leaders have now been arrested by the Communist regime in Poland—must be admired for their courage in defying the dictators who control their country. I am sure the sympathy of the American people is with the brave workers who are protesting the injustice and lack of freedom that have existed for 35 years in this so-called "workers' paradise."

But what about the federal government? While the sympathies of the American people are with the oppressed Polish workers, the sympathies of the federal government seem to be with the brutal masters of Poland. The American people sympathize with the Polish people, and the American government with the Polish government.

For example, **from the end of World War II until 1978, the federal government loaned and gave theCommunist regime in Poland $677**

3

million. In 1979, our federal government granted the Communist regime in Poland an additional $500 million in loans and loan guarantees. A recent study published in the Journal of Social and Political Studies pointed out: "The availability of these Western credits is probably relieving the Soviet Union from the expensive task of propping up the Polish economy."

Poland is, in fact, deeply in debt to Western countries, for the West, including the United States, has been propping up the Polish economy for decades. Poland's current debt is estimated at $20 billion. It has not yet repaid even its World War I debts to this country, and the present Communist government has no intention of doing so. **Why does our government continue to subsidize the Communists in Poland? Whose side is our government on, the Polish Communists or the Polish workers?**

I believe that we should have a consistent foreign policy of nonintervention in the affairs of other countries. We should certainly not be subsidizing a dictatorial regime that is not supported by its own people. It is outrageous that taxes paid by the American people—people who sympathize with the Polish workers, not the Communist government—have been and are being used to prop up that government. I have introduced legislation that would end such foreign subsidies, H.R. 3408, and I intend to push for its passage through Congress. Our irrational policy of subsidizing those who hate freedom must be stopped.

The turmoil in Poland dramatizes so well the wasted, worn-out slogans of the Communist state. The paradise promised to the worker has never materialized, and the source of discontent with the oppressive state is, as one would expect, expressed by the workers themselves. Neither our government nor our businessmen have expressed real sympathy for the protests and the support coming from our workers here in the United States. In contrast to what has been so long predicted—the revolt of the workers against a brutal capitalism—we see the opposite: The Polish workers demanding liberty and receiving support from working people throughout the world. All I can say is: "Workers of the world, unite; you have nothing to lose but your chains." ■

"We must guard against the acquisition of unwarranted influence, whether sought or unsought, by the military-industrial complex."
—Dwight D. Eisenhower

CHAPTER 3

The stage is often set for foreign intervention in so-called "non-binding" resolutions. Here the United States is making a dangerous commitment to Lebanon.

June 17, 1981
LEBANON: ANOTHER COMMITMENT?
HON. RON PAUL of TEXAS
IN THE HOUSE OF REPRESENTATIVES

Mr. Speaker, House Resolution 159 was passed almost unanimously yesterday, and it should have been.

Some parts of the resolution urge peace in the Middle East and praise the character of Philip Habib. I, of course, have no problem with these.

But toward the end of the resolution are some words that require a full debate, not a quick sense-of-Congress resolution brought up under unanimous consent, all too reminiscent of previous resolutions that have meant trouble.

House Resolution 159 states:

Resolved, That the House of Representatives strongly supports diplomatic efforts to resolve the current crisis in Lebanon,

5

and encourages the president to pursue, a comprehensive and coordinated policy in Lebanon, including the development of an effective cease-fire, resolution of the issue of Syrian missiles, and promotion of the independence, sovereignty, unity, and territorial integrity of Lebanon.

Since when have the people of the United States become the guarantor of Lebanon? Such a promise could require the use of troops, as well as billions of tax dollars.

Are we to solve the issue of Syrian missiles by force? Or use our troops to patrol a cease-fire?

This overbroad resolution, sponsored by the leadership of the Foreign Affairs Committee, has within it the seeds of possible trouble for the United States. Congress should not have considered it in such a fashion, with Members hardly even having time to read it.

We need less meddling in the internal affairs of other nations, not more.

But this resolution could be used to justify who-knows-what use of dollars and lives in a future conflict or peacekeeping operation.

House Resolution 159 is a bad resolution, brought up without sufficient time to study its implications. It is not in our country's interests. It should not have been passed. ■

October 14, 1981
HON. RON PAUL of TEXAS
IN THE HOUSE OF REPRESENTATIVES

Mr. Chairman, I am in opposition to the sale of the AWACS airplanes to Saudi Arabia. I happen to think that this particular sale is probably one of the least objectionable sales that we have had, because so often we give our weapons away and that is very, very expensive. So in comparison, I think this is certainly less objectionable.

But what I complain about and what I object to, and I think many Americans agree, it that I think it is time that we ought to quit being the supplier of weapons for everybody in the world. We are also not only providing AWACS for Saudi Arabia today, we are providing 1,177 Sidewinder missiles for the planes that Saudi Arabia has already purchased from us. I believe that it is very possible that those missiles will be used against American-built airplanes already in some other country, just as I believe there is a very great potential that the AWACS airplanes will be shot down in this decade by American-built airplanes. It is for this reason

6

that I object, and I believe that it should be a consistent policy for the security of this country that we provide security for this country and not try to be the policeman of the world, providing weapons for everybody.

For instance, in these last several decades, we helped build the trucks that the Russians used to invade Afghanistan. And our Corps of Engineers built the highway in Afghanistan that they marched in on. We give weapons to Greece, we give weapons to Turkey, and then they get together and fight. Now we are proposing we give weapons to Pakistan, yet we give aid to India. They are likely to end up in battle, since they are sworn enemies.

So I would say it is time that we looked at the policy in general of whether or not we are to be the supplier of weapons and the protector and the policeman of the world. Some suggest that the main reason is to protect the supplies of oil. Yet when you look at the statistics, we find out that only 5 percent of all our total energy needs come through the Straits of Hormuz. Even though Japan depends 100 percent on imports, and Europe nearly that much, their responsibility in securing the Mid-East is negligible. Why is it that the American taxpayer and the American soldier must assume this great burden and assume this great risk? The continuation of a policy of intervention throughout the world will one day, once again, drag America into another unnecessary war.

Mr. Chairman, while I find a sale of this nature more agreeable than an outright gift to the Saudi Arabian government, I think it is important to point out that this is not a clean sale. For example, the administration reports that the AWACS will be manned and operated by American servicemen. That means that there will be further and permanent American involvement in the Middle East. Some have sought to reassure Members of Congress by saying that the AWACS would remain under American control. I find this far from reassuring. Rather, it would more likely lead to an escalation of American involvement in any altercation in the Middle East. By permanently putting American soldiers there, we are making a commitment, whether explicit or not, that we may soon regret. So while this is a sale and not an outright gift, it is not a clean sale. That is my first reason for supporting this resolution of disapproval.

Second, there is the very real danger of this sophisticated technology falling into the hands of the enemy in the Middle East. Everyone knows what a volatile situation exists there, especially following the recent assassination of President Sadat of Egypt. We supplied the Shah of Iran with the latest in our weapons in order to shore up his government, but it

7

fell anyway, and those sophisticated weapons and radar installations were possessed by the Khomeini and, if reports are true, shared with some Socialist and Communist governments. Dare we risk the same thing with the AWACS? The Soviet Union has nothing comparable. Are we not making a fundamental mistake in thinking that it is weapons that shore up a government? Did we not learn from the example in Iran that it is not weapons but ideas?

Again, Mr. Chairman, **I believe that the American people are sick and tired of supplying, either deliberately or through accident, both sides in the conflicts since World War II.** We saw this happen in Vietnam. We were shipping both wheat and weapons to the Soviet Union, who, in turn, shipped them to North Vietnam, at the same time that we were shipping wheat and weapons to South Vietnam. We have seen this happen in the border wars between India and Pakistan. We have seen it happen in the wars between Israel and her neighbors. Are we about to see it happen again in the Middle East?

Of course, the reason given for this policy is that we must maintain a balance of power. But cannot that be done at a much lower level of power by not supplying either side with the sinews of war, rather than both sides? Cannot power be balanced at a much lower level—and without U.S. involvement—simply by our staying of the situation?

How much of a commitment are we making in this sale? Are we going to be building airbases for the AWACS? I believe that we will be maintaining them and furnishing replacement parts. How far does this commitment stretch into the future? Are we offering a 90-day warranty or a 90-year warranty?

For all these reasons, I believe that it is in the best interest of the American people to disapprove this sale of advanced technology and weapons to the Saudi government. I urge my colleagues to do so. ■

"Commerce wth all nations, alliances with none, should be our motto."—Thomas Jefferson

CHAPTER 4

Mutual defense pacts are a tricky business and can be very dangerous. When Britain and Argentina faced off, we actually had defense commitments with both sides.

April 27, 1982
THE FALKLAND CRISIS: NOT OUR BUSINESS
HON. RON PAUL of TEXAS
IN THE HOUSE OF REPRESENTATIVES

Mr. Speaker, in the Falkland Islands, America's foreign policy has once again gotten tangled in its own conflicting commitments. The NATO alliance commits us to the defense of Great Britain, and the Rio Treaty commits us to defending Argentina. These treaty commitments demonstrate so clearly how entangling alliances work to the detriment of the people of the United States. Fulfilling treaty obligations becomes impossible and the prime responsibility of defending our people becomes secondary to foreign involvements.

Thanks to NATO, we spend well over $100 billion per year subsidizing the defenses of wealthy Europeans. Our relations with Argentina have been more restrained, but we have still managed to help them finance the purchase of $200 million in military hardware over the last 30 years. The

9

Argentine submarine disabled off South Georgia is American, and their only aircraft carrier is also American.

I have spoken to the people in my district. They say: "Stay out of this conflict, it's none of our business." But there are those in the State Department who have suggested setting up a Sinai-type U.S. peacekeeping force. This would be sheer folly! Putting American boys between two warring factions, both using our weapons, is a sure-fire way of getting some of them killed, and of guaranteeing an ongoing, costly foreign commitment.

It is time we scrapped the foreign policy of treaties and interventionism, and began concentrating on the sorry state of our own defenses.

Our foreign policy should be that of nonintervention and armed neutrality. Grover Cleveland understood this when he said:

> *It is the policy of peace suitable to our interests. It is the policy of neutrality, rejecting any share in foreign brawls and ambitions on other continents, and repelling their intrusion here. It is the policy of Monroe and of Washington and Jefferson: Peace, commerce, and honest friendship with all nations; entangling alliances with none.* ■

To this day, NATO is a reminder that entangling alliances take on their own lives. With the Soviets now long gone, we still "protect" Europe. This stands as an example that "short term" troop commitments often become blank checks, with the tab paid by American taxpayers. The next two pieces consider this fact.

June 9, 1982
NATO RESOLUTION
HON. RON PAUL of TEXAS
IN THE HOUSE OF REPRESENTATIVES

Madam Speaker, today I am introducing a resolution for the planned withdrawal of American troops from Europe and Japan. It is humiliating for American presidents to continue begging our allies to ante-up and spend more on their own national defense. An effort to influence foreign governments' defense appropriations and to alter their economic relationship with Russia is a fruitless task. Subsidizing the defense budgets of rich European and Asian allies so they can use the funds saved on domestic social programs and pipelines to Russia is not in our best interest.

If the American taxpayer was not forced to indirectly pay for the cheap loans to Russia by our European friends, it would then be their own business as to how they deal with their Soviet neighbors. But that is not the case. And since Europe's and Japan's response for decades has been benign neglect to our request and public criticism for our policies, the time has come for a reassessment of our entire foreign policy. **The 20th Century notion that America has been chosen to police the world and pay all the bills, to make the world "safe for democracy" is no longer viable.** Economically, we no longer can afford it; militarily, it is of no value to us. In the past 65 years, this interventionist policy has given us four major military conflicts. The more we scatter our troops and the more dollars we spend, the more likely we are to have war and the worse our economic problems become.

The Falklands crisis demonstrates so well the failure and inconsistency of an interventionist foreign policy. Our commitment to the Rio Treaty and to NATO is impossible to fulfill. The recent UN vote and our attempt to change it after it was cast (seems like Jimmy Carter and Andy Young did something like that also) are symbolic of an overall policy that is contradictory and lacks direction and meaning. This comes about when American interests are confused with demands and manipulation by other nations. A vivid example of this confusion is given in a wire service story about Secretary of State Haig's remarks concerning the latest conflict in the Mideast. According to the official transcript of the briefing, Secretary Haig, speaking to reporters about the Israeli invasion of Lebanon, said, "We not only lost an aircraft and a helicopter yesterday, there's been a claim a second aircraft has been shot down, a second helicopter, and a number of army vehicles." It seems that the Secretary has so confused Israeli and American interests that he speaks broadly as "we."

It is ironic that we support Britain in the Falklands, while Israel, as recipient of billions of dollars of U.S. aid, continues selling weapons to Argentina and Iran. The American taxpayer remains the sacrificial lamb. What is wrong with a foreign policy based on American self-interest? Could it be that a policy like this just might also be a policy of humanitarianism and peace?

At the present time, 60 percent of our entire military budget is being spent on the defense of other nations. Nations we have, for all practical purposes, unilateral commitments to. The commitments, rather than reducing tension, increase it and aggravate the arms race. If Europe and Japan are unwilling to spend whatever is necessary to defend themselves,

11

our exorbitant sacrifice will not preserve their liberty. If we stop our financial and military commitments to allies, their decisions in dealing with the Soviets will suddenly become more objective and realistic. They would become stronger militarily, as we will also. We then would no longer have to plead with them to hold back easy credits to the Communists—which, of course, is an inconsistent request, since we ourselves continue to extend many credits to the Soviet bloc nations.

The military subsidies to our allies do not serve the cause of freedom; we frequently see the funds saved used in social programs that are less than free-market oriented. Since we practice the same kind of economic and political nonsense, it's difficult to be critical. If the funds saved by our allies on defense are not spent on trade assistance with the Soviets or aid to domestic socialistic programs, they can be used to subsidize car and steel companies by low taxes and export subsidies, cutting into our faltering market. And tragically, the worse the problem becomes, the more outcries we hear for tariff protection and more export subsidies—programs that contradict the notion of a free society and, in the past several decades, have contributed significantly to our weak economy, high interest rates, inflation, and unemployment.

NATO was strongly opposed by Mr. Republican himself, Senator Robert Taft of Ohio. At the time of its passage, he said:

It is clear that the pact is a military alliance, a treaty by which one nation undertakes to arm half the world against the other half, and in which all the pact members agree to go to war if one is attacked.

No matter how defensive an alliance may be, if it carries the obligation to arm, it means the building up of competitive offensive armaments. This treaty, therefore means inevitably an armaments race and armaments races in the past have led to war...It would strain the American economy; Europeans would be encouraged to depend upon Americans rather than themselves for their defense; the U.S.S.R. would be unnecessarily provoked; and Truman had no constitutional right to send American troops abroad in peacetime without prior congressional approval.

More recently, Dan Smoot restated clearly this belief in the *Review of the News*: "On the other hand, if the Soviets hit the United States, the European nations will not come to our defense, and the building up of European nation as nuclear threats to Russia will be stalemated and neutralized."

But the Soviets are stupid to believe NATO ever has or ever will be a threat to Russia. The United States has squandered something like a quarter of a trillion dollars on NATO, which has never provided a dime's worth of deterrence against Soviet imperialistic aggression, or a penny's worth of defense for the American homeland. It follows, therefore, that NATO has been a mighty boon to the Soviets in that it has drained off immense sums of money that could have been spent on weaponry to defend Americans against a Soviet surprise attack. I agree with the Soviet conclusion that none of our NATO allies will come to our aid if the Soviets attack us.

When Eisenhower was Commander of NATO forces, he said: "The large-scale permanent commitments of American troops to relatively fixed positions outside the continental limits would be costly beyond military returns."

These quotes are hardly from left-wing liberals.

What will it ever take for us to learn the lessons of history? When will we come to realize that a free nation—unhampered by government intervention, personally, economically, and internationally—is far superior to a coercive state? And if the people of the world are to eat, be housed and be clothed, we must recognize the value of productive effort, sound money, and a free market, and a foreign policy dedicated to strength with determination to defend our freedom while minding our own business. One thing I am convinced of is that more and more American people are coming to this conclusion—that it is time we let our rich allies take care of themselves, and that the lives of our young people and the dollars of our American taxpayers be used for the preservation of our security. ■

America has tried walking a dangerous tightrope in the Middle East, funding Israel then denouncing its actions, while angering Arab nations who also benefit from our largess. This has been going on for decades but safety and stability require we come down from the high wire.

July 14, 1982
THE MIDEAST CONFLICT
HON. RON PAUL of TEXAS
IN THE HOUSE OF REPRESENTATIVES

Mr. Speaker, our involvement in the Palestinian-Israel conflict poses a moral and political dilemma for all Americans. I have met no one eager to send troops to Lebanon or willing to assume the financial burden it is bound to create. If true peace could be bought with money or foreign commitments, many Americans, as they have in the past, would go along with continuing financial and military aid to the Mideast.

Many Americans, however, reject the entire notion of overseas adventurism and giveaways for both moral and constitutional reasons. This group is now joined by the growing number of those disillusioned with the rare success, and frequent harm, that comes from our interventionist foreign policy and masochistic foreign aid programs. They will no longer stand idly by and watch our young people get bamboozled into another no-win war by being put between two warring factions with the false hope that peace will be miraculously achieved. The only thing holding the Camp David accords together are billions of dollars of American taxpayers' money, and for this reason they are built on a shaky foundation, bound to crumble whenever the storm winds of conflict blow.

I find it inappropriate to criticize Israel for wanting to secure its borders. Yet if this means more military action than seems reasonable and it is financed entirely with American tax dollars, the U.S. Congress and the people of the United States who elect the Members of Congress bear a responsibility for what is happening.

Interventionism in the internal affairs of other nations and policing the world to "make it safe for democracy" do exactly the same thing as domestic economic intervention. They create many more problems than they solve. The Vietnam war is a good example of what is likely to result when intervention is pursued and our national security is not our only concern. Obviously our loss in Vietnam did not precipitate a war in Hawaii or California. It has been frequently argued that the reason why we stay in Europe, the Mideast, and the Far East is to prevent the battles from occurring on our own shores. In an age of ICBMs and space technology, this argument seems ludicrous. Yet the policies never change.

The absurdity of interventionism was clearly demonstrated by our participation in the Rio Treaty and in NATO. Obviously we could not perform both commitments except by making war against both Argentina and Britain. In the long run, it is anyone's guess what this will do to our relationship with our neighbors to the south. Neutrality obviously would have served our national interest to a much greater extent.

Now we witness again this same absurd policy in the Mideast—we supply all the weapons and tacitly endorse the invasion of Lebanon, at a significant dollar cost to all Americans. Because innocent Lebanese civilians have been injured and killed, we cannot stand idly by. A proposed $20 million grant to Lebanon is quickly increased to $50 million for "humanitarian" reasons. To refuse would mean that America and the U.S. Congress are heartless and enjoy seeing the innocent suffer.

Because of the war we helped create, we offer to risk not only more dollars but now American boys to rescue the PLO, an organization we have never recognized and have as a policy tried for decades to destroy. When will this ever end? Economically we are teetering on the brink of collapse, and militarily we remain weak, weak and defenseless from a Soviet missile attack. All this interventionist activity designed to make us look strong serves only to weaken and demoralize our people. The American people are tired of sacrificing themselves for the world. It never seems to help and the cost is now prohibitive. On top of it all, we are not respected, and generally condemned for our meddling.

The foreign policy debate that has existed for the past 45 years must be changed from a discussion of whom we should support—the Arab countries or Israel, Argentina or Britain, Greece or Turkey, North or South Vietnam—to a debate about interventionism or armed neutrality.

It is interventionism, inflation and trade wars that inevitably lead to economic isolationism and finally to war. The pattern of the 1930s is a typical pattern of interventionism and trade wars leading to war. A sound money, free trade, and "keep your guns at home" program can give us peace and prosperity. The inflation that has permitted a massive international debt to accumulate is clearly intertwined with all the military activities of recent years. Martial law was declared in Poland on the day many loans were due to be paid to the international bankers.

It appears that Argentina's $34 billion debt to Western banks and governments will never be paid. The massive debt of Brazil and Mexico, plus that of all the other Third-World nations, is indeed, a ticking time bomb. Subtle Arab threats not to renew their billions of dollars of short-term deposits in New York banks could easily influence our policy in the Mideast. Only through neutrality with strength can we hope once again to have a foreign policy of sense and direction.

But it is not the administration that is solely to blame; the Congress is equally culpable. It is so easy for Members of Congress to be critical of what the president is doing in the Mideast yet they themselves are as much to blame as he is. Why does Congress have a right to criticize the president for his daily decisions?

Last year the Congress encouraged the president to pursue a course he deemed necessary to stabilize the Mideast. By resolution the House— overwhelmingly 391 to 1—encouraged "the president to pursue a comprehensive and coordinated policy in Lebanon, including the development of an effective cease-fire, resolution of the issue of Syrian missiles, and promotion of the independence, sovereignty, unity, and territorial integrity of Lebanon." Although the resolution does not have the force of law, it implies that Congress endorses virtually whatever action the president deems necessary and encourages further involvement in the Mideast.

Although it is clear the president has acted in accordance with congressional intent, the bigger question remains: Are the Congress and the president acting in accordance with the intent of the American people? I am convinced the American people no longer endorse foreign adventurism and believe that our best interests are secured by a policy of armed neutrality.

This was the policy of our government from its founding until 1917. It is only in the 20th Century that interventionism has been accepted as a foreign policy, with the obvious consequences of unprecedented world wars and the loss of enormous numbers of American lives on foreign soil. **Our experiment with foreign policy interventionism has failed, just as our experience with domestic economic interventionism has failed.**

Let us learn from that experience and revive the polices of free trade, neutrality, and a strong defense that took this country from an underdeveloped agrarian economy to the world's major economic force. Only such policies will extricate us from absurd situations such as that which now prevails in the Mideast. ■

To this day we still prop up Communist China through the Export-Import Bank, thus subsidizing oppression while harming our own competitiveness.

September 14, 1982
EXPORT-IMPORT BANK LOAN
TO COMMUNIST CHINA IS A DISGRACE
HON. RON PAUL of TEXAS
IN THE HOUSE OF REPRESENTATIVES

Mr. Speaker, recently, the administration extended a $68,425,000 credit to the Communist dictator of Red China through the Export-Import Bank.

It is outrageous that the American taxpayers are being forced

to subsidize Communist China while domestic programs like Social Security are in jeopardy. Though the administration claims this loan credit is "in the national interest," common sense alone tells us that is not true.

Our own economy is in recession. Over 10 million Americans are unemployed. American small businesses are failing in record numbers. The American steel industry is in a depression, and tens of thousands of steelworkers have been laid off. Yet the administration contends that it is in our "national interest" to make a $68 million subsidized loan to help Communist China build steel plants that will then unfairly compete with our own steel industry. This kind of action is an insult to the American people. The Communist Chinese will receive these loans at below-market interest rates, yet our struggling American businesses must pay market rates.

Communist China is not one of our friends. Their repressive and tyrannical regime is the very opposite of everything America stands for. It is against our best interests, in every way, to use our tax dollars to help prop up Communist dictatorships. This $68 million Export-Import loan guarantee is a tragedy and a disgrace. ■

As I pointed out previously, it is often non-binding resolutions that start us down the road to unwise foreign entanglements. A favored trick of the interventionists is to slip in open-ended commitments on resolutions regarding humanitarian crises.

September 28, 1982
HON. RON PAUL of TEXAS
IN THE HOUSE OF REPRESENTATIVES

Mr. Speaker, I oppose House Concurrent Resolution 409, which concerns the massacre in the Palestinian refugee camps. It is said that a "yes" vote on the resolution is a vote against massacres. I disagree. Hardly anyone, surely, would accuse another of being in favor of such a massive disregard for human life. There are sound reasons, though for not passing a resolution of this kind without careful consideration of its entire meaning. The first section of the resolution—that condemns the immorality of ruthless killing—is a clear statement with which we all agree. However, section 5—which encourages the president to continue our involvement in the chaos in the Middle East in "every possible way"—just opens the door for more hostility, not less.

Urging the president to pursue peace by any means is an open-ended sanction to continue U.S. involvement in the problems that brought about the violence in the first place. This sanctioning of presidential power to pursue open-ended commitments reminds me of the Gulf of Tonkin resolution—at least in its thrust. It entrenches a foreign policy that we have followed for decades, one that led to the disastrous events of the Korea-Vietnam era. Endorsing international intervention is very different from just condemning massacres.

It is this very policy of interventionism that encouraged and permitted the invasion of Beirut and the massacre of civilians in Beirut and other Lebanese towns. **Through our endorsement, financing and providing of weapons to the government of Israel, we literally subsidized the invasion that set the stage for the weekend massacre.** And although our Pentagon did not plan the invasion, the fact that American dollars and American weapons were used means that we bear some responsibility for it.

And even as the bombs were falling on Beirut, we tripled our economic aid to Lebanon to rebuild the towns blown up by our weapons. To confuse matters even more, as the PLO—a declared enemy of the United States—appeared to be on the ropes, we risked life, limb and diplomacy to rescue them. For all of this the Arabs remain frustrated with us, and the Israeli-American relations worsen. The inevitable bad results of trying to be everything to everybody should surely persuade us to reassess our policy of intervention.

In June of 1981, we the Congress passed a resolution (House Resolution 159) praising Philip Habib for his efforts in the Middle East. At that time, we felt compelled to endorse our past involvement in the Mideast and to encourage even greater involvement by urging the president to "pursue a comprehensive and coordinated policy in Lebanon, including the development of an effective cease-fire, resolution of the issue of the Syrian missiles, and promotion of the independence, sovereignty, unity, and territorial integrity of Lebanon." These are good words prompted by good intentions, but they are hollow in substance and only encourage further fruitless involvement on our part. Nothing favorable has happened since June 1981; in fact, the problems have grown worse. Yet our financial and military commitment has also grown, while our relationships with Arabs and Jews continue to deteriorate

Condemning the killing is fine. But the fact that our policies can lead to and even promote the killing is a more crucial issue than any public pronouncement of this kind. Congressional denunciation of ruthless barbarism can certainly be justified, but if it is used as a stamp of approval for continuing a several-decades-old foreign policy that has helped produce this crisis, then it serves no useful purpose and can actually bring harm.

Congressional resolutions—House Concurrent Resolution 409 and House Resolution 159—are actually congressional stamps of approval for extensive presidential decisions to intervene with the use of troops, the use of dollars, the use of weapons. And once we are bogged down in a crisis like this one, it is difficult to withdraw gracefully. It seems we would have learned that lesson by now.

If the president decided next week to send in 50,000 troops from the Rapid Deployment Force—on a mission to maintain the peace—there would be little we in Congress could say. He would merely need to inform our congressional leaders of his decision, as required under the War Powers Act.

Yes, it is difficult to vote against a resolution that seems on the surface to be a simple condemnation of a massacre. But I am convinced that my position is consistent with a policy that would preclude our participation in setting the stage for the massacre in the first place. ■

"Our country is now geared to an arms economy bred in an artificially induced psychosis of war hysteria and an incessant propaganda of fear."—General Douglas MacArthur

CHAPTER 5

These next two speeches focus upon our current Middle East morass, which has been in the making for decades. Our policy has harmed our interests without adding stability to the region. In an attempt to "balance interests" we anger all sides, and that anger has consequences for our service members, as well as American civilians in the region.

February 24, 1983
U.S. INVOLVEMENT IN MIDDLE EAST
HON. RON PAUL of TEXAS
IN THE HOUSE OF REPRESENTATIVES

Mr. Speaker, this week President Reagan pledged U.S. border protection for Israel if Israel removes its troops from Lebanon. As Commander in Chief, the president certainly can respond militarily in an emergency, if our nation is attacked or our security threatened. But by no stretch of the imagination can it be said that such an elaborate arrangement in the Middle East is required for America's security. Moreover, the president has no authorization to make any such agreement.

This assumption of power, nevertheless, is the logical outgrowth of a decades-old foreign policy based on our extended commitments overseas. An interventionist foreign policy creates problems, the so-called solutions to which can only be found in further commitments and intervention. I do not believe the American people are happy with the ever-growing number of obligations we have assumed over the last several decades, but they feel helpless to change this policy.

Israel has not and will not benefit from our persistent involvement in the Mideast. Since our dollars flow to both Arabs and Israelis, we will not be inclined to allow either side to decide for itself what is in its own best interest.

Israel, under today's circumstances, cannot retain its sovereignty, for we will always feel compelled to criticize their actions if, in our opinion, these actions destabilize the area. This is true whether it involves their borders with Gaza in the south or the settlement on the West Bank. I think what they do in these areas is their business, not ours. How would we feel if a country halfway around the world told us how we should act in the face of what we believed to be a threat to our borders?

Committing unlimited troops and American dollars to secure a border between two warring factions who have fought for thousands of years does not make much sense. **Our presence in the Middle East helps neither the Arabs nor the Israelis, and it does little to increase the probability of peace in the long run. Although the proponents of these policies are sincere in their intent to bring peace, their actions in fact jeopardize America's interests.** They increase the likelihood of our being engulfed in a regional conflict in which we need not, and should not become entangled. In our attempt to befriend both Arab and Israel, we inevitably will alienate both. Giving military support to two sides of a conflict and then proclaiming neutrality is not a tenable policy.

It is like buying two tomcats, putting them in a cage and then insisting they should not fight since they belong to the same owner. Obviously, putting your hand between the two to stop the fighting while pleading for reason will not work either.

But even if it did work, which it will not, where is the moral and constitutional authority for such a grandiose assumption of responsibility? Quite frankly, there is none. The responsibility of the administration and the Congress is to promote security for our nation and to seek peace and

22

harmony with all nations. Pursuing a policy of free trade with all and not giving aid to allies or potential adversaries would do more to enhance peace and prosperity than any attempt to guarantee borders in the Middle East or anywhere else. Such a policy cannot achieve peace between enemies halfway around the world. There is neither authority nor popular mandate for it. There is no money for this kind of intervention either. We are broke, with $1 trillion debt staring us in the face. Expenditures of this sort will only hasten the day of our collapse.

We have already pumped a billion dollars into the Mideast in the name of peace, yet the powder keg is as hot and dangerous as ever. This policy has been costly beyond words. There are many more dollars hidden in our Pentagon budget over and above the direct foreign aid expenditures we all know about. But the real threat lies ahead.

Continued intervention in the Middle East will only guarantee greater problems for us in the future. It cannot enhance our security. It can only jeopardize peace and weaken our own defenses. ■

April 19, 1983
THE BOMBING OF THE AMERICAN EMBASSY IN LEBANON
HON. RON PAUL of TEXAS
IN THE HOUSE OF REPRESENTATIVES

Mr. Speaker, yesterday's abhorrent attack on the U.S. Embassy in Lebanon was a well-planned and willful attack on the U.S. government. The bomb was expertly planted to inflict maximum property damage and high loss of human life. The death toll currently stands at 39, but is expected to rise as high as 80.

We must not minimize the seriousness of this bombing. Under international law, an embassy and its grounds are considered to be the territory, not of the host country, but of the embassy's country. Therefore, this bombing must be viewed as an attack on U.S. territory. I am appalled that there are some who are attempting to minimize the impact that this attack will have on the U.S. presence in Lebanon.

We in this body have essentially endorsed our entire policy in the Mideast on two occasions. On June 16, 1981, the House approved House Resolution 159, a resolution commending Philip Habib for his efforts to negotiate a Mideast peace settlement. The resolution went further than simply patting Habib on the back. It encouraged the president to pursue a comprehensive and coordinated policy in Lebanon. Then on September 28, 1983, the House passed House Concurrent Resolution 409, a resolution regarding the massacre of Palestinians in Lebanon. I voted against this resolution for very specific reasons. While I abhorred the massacre of Palestinian refugees, I felt compelled to vote against the resolution because it granted carte blanche to President Reagan in the Mideast, stating that he should "pursue every possible effort to bring peace to the Middle East." This is a dangerous policy to pursue.

The murderous blast that ripped through the Embassy was not an act of random violence. It was a carefully planned response to the U.S. foreign policy of interventionism—a policy supported and encouraged by this body in resolutions such as the two I have just cited.

Since World War II, the United States has pursued an interventionist foreign policy. This policy has led to our involvement in distant regional conflicts that have no bearing on the genuine security interests of the United States. Often we have found ourselves in the awkward position of being allied to both sides of a conflict, as in the Falkland Islands crisis, and the Israeli-Lebanese conflict last summer. This policy has cost the United States $2 trillion since the end of World War II, and we have nothing to show for these huge expenditures.

In the Middle East, for example, we first gave economic and military aid to Israel; then we gave aid to Lebanon to help them rebuild from the Israeli attack on the PLO in Lebanon.

But the terrorist attack on our Embassy, while horrible and tragic, should come as no great surprise to anyone. There have been several attacks on U.S. Marines stationed in Lebanon that should have forewarned us that such an event was imminent.

I agree with the gentleman from Arizona in the other body who is calling for the withdrawal of U.S. Marines from Lebanon. As this gentleman wisely points out, the day that one U.S. Marine is killed, we will have to answer the question. What do we do? I believe that with this attack on U.S. territory, and the death of American citizens, the time to answer that question has arrived. **In order to avoid U.S. involvement in a Mideast war, we must remove our troops from the region immediately, and return to the historical and traditional American policy of nonintervention in the affairs of other nation.** ■

Trying to influence events in Central America with giveaway programs and trade barriers has repeatedly failed; a more positive approach would develop with more freedom and peaceful commerce.

June 6, 1983
CERTIFICATION OF CONDITIONS IN EL SALVADOR
HON. RON PAUL of TEXAS
IN THE HOUSE OF REPRESENTATIVES

Mr. Speaker, I would like to take this opportunity to explain my opposition to H.R. 1271. I do so not only to explain my own vote but to shed further light on this enormously complicated issue.

Let me make it clear that I, in no way, condone the violence in El Salvador. I think that those of my colleagues who support H.R. 1271 because they believe it would make it more difficult for El Salvador to receive further U.S. dollars are perfectly justified in doing so. But the bill does not challenge the notion of foreign aid itself.

My concern is that this bill would legitimize something my colleagues have denied for years. It legitimizes the concept of American foreign aid as a tool of American foreign policy. Of course, our foreign aid dollar is now and has always been a weapon. H.R. 1271 should lead my colleagues to admit this and to dispense with the humanitarian rhetoric in which we have indulged in this body. It should lead us to end this hypocrisy by ending our foreign aid program altogether.

As our imposition of conditions on El Salvador suggests, our foreign aid is a bribe by which we seek to impose our own will on other supposedly sovereign governments. Worse yet, successive administrations and successive Congresses have used this foreign aid bribe in a most hypocritical manner. In the case of El Salvador, we are not demanding that its government meet stringent conditions in exchange for relatively small amounts of foreign aid. Yet in the case of other less developed countries—that is, those ruled by Communists—the utter suppressing of the most basic human rights seems to matter not at all. We give them the money without a thought to internal conditions, in the vain hope of buying their friendship.

I oppose H.R. 1271 for another reason: H.R. 1271 and the section of the International Security and Development Cooperation Act of 1981 that it amend demand that the president certify certain conditions within El Salvador. How do we in Congress honestly expect the president of the

25

United States to know exactly what is going on within the government of another sovereign nation? We cannot. Since we cannot, this entire certification nonsense comes to little more than political grandstanding.

If the flow of U.S. foreign aid dollars is intended to boost the economies of our Latin American neighbors, and thus arrest the spread of communism, as some of our colleagues insist, then I would submit that there are more effective ways to accomplish both of these objectives.

After all, four decades of massive foreign aid giveaways have done nothing whatsoever to stop the growth of communism. Similarly, the flow of dollars from the taxpayers of this country to the dictators of the Third World have done nothing to stimulate economic growth in those backward economies, but a good deal to prevent it in our own.

Meanwhile, of course, my colleagues have introduced a barrage of protectionist legislation, imposing artificial barriers to trade that block any possibility of sustained economic growth in those countries. The economic stagnation that results increases the likelihood that these victimized countries will be economically and militarily vulnerable to communism. Our response, of course, will be to send them more dollars.

In closing, I would repeat that I deplore the killings in El Salvador. Unfortunately, the solution cannot be found in this hypocritical use of U.S. dollars. ∎

Ludwig von Mises wrote that interventionism simply breeds more interventionism. This was certainly true with regard to our policy toward the Communists. U.S. taxpayers were made to prop up red regimes and then financially support the people fighting against these very same governments.

July 28, 1983
AMENDMENT TO THE INTELLIGENCE AUTHORIZATION ACT FOR FISCAL YEAR 1983
HON. RON PAUL of TEXAS
IN THE HOUSE OF REPRESENTATIVES

Mr. Chairman, H.R. 2760 presents Members with only two options: covert aid or overt assistance to Central America. The bill fails to address the fundamental question of whether or not we should be sending any assistance to Central America. Throwing U.S. tax dollars at Central America is a shortsighted, regional response to the global problem of Soviet aggression.

I believe that aid to the region, which is supposedly designed to stop the spread of communism, would be unnecessary if the United States would quit subsidizing communism at its source—the Soviet Union and the Eastern bloc. At the present time, the Soviets and other Communist nations owe almost $100 billion to Western nations, particularly the United States; $100 billion buys a lot of arms for insurgents.

Many proponents of aid to Communist nations claim that the funds we give them are used only for peaceful purposes. However, funds are fungible. The grants, credits, and below-market loans the United States gives Communist nations for so-called peaceful reasons free up their own limited capital for fomenting revolution abroad.

All of us are concerned about the flow of arms from Cuba to Marxist rebels in Central America. Unfortunately, Congress has failed to examine the extent to which the Soviet Union is subsidizing Cuba. The amounts are staggering. In recent years, the Soviet Union has been spending over $10 million a day on Cuba. Soviet economic assistance to Cuba in 1982 amounted to $4.7 billion, accounting for almost 25 percent of Cuba's GNP. Further, Soviet military assistance to Cuba since 1961 is estimated at $10 billion. This massive flow of rubles into the Caribbean is being supported by the U.S. government's credit policies.

The Soviets are not foolhardy. They are actually cautious and quite calculating in their foreign policy. They have, however, reached the stage in their empire building where they are having trouble controlling their subjugated nations.

The point I am making is this: the Central American region is peripheral to Soviet interests. If the United States would cut off aid to the Eastern bloc, the resultant belt tightening would probably force the Soviets to end their military adventurism in the Caribbean and Central America in order to maintain control over the Warsaw Pact nations and Afghanistan.

While I would prefer an entirely different course of action to the one proposed in H.R. 2760, let me state that in the context of the bill I am opposed to any covert military actions by the U.S. government. Such actions have no place in a free society. Any action the government takes must be open to examination by all.

Beyond the ethical questions involved, there are practical considerations. Covert actions in the past have usually failed. And when these failures have been uncovered, they have been used against us by our enemies. In the struggle between freedom and tyranny in the Third World, the United States, as the freest nation in the world, is losing the battle of ideas. This

27

loss of stature is not for objective reasons. Our capitalist economy still provides the best model for development. Our largess has resulted in $2 trillion worth of foreign aid programs since the end of World War II. Yet we are viewed as an imperialist power by many wary, if not hostile, Third World nations. This is largely the result of effective Communist propaganda, and our own clumsy attempts at covert actions designed to bring about U.S. objectives.

While overt aid is always preferable to covert aid, the so-called interdiction assistance proposed in H.R. 2760 has many drawbacks. Many foreign policy experts believe that the $80 million called for in the bill is far too low to end the flow of arms to El Salvador. Further, the program's success rests completely on the cooperation of our Central American neighbors. I am also concerned because the bill would actually deepen U.S. involvement in the region. Covert assistance is currently going only to the rebels in Nicaragua. The interdiction assistance would be spread among friendly nations in the region.

The time has come to end the vicious cycle of funding communism and then funding those fighting communism. Instead of paying other nations to cut off the flow of arms into El Salvador, as H.R. 2760 proposes, let us simply stop paying for the arms. ∎

The next several statements focus on the tragedy that fell upon our troops in Lebanon. I had stood against sending them and questioned their being maintained there. Unfortunately, it took severe loss of life for us to follow a more rational policy.

September 15, 1983
TROOPS IN LEBANON
HON. RON PAUL of TEXAS
IN THE HOUSE OF REPRESENTATIVES

Mr. Speaker, it has been reported there is no sentiment in the Congress for the removal of the troops from Lebanon. If this is true, it is unfortunate because there certainly is a strong sentiment among the American people for their removal.

The motivation for sending in the Marines, that is to keep the peace, certainly cannot be questioned. However, good intentions in no way guarantee wisdom. The fact that we have assisted both factions in the war in the Mideast raises questions as to just why we have positioned ourselves

28

between the two warring factions. Already several Marines have been killed and many others wounded.

Since victory is not our goal but merely stability in an area that has been unstable for centuries, it makes the task of maintaining peace impossible. Our military presence and activity is escalating rapidly. At first it was a few Marines. Now we have sent in more Marines to stand by offshore. Naval and air power is now being used to intimidate certain factions of this civil war. Soon we will not be able to extricate ourselves from a deepening involvement that we may well be sorry for.

We should not have gone into Lebanon in the first place. We should not be escalating the military activity there, and we should leave Lebanon immediately. All we need now is for one Russian-built missile launched by the Syrians to sink one of our warships now shelling the Druzes' position and the big war will be started.

Now is the time to prevent that from happening. ■

September 20, 1983
WHY, I ASK, ARE WE THERE?
HON. RON PAUL of TEXAS
IN THE HOUSE OF REPRESENTATIVES

Mr. Speaker, the parents of Marines killed and wounded in Lebanon are asking: Why are we there? What is our goal? Where is the enthusiasm for the mission? What is our role?

Americans will support, and fight and rally together when the objectives are clear. They will grow discontented and divided if our goals are vague and untenable.

Now is the time to decide what the purpose for our Middle East involvement is. If we wait a day longer, we will become deeply mired in a conflict from which we cannot escape.

It has been said that we are a peace-keeping force, yet there is less peace now than when we went into Lebanon. We did not go in to fight, yet we fire our weapons daily to protect our Marines. But if our Marines were not there, there would be no reason to participate in the killing—nor have our own Marines killed and wounded.

Last year we rescued the PLO at great risk and expense. Today, those same PLO members are firing at our Marines.

Some have said that our Marines feel good about their mission in Lebanon. But Alexander Ortega, in his last letter home before

29

being killed, said: "I never knew how much I love America. I want to come home." Soon after he wrote that letter, he came home—in a box. And for what?

No—there is no peace, yet we are told there is no war. If there is no war, then victory can never be the goal.

It makes no sense. It is time we admit it and come home before a lot more Marines come home as Alexander Ortega did.

It would be a serious mistake for Congress to give approval for our troops to occupy Lebanon for an additional 18 months. Our involvement in Lebanon serves to escalate the war, jeopardizes our national security, and detracts from our ability to provide for a true defense of America. It is time to come home. ∎

September 21, 1983
LEBANESE WAR POWERS RESOLUTION
HON. RON PAUL of TEXAS
IN THE HOUSE OF REPRESENTATIVES

Mr. Speaker, it has been heralded as a compromise on the war powers issue. In my estimation it is nothing of the kind. It is complete capitulation to a continued active presence in the Mideast with a great possibility that the fighting will be escalated and more men and weapons will be required—just to maintain a status quo—of a continued no-win purposeless fight.

It is said to be bipartisan, yet it is just a continuation of our monolithic policy of decades of continued foreign intervention. This intervention is not required for our security and therefore fraught with great danger—danger of never achieving victory and never being able to gracefully withdraw.

We as a Congress are reneging on our responsibility to be the sole decision-maker in committing our people to war as directed by the Constitution.

How can we fix for 18 months the number of troops in an area of active hostility? It is totally untenable. More troops must be used to protect our men. If they are not, it would be rather simple to pick off and demoralize a fixed contingency of 1200 Marines—limited in their role to fight.

Security in this area is vital to Israel. Israel had nearly achieved this and had the PLO on the ropes, yet our policy makers decided to rescue the PLO who are now back in Lebanon—shooting at our Marines. It is an unworkable policy, doomed to fail. **It is with great risk that we**

30

remain in Lebanon with the chance that significant escalation of the conflict will come on the heels of some unforeseen incident— such as the sinking of a U.S. warship.

In the politics of war, compromise with precise goals ushers in tomorrow's unsolvable dilemmas. Let us have no part of this compromise of our responsibilities. ■

September 28, 1983
MULTINATIONAL FORCE IN LEBANON RESOLUTION
HON. RON PAUL of TEXAS
IN THE HOUSE OF REPRESENTATIVES

Mr. Chairman, I rise in strong opposition to this resolution. I think it is a serious mistake.

I would like to refer back to a little legislative history. In June of 1981, we were anxious to praise Ambassador Habib for the "peace" he brought about in the Mideast. In that resolution there was a statement that actually set the stage for what we are facing today. That resolution said:

The House of Representatives strongly encourages the president to pursue a comprehensive and coordinated policy in Lebanon including the development of an effective cease-fire, resolution of the issue of Syrian missiles, promotion of the independent sovereignty, unity and territorial integrity of Lebanon.

That resolution was passed 398 to 1 and literally set the stage for the involvement we have in Lebanon today.

This resolution, House Joint Resolution 364, I sincerely believe, is a capitulation. It is no compromise whatsoever on the war powers resolution. We are literally reneging on our responsibilities as Congressmen and Representatives of the people. We are reneging on our responsibility given only to Congress that only we can declare war. I do not see how we can prevent the escalation, if it is necessary in order to preserve the lives of the Marines in Lebanon. We, by passing this resolution, literally give license to the administration to pursue a more extended war.

The American people, I do not believe, endorse the involvement in Lebanon. If a referendum were taken, they would wholeheartedly endorse our getting out of Lebanon and not becoming increasingly involved, as we have been.

For the past couple of years, we have subsidized and helped both sides of the war over there. We have rescued the PLO when Israel was

31

about to do the PLO in. And what do we find now? The PLO is back in Lebanon, shooting at our Marines. And we actually financed both sides. Israel, at that time, was able to take care of the PLO, yet we marched in, rescued the PLO; now we still have them to contend with.

During the bombing of Beirut, bombing with weapons that we paid for, we had a bill on this House floor with foreign aid to Lebanon to rebuild Beirut during the time the bombs were still falling. This is a foolhardy policy.

It is time the American people woke up and decided there is a more sensible policy that we could pursue.

We have less peace in Lebanon now than a year ago. There is no peace, yet they say there is no war. If there is no war, there can be no victory. All we need today is one Russian-built missile to hit one of our ships and it sink. I believe we would face catastrophe, an international and world catastrophe. I do not know how we could prevent it.

Our purpose there is not definable because we do not know what our purpose is.

The policy of foreign involvement and interference is a policy the American people are questioning. It has failed us for the past 70 years, and the sooner we admit it the better.

The numerous mutual defense pacts that we have committed our sons and tax dollars to are unwise investments. How many believe that there is anything mutual about our allies coming to our aid in a time of need? Yet our citizens are continually being drained of their resources and their lives in order to attempt the unachievable. How can we expect to buy peace in the Mideast when there has been war there for so many centuries?

But most importantly, our unwise commitments and overextensions throughout the world serve to distract resources and energies that should be directed toward our national defense. Interference in the affairs of other nations precipitates conflicts and invites hostility directed toward the United States. It does not serve the interest of peace; it instead jeopardizes our security. The policy of global interference threatens the peace of the world and prevents the establishment of a policy based on adequate defense and self-confidence in our role in world affairs. It's time to bring the Marines home and reconsider our policy of foreign entanglements.

I thank the Chairman, and I rise to state my strong support for the Long-Obey amendment. It certainly does not do as much as I think we should do in restraining the activities we are performing over in the Middle East; but it does put on some of the needed controls that I think are necessary. It has been adequately explained here in the last several hours the great danger of having troops in the Middle East, but I think that there is another good reason why we should not be involved.

I think in many ways this justifies the use of Marines any place and every place. If we can put the Marines in the Middle East today and keep them on this so-called peace mission, we justify their use any place any time.

I think also that we must consider the fact that this represents a policy of interference. Interference in a place in the world where I do not think we should be interfering. It literally restrains Israel from doing the kind of thing that they need to do to secure their own country.

So, with the policy of interference, I think that we do great harm, not only to that area of the world by causing confusion and not allowing the balance of powers to develop adequately, but I think it literally harms and injures our own defense by taking resources and personnel that should be used for this purpose. ■

The idea of the President ignoring Congress regarding foreign policy is not new. Unfortunately, Congress often abrogates its duty, preferring to let the President take the political risks. When Congress does act, it is often based on partisan considerations rather than the national interest. As these two speeches suggest, contrasting the approach of some in Congress regarding Lebanon as compared with Grenada reveals this truth.

October 24, 1983
BLOWING HOT AND COLD ON
THE ISSUE OF COMMUNISM
HON. RON PAUL of TEXAS
IN THE HOUSE OF REPRESENTATIVES

Mr. Speaker, on the news this morning, the American people were informed that U.S. Marines are participating in a multinational force invading the island Grenada in the Caribbean. The purpose of the force is to rescue the American citizens there who wish to be rescued, and to restore peace and freedom to the chaotic nation.

News reports also indicate that the recent coup in Grenada was backed by the governments of the Soviet Union and Cuba, and that there are, in fact, Cuban and Russian troops on the island. Our Marines, according to the president, are there to depose the brutal leftist thugs who have murdered the Prime Minister and several other officials of the government of Grenada.

If this were not troubling enough, the news this morning also reports that our president has written a letter of apology to some Members of Congress who voted against cutting off a small part of our subsidy of Communist countries. In his letter of apology, the president said: "Enactment of any amendment that limits the use of IMF funds—including the amendment regarding "Communist dictatorships"—would unnecessarily tie the hands of the IMF."

Mr. Speaker, this administration blows hot and cold on the issue of communism. **Why are we engaged in military action against the Communists in which American lives are being lost when we cannot take the simple action of cutting off the flow of money to the Communists?** For decades we have pursued this immoral course of action, asking American men to die fighting an enemy the American government has financed. To have it announced on the same morning that American boys are dying and that this administration wants to continue financing communism is wrong.

Anti-Communist military action, such as an invasion to protect American citizens, may be legitimate, but it should be undertaken only after open consultation with the Congress and prior congressional approval as the Constitution prescribes. Certainly such action in the Caribbean, is much closer to our shores than Lebanon, and is strategically different. But to order men to die and then to continue sending our dollars to the Communists is immoral and an intolerable policy. ■

October 31, 1983
INVOKING SECTION 4(a)(1) OF WAR POWERS
RESOLUTION WITH RESPECT TO GRENADA
HON. RON PAUL of TEXAS
IN THE HOUSE OF REPRESENTATIVES

Mr. Speaker, the situations in Lebanon and Grenada have demanded the attention of both the American people and this Congress in the last few weeks. Not too long ago, this House was considering a war powers bill on the subject of Lebanon; today we have one before us on Grenada.

I find it ironic, Mr. Speaker, that the Congress wrote the president a blank check in the Lebanon matter, a check that is good for at least 18 months; but in the case of Grenada we are calling for, not an 18-month limitation, but a 2-month limitation. Nevertheless, **I believe that the president has no authority under the Constitution to engage U.S.**

troops without the consent of the Congress unless it is to repel an invasion of American territory or to rescue American citizens when Congress is not in session.

I find this action ironic, because the situation in Lebanon is quite different from the one in Grenada. First, in Lebanon, our Marines have no clearly defined objective. In Grenada, the objective of the invasion, or at least one of its objectives, is the rescue of American citizens. By contrast, our Marines were first used in Lebanon to rescue the PLO. Yet Congress leaps to reprimand the president for his action in Grenada, not Lebanon.

Second, 15 times as many Marines have died in Beirut as in the Caribbean. About 240 of our Marines have been killed in Lebanon; about 16 in Grenada. Yet Congress wants to reprimand the president for what he has done in Grenada, not Beirut.

Third, the United States has no clear interest in the Lebanese conflict 6,000 miles away, but the Caribbean is right on our shores. It now appears that there were troops and advisers in Grenada from Libya, Cuba, Bulgaria, the Soviet Union, East Germany, and North Korea. If that is the case, I fail to see how anyone can believe that Grenada posed no threat to our well-being.

Apparently the six foreign governments represented on the island thought differently. But Congress hastens to rebuke the president for what he did in Grenada, not Lebanon.

Fourth, the administration has repeatedly said that the Marines will be out of Grenada in a matter of weeks, but it has refused to place any time limit on our involvement in Lebanon. Yet the Congress is eager to impose a limit on the Grenada operation, but no meaningful limit on the Lebanon occupation.

Mr. Speaker, as I said earlier, I will vote for this resolution, for I believe the president should have come to Congress before committing troops to either Lebanon or Grenada. But I believe that the Congress is showing poor judgment in our foreign affairs by becoming more exercised over Grenada, in which we have a legitimate national interest, than it did over Lebanon in September, in which we have no legitimate national interest.

Congress does control the military, according to the Constitution. The president is Commander in Chief when we are at war. He has the power to conduct war, but the Congress has the exclusive power to initiate war. It is the failure of Congress to exercise its constitutional prerogatives to declare war that led to both Korea and Vietnam. I would hate to see either Lebanon or Grenada become another no-win undeclared war.

35

The War Powers Resolution itself, Mr. Speaker, is an imperfect instrument. It enshrined in law for the first time the claim some recent presidents have made that the president has the unilateral power to commit U.S. Armed Forces to war in the absence of a congressional declaration of war. Under the Constitution, the Congress has the exclusive right of initiating war, except in the two cases already noted, to repel invasion and to defend American citizens when Congress is not sitting. Not until June of 1950 did any president claim the right to start a war on his own. President Truman must go down in history for that novel and dangerous theory of executive power. What followed was a war in which we suffered 53,000 dead, 103,000 wounded. But Congress acquiesced in this bold usurpation of power. A little over 10 years later, the same thing happened in Southeast Asia, and 58,000 Americans died; 157,000 were wounded.

I suggest, Mr. Speaker, that we insist that the president abide by the explicit terms of the Constitution. Unfortunately, we ourselves have not done so, and we ought to put our own House in order first.

I am sorry that this resolution has come up under suspension of the rules. I think it would be highly appropriate to impose the same time limitation on the occupation of Lebanon that we are here imposing on the occupation of Grenada. But the procedure under which we are considering this resolution precludes the offering of an amendment to make a two-month limitation apply to our involvement in both Lebanon and Grenada. I pray that this action on our part does not usher in the same sort of conflict that we have forced on the American people twice in the past 30 years. ■

Congress seems at times to be incapable of letting any internal activity of foreign nations pass without some nanny-like comment from the body. Oddly, this often puts us at odds with one of America's founding principles, the right to self-determination.

November 17, 1983
CONDEMNING ACTION OF SO-CALLED TURKISH FEDERATED STATE OF CYPRUS IN DECLARING ITSELF TO BE AN INDEPENDENT STATE ON CYPRUS
HON. RON PAUL of TEXAS
IN THE HOUSE OF REPRESENTATIVES

Mr. Speaker, I rise in opposition to this resolution.
This does not mean that I necessarily approve of the unilateral

declaration of independence by the Turkish Cypriots. As a U.S. legislator, however, I have taken an oath to uphold the Constitution of the United States. My performance of this role does not include resolutions of condemnation such as the one before us today.

This resolution is a hastily conceived response to actions that took place in Cyprus on November 15. So hastily was it prepared that most Members did not even have access to the text until it was brought to the floor for debate. That is not responsible representation; that is a blind leap of faith.

Let us take a moment to examine House Concurrent Resolution 220 and its implications.

This resolution states that the U.S. government recognizes the government of the Republic of Cyprus as the sole legitimate government of Cyprus. I have no problems with this declaration. In international affairs, the recognition of a government carries with it profound implications, especially in this era of massive U.S. foreign aid giveaways. However, refusal to recognize a government is vastly different from the sort of condemnation contained in this resolution. It is, therefore, the stated reasons for this condemnation that I object to.

In one clause, the resolution states, "...this unjustified action clearly contradicts the stated U.S. objectives...." **The U.S. government seems to have stated objectives and strategic security interests in every nation in the world. We send planes, armaments, food, money and men all over the world in the hope of having things our way, yet rarely do we achieve our elusive goals.** Four decades of an interventionist foreign policy have not enhanced our security and/or our defensive capability. Instead, we have dissipated our energies and left ourselves militarily and economically weak by our indiscriminate actions.

The resolution is merely a reflection of our current bankrupt foreign policy—a policy we can no longer afford. We have spent over $2 trillion on foreign aid programs since the end of World War II, yet we have not bought peace, prosperity, or security.

The time has come to alter drastically our foreign policy. The sole legitimate function of our armed services and our foreign policy is to insure a strong and independent United States. By attempting to chaperone the entire world, we find U.S. forces committed indefinitely in areas from Western Europe to the Philippines, and everywhere in between.

We expect all these forces to be peacekeepers of sorts; their bodily presence is supposed to insure peace in our time. Yet our young men have died by the tens of thousands, and they are continuing to die in places where the United States has no genuine security interests.

Some Members of this body object strenuously to the foreign policy and military decisions made by the president. Yet we pass resolutions such as the one before us that gives him carte blanche and a green light.

Have my colleagues thought about the real message this resolution will send to the American people if approved? We are condemning the unilateral declaration of independence by the Turkish Cypriots. Is that as far as the resolution goes?

My colleagues, this resolution is dangerous. It leaves unanswered the question, "If we oppose this action, what do we plan to do about it?" That is a decision we will abdicate to the president if we approve this resolution.

If you think not, I would like to refresh your memories. In June 1981, we were anxious to praise Ambassador Habib for the "peace" he brought about in the Mideast. In that resolution—which the House overwhelmingly approved—there was a statement that actually set the stage for what we are facing in Lebanon today. That resolution said:

The House of Representatives strongly encourages the president to pursue a comprehensive and coordinated policy in Lebanon including the development of an effective cease-fire, resolution of the issue of Syrian missiles, promotion of the independent sovereignty, unity and territorial integrity of Lebanon.

That resolution passed 398 to 1. That seemingly innocuous resolution paved the way for U.S. Marine bunkers around Beirut Airport and the senseless deaths that followed.

We have no constitutional authority to impose our will on the people of Cyprus, nor do we have a moral authority for such action.

I urge my colleagues to oppose this resolution—also seemingly harmless —because it could become the rationale for deeper U.S. involvement in Cyprus. ■

"That we are to stand by the president, right or wrong is not only unpatriotic and servile, but is morally treasonable to the American public."—Theodore Roosevelt

CHAPTER 6

February 7, 1984
THE MIDDLE EAST SITUATION
HON. RON PAUL of TEXAS
IN THE HOUSE OF REPRESENTATIVES

(Mr. PAUL asked and was given permission to address the House for 1 minute and to revise and extend his remarks.)

Mr. PAUL. Mr. Speaker, it is said that we are in Lebanon today for the purpose of protecting our national interests in that area.

It was about 37 years ago that President Harry Truman stated a doctrine that became known as the Truman Doctrine. He essentially said that whenever and wherever aggression indirectly or directly threatens the peace, the U.S. interests are involved. A rather vague statement, but something that we have mechanistically followed. We have been robots since that policy was established.

Minor changes in troop locations in that area of the world will do nothing to change the situation. Basic policy must be addressed, basic policy must change.

Tactical adjustments with the troops will only keep us involve and committed in that area.

39

U.S. interests, if they are vaguely defined and we equate them with the U.S. security, we are bound to get into a lot more trouble before we can settle the difficult situation that we face in the Mideast.

As I prepared to end my first tenure in the House, I pointed out several of the irrational and contradictory policies we were pursuing, including those regarding our foreign entanglements.

September 19, 1984
SOME OBSERVATIONS ON FOUR TERMS IN CONGRESS
HON. RON PAUL of TEXAS
IN THE HOUSE OF REPRESENTATIVES

Mr. Speaker, I shall be soon leaving the House and have asked for this special order to make a few comments regarding the problems our nation faces and the actions needed to correct them. Having been honored by the 22nd District of Texas to represent them for four terms, I have grown to appreciate the greatness of this institution. I only wish the actions performed by the Congress in recent years could match the historic importance of this body.

Thousands of men and women have come and gone here in our country's history, and except for the few, most go unnoticed and remain nameless in the pages of history, as I am sure I will be. The few who are remembered are those who were able to grab the reins of power and, for the most part, use that power to the detriment of the nation. We must remember achieving power is never the goal sought by a truly free society. Dissipation of power is the objective of those who love liberty. Others, tragically, will be remembered in a negative way for personal scandals. Yet those individuals whose shortcomings prompted the taking of bribes or involvement in illicit sexual activities, have caused no more harm to society than those who used "legitimate" power to infringe upon individual liberty and expand the size of government. Morally the two are closely related. The acceptance of a bribe is a horrible act indeed for a public servant, but reducing liberty is an outrageous act that causes suffering for generations to come.

Since the time of our founding, few who have come to the Congress have been remembered for championing the cause of freedom. This is a sign of a declining nation and indicates that respect for freedom is on the wane.

Serving here has been a wonderful experience, and the many friendships will be cherished. I am, however, the first to admit the limited impact I've had on the legislative process. By conventional wisdom, I am "ineffective," unable to trade votes, and champion anyone's special privilege—even my own district's. It places me in a lonely category here in Washington. If the political career is not the goal sought, possibly the measuring of "effectiveness" should be done by using a different standard.

The most I can hope for is that someday a suggestion I've made is remembered: that the debate would shift to a different plane. Instead of asking which form of intervention and planning government should impose, perhaps someday Congress will debate intervention versus nonintervention, government versus voluntary planning, U.S. sovereignty versus internationalism—the pros and cons of true liberty. Today the debate basically is only that of deciding who will be the victims and who the beneficiaries. I hope the hours of debate over the mechanisms of the political system orchestrated by the special interests will give way to this more important debate on freedom. The lack of this debate was my greatest disappointment. Only rarely did I see small fragments of this discussion, and then merely as a tactic for short-term gain rather than because of a sincere belief in the principles of liberty and the Constitution.

Some have said my approach is not practical, but most concede, "At least he's consistent." Since I first came here in 1976, the number of lobbyists has doubled and the national debt has tripled—$550 billion to $1.59 trillion—to me a most impractical trend. Business cycles, unemployment, inflation, high interest rates, and trade wars are the real impracticalities brought about by unwise political and economic policies. I've been impressed over the years by those who concede to me the consistency of my views, yet evidently reject them in favor of inconsistent views. Who, I might ask, is served by the politicians of inconsistency—the special interests or the general welfare?

The petty partisan squabbles that are today more numerous and more heated serve no useful function. The rhetoric now becoming personal is not designed to solve problems, nor does it show a correct perception of our country's problems. All are motivated by good intentions, but that cannot suffice. The narrow partisan squabbles are a natural consequence of an intellectual bankruptcy, whereby correct solutions are not offered for our economic problems. The "good intentions" prompts those involved to "do something." It seems that narrow partisanship on the House floor contributes nothing to the solutions of today's problems.

Sadly, I have found that individual Members, even though we represent

41

our half-million constituents, are much less important than most of us would like to believe. The elite few who control the strings of power are the only ones who really count in the legislative process. Votes, of course, occur routinely after heated debate by all those who want to ventilate. But as C. Northcote Parkinson pointed out, the length of debate on an issue is inversely proportional to the importance of an issue. Many times debate is done either for therapy or as a ritual to force Members to make public commitments to those who wield the power, a mere litmus test of loyalty, thus qualifying some quietly to receive largess for their particular district.

More often than not, the floor debates are a charade without real issues being dealt with—a mere chance for grandstanding. Budgetary votes are meaningless in that continuing resolutions and supplemental appropriations are all that count. If covert aid to a nation is voted down, the CIA and the administration in power can find the means to finance whatever is desired. Emergencies are declared, finances are hidden, discretionary funds are found, foreign governments are used, and policy as desired is carried out, regardless of the will of the people expressed by Congress.

On occasion, a program requested by the administration is "stopped" or voted down. But this doesn't really change the course of events—the "price" is merely raised. The vote can be reversed on the House floor or in the conference, and the "enlightened" Member who cast the crucial vote will receive an ample reward for his or her district. These arrangements or deals are routine and accepted practice. The better one is at making them, the higher is one's "effectiveness" rating and the easier the next election.

Recently, the national Taxpayers' Union gave me their annual Taxpayers' Best Friend Award for voting for the least amount of taxes and spending of any Member of Congress. I realize this does not qualify as a news event, but I have, over the years, tried to emphasize how dangerous is the problem of overspending and have voted accordingly. This past year, I am recorded as having voted against 99 percent of all spending— to me that means voting *for* the taxpayer 99 percent of the time and *against* the tyranny of the state at the same percentage. I must confess, though, to the possible disappointment of the anarchists, that I endorse more than 1 percent of our expenditures—possibly even 20 percent. Due to the seriousness of the problems we face, I believe it's crucial to make the point that all programs are bloated, and overspending, deficits and monetary inflation are a mortal threat to a free society. Those not willing to vote for the cuts either must believe they are not a threat or do not care if they are. I suspect the former to be the case.

Deficits are in themselves very harmful, but it's what they represent that we must be concerned about. Deficits are a consequence of spending, and this tells us something about the amount of power gravitating into the hands of a centralized authority. As the deficits grow, so does the power of the state. Correspondingly, individual freedom is diminished.

It's difficult for one who loves true liberty and utterly detests the power of the state to come to Washington for a period of time and not leave a cynic. Yet I am not; for I believe in the goodness of my fellow man and am realistic enough to understand the shortcomings of all human beings. However, **I do believe that if the Democrats and the Republicans played more baseball and legislated a lot less, the country would be much better off. I am convinced the annual baseball game played by the Republicans and the Democrats must be considered one of the most productive events in which the Members of Congress participate.**

Mr. Speaker, I would like to take some time to point out some of the contradictions that I have observed in my four terms in the Congress. These I have found frustrating and exasperating and, if others agree, possibly this recognition will someday lead to policies designed to correct them. I find these contradictions in three areas: foreign policy, economic policy and social issues.

I have trouble believing that the foreign policy of the past 70 years has served the best interests of the United States. The policy of international intervention has been followed during this time, regardless of the party in power. The traditional American policy of strategic independence and neutrality based on strength has been replaced by an international policy of sacrifices, policy that has given us nearly a century of war. The last two wars were fought without formal declaration and without the goal of victory in mind. There are many specific examples to show how irrational this interventionist policy is.

We pump $40 billion a year into the Japanese economy by providing for essentially all of Japan's defense. At the same time, Japan out competes us in the market, in effect subsidizing their exports, which then undermines our domestic steel and auto industries. The result: greater deficits for us, higher taxes, more inflation, higher interest rates, and a cry by our producers for protectionism. We insist that Western Europe take our Pershing missiles. We get the bill, and the hostility of the people of Western Europe, and

43

then act surprised that the Soviets pull out of arms negotiations and send more modern nuclear submarines to our coastline. It's a sure guarantee that any conflict in Europe—even one between two socialist nations—will be our conflict.

Loyally standing by our ally Israel is in conflict with satisfying the Arab interests that are always represented by big business in each administration. We arm Jordan and Egypt, rescue the PLO (on two occasions), and guarantee that the America taxpayer will be funding both sides of any armed conflict in the Middle East. This policy prompts placing Marines, armed with guns without bullets, between two warring factions. Our F-15s shooting down our F-5s in the Persian Gulf War is our idea of neutrality and getting others to test our equipment. America's interests are forgotten under these circumstances.

We condemn the use of poison gas by Iraq at the same time we aid Iraq, along with the Soviets, in preventing an Iranian victory, forgetting that Iraq started the war. Inconsistently, the administration pressures Congress to manufacture new nerve gas so we have something with which to go to the Soviets and draw up some unworkable treaty regarding war gases. We allocate low-interest loans through the Export-Import Bank to build a pipeline for Iraq, giving huge profits to Shultz' Bechtel Corp., while hurting our domestic oil producers.

On the day we "stood firm" against Communist aggression in this hemisphere by invading Grenada, our president apologized to those liberal House Members who were "soft on communism" and pleaded for their vote to ensure the passage of the IMF bill, so the "Communist dictators" can continue to receive taxpayers' dollars—dollars used to support Castro's adventurism in the Carribean and in Central America.

Our official policy currently is to be tough on communism, but at the same time promote low-interest loans, allowing Red China to buy nuclear technology, F-16's and other military technology—all this by the strongest anti-Communist administration that we've had in decades. We participate in the bailout of bankrupt Argentina as she continues to loan money to Castro's Cuba, which then prompts us to send men, money and weapons to counteract the spread of communism formed by Castro. It's doubtful if any of these loans will be repaid, and the military equipment and technology will probably end up being used against us at a later date. We talk about a close alliance with Taiwan while subsidizing their hated enemy, Red China.

We subsidize Red China's nuclear technology; at the same time, we allow Jane Fonda to ruin ours.

We continuously sacrifice ourselves to the world by assuming the role of world policeman, which precipitates international crises on a regular basis, all the while neglecting our own defenses. New planes go overseas while our Air National Guard is forced to use planes 20 years old. We neglect our defenses by signing treaties like Salt I and the ABM Treaty that prevent us from building a non-nuclear defense system—and follow Salt II without even signing it. The result: a massive arms race based on a doctrine of mutual assured destruction.

Praising the greatness of the Vietnam veterans and honoring them can never remove the truth of our failed policy that took us there. Resurrecting heroes will never erase the pain and suffering of an interventionist foreign policy that prompted unnecessary military activities and a no-win strategy.

There are 42 wars now going on in the world, and it's reported we're involved in many of them—on both sides. We have troops in a total of 121 countries. National security is used as justification for all this activity, but rarely is it directly involved.

Our Export-Import Bank financed the building of the Kama River truck plant in Russia—trucks then used in the Soviet invasion of Afghanistan over a road built by our own Corps of Engineers. Our response? Draft registration and an Olympic boycott!

In pleading for the MX funds, the administration explains we need it as a bargaining chip. I guess to bargain away to the Soviets whom we can't trust anyway. We even modify the MX to conform with the Salt II Treaty—a treaty we never even signed.

If we look closely at the record, we find the conservative hawk is frequently the one who appeases and subsidizes the Communists, and never starts the war; the liberal dove is the one more likely to involve us in a war to protect democracy and stop Communist expansion. Images play tricks on us and policy is achieved by deception. Is this a mere coincidence, or is it contrived by those dedicated to internationalism?

The carnage of the 20th Century, as compared to the 19th Century, must someday make us aware of the difference between the two policies pursued. Does the modern age mandate that we reject a policy of self-interest and non-intervention, or is it just possible that worthwhile policies are of value, regardless of the age in which we live? It's an important question, because it will determine whether or not we will enjoy peace and prosperity in the generations to come.

Our economic policy is no less contradictory. It's fair to say that even with all the good intentions of the Members, the planned welfare state has been a complete and miserable failure. For the most part, the programs achieve exactly opposite results from those sought. There is a limit to how long the economy can tolerate these insults before we all suffer from the severe consequences. What we say and do are in conflict with each other. We talk boldly of balanced budgets, full employment, prosperity, low interest rates, and no inflation. So we either do not believe, as a body, what we say, or we are inept in our ability to pursue and achieve the goals that we seek. Either way, the results remain the same.

The economic contradictions are numerous. Conservatives, for years, preached balanced budgets—until in charge—then the deficits soared to $200 billion per year. Liberal big spenders who led the way to runaway spending quickly excoriate conservative deficits and nothing happens; the deficit financing continues and accelerates.

Campaigns are won on promising tax cuts; some are given, but are quickly canceled out by numerous tax increases associated with accelerated federal spending.

Congress and the administration are quick to blame the Federal Reserve System for high interest rates and do nothing about the huge deficits. Congress totally ignores their responsibility in maintaining the integrity of the money and refuses to exert their rightful authority over the Federal Reserve. We routinely preach about helping the poor, then plunder the working class to subsidize foreign socialist dictators and the welfare rich through abusive taxation and inflation.

Our government pursues a policy of currency debasement, causing steadily rising prices, and blindly treats only the symptoms while punishing, through regulations and taxation, those capable and willing to take care of themselves.

Vocal support for free trade is routinely heard, as protectionist measures march on. The steel, sugar, textile, shoe, copper, and automobile industries all come for help, and we do nothing to remove the burden of taxation, inflation, high interest rates and labor laws that put our companies at a competitive disadvantage. Our protectionist measures then hurt our trade partners, precipitating our need to send them more foreign aid to help out their weak economies and to relieve their debt burden.

Archconservatives champion tobacco subsidies, which are criticized by archconservatives who champion milk subsidies. Government then spends millions of dollars to regulate the tobacco industry and points out the hazards of smoking.

A liberal champion of the peace movement and disarmament pushes for the B-1 bomber as a reasonable alternative—and because it's good for the economy—the bomber, by coincidence, to be built in the Senator's home state.

The well-intentioned dogooder legislates minimum wage laws to help the poor and minorities, causing higher unemployment in the precise groups who were intended to be the beneficiaries.

We learned nothing from the Depression years and continue to pay farmers to raise crops not needed, then pay them to stop planting. Our policies drive prices of commodities down, so we prop up the prices and buy up the surpluses. The consumer suffers, the farmer suffers, the country suffers, but our policies never change; we just legislate more of the same programs that cause the problems in the first place.

Our steel plants are closing down, so we pursue protectionism and stupidly continue to subsidize the building of steel plants throughout the world through our foreign-aid projects.

We pay for bridges and harbors throughout the world and neglect our own. If we feel compulsion to spend and waste money, it would make more sense at least to waste it at home. We build highways around the world, raise gasoline taxes here, and routinely dodge potholes on our own highways.

Why do we cut funding for day care centers and Head Start programs before cutting aid to the Communists, Socialists, and international bankers?

A substantial number of businessmen demand the rigors of the free market for their competitors, and socialism/fascism for themselves.

Economic interventionism, a philosophy in itself and not a compromise with anything, is the cause of all these contradictions in the economy. Rejection of government planning, controlled by the powerful special interests, at the expense of the general welfare is necessary, and even inevitable, for that system will fall under its own weight. The question that remains is whether or not it will be replaced with a precise philosophy of the free market, rejecting all special interests and fiat money, or with a philosophy of socialism. The choice when the time comes should not be difficult, but freedom lovers have no reason for complacency or optimism.

Social issues are handled in a contradictory manner as well. A basic misunderstanding of the nature of rights and little respect for the Constitution has given us a hodgepodge of social problems that worsen each day.

At one time, we bused our children long distances from their homes to force segregation; now we bus them, against their will, to force integration.

We subsidize flood insurance in the low-lying areas of the country, prompting people to build where market-oriented insurance companies would have prevented it. When flooding problems worsen, land control and condemnation procedures become the only solution.

The Supreme Court now rules that large landowners must, against their wishes, sell to others to break up their holdings. This is being done in the name of "eminent domain." This is land reform "*a la* U.S.A."

Certain individual groups, against the intent of the Constitution and the sentiments of a free society, agitate to make illegal privately owned guns used for self-defense. At the same time, they increase the power of the state whose enforcement occurs with massive increase in government guns—unconstitutionally obtained at the expense of freedom. Taking away the individual's right to own weapons of self-defense and giving unwarranted power to a police state can hardly be considered progress.

We have strict drug laws written by those who generously use the drug alcohol. Our laws drive up the price of drugs a thousandfold, to the delight of the dealers, the pushers, and terrorist nations around the world who all reap huge illegal profits. Crimes are committed to finance the outrageous prices, and drug usage never goes down. Enforcement costs soar, and its success remains "mysteriously" elusive. The whole system creates an underground crime world worth billions of dollars; and addicts must then entice others to join, getting new customers to finance their habits—forever compounding a social problem epidemic in proportion. Any new suggestions for changing our drug laws— that is, liberalizing them—is seen as political suicide by the hypocritical politicians and a society legally hooked on alcohol, nicotine, caffeine, aspirin and valium.

Talk is cheap about freedom and civil liberties, while privacy and individual liberty are continuously undermined and government force is used to protect the privileges and illegal demands placed on government, by the special interest groups. Computers are routinely used to enforce draft registration, involving Selective Service, IRS, Social Security, HHS and ice cream parlor lists.

The shortcomings of South Africa's apartheid system are denounced continuously by the same politicians who ignore the fact that, in Communist countries, dissidents aren't segregated; they are shot or sent to concentration camps. In comparison, segregation is seen as more vicious than the exiling and the killing of the political dissidents in Russia. South Africa, for their defective system of civil liberties, is banned from the Olympics, while we beg the murdering Communists to come.

Government responsibility to protect life and liberty becomes muddled when the government and courts chosen to protect them, under the guise of privacy and civil liberties, totally ignore the real issue. The abortionist who makes a fortune dropping fetuses and infants into buckets, instead of being restrained by government, is encouraged by the courts and the law. Some show greater concern for the lives of seals than for the life of a human baby.

The government writes thousands of pages of regulations designed to protect workers in private industry—without proof of any beneficial results—and at the same time 50,000-plus are killed on government-engineered and operated highways.

Good conservatives explain why guns and teachers shouldn't be registered, and beg and plead and coerce the government into registering their own kids for the draft.

We have seen cases where harmless elderly women, having committed no act of violence, are arrested for: one, defending against an intruder with the use of a "Saturday night special;" two, raising marijuana in the yard to use for relief of severe arthritic pain; and three, selling chances in a numbers game—the fact that governments run the biggest crap games seems to have no moral significance.

Federal officials—IRS agents and drug enforcement agents—have been known to destroy the property and lives of totally innocent people as homes are entered mistakenly without search warrants. Confiscation of property without due process of law is becoming more commonplace everyday with the tactics of the IRS.

The products produced by businessmen are regulated to the extreme by so-called liberals who would never accept similar regulations on the products of the mind and the media. Yet the ill effect of bad economic ideas and bad education is much more damaging to one's economic health than are the products manufactured in a totally free and unregulated market. The conservative's answer to regulating ideas in a similar way to regulating goods and services is the risk of pointing out this inconsistency.

THE PROBLEMS WE FACE

Contradictions are all about us, but we must realize they are merely the manifestations of more basic problems. Some of these problems are general, others specific; but all are a consequence of the precise ideology to which the nation's intellectuals ascribe. Understanding this is imperative if we ever expect to reverse the trend toward statism in which we find ourselves.

Our government officials continue to endorse, in general, economic interventionism, control of interventionist individuals, a careless disregard for our property rights, and an international foreign policy. The ideas of liberty for the individual, freedom for the markets, both domestic and international, sound money, and a foreign policy of strategic independence based on strength are no longer popularly endorsed by our national leaders. Yet support by many Americans for these policies exists. The current conflict is over which view will prevail.

The concept of rights is rarely defined, since there is minimal concern for them as an issue in itself. Rights have become nothing more than the demands of special-interest groups to use government coercion to extract goods and services from one group for the benefit of another. The moral concept of one's natural right to life and liberty without being molested by State intervention in one's pursuit of happiness is all but absent in Washington. Carelessly the Congress has accepted the concept of "public interest" as being superior to "individual liberty" in directing their actions. But the "public" is indefinite and its definition varies depending on who and which special interest is defining it. It's used merely as an excuse to victimize one individual for the benefit of another. The dictatorship of the majority, now a reality, is our greatest threat to the concept of equal rights

Careless disregard for liberty allows the government to violate the basic premise of a free society; there shall be no initiation of force by anyone, particularly government. Use of force for personal and national self-defense against initiators of violence is its only proper use in a moral and free society. Unfortunately this premise is rejected—and not even understood—in its entirety in Washington. The result is that we have neither a moral nor a free society.

Rejecting the notion that government should not coerce and force people to act against their wishes prompts Congress to assume the role of central economic and social planner. Government is used for everything from subsidized farming to protecting cab monopolies; from the distribution of food stamps to health care; from fixing the price of labor to the fixing the price of gasoline. Always the results are the same, opposite to what was intended: chaos, confusion, inefficiency, additional costs and lines.

The more that is spent on housing or unemployment problems, the worse the housing and unemployment problems become. Proof that centralized economic planning always fails, regardless of the good intentions behind it, is available to us. It is tragic that we continue to ignore it.

Our intervention and meddling to satisfy the powerful well-heeled special interests have created a hostile atmosphere, a vicious struggle for a shrinking economic pie distributed by our ever-growing inefficient government bureaucracy. Regional class, race, age and sex disputes polarize the nation. This probably will worsen until we reject the notion that central planning works.

As nations lose respect for liberty, so too do they lose respect for individual responsibility. Laws are passed proposing no-fault insurance for injuries for which someone in particular was responsible. Remote generations are required to pay a heavy price for violations of civil liberties that occurred to the blacks, to the Indians, and to Japanese-Americans. This is done only at the expense of someone else's civil liberties and in no way can be justified

Collective rights—group rights, in contrast to individual rights—prompt laws based on collective guilt for parties not responsible for causing any damage. The Superfund is a typical example of punishing innocent people for damages caused by government/business. Under a system of individual rights where initiation of force is prohibited, this would not occur.

Short-run solutions enhance political careers and motivate most legislation in Washington, to the country's detriment. Apparent economic benefits deceive many Members into supporting legislation that in the long run is devastating to the economy. Politics unfortunately is a short-run game—the next election. Economics is a long-run game and determines the prosperity and the freedoms of the next generation. Sacrificing future wealth for present indulgence is done at the expense of liberty for the individual.

Motivations of those who lead the march toward the totalitarian state can rarely be challenged. Politicians' good intentions, combined with the illusion of wisdom, falsely reassure the planners that good results will be forthcoming. Freedom endorses a humble approach toward the idea that one group of individuals by some quirk of nature knows what is best for another. Personal preferences are subjectively decided upon. Degrees of risk that free individuals choose to take vary from one individual to another. Liability and responsibility for one's own acts should never be diminished by government edicts. Voluntary contracts should never be interfered with in a free society except for their enforcement. Trust in a free society— even with its imperfections—if we're to strive for one, must be superior to our blind faith in government's ability to solve our problems for us.

51

Government in a free society is recognized to be nothing more than in embodiment of the people. The sovereignty is held by the people. A planned coercive society talks vaguely of how government provides this and that, as if government were equivalent to the Creator. Distribution is one thing—production is another. Centralized control of the distribution of wealth by an impersonal government that ignores the prescribed role of guaranteeing the equal protection of liberty assures that one day freedom will disappear and take with it the wealth that only free men can create.

Today the loss of the people's sovereignty is clearly evident. Lobbyists are important, if not the key figures, in all legislation—their numbers are growing exponentially. It's not an accident that the lobbyist's and chief bureaucrat's salaries are higher than the Congressman's—they are literally "more important." The salary allocation under today's conditions are correct. Special interests have replaced the concern that the Founders had for the general welfare. Conference committees' intrigues are key to critical legislation. The bigger the government, the higher the stakes, the more lucrative the favors granted. Vote trading is seen as good politics, not as an immoral act. The errand-boy mentality is ordinary—the defender of liberty is seen as bizarre. The elite few who control our money, our foreign policy, and the international banking institutions—in a system designed to keep the welfare rich in diamonds and Mercedes—make the debates on the House and Senate floors nearly meaningless.

The monetary system is an especially important area where the people and Congress have refused to assume their responsibilities. Maintaining honest money—a proper role for government—has been replaced by putting the counterfeiters in charge of the government printing press. This system of funny money provides a convenient method whereby Congress' excessive spending is paid for by the creation of new money. Unless this is addressed, which I suppose it will be in due time, monetary and banking crises will continue and get much worse during this decade.

Congress assumes that it can make certain groups economically better off by robbing others of their wealth. The business and banker welfare recipient justifies the existence of the system by claiming that it is good for jobs, profits and sound banking. The welfare poor play on the sympathies of others, and transfer programs based on government force and violence are justified as "necessary" to provide basic needs to all—at the expense of liberty needed to provide for the prosperity everyone desires.

Government cannot make people morally better by laws that interfere with nonviolent personal acts that produce no victims.

52

Disapproving of another's behavior is not enough to justify a law prohibiting it. Any attempt to do so under the precepts of liberty is an unwarranted use of government force.

Congress reflects prevailing attitudes developed by an educational system and the conventional media, and in this sense Congress rarely leads, but is merely pushed and manipulated by public opinion. This is even done with scientific use of public-opinion polls. "Show me the direction the crowd is going and I will lead them," is sadly the traditional cry of the politician. Statesmanship is not the road to reelection. Statesmanship is reserved for a rare few at particular times in history unknown to most of us. Leadership in great movements is infrequently found in official capacities. Lech Walesa, Alexander Solzhenitsyn, et al are not legal officials, but are nevertheless great leaders

Today the deficits, the skyrocketing real interest rates, total government spending, and the expansionist foreign policy have delivered to us a crisis of confidence. The politicians' worries and concerns on the short run reflect the lack of plans made for the future. The interest rates on 30-year bonds tell a lot about the trust in the economic system and especially the integrity of the money.

It's become traditional, especially during the last 70 years, for foreign policy to be pawned off as "bipartisan," meaning no dissent is permissible and all true debate is squelched. Congress, it is said, has no role in formulating foreign policy, for the Constitution gives this power to the president. Nowhere is this written. **Many more powers and responsibilities are to be assumed by the Congress than by the president in the foreign policy area, according to my reading of the Constitution.** Monopoly power for a president to wage war without declaration, as was done in Korea and Vietnam, is a blatant attack on constitutionally guaranteed liberty. I hope the caution shown by the Congress in recent years will prevail—yet the Grenada invasion was not reassuring.

Unfortunately, economic egalitarianism has taken over as the goal of most congressional legislation. Any equality achieved will come about by leveling—a lowering of everyone's standard of living—not by raising it. It is achieved by ignoring the sanctity of the voluntary contract and the prohibitions that should exist against government initiating force against the citizen. This concept must be rejected if we're to reverse the trend toward the Orwellian state.

Many Members of Congress defend liberty, but only in minute bits and pieces as it appears convenient. I find in Washington the total absence of a consistent defense of liberty, as this principle applies to the marketplace, our personal lives, and international relations. Bits and pieces of liberty will never suffice for the defense of an entire concept. **Consistency in defense of freedom is necessary to counteract the consistent aggressive militancy of interventionism, whether it's of liberal or conservative flavor.**

Government today perpetuates violence in epidemic proportions. Most of the time, the mere "threat" of violence by the agencies, the bureaucrats, the officials in charge of writing the final drafts of legislation, is enough to intimidate the staunchest resister. Courts, legal costs, government arrests, government guns, and long-term imprisonments have created a society of individuals who meekly submit to the perpetual abuse of our liberties. All this in the name of the "social good," "stability," "compromise," the "status quo," and the "public interest." The IRS, the EPA and other agencies now carry guns. The colonists would have cringed at the sight of such abuse of our rights to live free. They complained about a standing army that carried guns; we now have a standing bureaucracy that carries guns.

Government today has accumulated massive power that can be used to suppress the people. How is it that we grant our government power to do things that we as individuals would never dream of doing ourselves, declaring such acts as stealing wealth from one another as immoral, and unconscionable? If a free nation's sovereignty is held in the hands of the people, how is it that the state now can do more than the people can do themselves? Planning our people's lives, the economy, and meddling throughout the world change the role of government from the guarantor of liberty to the destroyer of liberty.

Our problems have become international in scope due to the nature of the political system and our policies. This need not be, but it is. The financial problems of the nation, although clearly linked to our deficits and domestic monetary policy, cannot be separated from the international schemes of banking as promoted by the IMF, the World Bank and the Development Banks. It is much clearer to me now, having been in Washington for seven years, how our banking and monetary policies are closely linked to our foreign policy and controlled by men not motivated to protect the sovereignty of America, nor the liberties of our citizens. It's not that they are necessarily inclined to deliberately destroy our freedom, but they place a higher priority on internationalism and worldwide inflation—a system of government and finance that serves the powerful elite.

All the military might in the world will not protect us from deteriorating economies and protectionism, and will not assure peace. Policies are much more important than apparent military strength. The firepower used in Vietnam and the lives sacrificed did nothing to overcome the interventionist policies of both the Republicans and the Democratic administrations. When foreign policies are right, money sound, trade free, and respect for liberty prevalent, strong economies and peace are much more likely to evolve. **The armaments race, and the funding of enemies and wealthy allies, only contribute to the fervor with which our tax dollars are churned through the military-industrial complex.**

The crisis we face is clearly related to a loss of trust—trust in ourselves, in freedom, in our own government and in our money. We are a litigious welfare society gone mad. Everyone feels compelled to grab whatever he can get from government or by suit. The "something for nothing" obsession rules our every movement, and is in conflict with the other side of man's nature—that side that values self-esteem and pride of one's personal achievement. Today the pride of self-reliance and personal achievement is buried by the ego-destroying policies of the planned interventions of big government and replaced by the "satisfaction" of manipulating the political system to one's own special advantage. Score is kept by counting the federal dollars allocated to the special group or the congressional district to which one belongs. This process cannot continue indefinitely. Something has to give—we must choose either freedom and prosperity or tyranny and poverty. ■

"It is our true policy to steer clear of entangling alliances with any portion of the foreign world."—George Washington

CHAPTER 7

Between stints in Congress, I wrote a petition to the body. These excerpts focus on foreign policy issues and indicate how the turn away from traditional American policy led us to where we are today.

While Out of Congress
Excerpt from Petition to the 103rd Congress
THE PROBLEMS WE FACE - JANUARY 1993

Foreign policy needs a total reassessment. Foreign aid, one of the most unpopular programs among American taxpayers, continues to expand annually for special reasons known only to powerful politicians.

We must recognize that the U.S.'s ability to act as the policeman of the world will soon come to an end. We have neither the wisdom nor the money to continue. If we carefully review the history of Noriega, Kadafi, Hussein, Panama, Mexico, Lebanon, the Persian Gulf, Vietnam, Korea, Bosnia, Somalia, etc., we can only conclude that something is seriously wrong with this un-American, interventionist foreign policy. Authority to be the world's policeman and social worker cannot be found in the Constitution. It has only become acceptable policy in the 20th Century.

Internationalism is now an accepted principle by most politicians in Washington, yet many Americans cling to the notion that national sovereignty is worth preserving. In our early history, it was thought that the states were merely "countries" that were loosely bound together. Today the United Nations delivers marching orders from our military in the Persian Gulf War and in Somalia at Bush's request.

Won't anyone in Washington question the wisdom and arrogance of shooting down Iraqi planes over Iraq as if Hussein were the only criminal in power in the world? If this policy makes sense, why aren't we shooting down Cuban planes over Cuba? Is Bosnia next? President Bush said he would go to the Persian Gulf regardless of what Congress said.

We can expect continual international meddling overseas by the new administration. Though we hear inane arguments that Somalia is different from Ethiopia, and Kuwait is different from Bosnia or Herzegovina, the principle of unwise interference is endorsed by the majority of those in leadership positions in both parties. Our only "hope" of thwarting these efforts is U.S. bankruptcy.

Nevertheless, the great danger of a worldwide armed conflict continues. A new world power is bound to develop in the near future to fill the vacuum left by the disintegration of the Soviet Union. This new power very well could grow out of the old Soviet bloc nations or from a radical Islamic fundamentalism centered around the growing military strength of Iran. And China cannot be ignored as it evolves from its old Communist past toward a more fascist state.

"[T]he essence of so-called war prosperity; it enriches some by what it takes from others. It is not rising wealth but a shifting of wealth and income."—Ludwig von Mises

CHAPTER 8

During my second tenure in Congress I began to once again seriously question our foreign interventionism on the floor of the House, focusing attention on how our policies were combining with the breakdown of the constitutional separation of powers to bring about a very dangerous situation.

July 15, 1997
AMERICA'S FOREIGN POLICY
HON. RON PAUL of TEXAS
IN THE HOUSE OF REPRESENTATIVES

Mr. Speaker, it is currently an accepted cliché to say foreign policy is a presidential matter and Congress should not meddle. Frequently we hear the plea to remain bipartisan with no dissent, especially when troops are placed in harm's way. Yet no place in the Constitution do we find any such explicit instruction. Instead, we find no mention of foreign policy.

To the contrary, we find strict prohibitions placed on the president when it comes to dealing with foreign nations.

The Constitution is clear. No treaties can be entered into without the consent of the Senate. No war may be fought without the declaration of war by the Congress.

No money shall be spent overseas without Congress first raising the money and then authorizing it and appropriating these funds for specific purposes.

Since the Constitution does not even assume a standing army, let alone stationing troops in peacetime in over 100 countries, with CIA clandestine activities in even more, the current foreign policy that has evolved over the past 100 years would surely be unrecognizable by the authors of that document.

The Founders of this country were opposed to standing armies for fear they would be carelessly used. They were right.

The U.S. record of foreign intervention and its failures has not yet prompted a serious discussion of the need for an overall reassessment of this dangerous and out-of-control policy. Not only has Congress failed in its responsibilities to restrain our adventurous presidents in pursuing war, spying, and imposing America's will on other nations by installing leaders, and at times eliminating others, throughout the world these past 50 years, we now, by default, have allowed our foreign policy to be commandeered by international bodies like NATO and the United Nations. This can only lead to trouble for the United States and further threaten our liberties, and we have already seen plenty of that in this century.

It looks like our current president, who was less than excited about serving in the military himself, was quite eager to promote U.S. complicity in the escalating dangerous activity in Bosnia. What has been done so frequently in the name of peace more often than not has led to war and suffering, considering Korea, Vietnam, Somalia, and even the Persian Gulf War.

Clinton has not been willing to phase out the Selective Service Department and has actually asked for additional funding to include the Selective Service process in his domestic so-called voluntary AmeriCorps program.

But this failed policy of foreign intervention is being pursued once again in Bosnia, with full acknowledgment and funding by the Congress. Congress has failed to exert its veto over this dangerous game our president is determined to play in this region.

Sensing that maybe soon the Congress will finally cut the purse strings on this ill-advised military operation, pushed hard by Secretary of State Albright, policymakers are quietly and aggressively escalating the tension— placing our nearly 8,000 troops in even greater danger—while further destabilizing a region never prone to be stable over this century, with the certain outcome that Congress will further capitulate and provide funding for extension and escalation of the military operation.

In spite of some resistance in the Congress, the current escalation is likely to prevent any chance of withdrawal of our troops by next summer.

The recent $2 billion additional funds in the supplemental appropriation bill were the cue to the president that the Congress will not act to stop the operation when under pressure to support the troops. Of course, common sense will tell us that the best way to support our troops is to bring them home as quickly as possible. **This idea, that support for the troops once they are engaged means we must continue the operation, no matter how ill-advised, and perpetuate a conflict that makes no sense** is what President Clinton is depending on.

Last week the whole operation in Bosnia changed. The arrest and killing of war criminals by occupation forces coming from thousands of miles away is a most serious escalation of the Bosnia conflict. For outside forces to pronounce judgment on the guilt or innocence of warring factions in a small region of the world is a guarantee that the conflict will escalate. I think those pursuing this policy know this. Prosecuting war criminals is so fraught with danger it seems that the need to escalate surpassed all reason.

Yet immediately after the NATO operation—supported by the United States—that resulted in the death of a Serb leader, Clinton strongly suggested that the troops may well not be able to leave in June of 1998, as promised. They were first supposed to leave in December of 1996, and now 18 months after their arrival, the departure date is indefinite. We in the Congress tragically continue to fund the operation.

This illegal and dangerous military operation will not go unnoticed and will embolden the Serbs and further stir the hatred of the region. Is this policy based on stupidity, or is there a sinister motive behind what our world leaders do?

Must we have perpetual war to keep the military appropriations flowing? Does our military work hand in glove in securing new markets? It is not a hidden fact that our own CIA follows our international corporate interests around the globe, engaging in corporate espionage and installing dictators when they serve these special interests.

Why would an Air Force plane, with a dozen leading industrialists, be flying into a war-torn region like Bosnia, along with the Secretary of Commerce? I doubt they were on a

humanitarian mission to feed the poor and house the homeless.

The lobbyists who pushed the hardest to send troops to Bosnia came from corporations who are now reaping great profits from construction work in Bosnia. It may be the calculation is for a slight escalation of the conflict that inevitably will accompany any attempt to try war criminals—and no one plans for another great war breaking out in this region.

What might be planned is just enough conflict to keep the appropriations coming. But the possibility of miscalculation is very real. The history of this region should surely warn us of the dangers that lurk around the corner.

We, in the Congress, have a great responsibility in reversing this policy. We must once again assume this responsibility in formulating foreign policy and not acquiesce to the president's pressure to perpetuate a serious misdirected policy of foreign meddling 4,000 miles away from home. We must not fall for the old line that we cannot leave, because to do so would not be patriotically 'supporting our troops.' That is blatant nonsense!

We have already invested $7.7 billion in this ill-advised military adventure. That money should have either remained in the pockets of working Americans or been spent here in the United States.

The *New York Times* has praised this recent action by Clinton and the NATO forces and has called for more of the same. The *New York Times* and the *Washington Post* also support the notion that our troops will have to stay in this region for a lot longer than the middle of next year.

The military-industrial complex and its powerful political supporters continue to be well-represented in the media and in Washington. Unfortunately the idea that America is responsible to police the world, and provide the funding and the backup military power to impose 'peace' in all the disturbed regions of the world, remains a policy endorsed by leaders in both parties.

The sooner this policy is challenged and changed, the better off we will be. Our budget will not permit it; it threatens our national security, and worst of all, it threatens our personal liberties. ■

Several of us understood that our policy regarding Bosnia was a real problem. This would result in a serious entanglement, as well as NATO's first offensive war. I believe the precedent set by this action will have significant consequences in the future.

September 4, 1997
THE SOONER WE GET OUT OF BOSNIA, THE BETTER
HON. RON PAUL of TEXAS
IN THE HOUSE OF REPRESENTATIVES

Mr. Speaker, NATO has announced it will now use lethal force in Bosnia. NATO, of course, means the United States, both our dollars and our troops. Little concern is shown here in Congress as we appropriate billions of dollars more for Bosnia with no end in sight.

Policing this area is an impossible task as NATO interferes with TV broadcasts and arresting and trying so-called war criminals. Current policy is only leading to an escalation of the conflict. Ethnic hatred and border fights have been going on in this region for centuries.

Mr. Speaker, the United States will not solve these problems. It is impossible for us to do so. We are already being blamed by the Bosnians while our troops are being attacked with stones and homemade weapons. Congress must bear some of the responsibility for the coming policy disaster. The president cannot act without funds, funds which only Congress can appropriate. Our efforts in Bosnia have nothing to do with national security. We have a responsibility to our troops, and our current policy exposes them to unwarranted danger.

Congress must defund the Bosnian conflict. The sooner we get out of Bosnia, the better. ∎

September 5, 1997
ON BOSNIA
HON. RON PAUL of TEXAS
IN THE HOUSE OF REPRESENTATIVES

Mr. Speaker, I have asked for this time today to express my deep concern for the recent military buildup in Bosnia.

I think this is a dangerous situation, and I would like to call it to the attention of my colleagues here in the Congress. This is something that has been going on for a long time.

Many of us have tried to get our troops out of Bosnia and out of harm's way, but so far that has not been the case. Yesterday, the U.S. Defense Department announced that they would be adding more aircraft in this region. There will be 6 more F-16's sent to this region, taking the total number up to 24. They will be flying out of Ariano, Italy, and the purpose is to patrol the Bosnian skies.

The purpose that is stated is to provide deterrence and to provide a peaceful situation to a very difficult problem that has existed, not for a few months or for a few years, but for decades, if not hundreds of years, in this region.

Instead of providing deterrence and a peaceful effort being made here, I believe our contribution is going to do nothing more than escalate the problems of that region.

The recent buildup has also been said to be necessary, because it is supposed to guarantee an election process. During the last year, there were two attempts to hold elections in this region but, due to the political turmoil there, the elections have had to be canceled. Again they are trying to have another election. Our presence there is supposed to provide the stability to a region that is inherently unstable, and I challenge this notion whether or not this can even be achieved.

In addition to the troops and the aircraft that have gone in which we are sending, the international bodies have sent in 2,600 election monitors. The odds of this providing stability to an election are very, very slim.

Last month there were some additional troops sent into Bosnia. Not much was said about this. There were not very many reports in the media regarding this, and certainly no discussion here in the Congress. But we have had 8,000 troops stationed in Bosnia. We have added 1,600 more. So we are now in the process of adding aircraft and adding personnel in a situation which puts our troops in jeopardy. It was not too long ago that our troops were stoned and homemade weapons were used against them.

The NATO forces just recently took control of a television transmitter and said that the information over this transmitter was not acceptable. Just recently that transmitter was returned in hopes that the return of the transmitter to the Serbs would calm the personnel there, the people there, so that the elections could be carried out. But just the thought of taking over the transmitter is one thing. But the conditions that were placed on the Serbs in the return of the transmitter are something else again.

Our Pentagon official threatened the Serbs that if they violated the instructions that were given the television station, it would be a clear-cut justification for NATO forces to retaliate. In the best of diplomatic jingoism, our Pentagon official, as quoted in the *Washington Post*, said, if they do not comply, we will "whack" them.

Hardly do I think this policy will lead to peace and a wonderful election. I really challenge the Congress, in the continuation of the funding of a military operation that is doomed to fail. It is a real tragedy that we get promises made by the administration.

The troops were supposed to be in there until December 1996, and here they are, another year, and supposedly they are supposed to come out next July. But the way things are going there, and by the way we comply, we are complicit in this operation and provide the funds, the odds of our troops being out of there next July are very, very slim.

This raises the question about overall policy. Traditionally the American foreign policy, up until the latter part of this century, has been a policy of noninterference, nonintervention in the affairs of other nations, and also that of neutrality with all nations.

This is proper under the Constitution. This has been traditional. Instead, we should be concentrating on national security issues. We should be concerned about what the American position is, and we should not pretend that we know what is best for everybody, because we do not. ■

November 5, 1997
INCONSISTENCY IN AMERICA'S FOREIGN POLICY
HON. RON PAUL of TEXAS
IN THE HOUSE OF REPRESENTATIVES

Mr. Speaker, the Congress has never earned high marks for consistency. We do spend many hours debating the minor differences in the management of many centralized programs that are generally unwarranted. But when it comes to foreign policy, I see both sides of the aisle are eagerly agreeing with the president that we must threaten force and use of force in Iraq.

Yet, Mr. Speaker, there is no indication that this is a proper position. **We have been told by the Ambassador to the United Nations that the reason we must threaten force in this area is that Iraq is a direct threat to the security of the United Nations. Here all along, I thought I was here in the Congress to protect the security of the United States.**

We are inconsistent, because the majority of Americans want us out of Bosnia. Most Members of Congress argue and vote to get us out of Bosnia. There is no indication that we are going to get out of Bosnia. Yet here we are, chanting away that we should use force and threaten force in Bosnia. We do not have that same policy with China, a country many see as a threat to our security. ■

"Of all the enemies to public liberty, war is perhaps the most to be dreaded because it comprises and develops the germ of every other."
—James Madison

CHAPTER 9

My concern regarding our policy toward Iraq began long before the current conflict. I spoke out against President Clinton's actions, and note below that Iraq was also a client state of adversaries we had long subsidized.

January 27, 1998
BOMBING IRAQ WOULD BE THE RESULT OF FLAWED FOREIGN POLICY
HON. RON PAUL of TEXAS
IN THE HOUSE OF REPRESENTATIVES

Mr. Speaker, it appears the administration is about to bomb Iraq. The stated reason is to force UN inspections of every inch of Iraqi territory to rule out the existence of any weapons of mass destruction. The president's personal problems may influence this decision, but a flawed foreign policy is behind this effort.

Why is Iraq a greater threat to U.S. security than China, North Korea, Russia or Iran? They all have weapons of mass destruction. This makes no sense.

There was a time in our history that bombing foreign countries was considered an act of war, done only with a declaration by this Congress. Today, tragically, it is done at the whim of presidents and at the urging of congressional leaders without a vote, except maybe by the UN Security Council.

But the president is getting little support and a lot of resistance from our allies for this aggressive action.

Sadly, our policy in the Middle East has served to strengthen the hand of Hussein, unify the Islamic fundamentalists and expose American citizens to terrorist attacks. Hussein is now anxious for the bombs to hit to further stir the hatred and blame toward America for all the atrocities he has inflicted on his people. ■

January 28, 1998
HON. RON PAUL of TEXAS
IN THE HOUSE OF REPRESENTATIVES

Mr. Speaker, the morning papers today recorded that Russia was providing weapon technology to Iraq. We have known for years that China has done the same thing. Does this mean that we must attack them as well as Iraq?

Instead, though, we give foreign aid to both China and to Russia, so indirectly we are subsidizing the very weapons that we are trying to eliminate.

I would like to remind my colleagues that bombing a country, especially one halfway around the world that is not a direct threat to our security, is not a moral act. A moral war is one that is defensive and a legal war is one that is declared by Congress. We should only pursue an act of war when our national security is threatened.

Bombing will solve nothing. It will open up a can of worms. We should not condone it. We should not endorse it. We should not encourage it.

Please think carefully before we permit our president to pursue this war adventure. ■

In response to President Clinton's State of the Union Address, I analyzed the status of our republic. Here excerpted are portions dealing with foreign affairs.

January 28, 1998
STATE OF THE REPUBLIC
HON. RON PAUL of TEXAS
IN THE HOUSE OF REPRESENTATIVES

Mr. Speaker, the first session of the 105th Congress has been completed, and the third year of the conservative revolution has passed. Current congressional leadership has declared victory and is now debating how to spend the excess revenues about to flow into the Treasury.

As the legislative year came to a close, the only serious debate was over the extent of the spending increases negotiated into the budget. The more things changed, the more they stayed the same. Control over the Congress is not seriously threatened, and there has been no clear-cut rejection of the 20th Century welfare state. But that does not mean there is no effort to change the direction of the country. It is just that it is not yet in progress.

But many taxpayers throughout the country are demanding change. Today there are more people in Washington expressing a sincere desire to shrink the welfare state than there were when I left 13 years ago. The final word on this has not yet been heard.

In contemplating what needs to be done and why we have not done better, we should consider several philosophic infractions in which Members of Congress participate that encourage a loss of liberty and endanger our national security and the Republic while perpetuating the status quo.

Following are some of the flaws or errors in thinking about issues that I find pervasive throughout the Congress:

Although foreign affairs was not on the top of the agenda in the last session, misunderstanding in this area presents one the greatest threats to the future of America. There is near conformity and uniformity of opinion in the Congress for endorsing the careless use of U.S. force to police the world. Although foreign policy was infrequently debated in the past year and there are no major wars going on or likely to start soon, the danger inherent in foreign entanglements warrants close scrutiny.

The economy, crime, the environment, drugs, currency instability, and

69

many other problems are important. But it is in the area of foreign policy and for interventionism that provokes the greatest threat to our liberties and sovereignty. Whenever there are foreign monsters to slay, regardless of their true threat to us, misplaced patriotic zeal is used to force us to look outward and away from domestic problems and the infractions placed on our personal liberties here at home.

Protecting personal liberties in any society is always more difficult during war. The uniformity of opinion in Congress is enshrined with the common clichés that no one thinks through, like foreign policy is bipartisan; only the president can formulate foreign policy; we must support the troops and, therefore, of course, the war, which is usually illegal and unwise but cannot be challenged; we are the only world superpower; we must protect our interests, like oil. However, it is never admitted, although most know, our policy is designed to promote the military-industrial complex and world government.

Most recently, the **Congress almost unanimously beat the drums for war, i.e., to kill Hussein. Any consideration of the facts involved elicited charges of anti-patriotism.** Yet in the midst of the clamor to send our planes and bombs to Baghdad, cooler heads were found in, of all places, Kuwait.

A Kuwaiti professor, amazingly, was quoted in a proper pro-government Kuwaiti newspaper saying, "The U.S. frightens us with Saddam to make us buy weapons and sign contracts with American companies…" thus ensuring a market for American arms manufacturers and United States continued military presence in the Middle East.

A Kuwaiti legislator was quoted as saying, "The use of force has ended up strengthening the Iraqi regime rather than weakening it."

Other Kuwaitis have suggested that the U.S. really wants Hussein in power to make sure his weak neighbors fear him and are forced to depend on the United States for survival.

In spite of the reservations and reasons to go slow, the only criticism coming from congressional leaders was that Clinton should do more, quicker, without any serious thought of the consequences, which would be many.

The fact that, of the original 35 allies in the Persian Gulf War, only one remains—Great Britain—should make us question our policy in this region. This attitude in Washington should concern all Americans. It makes it too easy for our presidents to start a senseless war without considering dollar costs or threats to liberty here and abroad. Even without a major war, this policy enhances the prestige and the influence of the United Nations.

These days, not even the United States moves without permission from the UN Security Council. In checking with the U.S. Air Force about the history of U-2 flights in Iraq, over Iraq, and in their current schedules, I was firmly told the Air Force was not in charge of these flights, the UN was. The Air Force suggested I call the Defense Department.

There is much to be concerned about with our current approach to foreign policy. It is dangerous because it can lead to a senseless war, like Vietnam, or small ones with bad results, like Somalia.

Individual freedom is always under attack. Once there is any serious confrontation with a foreign enemy, we are all required to rally around the president, no matter how flawed the policy. Too often, the consequences are unforeseen, like making Hussein stronger, not weaker after the Persian Gulf War.

The role of the military-industrial complex cannot be ignored; and since the marching orders come from the United Nations, the industrial complex is more international than ever.

But there is reason to believe the hidden agenda of our foreign policy is less hidden than it had been in the past. Referring to the United States in the international oil company success in the Caspian Sea, a Houston newspaper recently proclaimed, "U.S. views pipelines as a big foreign policy victory."

This referred to the success of major deals made by giant oil companies to build pipelines to carry oil out of the Caspian Sea while also delivering a strong message that, for these projects to be successful and further enhance foreign policy, it will require government subsidies to help pay the bill. Market development of the pipelines would be cheaper, but would not satisfy our international government planners.

So we must be prepared to pay, as we already have started to, through our foreign aid appropriations. This promotes, on a grand scale, a government business partnership that is dangerous to those who love liberty and detest fascism. Yet most Members of Congress will say little, ask little, and understand little, while joining in the emotional outburst directed toward the local thugs running the Mideastern fiefdoms like Iraq and Libya.

This attitude, as pervasive as it is in Washington, is tempered by the people's instincts for minding our own business, not wanting Americans to be the policemen of the world, and deep concern for American sovereignty. The result, not too unusual, is for the politicians to be doing one thing in

Washington while saying something else at home.

At home, virtually all citizens condemn U.S. troops serving under UN command, yet the financing and support for expanding the United Nations' and NATO's roles continue as the hysteria mounts on marching on Baghdad or Bosnia or Haiti, or wherever our leaders decide the next monster is to be found.

The large majority of House Members claim they want our troops out of Bosnia. Yet the president gets all the funding he wants. The Members of Congress get credit at home for paying lip service to a U.S. policy of less intervention, while the majority continue to support the troops, the president, the military-industrial complex, and the special interests who drive our foreign policy, demanding more funding while risking the lives, property, peace, and liberty of American citizens.

Congress casually passes resolution after resolution, many times nearly unanimously, condemning some injustice in the world, and for the most part there is a true injustice. But along with the caveat that threatens some unconstitutional U.S. military interference, financial assistance—or withdrawal of assistance or sanctions—in order to force our will on someone else is all done in the name of promoting the United Nations and one-world government.

Many resolutions on principle are similar to the Gulf of Tonkin resolution, which became equivalent to a declaration of war and allowed for a massive loss of life in the Vietnam fiasco. Most Members of Congress fail to see the significance of threatening violence against countries like Libya, Somalia, Rwanda, Bosnia, Iraq, Iran, or Haiti. But our credibility suffers since our policies can never satisfy both sides of each regional conflict.

In the Middle East, even with all our announced intentions and military effort to protect Kuwait, our credibility is questioned as most Arabs still see us as pro-Israel, anti-Arab, and motivated by power, oil and money.

America's effort to prevent a million casualties in Rwanda does not in any way compare to our perennial effort to get Hussein. It is hardly violations of borders or the possession of weapons of mass destruction that motivate us to get Hussein or drive our foreign policy.

We were allies of Iraq when it used poison gas against the Kurds and across the border into Iran. We support the Turks, even though they murdered Kurds, but we condemn the Iraqis when they do the same thing.

There are more than 25,000 Soviet nuclear warheads that cannot be accounted for, and all we hear about from the politicians is Iraq's control of weapons of mass destruction.

Our policy in the Middle East is totally schizophrenic and driven by Arab oil, weapon sales, and Israel. This is especially dangerous, because the history of the West's intrusion into the Middle East for a thousand years in establishing the artificial borders that exist today has created a mindset among Islamic fundamentalists guaranteeing friction will persist in this region, no matter how many Husseins or Ayatollahs we kill. That would only make things worse for us.

As much as I fear and detest one-world government, this chaos that we contribute to in the Middle East assures me that there is no smooth sailing for the new world order. Rough seas are ahead for all of us. If the UN's plans for their type of order is successful, it will cost American citizens money and freedom. If significant violence breaks out, it will cost American citizens money, freedom and lives.

Yes, I fear a biological, even a nuclear accident. But I see our cities at a much greater risk because of our policy than if we were neutral and friends with all factions, instead of trying to be a financial and military ally of all factions depending on the circumstances.

The way we usually get dragged into a shooting war is by some unpredictable incident, where innocent Americans are killed after our government placed them in harm's way and the enemy was provoked. Then the argument is made that once hostilities break out, debating the policy that created the mess is off limits. Everybody then must agree to support the troops.

But **the best way to support our troops and our liberties is to have a policy that avoids unnecessary confrontation.** A pro-American constitutional policy of nonintervention would go a long way toward guaranteeing maximum liberty and protection of life and property for all Americans.

American interests around the world could best be served by friendship and trade with all who would be friends, and subsidies to none. ■

The lead up to the current Iraq debacle was a long time coming, and even in the Clinton years, Congress was laying the ground work, which only a few of us in the body questioned.

February 5, 1998
CONGRESS SHOULD MOVE CAUTIOUSLY ON RESOLUTION REGARDING IRAQ
HON. RON PAUL of TEXAS
IN THE HOUSE OF REPRESENTATIVES

Madam Speaker, in 1964, a resolution passed this Congress urging the president to take all necessary measures to repel any armed attack against the forces of the United States and to prevent further aggression, the Gulf of Tonkin Resolution.

Today there is a resolution floating around this Congress that urges the president to take all necessary and appropriate actions to respond to the threat posed by Iraq. We should remember history. We lost 50,000 men after we passed that last resolution. **We do not have a sensible policy with Iraq.** We should move cautiously.

Madam Speaker, I would also urge other Members to be cautious when they talk about a surgical strike and assassination. Assassination of foreign leaders is still illegal under our law.

I urge my fellow colleagues, please, be cautious, be careful, and be wise when it comes to giving this president the right to wage war. Ironically, this president did not respond in the same manner with the Gulf of Tonkin resolution as he expects the young people to respond today. ■

Sending and maintaining troops abroad is a major component of our current interventionist policies that not only violate our deeply held principles but also leads to practical problems

March 10, 1998
U.S. OBSESSION WITH WORLDWIDE MILITARY OCCUPATION POLICY
HON. RON PAUL of TEXAS
IN THE HOUSE OF REPRESENTATIVES

Mr. Speaker, **last week it was Saddam Hussein and the Iraqis. This week's Hitler is Slobodon Milosevic and the Serbs. Next week,**

who knows? Kim Jong il and the North Koreans? Next year, who will it be, the Ayatollah and the Iranians? Every week we must find a foreign infidel to slay, and, of course, keep the military-industrial complex humming.

Once our ally, Saddam Hussein, with encouragement from us, invaded Iran, was it not logical that he might believe that we condone border crossings and invasions, even into what Iraqis believe rightfully theirs—Kuwait—especially after getting tacit approval from U.S. Ambassador Glaspie?

Last week, U.S. Special Envoy to the Balkans, Robert Gelbard, while visiting Belgrade, praised Milosevic for his cooperation in Bosnia and called the separatists in Kosovo "without question, a terrorist group." So how should we expect a national government to treat its terrorists?

Likewise, our Secretary of State, in 1991, gave a signal to Milosevic by saying, "All Yugoslavia should remain a monolithic state." What followed was to be expected: Serb oppression of the Croats and the Muslims.

All our wise counsel so freely given to so many in this region fails to recognize that the country of Yugoslavia was an artificial country created by the Soviet masters, just as the borders of most Middle Eastern countries were concocted by the British and UN resolutions.

The centuries-old ethnic rivalries, inherent in this region and aggravated by persistent Western influence as far back as the Crusades, will never be resolved by arbitrary threats and use of force from the United States or the United Nations. All that is being accomplished is to further alienate the factions, festering hate and pushing the region into a war of which we need no part.

Planning any military involvement in Kosovo is senseless. Our security is not threatened, and no one has the foggiest notion whether Kofi Annan or Bill Clinton is in charge of our foreign policy. The two certainly do not speak in unison on Iraq.

But we cannot maintain two loyalties, one to a world government under the United Nations and the other to U.S. sovereignty protected by an American Congress. If we try, only chaos can result, and we are moving rapidly in that direction.

Instead of bringing our troops home from Bosnia, as many Members of Congress have expressed an interest in doing, over the president's objection, we are rapidly preparing for sending more troops into Kosovo. This obsession with worldwide military occupation by U.S. troops is occurring at the very time our troops lack adequate training and preparation.

This is not a result of too little money by a misdirected role for our military, a role that contradicts the policy of neutrality, friendship, trade and nonintervention in the affairs of other nations. The question we should ask is: are we entitled to, wealthy enough, or even wise enough to assume the role of world policemen and protector of the world's natural resources?

Under the Constitution, there is no such authority. Under rules of morality, we have no authority to force others to behave as we believe they should, and force American citizens to pay for it, not only with dollars, but with life and limb as well. By the rules of common sense, the role of world policemen is a dangerous game and not worth playing.

Acting as an honest broker, the U.S. may help bring warring factions to the peace table, but never with threats of war or bribes paid for by the American taxpayers. We should stop sending money and weapons to all factions. Too often our support finds its way into the hands of both warring factions. We never know how long it will be for our friends and allies of today to become our enemy and targets of tomorrow.

Concern for American security is a proper and necessary function of the U.S. Congress. The current policy, and one pursued for decades, threatens our security, drains our wallets—and worst of all—threatens the lives of young Americans to stand tall for Americans defense, but not for Kofi Annan and the United Nations. ■

Tom Campbell of California introduced a resolution to remove our troops from Bosnia. We got nearly 200 votes, including a vast majority of Republicans. A year later we would be engaged in bombing in the region.

March 17, 1998
REMOVING U.S. ARMED FORCES FROM BOSNIA AND HERZEGOVINA
HON. RON PAUL of TEXAS
IN THE HOUSE OF REPRESENTATIVES

Mr. Speaker, I would like to draw the attention of my colleagues to two House Concurrent Resolutions that we will be voting on, one today and one tomorrow.

The one tomorrow is offered by the gentleman from California (Mr. Campbell), which I think we should pay close attention to and, hopefully, support. This is H. Con. Res. 227. It is a concurrent resolution directing the president, pursuant to section 5(c) of the War Powers Resolution, to remove United States Armed Forces from the Republic of Bosnia and Herzegovina.

The troops should never have been sent there in the first place. There was a lot of controversy. It was far from unanimous consent from the Congress to send the troops there. They were sent there in 1995, and they were to be there for 18 months. Each time we came upon a date for removing the troops, they were extended.

Currently, it is the president's position that the troops will stay indefinitely. He has not set a date, although the Congress has set a date of this June for all funding to be removed as of June and the troops should come home. This resolution more or less states that same position. I strongly favor this, and I believe that the Congress should send a strong message that we should not casually and carelessly send troops around the world to police the world. This is a good way for us to get into trouble.

Our national security is not threatened. There was no justification for our troops to be sent there. There are always good reasons given, though, because there are problems. Well there are problems every place in the world. If we try to solve all the problems of the world, we would not have troops in a hundred countries like we have now, we would have them in three or four hundred countries. But it is true that we send troops with the most amount of pressure put upon us to do it.

There are certain countries, like in Rwanda, Africa, we certainly did not apply the same rules to that country as we did to Bosnia and the Persian Gulf and Iraq. We did not do this when we saw the mass killings in the Far East under Pol Pot.

Under certain circumstances where there is political pressure made by certain allies or by interests of oil, we are likely to get involved. But the principle of a noninterventionist foreign policy should make certain that we, the Congress, never condone, never endorse, never promote the placement of troops around the world in harm's way because it is a good way for men to get killed. For most purposes, the lives of our American soldiers are too valuable to be put into a situation where there is so much harm and danger.

Fortunately there have been no American deaths in this region, but there is a good reason for those troops to come out. The peace has not been settled there, and it is not going to be. And the 16,000 to 20,000 troops that we have had there will not be able to maintain the peace as long as these warring factions exist. They have existed, not for months, not for a few years, but literally for hundreds, if not thousands, of years that people in this region have been fighting among themselves.

It is not our responsibility. Yes, we can condemn the violence; and who would not? But does that justify the taxing of American citizens and imposing a threat to American lives by sending our troops to all these hot spots around the region?

I strongly urge my fellow colleagues to look carefully at this resolution tomorrow and assume congressional responsibility. It is not the responsibility of the president to wage war, to put troops around the world. That is a *congressional* responsibility.

Although there has been no declaration of war, we are sitting ducks for a war to be started. So let us stop the war before it gets started.

I think we should strongly endorse this resolution and make sure these troops come home. It is interesting that there is a fair amount of support for this, and we obviously won the vote on this last year to say the troops should come home in June of this year. I suspect and hope that this will be restated, and there will be no excuse to extend their stay in this region.

But at the same time we win those kind of votes, there is a strong sentiment here in the Congress when we are required to vote, and there is certainly a strong sentiment among the American people that we ought to be dealing with our problems here at home. We ought not to assume the role of world policemen. And we ought to mind our own business, and we ought to be concerned about the sovereignty of the United States, rather than sending our troops around the world under the auspices of the United Nations and NATO and literally giving up our sovereignty to international bodies. We were very confused as to who was really in charge of foreign policy in Iraq, whether it was Kofi Annan or whether it was our president. ■

The Iraq Liberation Act set the stage for war. Passed during Bill Clinton's term, it was, like the later bill to give President Bush authority to invade, passed with strong bipartisan support

October 5, 1998
SETTING THE STAGE FOR WAR
HON. RON PAUL of TEXAS
IN THE HOUSE OF REPRESENTATIVES

Mr. Speaker, understand this legislation came before the committee on Friday, one legislative day prior to today. There has been no committee report filed, and it was brought up under suspension. I believe this legislation is very serious legislation. It is not a casual piece of legislation condemning a leader in another country that is doing less than honorable things.

I see this piece of legislation as essentially being a declaration of virtual war. It is giving the president tremendous powers to pursue war efforts against a sovereign nation. It should not be done casually. I think it is another example of a flawed foreign policy we have followed for a good many decades.

For instance, at the beginning of this legislation is cited one of the reasons why we must do something. It says on September 22, 1980, *Iraq* invaded Iran starting an eight-year war in which *Iraq* employed chemical weapons against Iranian troops, very serious problems. We should condemn that. But **the whole problem is we were *Iraq*'s ally at that time, giving him military assistance, giving him funds and giving him technology for chemical weapons.**

So here we are now deciding that we have to virtually declare war against this individual. It is not like he is the only hoodlum out there. I could give my colleagues a list of 15 or 20. I do not like the leadership of China. Why do we not do something about China? I do not like the leadership of Sudan. But all of a sudden we have to decide what we are going to give this president to pursue getting rid of Saddam Hussein.

Just a few months ago, or last November, we passed a resolution, and the resolution was HR137. It sounded very general and very benign, and it talked about the atrocities caused by Saddam Hussein, and we asked to condemn, and also to set up a UN commission to study this and give the UN authority to pursue arrests and convict and try Saddam Hussein. This is not something we are doing for the interests of the United States. We are doing this under the interests of the United Nations; we are the spokesperson for them.

Not too long ago, a few years back in the 1980s, in our effort to bring peace and democracy to the world, we assisted the freedom fighters of Afghanistan. In our infinite wisdom, we gave money, technology and training to Bin Laden, and now, this very year, we have declared that Bin Laden was responsible for the bombing in Africa. So what is our response, because we allow our president to pursue war too easily? What was the president's response? Some even say that it might have been for other reasons than for national security reasons. So he goes off and bombs Afghanistan, and he goes off and bombs Sudan, and now the record shows that very likely the pharmaceutical plant in

Sudan was precisely that, a pharmaceutical plant.

I say we should stop and think for a minute before we pursue and give the president more authority to follow a policy that to me is quite dangerous. This to me is equivalent to declaring war and allowing the president to pursue this.

Another complaint listed on this legislation: in February 1988 Iraq forcibly relocated Kurdish civilians from their homes. Terrible thing to do, and they probably did; there is no doubt about it. But what did we do after the Persian Gulf War? We encouraged the Kurdish people to stand up and fight against Saddam Hussein, and they did, and we forgot about them. They were killed by the tens of thousands. There is no reason for them to trust us. There is no reason for the Sudanese people to believe and trust in us, in what we do when we rain bombs on their country and they have done nothing to the United States. **The people of Iraq certainly have not done anything to the United States, and we certainly can find leaders around the world that have not done equally bad things. I think we should stop and think about this.**

Just today it was announced that the Turks are lined up on the Syrian border. What for? To go in and kill the Kurds because they do not like the Kurds. I think that is terrible. But what are we doing about it? Who are the Turks? They are our allies, they are our friends. They get military assistance. The American people are paying the Turks to keep their military up. So we are responsible for that.

This policy makes no sense. Some day we have to think about the security of the United States. We spend this money. We spent nearly $100 million bombing nobody and everybody for who knows what reason last week. At the same time our military forces are under trained and lack equipment, we are wasting money all around the world trying to get more people, see how many people we can get to hate us. Some day we have to stop and ask why are we pursuing this. Why do we not have a policy that says that we should, as a Congress, defend the United States, protect us, have a strong military, but not to police the world in this endless adventure of trying to be everything to everyone? We have been on both sides of every conflict since World War II. Even not too long ago they were talking about bombing in Kosovo. As a matter of fact, that is still a serious discussion. But a few months ago they said, well, we are not quite sure who the good guys are, maybe we ought to bomb both sides. It makes no sense. Why do we not become friends to both sides?

There are people around the world that we deal with that are equally repulsive to Saddam Hussein. I believe very sincerely that the Founders of this country were on the right track when they said stay out of entangling alliances. We should trade with people; we would get along with them better. We have pursued this type of policy in Cuba for 40 years, and it has served Castro well. Why do we not go down and get rid of Castro? Where do we get this authority to kill a dictator? We do not have that authority, and to do it under one day of hearings, mark it up, bring it up the next day under suspension; I do not understand why anybody could vote for this just on the nature of it.

We should not be doing this. We should stop and think about it and try to figure out a much better way. I, for instance, am on a bill to trade with Cuba. Oh, how horrible, we should not trade with Cuba, they are a bunch of Commies down there. But we should be selling them rice, and we should be selling them our crops. We should not be bombing these people. As my colleagues know, at the end of this bill I think we get a hint about why we do not go to Rwanda for humanitarian reasons. Now there are some atrocities. Why do we not clean that mess up? Because I believe very sincerely that there is another element tied into this, and I think it has something to do with money. I think it has something to do with oil. The oil interests need the oil in *Iraq*, and he does not, Saddam Hussein does not, comply with the people of the West. So he has to go.

Also at the end of this legislation is something about what might be going on. They are asking to set up and check into the funds that Saddam Hussein owes to the West. Who is owed? They do not owe me any money. But I will bet my colleagues there are a lot of banks in New York who are owed a lot of money, and this is one of the goals, to set up and make sure Saddam Hussein pays his bills.

All I do is ask my colleagues to think about it, urge them to go slowly. Nothing is so pressing that we should give the president this much authority to go to war.

Under the appropriations it is endless, it is open, endless, and here we are concerned about saving Social Security. Any amount of money spent on this bill comes out of Social Security. Yes, there was yelling and screaming about a tax cut. Oh, it is coming out of Social Security? Well, this money is not appropriated, and it is such sums as necessary for military and economic benefits. After we get rid of one thug, we are going to have it in. I hope we make a better choice than we did with Bin Laden. I mean, he was our close ally.

Please think twice, slow up, vote against this bill. We do not need this. ■

"It is unpatriotic not to tell the truth, whether about the president or anyone else."—Theodore Roosevelt

CHAPTER 10

The UN inspired war with Iraq continued during the Clinton Administration without congressional authorization and without any real accountability as Congress forsook its constitutional duties.

February 2, 1999
HOW LONG WILL THE WAR WITH IRAQ GO ON BEFORE CONGRESS NOTICES?
HON. RON PAUL of TEXAS
IN THE HOUSE OF REPRESENTATIVES

Mr. Speaker, I ask my fellow colleagues, how long will the war go on before Congress notices? **We have been bombing and occupying Iraq since 1991, longer than the occupation of Japan after World War II. Iraq has never committed aggression against the United States.** The recent escalation of bombing in Iraq has caused civilian casualties to mount. The Clinton administration claims UN resolution 687, passed in 1991, gives him the legal authority to continue this war. We have perpetuated hostilities and sanctions for more than 8 years on a country that has never threatened our security, and the legal justification comes not from the U.S. Congress, as the Constitution demands, but from a clearly unconstitutional authority, the United Nations.

In the past several months, the airways have been filled with Members of Congress relating or restating their fidelity to their oath of office to uphold the Constitution. That is good, and I am sure it is done with the best of intentions. But when it comes to explaining our constitutional responsibility to make sure unconstitutional sexual harassment laws are thoroughly enforced, while disregarding most people's instincts towards protecting privacy, it seems to be overstating a point, compared to our apathy toward the usurping of congressional power to declare and wage war. That is something we ought to be concerned about.

A major reason for the American Revolution was to abolish the King's power to wage war, tax, and invade personal privacy without representation and due process of law. For most of our history, our presidents and our congresses understood that war was a prerogative of the congressional authority alone. Even minimal military interventions by our early presidents were, for the most part, only with constitutional approval.

This all changed after World War II with our membership in the United Nations. As bad as it is to allow our presidents to usurp congressional authority to wage war, it is much worse for the president to share this sovereign right with an international organization that requires us to pay more than our fair share while we get a vote no greater than the rest.

The Constitution has been blatantly ignored by the president, while Congress has acquiesced in endorsing the eight-year war against Iraq. The War Powers Resolution of 1973 has done nothing to keep our presidents from policing the world, spending billions of dollars, killing many innocent people, and jeopardizing the very troops that should be defending America.

The continual ranting about stopping Hussein—who is totally defenseless against our attacks—from developing weapons of mass destruction ignores the fact that more than 30,000 very real nuclear warheads are floating around the old Soviet empire.

Our foolish policy in Iraq invites terrorist attacks against U.S. territory and incites Islamic fundamentalists against us. As a consequence, our efforts to develop long-term peaceful relations with Russia are now ending. This policy cannot enhance world peace. Instead of changing it, the president is about to expand it in another no-win centuries-old fight in Kosovo.

It is time for Congress to declare its interest in the Constitution and take responsibility on issues that matter, like the war powers. ■

My "State of the Republic" for 1999 was a broad overview of federal policy, but specifically looked at the drift of the war-making power from Congress, where the Constitution places it, to the Executive. I also consider how our foreign policy dovetails with the general trend toward bigger government.

February 2, 1999
THE STATE OF THE REPUBLIC
or CONGRESS RELINQUISHING THE
POWER TO WAGE WAR
HON. RON PAUL of TEXAS
IN THE HOUSE OF REPRESENTATIVES

Madam Speaker, I have great concern for the future of the American Republic. Many Americans argue that we now enjoy the best of times. Others concern themselves with problems less visible but smoldering beneath the surface. Those who are content point out that the economy is booming, we are not at war, crime rates are down, and the majority of Americans feel safe and secure in their homes and community. Others point out that economic booms, when brought about artificially with credit creation, are destined to end with a bang. The absence of overt war does not negate the fact that tens of thousands of American troops are scattered around the world in the middle of ancient fights not likely to be settled by our meddling and which may escalate at any time.

Madam Speaker, the relinquishing of the power to wage war by Congress to the President, although ignored or endorsed by many, raises serious questions regarding the status of our Republic, and although many Americans are content with their routine activities, much evidence demonstrating that our personal privacy is routinely being threatened. Crime still remains a concern for many with questions raised as to whether or not violent crimes are accurately reported, and ironically there are many Americans who now fear that dreaded federal bureaucrat and possible illegal seizure of their property by the government more than they do the thugs in the street. I remain concerned about the economy, our militarism and internationalism, and the systemic invasion of our privacy in every aspect of our lives by nameless bureaucrats. I am convinced that if these problems are not dealt with, the Republic for which we have all sworn an oath to protect will not survive.

Madam Speaker, all Members should be concerned about the war

85

powers now illegitimately assumed by the president, the financial bubble that will play havoc with the standard of living of most Americans when it bursts, and the systemic undermining of our privacy even in this age of relative contentment.

The Founders of this great nation abhorred tyranny and loved liberty. The power of the King to wage war, tax and abuse the personal rights of the American colonists drove them to rebel, win a revolution, and codify their convictions in a new Constitution. It was serious business, and every issue was thoroughly debated and explained most prominently in the Federalist Papers. Debate about trade among the States and with other countries, sound money, and the constraints on presidential power occupied a major portion of their time.

Initially the Articles of Confederation spoke clearly of just who would be responsible for waging war. It gave the constitutional Congress, "sole and exclusive right and power of determining on peace and war." In the debate at the Constitutional Convention, it was clear that this position was maintained as the power of the British King was not to be "a proper guide in defining executive war powers" for the newly formed Republic. The result was a Constitution that gave Congress the power to declare war, issue letters of mark and reprisal, call up the militia, raise and train an Army and Navy, and regulate foreign commerce, a tool often used in international conflict. The president was also required to share power with the Senate in ratifying treaties and appointing ambassadors.

Let there be no doubt: the president, according to the Constitution, has no power to wage war. However it has been recognized throughout our history that certain circumstances might require the president to act in self-defense if Congress is not readily available to act if the United States is attacked.

Recent flagrant abuse of the power to wage war by modern-day presidents—including the most recent episodes in Iraq, Afghanistan and Sudan—should prompt this Congress to revisit this entire issue of war powers. Certain abuses of power are obviously more injurious than others. The use of the FBI and the IRS to illegally monitor and intimidate citizens is a power that should be easy to condemn, yet it continues to thrive. The illegal and immoral power to create money out of thin air for the purpose of financing a welfare-warfare state serving certain financial interests, while causing the harmful business cycle, is a process that most in Washington do not understand nor care about. These are ominous powers of great magnitude that were never meant to be permitted under the Constitution.

But as bad as these abuses are, the power of a single person, the president, to wage war is the most egregious of all presidential powers: and Congress deserves the blame for allowing such power to gravitate into the hands of the president. The fact that nary a complaint was made in Congress for the recent aggressive military behavior of our president in Iraq for reasons that had nothing to do with national security should not be ignored. Instead, Congress unwisely and quickly rubber-stamped this military operation. We should analyze this closely and decide whether or not we in the Congress should promote a war powers policy that conforms to the Constitution or continue to allow our presidents ever greater leverage to wage war any time, any place and for any reason.

This policy of allowing our presidents unlimited authority to wage war has been in place since the end of World War II, although abuse, to a lesser degree, has occurred since the beginning of the 20th Century. Specifically since joining the United Nations, congressional authority to determine when and if our troops will fight abroad has been seriously undermined. From Truman's sending of troops to Korea to Bush's Persian Gulf War, we have seen big wars fought, tens of thousands killed, hundreds of thousands wounded, and hundreds of billions of dollars wasted. U.S. security, never at risk, has been needlessly jeopardized by the so-called peacekeeping missions and police exercises, while constitutional law has been seriously and dangerously undermined.

Madam Speaker, something must be done. The cost of this policy has been great in terms of life and dollars and our constitutional system of law. Nearly 100,000 deaths occurred in the Vietnam and Korean Wars. If we continue to allow our presidents to casually pursue war for the flimsiest of reasons, we may well be looking at another major conflict somewhere in the world in which we have no business or need to be involved.

The correction of this problem requires a concerted effort on the part of Congress to reclaim and reassert its responsibility under the Constitution with respect to war powers. Efforts were made to do exactly that after Vietnam in 1973 and more recently in 1995. Neither effort was successful, and ironically, the president emerged with more power, with each effort being undermined by supporters in the Congress of presidential authoritarianism and internationalism. Few objected to the Truman-ordered UN police actions in Korea in the 1950s, but they should have. This illegal and major war encouraged all subsequent presidents to assume greater authority to wage war than was ever intended by the Constitution, or assumed by all the presidents prior to World War II. **It is precisely because of the way we have entered in each military action since the 1940s without declaring war that their purposes have been vague and victory elusive; yet pain, suffering and long-term negative consequences have resulted.** The road on which this country embarked 50 years ago has led to the sacrifice of a lot of congressional prerogatives and citizen control over the excessive powers that have fallen into the hands of presidents quite willing to abuse this authority. No one person, if our society is to remain free, should be allowed to provoke war with aggressive military acts. Congress and the people are obligated to rein in this flagrant abuse of presidential power.

Not only did we suffer greatly from the unwise and illegal Korean and Vietnam wars, Congress has allowed a continuous abuse of military power by our presidents in an ever-increasing frequency. We have seen: troops needlessly die in Lebanon; Grenada invaded for questionable reasons; Libya bombed with innocent civilians killed; persistent naval operations in the Persian Gulf; Panama invaded; Iraq bombed on numerous occasions; Somalia invaded; a secret and illegal war fought in Nicaragua; Haiti occupied; and troops stationed in Bosnia, and now possibly soon in Kosovo.

Even the congressional permission to pursue the Persian Gulf War was an afterthought, since President Bush emphatically stated that it was unnecessary, since he received his authority from the United Nations.

Without an actual declaration of war and support from the American people, victory is unachievable. This has been the case with the ongoing war against Iraq. Without a legitimate concern for our national security, the willingness to declare war and achieve victory is difficult. The war effort becomes narrowly political, serving special interests, not fought for the defense of the United States against a serious military threat. If we can win a Cold War against the Soviets, we hardly need a *hot war* with a third-world nation unable to defend itself, Iraq.

Great concern in the 1960s over the excessive presidential war powers was expressed by the American people, and, thus, the interests of the U.S. Congress after Vietnam in the early 1970s. The War Powers Resolution of 1973 resulted, but due to shrewd manipulation and political chicanery, the effort resulted in giving the president more authority, allowing him to wage war for 60 to 90 days without congressional approval.

Prior to the Korean War, when the Constitution and historic precedent had been followed, the president could not and, for the most part, did not engage in any military effort not directly defensive in nature without explicit congressional approval.

The result of the passage of the War Powers Resolution was exactly opposite to its authors' intentions. More power is granted to the president to send troops hither and yon, with the various presidents sometimes reporting to the Congress and sometimes not. But Congress has unwisely and rarely objected, and has not in recent years demanded its proper role in decisions of war, nor hesitated to continue the funding that the various presidents have demanded.

Approval of presidentially directed aggression, disguised as "support for the troops," comes routinely, and if any Member does not obediently endorse every action a president might take, for whatever reason, it is implied the Member lacks patriotism and wisdom. It is amazing how we have drifted from the responsibility the Founders imagined that the Congress and the people would jealously protect.

It is too often and foolishly argued that we must permit great flexibility for the president to retaliate when American troops are in danger. But this is only after the president has invaded and placed our troops in harm's way.

By what stretch of the imagination can one say that these military actions can be considered defensive in nature? **The best way we can promote support for our troops is to employ them in a manner that is the least provocative. They must be given a mission confined to defending the United States, not policing the world or taking orders from the United Nations, or serving the special commercial interests of U.S. corporations around the world.**

The 1995 effort to repeal the War Powers Resolution failed because it was not a clean repeal, but one still requiring consultation and reporting to the Congress. This led to enough confusion to prevent its passage.

What is needed is a return to the Constitution as a strict guide to who has the authority to exert the war powers and, as has been scrupulously followed in the 19th Century by essentially all political parties and presidents.

The effort to curtail presidential powers, while requiring consultation and reporting to the Congress, implies that is all that is needed to avoid the strict rules laid out by the Constitution.

It was admitted in the House debate by the House leadership that the repeal actually gave the president more power to use troops overseas and they, therefore, urged passage of the measure. This accurate assessment prompted antiwar, pro-peace Republicans and Democrats to narrowly reject the proposal.

The message here is that clarification of the War Powers Resolution and a return to constitutional law are the only way presidential authority to wage war can be curtailed. If our presidents do not act accordingly, Congress must quickly and forcefully meet its responsibility by denying funds for foreign intervention and aggression initiated by the president.

The basic problem here is that there are still too many Members of Congress who endorse a presidency armed with the authority of a tyrant to wage war. But if this assumption of power by the president with Congress' approval is not reversed, the Republic cannot be maintained.

Putting the power in the hands of a single person, the president, to wage war, is dangerous and costly, and it destroys the notion that the people, through their congressional representatives, decide when military action should start and when war should take place.

The sacrifice of this constitutional principle, guarded diligently for 175 years and now severely eroded in the past 50, must be restored if we hope to protect our liberties and avoid yet another unnecessary and, heaven-forbid, major world conflict. Merely changing the law will not be enough to guarantee that future presidents will not violate their trust.

A moral commitment to the principle of limited presidential war powers in the spirit of the Republic is required. Even with the clearest constitutional restriction on the president to wage undeclared wars, buffered by precise legislation, if the sentiment of the Congress, the courts and the people or the president is to ignore these restraints, they will.

The best of all situations is when the spirit of the Republic is one and the same as the law itself, and honorable men are in positions of responsibility to carry out the law. Even though we cannot guarantee the moral commitment of future congresses or our presidents to the principles of liberty by changing the law, we still must make every effort possible to make the law and the Constitution as morally sound as possible.

Our responsibility here in the Congress is to protect liberty and do our best to ensure peace and trade with all who do not aggress against us. But peace is more easily achieved when we reject the notion that some Americans must subsidize foreign nations for a benefit that is intended to flow back to a select few Americans. Maintaining an empire or striving for a world government, while allowing excessive war powers to accrue to an imperial president, will surely lead to needless military conflicts, loss of life and liberty, and a complete undermining of our constitutional republic.

On another issue, privacy is the essence of liberty. Without it, individual rights cannot exist. Privacy and property are interlocked. If both were protected, little would need to be said about other civil liberties. If one's home, church or business is one's castle, and the privacy of one's person, papers and effects are rigidly protected, all rights desired in a free society will be guaranteed. Diligently protecting the right to privacy and property guarantees religious, journalistic and political experience, as well as a free market economy and sound money. Once a careless attitude emerges with respect to privacy, all other rights are jeopardized.

Today we find a systematic and pervasive attack on the privacy of American citizens, which undermines the principle of private property ownership. Understanding why the attack on privacy is rapidly expanding and recognizing a need to reverse this trend are necessary if our Republic is to survive.

Lack of respect for the privacy and property of the American colonists by the British throne was a powerful motivation for the American Revolution and resulted in the strongly worded and crystal-clear Fourth Amendment.

Emphatically, searches and seizures are prohibited except when warrants are issued upon probable cause supported by oath or affirmation, with details given as to place, person and things to be seized.

This is a far cry from the routine seizure by the federal government and forfeiture of property which occurs today. Our papers are no longer considered personal and their confidentiality has been eliminated. Private property is searched by federal agents without announcement. Huge fines are levied when federal regulations appear to have been violated, and proof of innocence is demanded if one chooses to fight the abuse in court and avoid the heavy fines.

Eighty thousand armed federal bureaucrats and law enforcement officers now patrol our land and business establishments. Suspicious religious groups are monitored and sometimes destroyed without due process of law, with little or no evidence of wrongdoing. Local and state jurisdiction is rarely recognized once the feds move in.

Today, it is routine for government to illegally seize property, requiring the victims to prove their innocence in order to retrieve their property. Many times they fail due to the expense and legal roadblocks placed in the victim's way.

Although the voters in the 1990s have cried out for a change in direction and demanded a smaller, less-intrusive government, the attack on privacy by the Congress, the administration and the courts has, nevertheless, accelerated. Plans have now been laid or implemented for a national I.D.

card, a national medical data bank, a data bank on individual MDs, deadbeat dads, intrusive programs monitoring our every financial transaction.

The Social Security number has been established as the universal identifier. The Social Security number is now commonly used for just about everything: getting a birth certificate, buying a car, seeing an MD, getting a job, opening up a bank account, getting a driver's license, making many routine purchases, and, of course, a death certificate. Cradle-to-the-grave government surveillance is here and daily getting more pervasive.

The attack on privacy is not a coincidence or an event that arises for no explainable reason. It results from a philosophy that justifies it and requires it. A government not dedicated to preserving liberty must, by its very nature, allow this precious right to erode.

A political system designed as ours was to protect life, liberty and property would vigorously protect all citizens' rights to privacy; this cannot occur unless the property and the fruits of one's labor, of every citizen, is protected from confiscation by thugs in the street as well as those in our legislative bodies.

The promoters of government intrusion into our privacy characteristically use wornout clichés to defend what they do. The most common argument is that if you have nothing to hide, why worry about it?

This is ludicrous. We have nothing to hide in our homes or our bedrooms, but that is no reason why Big Brother should be permitted to monitor us with a surveillance camera.

The same can be argued about our churches, our businesses, or any peaceful action we may pursue. Our personal activities are no one else's business. We may have nothing to hide, but, if we are not careful, we have plenty to lose—our right to be left alone.

Others argue that to operate government programs efficiently and without fraud, close monitoring is best achieved with a universal identifier, the Social Security number.

Efficiency and protection from fraud may well be enhanced with the use of a universal identifier, but this contradicts the whole notion of the proper role for government in a free society.

Most of the federal programs are unconstitutional to begin with, so eliminating waste and fraud and promoting efficiency for a program that requires a violation of someone else's rights should not be a high priority of the Congress. But the temptation is too great, even for those who question the wisdom of the government programs, and compromise of the Fourth

Amendment becomes acceptable.

I have never heard of a proposal to promote the national I.D. card, or anything short of this for any reasons other than a good purpose. Essentially all those who vote to allow the continual erosion of our privacy and other constitutional rights never do it because they consciously support a tyrannical government; it is always done with good intentions.

Believe me, most of the evil done by elected congresses and parliaments throughout all of history has been justified by good intentions. But that does not change anything. It just makes it harder to stop.

Therefore, we cannot ignore the motivation behind those who promote the welfare state. Bad ideas, if implemented, whether promoted by men of bad intentions or good, will result in bad results.

Well-intentioned people, men of goodwill, should, however, respond to a persuasive argument. Ignorance is the enemy of sound policy, every bit as much as political corruption.

Various management problems in support of welfarism motivate those who argue for only a little sacrifice of freedom to achieve a greater good for society. Each effort to undermine our privacy is easily justified.

The national I.D. card is needed, it is said, to detect illegal aliens, yet all Americans will need it to open up a bank account, get a job, fly on an airplane, see a doctor, go to school or drive a car.

Financial privacy must be sacrificed, it is argued, in order to catch money launderers, drug dealers, mobsters and tax cheats. Privacy for privacy's sake, unfortunately for many, is a nonissue.

The recent know-your-customer plan was designed by Richard Small, Assistant Director of the Division of Banking Supervision Regulation at the Federal Reserve. He is not happy with all of the complaints that he has received regarding this proposal. His program will require that every bank keep a detailed profile on every customer, how much is deposited, where it comes from, and when and how the money is spent. If there is any deviation from the profile on record, the bank is required to report this to a half dozen government agencies, which will require the customer to do a lot of explaining. This program will catch a few drug dealers, but will surely infringe on the liberty of every law-abiding citizen.

After thousands of complaints were registered at the Federal Reserve and the other agencies, Richard Small was quoted as saying that, in essence, the complaints were coming from these strange people who are overly concerned about the Constitution and privacy. Legal justification for the program, Small explained, comes from a court case that states that our personal papers, when in the hands of a third party like a bank, do not qualify for protection under the Fourth Amendment.

He is accurate in quoting the court case, but that does not make it right. Courts do not have the authority to repeal a fundamental right as important as that guaranteed by the Fourth Amendment. Under this reasoning, when applied to our medical records, all confidentiality between the doctor and the patient is destroyed.

For this reason, the proposal for a national medical data bank to assure us there will be no waste or fraud, that doctors are practicing good medicine, that the exchange of medical records between the HMOs will be facilitated and statistical research made easier, should be strenuously opposed. The more the government is involved in medicine or anything else, the greater the odds that personal privacy will be abused.

The IRS and the DEA, with powers illegally given them by the Congress and the courts, have prompted a flood of seizures and forfeitures in the last several decades without due process and, frequently, without search warrants or probable cause. Victims then are required to prove themselves innocent to recover the goods seized.

This flagrant and systematic abuse of privacy may well turn out to be a blessing in disguise. Like the public schools, it may provide the incentive for Americans finally to do something about the system.

The disaster state of the public school system has prompted millions of parents to provide private or home schooling for their children. The worse the government schools get, the more the people resort to private option, even without tax relief from the politicians. This is only possible as long as some remnant of our freedom remains, and these options are permitted. We cannot become complacent.

Hopefully, a similar reaction will occur in the area of privacy, but overcoming the intrusiveness of government into our privacy in nearly every aspect of our lives will be difficult. Home schooling is a relatively simple solution compared to avoiding the roving and snooping eye of Big Brother. Solving the privacy problem requires an awakening by the American people, with a strong message being sent to the U.S. Congress that we have had enough.

Eventually, stopping this systematic intrusion into our privacy will require challenging the entire welfare state. Socialism and welfarism self-destruct after a prolonged period of time due to their natural inefficiencies and national bankruptcy. As the system ages, more and more efforts are made to delay its demise by borrowing, inflating and coercion. The degree of violation of our privacy is a measurement of the coercion thought necessary by the proponents of authoritarianism to continue the process.

The privacy issue invites a serious discussion between those who seriously believe welfare redistribution helps the poor and does not violate anyone's rights, and others who promote policies that undermine privacy in an effort to reduce fraud and waste to make the programs work efficiently, even if they disagree with the programs themselves. This opportunity will actually increase as it becomes more evident that our country is poorer than most believe and sustaining the welfare state at current levels will prove impossible. An ever-increasing invasion of our privacy will force everyone eventually to reconsider the efficiency of the welfare state, if the welfare of the people is getting worse and their privacy invaded.

Our job is to make a principled, moral, constitutional and practical case for respecting everyone's privacy, even if it is suspected some private activities, barring violence, do not conform to our own private moral standards. We could go a long way to guaranteeing privacy for all Americans if we, as Members of Congress, would take our oath of office more seriously and do exactly what the Constitution says.

THE FINANCIAL BUBBLE

On a third item, the financial bubble: a huge financial bubble engulfs the world financial markets. This bubble has been developing for a long time, but has gotten much larger the last couple of years. Understanding this issue is critical to the economic security of all Americans that we all strive to protect.

Credit expansion is the root cause of all financial bubbles. Fiat monetary systems inevitably cause unsustainable economic expansion that results in a recession and/or depression. A correction always results, with the degree and duration being determined by government fiscal policy and central-bank monetary policy. If wages and prices are not allowed to adjust and the correction is thwarted by invigorated monetary expansion, new and sustained economic growth will be delayed or prevented. Financial dislocation caused by central banks in the various countries will differ from one another due to political perceptions, military considerations, and reserve currency status.

The U.S.'s ability to inflate has been dramatically enhanced by other countries' willingness to absorb our inflated currency, our dollar being the reserve currency of the world. Foreign central banks now hold in reserve over $600 billion, an amount significantly greater than that even held by our own Federal Reserve System. Our economic and military power gives us additional license to inflate our currency, thus delaying the inevitable correction inherent in a paper money system. This only allows for a larger bubble to develop, further jeopardizing our future economy.

Because of the significance of the dollar to the world economy, our inflation and the dollar-generated bubble is much more dangerous than single currency inflation such as that of Mexico, Brazil, South Korea, Japan and others. The significance of these inflations, however, cannot be dismissed.

Federal Reserve Board Chairman Alan Greenspan, when the Dow was at approximately 6,500, cautioned the nation about irrational exuberance; and for a day or two, the markets were subdued. But while openly worrying about an unsustained stock market boom, he nevertheless accelerated the very credit expansion that threatened the market and created the irrational exuberance.

From December 1996, at the time that Greenspan made this statement, to December 1998, the money supply soared. Over $1 trillion of new money, as measured by M-3, was created by the Federal Reserve. MZM, another monetary measurement, is currently expanding at a rate greater than 20 percent. This generous dose of credit has sparked even more irrational exuberance, which has taken the Dow to over 9,000 for a 30 percent increase in just two years.

When the foreign registered corporation long-term capital management was threatened in 1998; that is, the market demanding a logical correction to its own exuberance with its massive $1 trillion speculative investment in the derivatives market, Greenspan and company quickly came to its rescue with an even greater acceleration of credit expansion.

The pain of market discipline is never acceptable when compared to the pleasure of postponing hard decisions and enjoying, for a while longer, the short-term benefits gained by keeping the financial bubble inflated. But the day is fast approaching when the markets and Congress will have to deal with the attack on the dollar, once it is realized that exporting our inflation is not without limits.

A hint of what can happen when the world gets tired of holding too many of our dollars was experienced in the dollar crisis of 1979 and 1980, and we saw at that time interest rates over 21 percent. There is abundant evidence around warning us of the impending danger. According to Federal Reserve statistics, household debt reached 81 percent of personal income in the second quarter of 1998. For 20 years prior to 1985, household debt averaged around 50 percent of personal income. Between 1985 and 1998, due to generous Federal Reserve credit, competent American consumers increased this to 81 percent; now it is even higher. At the same time, our savings rate has dropped to zero percent.

The conviction that stock prices will continue to provide extra cash and confidence in the economy have fueled wild consumer spending and personal debt expansion. The home refinance index between 1997 and 1999 increased 700 percent. Secondary mortgages are now offered up to 120 percent of a home's equity, with many of these funds finding their way into the stock market. Generous credit and quasi-government agencies make these mortgage markets robust, but a correction will come when it is realized that the builders and the lenders have gotten ahead of themselves.

The willingness of foreign entities to take and hold our dollars has generated a huge current account deficit for the United States. It is expected that the $200 billion annual deficit that we are running now will accelerate to over $300 billion in 1999, unless the financial bubble bursts.

This trend has made us the greatest international debtor in the world, with a negative net international asset position of more than $1.7 trillion. A significantly weakened dollar will play havoc when this bill comes due and foreign debt holders demand payment.

Contributing to the bubble and the dollar strength has been the fact that even though the dollar has problems, other currencies are even weaker and thus make the dollar look strong in comparison. Budgetary figures are frequently stated in a falsely optimistic manner. In 1969, when there was a surplus of approximately $3 billion, the national debt went down approximately the same amount. In 1998, however, with a so-called surplus of $70 billion, the national debt went up $113 billion. Instead of the surpluses which are not really surpluses running forever, the deficits will rise with a weaker economy and current congressional plans to increase welfare and warfare spending.

Government propaganda promotes the false notion that inflation is no longer a problem. Nothing could be further from the truth. The dangerous financial bubble, a result of the Federal Reserve's deliberate policy of inflation, and the Fed's argument that there is no inflation according to government-concocted CPI figures, is made to justify a continuous policy of monetary inflation, because they are terrified of the consequence of deflation. The Federal Reserve may sincerely believe maintaining the status quo, preventing price inflation and delaying deflation is possible, but it really is not.

The most astute money manager cannot balance inflation against deflation as long as there is continued credit expansion. The system inevitably collapses, as it finally did in Japan in the 1990s. Even the lack of CPI inflation as reported by the Federal Reserve is suspect.

A CPI of all consumer items measured by the private source shows an approximate 400-percent increase in prices since 1970. Most Americans realize their dollars are buying less each year and no chance exists for the purchasing power of the dollar to go up. Just because prices of TVs and computers may go down, the cost of medicine, food, stocks and entertainment, and of course, government, certainly can rise rapidly.

One characteristic of an economy that suffers from a constantly debased currency is sluggish or diminished growth in real income. In spite of our so-called great economic recovery, two-thirds of U.S. workers for the past 25 years have had stagnant or falling wages. The demands for poverty relief from government agencies continue to increase. Last year alone, 678,000 jobs were lost due to downsizing. The new service sector jobs found by many of those laid off are rarely as good paying.

In the last year and a half, various countries have been hit hard with deflationary pressures. In spite of the IMF-led bailouts of nearly $200 billion, the danger of a worldwide depression remains. Many countries, even with the extra dollars sent to them courtesy of the American taxpayer, suffer devaluation and significant price inflation in their home currency.

Although helpful to banks lending overseas, this has clearly failed, has cost a lot of money, and prevents the true market correction of liquidation of debt that must eventually come. The longer the delay and the more dollars used, the greater the threat to the dollar in the future.

There is good reason why we in the Congress should be concerned. A dollar crisis is an economic crisis that will threaten the standard of living of many Americans. Economic crises frequently lead to political crises, as is occurring in Indonesia.

Congress is responsible for the value of the dollar. Yet, just as we have done too often in other areas, we have passed this responsibility on to someone else; in this case, to the Federal Reserve.

The Constitution is clear that the Congress has responsibility for guaranteeing the value of the currency, and no authority has ever been given to create a central bank. Creating money out of thin air is counterfeiting, even when done by a bank that the Congress tolerates.

It is easy to see why Congress, with its own insatiable desire to spend money and perpetuate a welfare and military state, cooperates with such a system. A national debt of $5.6 trillion could not have developed without a willing Federal Reserve to monetize this debt and provide for artificially low interest rates. But when the dollar crisis hits and it is clearly evident that the short-term benefits were not worth it, we will be forced to consider monetary reform.

Reconsidering the directives given us in the Constitution with regard to money would go a long way toward developing a sound monetary system that best protects our economy and guides us away from casually going to war. Monetary reform is something we ought to be thinking about now.

Mr. Speaker, let me summarize. We in the Congress, along with the President, will soon have to make a decision that will determine whether or not the American Republic survives. Allowing our presidents to wage war without the consent of Congress, ignoring the obvious significance of fiat money to a healthy economy, and perpetuating pervasive government intrusion into the privacy of all Americans will surely end the American experiment with maximum liberty for all unless we reverse this trend.

Too often the American people have chosen security over liberty. Allowing the president a little authority to deal with world problems under a UN banner has been easier than reversing the trend of the past 50 years. Accepting the financial bubble, when on the short run, it helps everyone's portfolio and helps to finance government spending is easy, even if it only delays the day of reckoning when the bills come due, as they already have in so many other countries in the world.

Giving up a little privacy seems a small price to pay for the many who receive the generous benefits of big government, but when the prosperity comes to an end and the right to privacy has been squandered, it will be most difficult to restore the principles of a free society.

Materialistic concerns and complacency toward the principles of liberty will undo much of what has been built in America over the past 200 years, unless there is a renewed belief that our God-given rights to life and liberty are worth working for. False economic security is no substitute for productive effort in a free society, where the citizens are self-reliant, generous and nonviolent. Insisting on a limited government designed to protect life and property, as is found in a republic, must be our legislative goal. ■

As we moved toward direct military conflict with Serbia and the NATO bombing campaign, I made several statements indicating the folly of interventionism and the constitutionally suspect means by which we were undertaking these policies.

February 24, 1999
PRESIDENT HAS NO AUTHORITY TO WAGE WAR WITHOUT CONGRESSIONAL APPROVAL
HON. RON PAUL of TEXAS
IN THE HOUSE OF REPRESENTATIVES

Mr. Speaker, the threats of bombing did not bring a peace agreement to Kosovo. The president has no authority to wage war, yet Congress says nothing. When will Congress assume its war power authority to rein in the president? An endless military occupation of Bosnia is ignored by Congress, and the spending rolls on, yet there is no lasting peace.

For nine years, bombing Iraq and killing innocent Iraqi children with sanctions has done nothing to restore stability to Iraq, but it has served to instill an ever-growing hatred toward America. It is now clear that the threats of massive bombing of Serbia have not brought peace to Kosovo.

Congress must assume its responsibility. It must be made clear that the president has no funds available to wage war without congressional approval. This is our prerogative. Therefore, the endless threats of bombing should cease. Congress should not remain timid.

Merely telling the president to reconsider his actions will have little effect. We must be firm and deny the funds to wage war without our consent. We live in a republic, not a monarchy. ■

March. 9, 1999
WAR POWER AUTHORITY SHOULD BE RETURNED TO CONGRESS
HON. RON PAUL of TEXAS
IN THE HOUSE OF REPRESENTATIVES

Mr. Speaker, the president has stated that should a peace treaty be signed between Serbia and Kosovo he plans to send in at least 4,000 American soldiers as part of a NATO peacekeeping force.

We, the Congress, have been informed—through a public statement by the president—that troops will be sent. We have not been asked to act in a constitutional fashion to grant the president permission to act. He is not coming to us to fully explain his intentions. The president is making a public statement as to his intentions and we are expected to acquiesce, to go along with the funding, and not even debate the issue, just as we are doing in Iraq.

That is not a proper constitutional procedure, and it should be condemned. Silence in the past, while accommodating our presidents in all forms of foreign adventurism—from Korea and Vietnam to Iraq and Bosnia—should not be the standard Congress follows.

The Constitution is clear: Our presidents, from Washington to Roosevelt, all knew that initiating war was clearly the prerogative of the Congress, but our memories are flawed and our reading of the law is careless. The president should not be telling us what he plans to do; he should be giving us information and asking our advice. We are responsible for the safety of our troops, how taxpayers' dollars are spent, the security of our nation, and *especially* the process whereby our nation commits itself to war.

Citing NATO agreements or UN resolutions as authority for moving troops into war zones should alert us all to the degree to which the rule of law has been undermined. The president has no war power; only the Congress has that. When one person can initiate war, by its definition, a republic no longer exists.

The war power, taken from the Congress 50 years ago, must be restored. If not, the conclusion must be that the Constitution of the United States can and has been amended by presidential fiat or treaty—both excluding the House of Representatives from performing its duty to the American people in preventing casual and illegal wars.

Some claim that the Kosovo involvement must be clarified as to where the money will come to finance it, the surplus or Social Security. This misses the point. We have and should exert the power of the purse, but a political argument over surpluses versus Social Security is hardly the issue.

Others have said that support should be withheld until an exit strategy is clearly laid out. But the debate should not be over the exit strategy. It is the entry process that counts.

The war powers process was set early on by our presidents in dealing with the North African pirates in the early 19th Century. Jefferson and Madison, on no less than 10 occasions, got Congress to pass legislation endorsing each military step taken. It has clearly been since World War II that our presidents have assumed power not granted to them by the

101

Constitution, and Congress has been negligent in doing little to stop this usurpation.

In the case of Kosovo, no troops should be sent without the consent of Congress. Vague discussion about whether or not the money will come out of Social Security or the budget surplus or call for an exit strategy will not suffice. If the war power is taken from the president and returned to the Congress, we would then automatically know the funds would have to be appropriated and the exit strategy would be easy: *when we win the war.*

Vague police actions authorized by the United Nations or NATO, and implemented by the president without congressional approval, invite disasters with perpetual foreign military entanglements. The concept of national sovereignty and the rule of law must be respected, or there is no purpose for the Constitution. ■

March 11, 1999
PEACEKEEPING OPERATIONS IN KOSOVO RESOLUTION
HON. RON PAUL of TEXAS
IN THE HOUSE OF REPRESENTATIVES

Mr. Chairman, I want to thank the leadership for allowing this debate to come to the floor. I have, for quite a few weeks, advocated that we talk about this and have urged that the troops never be sent to Kosovo without our consent. I do believe, though, that the process here is less than perfect. The fact that we are talking about a House Concurrent Resolution at the same time we are authorizing troop deployment raises serious questions.

Since World War II, we have not been diligent here in the Congress to protect our prerogatives with respect to the declaration of war. The Korea and Vietnam Wars were fought without a declaration of war. And these wars were not won.

Since 1973, since the War Powers Resolution was passed, we have further undermined the authority of the Congress and delivered more authority to the president, because the resolution essentially has given the president more power to wage war up to 90 days without the Congress granting authority. It is to our credit at least that we are bringing this matter up at this particular time.

We must remember that there are various things involved here. First, whether or not we should be the world policeman. That answer should be easy. We should not be. It costs a lot of money to do what we are doing,

102

and it undermines our military strength. So we should consider that.

We should consider the law and the process in the War Powers Resolution, and just exactly how we grant authority to the president to wage war. We should be more concerned about the Constitution and how we should give this authority. We should be concerned about this procedure.

The bigger question here, however, is if we vote for this—and I strongly oppose passing this, because if we vote for this, we authorize the moving of troops into a dangerous area. We should ask ourselves, if we are willing to vote for this resolution; are we ourselves willing to go to Kosovo and expose our lives on the front lines? Are we willing to send our children, or our grandchildren, to not only be exposed to the danger, with the pretext we are going to save the world, but with the idea that we may lose our life? That is what we have to consider. ■

March 17, 1999
WAR POWERS RESOLUTION
HON. RON PAUL of TEXAS
IN THE HOUSE OF REPRESENTATIVES

Mr. Speaker, last week the House narrowly passed a watered-down House Concurrent Resolution originally designed to endorse President Clinton's plan to send U.S. troops to Kosovo. A House Concurrent Resolution, whether strong or weak, has no effect of law. It is merely a sense of Congress statement.

If last week's meager debate and vote are construed as merely an endorsement, without dissent, of Clinton's policy in Yugoslavia, the procedure will prove a net negative. It will not be seen as a congressional challenge to unconstitutional presidential war power. If, however, the debate is interpreted as a serious effort to start the process to restore congressional prerogatives, it may yet be seen as a small step in the right direction. We cannot know with certainty which it will be. That will depend on what Congress does in the future.

Presently, those of us who argued for congressional responsibility with regards to declaring war and deploying troops cannot be satisfied that the trend of the last 50 years has been reversed. Since World War II, the war power has fallen into the hands of our presidents, with Congress doing little to insist on its own constitutional responsibility. From Korea and Vietnam, to Bosnia and Kosovo, we have permitted our presidents to "wag the Congress," generating a perception that the United States can and should police the world. Instead of authority to move troops and fight wars coming from the people through a vote of their congressional representatives, we now permit our presidents to cite NATO declarations and UN resolutions.

This is even more exasperating, knowing that upon joining both NATO and the United Nations it was made explicitly clear that no loss of sovereignty would occur and all legislative bodies of member States would retain their legal authority to give or deny support for any proposed military action.

Today it is erroneously taken for granted that the president has authority to move troops and fight wars without congressional approval. It would be nice to believe that this vote on Kosovo was a serious step in the direction of Congress once again reasserting its responsibility for committing U.S. troops abroad. But the president has already notified Congress that, regardless of our sense of Congress resolution, he intends to do what he thinks is right—not what is legal and constitutional, only what he decides for himself.

Even with this watered-down endorsement of troop deployment with various conditions listed, the day after the headlines blared, "The Congress approves troop deployments to Kosovo."

If Congress is serious about this issue, it must do more. First, Congress cannot in this instance exert its responsibility through a House Concurrent Resolution. The president can and will ignore this token effort. If Congress decides that we should not become engaged in the civil war in Serbia, we must deny the funds for that purpose. That we can do. Our presidents have assumed the war power, but as of yet, Congress still controls the purse.

Any effort on our part to enter a civil war in a country 5,000 miles away for the purpose of guaranteeing autonomy and/or a separate state against the avowed objections of the leaders of that country involved—that is, Yugoslavia—can and will lead to a long-term serious problem for us.

Our policy, whether it is with Iraq or Serbia, of demanding that if certain actions are not forthcoming, we will unleash massive bombing attacks on them, I find reprehensible, immoral, illegal, and unconstitutional. We are seen as a world bully, and a growing anti-American hatred is the result. This policy cannot contribute to long-term peace. Political instability will result and innocent people will suffer. The billions we have spent bombing Iraq, along with sanctions, have solidified Saddam Hussein's power, while causing the suffering and deaths of hundreds of thousands of innocent Iraqi children. Our policy in Kosovo will be no more fruitful.

The recent flare-up of violence in Serbia has been blamed on the United States' plan to send troops to the region. The Serbs have expressed outrage at the possibility that NATO would invade their country with the plan to reward the questionable Kosovo Liberation Army. If ever a case could be made for the wisdom of non-intervention, it is here. Who wants to defend all that the KLA had done and at the same time justify a NATO invasion of a sovereign nation for the purpose of supporting secession? "This violence is all America's fault," one Yugoslavian was quoted as saying. And who wants to defend Milosevic?

Every argument given for our bombing Serbia could be used to support the establishment of Kurdistan. Actually a stronger case can be made to support an independent Kurdistan, since their country was taken from them by outsiders. But how would Turkey feel about that? Yet the case could be made that the mistreatment of the Kurds by Saddam Hussein and others compel us to do something to help, since we are pretending that our role is an act as the world's humanitarian policeman.

Humanitarianism, delivered by a powerful government through threats of massive bombing attacks, will never be a responsible way to enhance peace. It will surely have the opposite effect.

It was hoped that the War Powers Resolution of 1973 would rein in our president's authority to wage war without congressional approval. It has not happened, because all subsequent presidents have essentially ignored its mandates. Unfortunately the interpretation, since 1973, has been to give the president greater power to wage war with congressional approval for at least 60 to 90 days as long as he reports to the Congress. These reports are rarely made, and the assumption has been, since 1973, that Congress need not participate in any serious manner in the decision to send troops.

It could be argued that this resulted from a confused understanding of the War Powers Resolution, but more likely it's the result of the growing imperial Presidency that has developed with our presidents assuming power, not legally theirs, and Congress doing nothing about it.

Power has been gravitating into the hands of our presidents throughout this century, both in domestic and foreign affairs. Congress has created a maze of federal agencies, placed under the president, that have been granted legislative, police, and judicial powers, thus creating an entire administrative judicial system, outside our legal court system, where constitutional rights are ignored. Congress is responsible for this trend, and it's Congress' responsibility to restore constitutional government.

As more and more power has been granted in international affairs, presidents have readily adapted to using Executive Orders, promises and quasi-treaties to expand the scope and size of the presidency far above anything even the federalist ever dreamed of.

We are at a crossroads, and if the people and the Congress do not soon insist on the reining in of presidential power, both foreign and domestic, individual liberty cannot be preserved.

Presently, unless the people exert a lot more pressure on the Congress to do so, not much will be done. Specifically, Congress needs a strong message from the people insisting that the Congress continues the debate over Kosovo before an irreversible quagmire develops. The president today believes he is free to pursue any policy he wants in the Balkans and the Persian Gulf without congressional approval. It shouldn't be that way. It's dangerous politically, militarily and morally, and above all else, it undermines our entire system of the rule of law. ■

March 24, 1999
U.S. MILITARY ACTION TAKING PLACE IN SERBIA IS UNCONSTITUTIONAL
HON. RON PAUL of TEXAS
IN THE HOUSE OF REPRESENTATIVES

Mr. Speaker, U.S. military forces are now bombing a foreign nation halfway around the world. This cannot be a proud moment for America. The reason given for doing so is that Serbian leaders have not done what we have told them to do.

Serbia has not invaded another country but is involved in a nasty civil war, with both sides contributing to the violence. There is no American security interest involved in Serbia. Serbia has not threatened us nor used any force against any American citizen.

As bad as the violence is toward the ethnic Albanians in Kosovo, our ability to police and stop all ethnic fighting around the world is quite limited and the efforts are not permitted under constitutional law. We do not even pretend to solve the problems of sub-Saharan Africa, Tibet, East Timor, Kurdistan, or many other places around the world where endless tragic circumstances prevail.

106

Our responsibility as U.S. Members of Congress is to preserve liberty here at home and uphold the rule of law. Meddling in the internal and dangerous affairs of a nation involved in civil war is illegal and dangerous. Congress has not given the president authority to wage war.

The House resolution regarding Kosovo was narrowly, reluctantly, and conditionally passed. It was a nonbinding resolution and had no effect of law. Even if it did, the resolution dealt with sending troops as a peacekeeping force to Kosovo only if a peace agreement was signed. There was no mention of endorsing an act of war against Serbia. Besides, the resolution was not the proper procedure for granting war powers to a president.

The Senate resolution, now claimed to be congressional consent for the president to wage war, is not much better. It, too, was a sense of Congress resolution without the force of law. It implies the president can defer to NATO for authority to pursue a war effort.

Only Congress can decide the issue of war. Congress cannot transfer the constitutional war power to the president or to NATO or to the United Nations. The Senate resolution, however, specifically limits the use of force to air operations and missile strikes, but no war has ever been won with air power alone. The Milosevic problem will actually get worse with our attacks, and ground troops will likely follow.

It has been argued that we are needed to stop the spread of war throughout the Balkans. Our presence will do the opposite, and it will certainly help the military-industrial complex. Peaceful and cooperative relations with Russia, a desired goal, have now ended; and we have provoked the Russians into now becoming a much more active ally of Serbia.

U.S. and NATO policy against Serbia will certainly encourage the Kurds. Every argument for Kosovo's independence can be used by the Kurds for their long-sought-after independence. This surely will drive the Turks away from NATO.

Our determination to be involved in the dangerous civil war may well prompt a stronger Greek alliance with their friends in Serbia, further splitting NATO and offending the Turks, who are naturally inclined to be sympathetic to the Albanian Muslims. No good can come of our involvement in this Serbian civil war, no matter how glowing and humanitarian the terms used by our leaders.

Sympathy and compassion for the suffering and voluntary support for the oppressed is commendable. The use of force and acts of war to pick and choose between two sides fighting for hundreds of years cannot achieve peace. It can only spread the misery and suffering, weaken our defenses and undermine our national sovereignty.

Only when those who champion our war effort in Serbia are willing to volunteer for the front lines and offer their own lives for the cause will they gain credibility. Promoters of war never personalize it. It is always some other person or some other parent's child whose life who will be sacrificed, not their own.

With new talk of reinstating the military draft, since many disillusioned military personnel are disgusted with the morale of our armed forces, Americans should all pay close attention as our leaders foolishly and carelessly rush our troops into a no-win war of which we should have no part. ■

While NATO's Serbia campaign was ongoing, I became acquainted with some speeches of past conservative thinkers, such as Edmund Burke, who clearly stated the principles of non-intervention. By applying these ideas to current events, my hope was to renew truths that are timeless.

March 25, 1999
CLOSER TO EMPIRE
HON. RON PAUL of TEXAS
IN THE HOUSE OF REPRESENTATIVES

Mr. Speaker, I rise again today to consider the effect of our current actions in Kosovo, but this time I do not wish to address the folly of war, for attempts to prevent war measures against that nation are now futile. Mr. Speaker, today I rise to address a long-term concern, a problem larger even than war. I am referring to the folly of empire.

Our involvement in Kosovo and in Iraq and in Bosnia—when combined with America's role in Korea, and in the Middle East and other places around the world—is now lurching our republic ever closer to empire. Empire is something that all Americans ought to oppose.

I remind those who believe in the Judeo-Christian tradition that opposition to empire is to be found in the warnings found in the Book of Ezekiel, warnings against the empowerment of a king. And it is this same principle which is evident in the story of the Tower of Babel, and in that admonition of Christ, which reminds us that those things which are of Caesar are not of God.

To pragmatists, agnostics and such, I point to the decline and fall which has historically attended every other empire. The Ottomans and Romans, the Spanish and the British, all who have tried empire have faltered, and at great costs to their own nations.

Mr. Speaker, to liberals I would remind that these interventions, however well-intended, all require the use of forces of occupation. This is the key step toward colonialism, itself always leading to subjugation and to oppression.

To conservatives, I want to recall the founding of our Republic, our nation's breaking from the yoke of empire in order that we might realize the benefits of liberty and self-determination, and that we might obtain the blessings that flow naturally from limitations on centralized power—empire reflecting the most perfect means yet devised to concentrate power in the fewest hands.

Now, Mr. Speaker, our own nation faces a choice, and we may well be at the very precipice. Indeed, to move even one step further down the road to empire may mean that there will be no turning back, short of the eventual decline and fall. Will we act now to restore our Republic?

It is oft repeated that we do not realize the import of our most critical actions at the time that we begin to undertake them. How true, Mr. Speaker, this statement is. Were Mr. Townshend, or the King in England in the least contemplative of the true cost which would eventuate as a result of the tea tax or the stamp act?

Now we must ask, is our nation on the verge of empire? Some will say no, because, they say we do not seek to have direct control over the governments of foreign lands. But how close are we to doing just that? And is it so important whether the dictates of empire come from the head of our government or from the Secretary General of some multilateral entity which we direct?

Today we attempt, directly or indirectly, to dictate to other sovereign nations who they ought and ought not have as leader, which peace accords they should sign, and what form of government they must enact. How limited is the distinction between our actions today and those of the emperors of history? How limited indeed. In fact, one might suggest that this is a distinction without a substantive difference.

Where now are we willing to commit troops and under what conditions? If we are to stop all violations of human rights, what will we do of Cuba, which recently announced new crackdowns?

And what of Communist China? Not only do they steal our secrets, but they violate their own citizens. Who should be more upset, for example, about forced abortion? Is it those who proclaim the inviolable right to life or those who argue for so-called reproductive rights? Even these polar opposites recognize the crimes of the Chinese government in forced abortion. Should we then stop this oppression of millions? Are we committed to lob missiles at this massive nation until it ceases this program?

Will the principle upon which we are now claiming to act lead us to impose our political solutions upon the nations that now contain Tibet and Kurdistan, and should the sentiment bear, even Quebec and Chechnya?

The most dangerous thing about where we are headed is our lack of historical memory and our disastrous inattention to the effect of the principles upon which we act, for ideas do indeed have consequences, Mr. Speaker, and they pick up a momentum that becomes all their own.

I do believe that we are on the brink, Mr. Speaker, but it is not yet too late. Soon I fear the train, as it is said, will have left the station. We stand on the verge of crossing the line that so firmly distinguishes empire from republic. This occurs not so much by an action, or series of actions, but by the acceptance of an idea, the idea that we have a right, a duty, an obligation, or a national interest to perfect foreign nations, even while we remain less than principled ourselves.

When will we, as a people and as an institution, say "We choose to keep our Republic; your designs for empire interest us not in the least." I can only hope it will be soon, for it is my sincerest fear that failing to do so much longer will put us beyond this great divide. ■

March 25, 1999
PEACE
HON. RON PAUL of TEXAS
IN THE HOUSE OF REPRESENTATIVES

Mr. Speaker, today I rise with gratitude to Edmund Burke and paraphrase words he first spoke 224 years ago this week. It is presently true that to restore liberty and dignity to a nation so great and distracted as ours is indeed a significant undertaking. For, judging of what we are by what we ought to be, I have persuaded myself that this body might accept this reasonable proposition.

The proposition is peace. Not peace through the medium of war, not peace to be hunted through the labyrinth of intricate and endless negotiations; not peace to arise out of universal discord, fomented from principle, in all part of the earth; not peace to depend on juridical determination of perplexing questions, or the precise marking the shadowy boundaries of distant nations. It is simply peace, sought in its natural course and in its ordinary haunts.

Let other nations always keep the idea of their sovereign self-government associated with our Republic and they will befriend us, and no force under heaven will be of power to tear them from our allegiance. But let it be once understood that our government may be one thing and their sovereignty another; that these two things exist without mutual regard one for the other—and the affinity will be gone, the friendship loosened and the alliance hastened to decay and dissolution. As long as we have the wisdom to keep this country as the sanctuary of liberty, the sacred temple consecrated to our common faith, wherever mankind worships freedom, they will turn their faces toward us. The more they multiply, the more friends we will have; the more ardently they love liberty, the more perfect will be our relations. Slavery they can find anywhere, as near to us as Cuba or as remote as China. But until we become lost to all feeling of our national interest and natural legacy, freedom and self-rule they can find in none but the American founding. These are precious commodities, and our nation alone was founded on them. This is the true currency which binds to us the commerce of nations and through them secures the wealth of the world. But deny others their national sovereignty and self-government, and you break that sole bond which originally made, and must still preserve, friendship among nations. Do not entertain so weak an imagination as that UN Charters and Security Councils, GATT and international laws, World Trade Organizations and General Assemblies are what promote commerce and friendship. Do not dream that NATO and peacekeeping forces are the things that can hold nations together. It is the spirit of community that gives nations their lives and efficacy. And it is the spirit of the Constitution of our Founders that can invigorate every nation of the world, even down to the minutest of these.

For is it not the same virtue which would do the thing for us here in these United States? Do you imagine then that it is the Income Tax that pays our revenue? That it is the annual vote of the Ways and Means Committee that provide us an army? Or that it is the Court Martial that inspires it with bravery and discipline? No! Surely, no! It is the private activity of citizens which gives government revenue, and it is the defense of our country that encourages young people to not only populate our Army and Navy, but also has infused them with a patriotism, without which our Army will become a base rubble and our Navy nothing but rotten timber.

All this, I know well enough, will sound wild and chimerical to the profane herd of those vulgar and mechanical politicians who have no place among us: a sort of people who think that nothing exists but what is gross and material, and who, therefore, far from being qualified to be directors of the great movement of this nation, are not fit to turn a wheel in the machinery of our government. But to men truly initiated and rightly taught these ruling and master principles, which in the opinion of such men as I have mentioned have no substantial existence, are in truth everything. Magnanimity in politics is often the truest wisdom, and a great nation and little minds go ill together. If we are conscious of our situation, and work zealously to fill our places, as becomes the history of this great institution, we ought to auspicate all our public proceedings on Kosovo with the old warning of the Church, *Sursum corda!* We ought to elevate our minds to the greatness of that trust to which the order of Providence has called us. By averting to the dignity of this high calling, our forefathers turned a savage wilderness into a glorious nation, and have made the most extensive and the only honorable conquests, not by bombing and sabre-rattling, but by promoting the wealth, the liberty, and the peace of mankind. Let us gain our allies as we obtain our own liberty. Respect of self-government has made our nation all that it is. Peace and neutrality alone will make ours the Republic that it can yet still be. ■

NATO was an institution I had long pointed to as a potential problem. This series of talks focuses attention on the role of NATO in the current conflict, and the pitfalls of a continued U.S. role in NATO.

April 12, 1999
IF NATO HAS ITS WAY, ALBANIAN KOSOVORS WILL NOT REMAIN PART OF SERBIA
HON. RON PAUL of TEXAS
IN THE HOUSE OF REPRESENTATIVES

Madam Speaker, the U.S.-NATO war against Serbia is illegal by all standards. Congress has not declared war. Therefore, the president has no authority to wage war. Attacking a sovereign nation violates long-standing international law as well as the NATO and UN charters.

NATO's aggression is immoral as well. It forces U.S. citizens and

112

others in Europe opposed to the war to pay for it, and some are even forced to fight in it against their will. If the war expands, we can expect the return of the draft to make sure there are enough soldiers to participate.

As ugly as the Yugoslavian civil war may be in Kosovo, and as heart-wrenching as the pictures of mass refugees fleeing their homeland is, one evil can never justify another. If one is disinclined to be persuaded by law and morality and responds only to emotions, propaganda and half-truths, then one must consider the practical failure of compulsive intervention in the affairs of other nations.

Prior to NATO's expanding the war in Yugoslavia, approximately 2,000 deaths in the past year were recorded in Kosovo. As a consequence of NATO's actions, the killing has now escalated, and no one can be pleased just because now Serbs, our once-valiant allies against the Nazis, are dying. Those who are motivated by good intentions while ignoring facts cannot be excused for the escalating and dangerous crisis in Yugoslavia.

The humanitarian concerns for Albanian refugees is justified, but going to war because of emotional concerns while ignoring other millions of refugees around the world only stirs the passions of the oppressed—whether they are Kurds, Palestinians, Tibetans, East Timorans or Rwandans.

When NATO talks of returning Albanians to their homes in Kosovo, I wonder why there is no reference or concern for the more than 50,000 Serbs thrown out of their homes in Bosnia, Slovenia and Croatia. Current NATO policy in Yugoslavia will surely encourage more ethnic minorities around the world to revolt and demand independence.

Some in Congress are now saying that although they were strongly opposed to the administration's policy of bombing in Yugoslavia prior to its onset, conditions are now different and an all-out effort to win with ground troops, if necessary, must be undertaken. This, it is said, is required to preserve NATO's credibility.

Who cares about NATO's credibility? Are American lives to be lost and a greater war precipitated to preserve NATO's credibility? Should the rule of law and morality be thrown out in an effort to preserve NATO's credibility? Can something be wrong and misguided before it is started and all of a sudden deserve to be blindly supported?

This reasoning makes no sense.

No one has quite figured out the secret motivation of why this war must be fought, but I found it interesting that evidence of our weapons shortage is broadcast to the world and to the Serbs. Surely one result of the war will be a rapid rush by Congress this year to massively increase the military budget. But a serious discussion of our flawed foreign policy of intervention that has served us so poorly unfortunately will not occur.

Political leaders and pundits are struggling to define an exit strategy for the war. In the old days when wars were properly declared for national security reasons, no one needed to ask such a question. A moral war fought against an aggressor for national security reasons was over when it was won. It has only been since Congress has reneged on its responsibility with regards to war power that it has become necessary to discuss how we exit a war not legitimately entered into and without victory as a goal.

The political wars, fought without declaration, starting with the Korean War to the present, have not enhanced the long-term security and liberty of the American people. Institutionalizing a collective approach to war seems a result of the obsession to save face for NATO. Never before in our history have we Americans accepted so casually the turning over of a military operation to foreign control with non-American spokesmen briefing us each day.

This is a major step in further solidifying the world-government approach to all political problems. There is, however, one major contradiction to the internationalists' desire to assimilate all countries and ethnic groups and have them governed by a single world government.

Quite ironically, ethnic diversity will surely be the casualty of all of this mischief. NATO and the U.S. are co-conspirators and military allies of a Serbian province that is seeking to become a separate ethnic country. Let there be no doubt, if NATO has its way, Albanian Kosovors will not remain part of Serbia.

Current NATO and U.S. policy completely contradict the professed goal of multi-ethnicity and assimilation of all people. NATO's operation, by its very nature, is bureaucratically burdened by the effort to appease the political concerns of 19 different countries. This inefficiency and the contradiction of supporting the establishment of an ethnic state will guarantee NATO's deserved demise. The sooner we get out of Yugoslavia the better off everyone will be. ■

April 14, 1999
CRISIS IN KOSOVO
HON. RON PAUL of TEXAS
IN THE HOUSE OF REPRESENTATIVES

Mr. Speaker, I rise this evening to address the crisis that is ongoing now in Yugoslavia. For a war to be moral, we must have a reason to go in. National defense is a moral justification. If we are attacked, it is a moral war. Getting involved in any other kind of war is not considered to be moral.

A legal war in this country is one that is declared, declared by the Congress. Any other war is illegal. The war in Yugoslavia now pursued by our administration and with NATO is both immoral and illegal, and it should not be pursued. We will soon be voting on an appropriation, probably next week. There may be a request for $5 billion to pursue the war in Yugoslavia. I do not believe that we should continue to finance a war that is both immoral and illegal.

It has been said that we are in Yugoslavia to stop ethnic cleansing, but it is very clear that the goal of the NATO forces is to set up an ethnic state.

It is totally contradictory. There is a civil war, and it is horrible, going on in Yugoslavia today, but this is no justification for outsiders, and especially United States of America, to become involved without the proper proceedings.

I believe that our colleague, the gentleman from California (Mr. Campbell), deserves to be complemented because he is making a determined effort to put the burden on the Members of Congress to vote one way or the other. Since World War II we have fought numerous wars, and they have never been fought with a declaration of war. It is precisely for that reason, because they have not been fought for truly national security reasons, that we have not won these wars. If a war is worth fighting, it is worth declaring, and it is worth winning.

I am delighted that this effort is being made by the gentleman from California (Mr. Campbell) and others here in the Congress, because for so long, for 50 years now, we have permitted our presidents to casually and carelessly involve our troops overseas. So I see this trend as putting more pressure on the Congress to respond to their responsibilities. I think this is a very, very good move and going in the right direction.

It has been asked why in the world might we be there if it is not a concern for the refugees, because obviously we have hundreds of

115

thousands, if not millions, of refugees in many, many places around the world. We do not go to Rwanda to rescue the refugees, we did not go into Yugoslavia to rescue the Serbian refugees when they were being routed from Bosnia and Croatia, but all of a sudden the refugees seem to have an importance.

Most people know why we went to the Persian Gulf. It was not because we were attacked. It was because of a financial commercial interest: oil. But what is the interest in this area in Yugoslavia? I am not sure exactly what it is. There have been a lot of postulations about this, but I am not convinced that it is all of a sudden the concern for the refugees.

Yesterday in the *Washington Post,* an interesting article occurred on this subject; but it was not in the news section; it was in the business section. The headline yesterday said: "Count Corporate America Among NATO's Staunchest Allies." Very interesting article because it explains why so many corporations have an intense interest in making sure that the credibility of NATO is maintained, and they go on to explain that it is not just the arms manufacturers but the technology people who expect to sell weapons in Eastern Europe, in Yugoslavia. They are very interested in making use of the NATO forces to ensure that their interests are protected. I think this is not the reason for us to go to war.

There is talk now of calling up all our Reserves, or many of our Reserves, at the same time there are hints now that there may be the institution of the draft. So this is a major problem that this country is facing, the world is facing; and up until now we, the Congress, have not spoken.

On February 9 of this year, I introduced a bill that would have prevented this by prohibiting any funds being spent on a war in Yugoslavia. I say it is too bad we did not pass that legislation a long time ago. ∎

April 21, 1999
U.S. FOREIGN POLICY AND NATO'S INVOLVEMENT IN YUGOSLAVIA AND KOSOVO
HON. RON PAUL of TEXAS
IN THE HOUSE OF REPRESENTATIVES

Mr. Speaker, supporters of internationalism celebrated NATO's 50th anniversary with the Senate's 1998 overwhelming approval for expanding NATO to include Eastern European countries. This year's official inclusion of Poland, Hungary, and the Czech Republic made all NATO's supporters proud, indeed. But in reality, NATO now is weaker and more chaotic than ever.

In the effort to expand NATO and promote internationalism, we see reaction in the rise of ugly nationalism. The U.S. and NATO policy of threats and intimidation to establish an autonomous Kosovo without true independence from Serbia, and protected by NATO's forces for the foreseeable future, has been a recipe for disaster. This policy of nation-building and interference in a civil war totally contradicts the mission of European defense set out in the NATO charter.

Without the Soviet enemy to justify the European military machine, NATO had to find enemies and humanitarian missions to justify its existence. The centuries-old ethnic hatreds found in Yugoslavia and the militant leaders on all sides have served this purpose well. Working hard to justify NATO's policy in this region has totally obscured any objective analysis of the turmoil now raging.

Some specific policy positions of NATO guaranteed that the ongoing strife would erupt into a full-fledged and dangerous conflict. Once it was determined in the early 1990s that outsiders would indict and try Yugoslavian war criminals, it was certain that cooperation with Western negotiators would involve risks. Fighting to the end became a practical alternative to a mock international trial. Forcing a treaty settlement on Serbia where Serbia would lose the sovereign territory of Kosovo guaranteed an escalation of the fighting and the forced removal of the Kosovors from their homes.

Ignoring the fact that more than 500,000 Serbs were uprooted from Croatia and Bosnia with the encouragement of NATO intervention did great harm to the regional effort to reestablish more stable borders.

The sympathy shown Albanian refugees by our government and our media, although justified, stirred the flames of hatred by our refusing to admit that over a half million Serbs suffered the same fate, yet elicited no concern from the internationalists bent on waging war. No one is calling for the return of certain property and homes.

Threatening a country to do what we the outsiders tell them or their cities will be bombed is hardly considered good diplomacy. Arguing that the Serbs must obey and give up what they see as sovereign territory after suffering much themselves, as well as face war crimes trials run by the West, makes no sense. Anyone should have been able to predict what the results would be.

The argument that, because of humanitarian concerns for the refugees, we were forced to act is not plausible. Our efforts dramatically increased the refugee problem. Milosevic, as he felt cornered by the Western threats, reacted the only way he could to protect what he considered Serbia, a position he defends with international law while being supported by unified Serb people.

If it is the suffering and the refugees that truly motivate our actions, there is no answer to the perplexing question of why no action was taken to help the suffering in Rwanda, Sudan, East Timor, Tibet, Chechnya, Kurdish Turkey, and for the Palestinians in Israel. This is not a reason; it is an excuse.

Instead, we give massive foreign aid to the likes of China and Russia, countries that have trampled on the rights of ethnic minorities.

How many refugees, how many children's deaths has U.S. policy caused by our embargo and bombing for nine years of a defenseless, poverty-ridden Iraq. Just as our bombs in Iraq have caused untold misery and death, so have our bombs in Serbia killed the innocent on both sides, solidified support for the ruthless leaders, and spread the war.

This policy of intervention is paid for by the U.S. taxpayer and promoted illegally by our president without congressional authority, as required by the Constitution.

The United States government has, in the past, referred to the Kosovo Liberation Army leaders as thugs, terrorists, Marxists, and drug dealers. This current fight was initiated by Kosovo's desire for independence from Serbia.

The KLA took on the Serbs, not the other way around. Whether or not one is sympathetic to Kosovo's secession is irrelevant. I, for one, prefer many small independent governments pledged not to aggress against their neighbors over the international special-interest authoritarianism of NATO, the CIA, and the United Nations.

But my sympathies do not justify our taxing and sending young Americans to fight for Kosovo's independence. It is wrong legally and morally; and besides, the KLA is not likely to institute a model nation respecting civil liberties of all its citizens.

The biggest irony of this entire mess is to see the interventionists, whose goal is one world government, so determined to defend a questionable group of local leaders, the KLA, bent on secession. This action will not go unnoticed and will provide the philosophic framework for the establishment of a Palestinian state, Kurdistan, and independent Tibet; and it will encourage many other ethnic minorities to demand independence.

Our policy of intervention in the internal affairs of other nations and their border disputes is not one that comes from American tradition or constitutional law. It is a policy based on our current leaders' belief that we are the policemen of the world, something we have earnestly and foolishly pursued since World War II, and in a more aggressive fashion since the demise of the Soviet Union.

Interventionism is done with a pretense of wisdom believing we always know the good guys from the bad guys and that we will ignore the corporate and political special interests always agitating for influence. Nothing could be further from the truth.

Instead of being lucky enough on occasion to pick the right side of a conflict, we instead end up supporting both sides of nearly every conflict. In the 1980s, we helped arm, and allied ourselves with, the Iraqis against Iran. Also in the 1980s we supported the Afghan freedom fighters, which included Osama bin Laden. Even in the current crisis in Yugoslavia, we have found ourselves on both sides.

The United States, along with the United Nations, in 1992, supported an arms embargo against Kosovo essentially making it impossible for the Kosovors to defend themselves against Serbia. Helping the Albanian Muslims is interpreted by some as token appeasement to the Arab oil countries unhappy with the advantage the Serbs got from the arms embargo.

This balancing act between three vicious warring factions was doomed to fail and has only led to more instability and the spread of the war in the region.

Instead of pretending to be everything to everyone, while shifting alliances and blindly hoping for good to come of it, we should reconsider the advice of the Founders and take seriously the strict restraints on waging war placed in the Constitution.

Not much long-term good can come of a foreign policy designed to meddle and manipulate in places where we have no business or authority. It cannot help the cause of peace.

Unfortunately, our policies usually backfire and do more harm than good. When weaker nations are intimidated by more powerful ones, striking back very often can be done only through terrorism, a problem that will continue to threaten all Americans as our leaders incite those who oppose our aggressive stands throughout the world.

War has been used throughout history to enhance the state against the people. Taxes, conscription and inflation have been used as tools of the state to pursue wars not popular with the people. Government size and authority always grows with war, as the people are told that only the sacrifice of their liberties can save the nation. Propaganda and threats are used to coerce the people into carelessly giving up their liberties.

This has always been true with military wars, but the same can be said of the war mentality associated with the war on drugs, the war on poverty, the war against illiteracy, or any other war proposed by some social do-gooder or intentional mischief-maker.

But **when a foreign war comes to our shores in the form of terrorism, we can be sure that our government will explain the need for further sacrifice of personal liberties to win this war against terrorism as well.** Extensive preparations are already being made to fight urban and domestic violence, not by an enhanced local police force, but by a national police force with military characteristics.

Even the war against national disasters led by FEMA usurps local authority while imposing restraints on movement and controlling recovery efforts that should be left to local police, private insurance, and voluntary groups.

Our overseas efforts to police the world imply that, with or without success, resulting injuries and damage imposed by us and others will be rectified with U.S. tax dollars in the form of more foreign aid, as we always do. Nation building and international social work have replaced national defense as the proper responsibility of our government.

What will the fate of NATO be in the coming years? Many are fretting that NATO may dissolve over a poor showing in Yugoslavia, despite the 50th anniversary hype and its recent expansion. Fortunately for those who cherish liberty and limited government, NATO has a questionable future.

When our leaders sanctioned NATO in 1949, there were many patriotic Americans who questioned the wisdom and the constitutionality of this organization. It was by its charter to be strictly a defensive organization designed to defend Western Europe from any Soviet threat. The NATO charter clearly recognized the Security Council of the United Nations was responsible for the maintenance of international peace and security.

Likewise, the legislative history and congressional testimony maintained NATO could not usurp from Congress and the people the power to wage war. We have drifted a long way from that acknowledgment; the fears expressed by Robert Taft and others in 1949 were certainly justified.

The United States and NATO, while deliberately avoiding a UN vote on the issue, have initiated war against a sovereign state in the middle of a

120

civil war. A civil war that caused thousands of casualties and refugees on both sides has been turned into a war with hundreds of thousands of casualties and refugees with NATO's interference. The not-so-idle U.S. threats cast at Milosevic did not produce compliance. It only expanded the violence and the bloodshed.

The foolishness of this policy has become apparent, but Western leaders are quick to justify their warmongering. It was not peace or liberty or national security they sought as they sent the bombs flying. It was to save face for NATO.

Without the Soviets to worry about, NATO needed a mission, and stopping the evil Serbs fit the bill. It was convenient to ignore the evil Croates and the Kosovors, and it certainly was easy to forget the United Nations', NATO's, and the United States' policies over the past decade that contributed to the mess in Yugoslavia.

It was soon apparent that bombing was no more a successful diplomatic tool than were the threats of dire consequences if the treaty, unfavorable to the Serbs, was not quickly signed by Milosevic. This drew demands that policy must be directed toward saving NATO by expanding the war. NATO's credibility was now at stake. How could Europe or the United States war machine survive if NATO were to disintegrate?

Hopes as expressed by Ron Brown and his corporate friends were not extinguished by the unfortunate and mysterious Air Force crash while on their way to Bosnia to do business deals. Nobody even bothers to find out what U.S. policy condones business trips of our corporate leaders in a war zone on an Air Force aircraft. **Corporate interests and the military-industrial complex continue to play a role in our Yugoslavian war policy. Corporate America loves NATO.**

Most politicians and the public do not know what NATO's real mission is, and today's policy cannot be explained by reading its mission statement written in 1949. Certainly our vital interests and national security cannot justify our escalation of the war in Yugoslavia.

The excuse that we are the only superpower is hardly a moral reason to justify bombing nations that are seen as uncooperative. Military strength gives neither a right to bully nor a monopoly on wisdom. This strength too often, when held by large political entities, is used criminally to serve the powerful special interests.

The Persian Gulf and Yugoslavia obviously are much more economically intriguing than Rwanda and Sudan. There are clearly no business benefits for taking on the Chinese over its policy toward Tibet. Quite the contrary, we do business with China and subsidize her, to boot.

In spite of the powerful political and industrial leaders' support behind NATO, and the budgets of 19 Western countries, NATO's days appear numbered. **We shall not weep when NATO goes the way of the Soviet Empire and the Warsaw Pact.** Managing a war with 19 vetoes makes it impossible for a coherent strategy to evolve. Chaos, bickering, bureaucratic blundering, waste and political infighting will surely result.

There is no natural tendency for big government to enjoy stability without excessive and brute force, as was used in the Soviet system. Eventually the natural tendency towards instability, as occurred in the Soviet Empire, will bring about NATO's well-deserved demise. NATO, especially since it has embarked on a new and dangerous imperialistic mission, will find using brute force to impose its will on others is doomed to fail.

It has been said that, in numbers, there is strength. But in politics, it can also be said that, in numbers, there is confusion as differences become magnified.

Nationalism is alive and well even within the 19-member NATO group. When nationalism is non-militaristic, peace-loving, and freedom-oriented, it is a force that will always undermine big-government planners, whether found in a Soviet system or a NATO/UN system.

The smaller the unit of government, the better it is for the welfare of all those who seek only peace and freedom. NATO no longer can hide its true intent behind an anti-Communist commitment.

Some have wondered how a 1960s generation administration could be so prone to war. The 1960s were known for their rebellion against the Vietnam War and a preference for lovemaking and drugs over fighting, even Communists. **In recent months, four separate sovereign nations were bombed by the United States. This has to be some kind of a record.** Bombing Belgrade on Easter has to tell us something about an administration that is still strangely seen by some as not having the determination to fight a real war. There is a big difference between being anti-war when one's life is at risk as compared to when it is someone else's. That may tell us something about character, but there is more to it than that.

Many who were opposed to the Persian Gulf and Vietnam Wars are now strongly supporting this so-called just and humanitarian war to punish those who are said to be totally responsible for the Yugoslavian refugee problem. The fact that Serbia is not Communist in the sense of North Vietnam may play a part for some in making the decision to support this war, but not the war in Vietnam. But the Persian Gulf War was not at all about communism; it was about oil.

Some from the left, if strongly inclined toward internationalism, supported the Persian Gulf War, but for the most part, the opposition came from those who chose not to support a president of the opposite party, while today, supporting one's own party's position to bomb the Serbs becomes politically correct.

The same can be said of those who are opposed to the Yugoslavian war. Where they supported the Persian Gulf War, this administration has not garnered their support for partisan reasons. The principles of interventionism, constitutionality and morality have not been applied consistently to each war effort by either political party; and there is a precise reason for this, over and above the petty partisanship of many.

The use of government force to mold personal behavior, manipulate the economy and interfere in the affairs of other nations is an acceptable practice endorsed by nearly everyone in Washington, regardless of party affiliation. Once the principle of government force is acknowledged as legitimate, varying the when and to what degree becomes the only issue. It is okay to fight Communists overseas but not Serbs; it is okay to fight Serbs but not Arabs. The use of force becomes completely arbitrary and guided by the politicians' good judgment. When it pleases one group to use constitutional restraint, it does, but forget about the restraints when it is not convenient.

The 1960s crowd, although having a reputation for being anti-war due to their position on Vietnam, has never been bashful about its bold authoritarian use of force to mold economic conditions, welfare, housing, medical care, job discrimination, environment, wages and working conditions, combined with a love for taxes and inflation to pay the bills. When in general the principle of government force to mold society is endorsed, using force to punish Serbs is no great leap of faith, and for the interventionists is entirely consistent—likewise, the interventionists who justified unconstitutional fighting in Vietnam, Panama, Nicaragua, Grenada, Libya and the Persian Gulf, even if they despise the current war in Yugoslavia, can easily justify using government force when it pleases them and their home constituency.

Philosophic interventionism is a politician's dream. It allows arbitrary intervention, domestic or international, and when political circumstances demand opposition, it is easy to cite the Constitution, which always and correctly rejects the use of government force, except for national self-defense and for the protection of life, liberty and property.

Politicians love interventionism and pragmatism—the prevailing philosophy of our age and a philosophy based on relative ethics. No rigid adherence to law or morality is required. Even the Constitution can be used in this delicate debate of just when and for whom we go to war. The trick is to grab the political moral high ground while rejecting the entire moral foundation upon which the law rests, natural rights, rejection of force and the requirement that politicians be strictly bound by a contract which all of us take an oath to uphold.

What does this hodgepodge philosophy here in the Congress mean for the future of peace and prosperity in general, and NATO and the United Nations in particular? Pragmatism cannot prevail. Economically and socially, it breeds instability, bankruptcy, economic turmoil and factionalism here at home. Internationally it will lead to the same results.

NATO's days are surely numbered. That is the message of the current chaos in Yugoslavia. NATO may hold together in name only for a while, but its effectiveness is gone forever. The U.S. has the right to legally leave NATO with a one-year's notice. We should leave, but we will not. We will continue to allow ourselves to bleed financially and literally for many years to come before it is recognized that governance of diverse people is best done by diverse and small governments—not by a one-world government dependent on the arbitrary use of force determined by politically correct reasons and manipulated by the powerful financial interests around the world.

Our more immediate problem is the financing of the ongoing war in Yugoslavia. On February 9 of this year I introduced legislation to deny funds to the president to wage war in Yugoslavia. The Congress chose to ignore this suggestion and missed an opportunity to prevent the fiasco now ongoing in Yugoslavia.

The president, as so many other presidents have done since World War II, took it upon himself to wage an illegal war against Yugoslavia under NATO's authority, and Congress again chose to do nothing. By ignoring our constitutional responsibility with regards to war power, the Congress implicitly endorsed the president's participation in NATO's illegal war against Yugoslavia. We neither declared war nor told the president to cease and desist.

Now we have a third chance, and maybe our last, before the war gets out of control. We are being asked to provide all necessary funding for the war. Once we provide funds for the war, the Congress becomes an explicit partner in this ill-conceived NATO-inspired intervention in the civil war of a sovereign nation, making Congress morally and legally culpable.

Appropriating funds to pursue this war is not the way to peace. We have been bombing, boycotting and killing thousands in Iraq for nine years with no end in sight. We have been in Bosnia for three years, with no end in sight. And once Congress endorses the war in Yugoslavia with funding, it could take a decade, billions of dollars, and much more suffering on both sides, before we put it to an end.

Bellicosity and jingoism associated with careless and illegal intervention can never replace a policy of peace and friendship whenever possible—and when it is not, at least neutrality. NATO's aggressive war of destruction and vengeance can only make the situation worse. The sooner we disengage ourselves from this ugly civil war, the better. It is the right thing to do. ■

In 1999 Chairman James Walsh of New York made an effort to end the Selective Service System. We worked closely with Citizens Against Government Waste and other groups but were opposed by Duke Cunningham of California. On September 8, 1999, we won the vote 232-187. Unfortunately, the Senate restored the funding in conference committee.

September 8, 1999
THE APPROPRIATION FOR THE SELECTIVE SERVICE SYSTEM SHOULD NOT BE REINSTATED
HON. RON PAUL of TEXAS
IN THE HOUSE OF REPRESENTATIVES

Madam Speaker, later today we will be dealing with the VA HUD bill, and I want to compliment the Committee on Appropriations for deleting the $24.5 million for the selective service system. There will be an attempt to put that money back into the bill. I think that is a serious mistake.

The military has not asked for the selective service to continue. We do not need it. It is a serious abuse of the civil liberties of all 18- and 19-year-olds to continue this registration. The registration is totally unnecessary. This $24.5 million could be better spent on veterans' affairs or some other worthy cause, but to put the money back in is a serious mistake.

I would like to remind my conservative colleagues that Ronald Reagan had a very strong position on the draft and selective service. He agreed that it was a totalitarian notion to conscript young people and strongly spoke out against the draft whenever he had the opportunity.

I also would like to remind my conservative colleagues that if somebody came to the House floor and asked that we register all the guns of America, there would be a hue and cry about why this would be unconstitutional and unfair, yet they are quite willing to register their 18- and 19-year-olds. I do not understand why there is less respect given for 18- and 19-year-olds than for their own guns.

I strongly urge that we not fund the selective service system today. ■

In 1999 events seemed to me to be providing an impetus and excuse for foreign terrorists to strike at us again. My hope was tha,t by reconsidering our policy, we might avoid a disaster on our own shores.

November 17, 1999
U.S. FOREIGN POLICY OF MILITARY INTERVENTIONISM BRINGS DEATH, DESTRUCTION, AND LOSS OF LIFE
HON. RON PAUL of TEXAS
IN THE HOUSE OF REPRESENTATIVES

Mr. Speaker, demonstrators are once again condemning America in a foreign city. This time, it is in Kabul, Afghanistan. Shouting "Death to America," burning our flag, and setting off bombings, the demonstrators express their hatred toward America.

The United States has just placed sanctions on yet another country to discipline those who do not obey our commands. The nerve of them! Do they not know we are the most powerful nation in the world and we have to meet our responsibilities? They should do as we say and obey our CIA directives.

This process is not new. It has been going on for 50 years, and it has brought us grief and multiplied our enemies. Can one only imagine what the expression of hatred might be if we were not the most powerful nation in the world?

Our foreign policy of military interventionism has brought us death and destruction to many foreign lands and loss of life for many Americans. From Korea and Vietnam to Serbia, Iran, Iraq and now Afghanistan, we have ventured far from our shores in search of wars to fight. Instead of more free trade with our potential adversaries, we are quick to slap on sanctions that hurt American exports and help to solidify the power of the

126

tyrants, while seriously penalizing innocent civilians in fomenting anti-America hatred.

The most current anti-American demonstrations in Kabul were understandable and predictable. **Our one-time ally, Osama bin Laden, who served as a freedom fighter against the Soviets in Afghanistan and when we bombed his Serbian enemies while siding with his friends in Kosovo, has not been fooled and knows that his cause cannot be promoted by our fickle policy.**

Sanctions are one thing, but seizures of bank assets of any related business to the Taliban government infuriates and incites the radicals to violence. There is no evidence that this policy serves the interests of world peace. It certainly increases the danger to all Americans as we become the number one target of terrorists. Conventional war against the United States is out of the question, but acts of terrorism, whether it is the shooting down of a civilian airliner or bombing a New York City building, are almost impossible to prevent in a reasonably open society.

Likewise, the bombings in Islamabad, and possibly the UN plane crash in Kosovo, are directly related to our meddling in the internal affairs of these nations.

General Musharraf's successful coup against Prime Minister Sharif of Pakistan was in retaliation for America's interference with Sharif's handling of the Pakistan-India border war. The recent bombings in Pakistan are a clear warning to Musharraf that he, too, must not submit to U.S.-CIA directives.

I see this as a particularly dangerous time for a U.S. president to be traveling to this troubled region, since many blame us for the suffering, whether it is the innocent victims in Kosovo, Serbia, Iraq, or Afghanistan. It is hard for the average citizens of these countries to understand why we must be so involved in their affairs, and resort so readily to bombing and boycotts in countries thousands of miles away from our own.

Our foreign policy is deeply flawed and does not serve our national security interest. In the Middle East, it has endangered some of the moderate Arab governments and galvanized Muslim militants.

The recent military takeover of Pakistan and the subsequent anti-American demonstration in Islamabad should not be ignored. It is time we in Congress seriously rethink our role in the region and in the world. We ought to do more to promote peace and trade with our potential enemies, rather than resorting to bombing and sanctions. ■

"No nation could preserve its freedom in the midst of continual warfare."—James Madison

CHAPTER 11

Columbia has not gotten very much attention since 9/11, but our intervention there may well end up being more lengthy than Iraq, and more devastating in the long run.

September 6, 2000
MINDING OUR OWN BUSINESS REGARDING COLOMBIA IS IN THE BEST INTEREST OF AMERICA
HON. RON PAUL of TEXAS
IN THE HOUSE OF REPRESENTATIVES

Mr. Speaker, those of us who warned of the shortcomings of expanding our military presence in Colombia were ignored when funds were appropriated for this purpose earlier this year. We argued at that time that clearly no national security interests were involved; that the Civil War was more than 30 years old, complex with three factions fighting, and no assurance as to who the good guys were; that the drug war was a subterfuge, only an excuse, not a reason, to needlessly expand our involvement in Colombia; and that special interests were really driving our policy: Colombia Oil Reserves owned by American interests, American weapons manufacturers, and American corporations anxious to build infrastructure in Colombia.

Already our foolishly expanded pressure in Colombia has had a perverse effect. The stated purpose of promoting peace and stability has been undermined. Violence has worsened as factions are now fighting more fiercely than ever before for territory while they anticipate the full force of U.S. weapons arriving.

The already-weak peace process has been essentially abandoned. Hatred toward Americans by many Colombians has grown. The presidents of 12 South American countries rejected outright the American-backed military operation amendment aimed at the revolutionary groups in Colombia.

This foolhardy effort to settle the Colombian civil war has clearly turned out to be a diplomatic failure. The best evidence of a seriously flawed policy is the departure of capital. Watching money flows gives us a market assessment of policy; and by all indications, our policy spells trouble.

There is evidence of a recent large-scale exodus of wealthy Colombians to Miami. Tens of thousands of Colombians are leaving for the U.S., Canada, Costa Rica, Spain, and Australia. These are the middle-class and upper-class citizens, taking their money with them. Our enhanced presence in Colombia has accelerated this exodus.

Our policy, unless quickly and thoroughly reversed, will surely force an escalation of the civil war and a dangerous increase in our involvement with both dollars and troops. All this will further heighten the need for drug sales to finance all factions of the civil war. So much for stopping the drug war.

Our policy is doomed to fail. There is no national security interest involved; therefore, no goals can be set and no victory is achievable. A foreign policy of non-intervention designed only to protect our sovereignty with an eagerness to trade with all nations willing to be friends is the traditional American foreign policy and would give us the guaranteed hope of peace, the greatest hope of peace and prosperity.

Let us think seriously about our foreign policy, and hopefully someday we will pursue a policy in the best interest of America by minding our own business. ■

I have crafted several pieces of legislation highly critical of the UN, the International Criminal Court and other entities that not only tend to be corrupt and ineffective, but also threaten our national independence.

September 18, 2000
AMERICA'S ROLE IN THE UNITED NATIONS
HON. RON PAUL of TEXAS
IN THE HOUSE OF REPRESENTATIVES

Mr. Speaker, over a half a century has transpired since the United States of America became a member of the United Nations. Purporting to act pursuant to the treaty powers of the Constitution, the president of the United States signed, and the United States Senate ratified, the charter of the United Nations. Yet, the debate in government circles over the United Nations' charter scarcely has touched on the question of the constitutional power of the United States to enter such an agreement. Instead, the only questions addressed concerned the respective roles that the president and Congress would assume upon the implementation of that charter.

On the one hand, some proposed that once the charter of the United States was ratified, the president of the United States would act independently of Congress pursuant to his executive prerogatives to conduct the foreign affairs of the nation. Others insisted, however, that the Congress played a major role of defining foreign policy, especially because that policy implicated the power to declare war, a subject reserved strictly for Congress by Article I, Section 8 of the U.S. Constitution.

At first, it appeared that Congress would take control of America's participation in the United Nations. But in the enactment of the United Nations' participation act on December 20, 1945, Congress laid down several rules by which America's participation would be governed. Among those rules was the requirement that, before the president of the United States could deploy United States Armed Forces in service of the United Nations, he was required to submit to Congress for its specific approval the numbers and types of Armed Forces, their degree of readiness and general location, and the nature of the facilities and assistance, including rights of passage to be made available to the United Nations Security Council on its call for the purpose of maintaining international peace and security.

Since the passage of the United Nations Participation Act, however, congressional control of presidential foreign policy initiatives, in cooperation with the United Nations, has been more theoretical than real. Presidents

131

from Truman to the current president have again and again presented Congress with already-begun military actions, thus forcing Congress's hand to support United States troops or risk the accusation of having put the nation's servicemen and service women in unnecessary danger. **Instead of seeking congressional approval of the use of the United States Armed Forces in service of the United Nations, presidents from Truman to Clinton have used the United Nations Security Council as a substitute for congressional authorization of the deployment of United States Armed Forces in that service.**

This transfer of power from Congress to the United Nations has not, however, been limited to the power to make war. Increasingly, presidents are using the UN not only to implement foreign policy in pursuit of international peace, but also domestic policy in pursuit of international, environmental, economic, education, social welfare and human rights policy, both in derogation of the legislative prerogatives of Congress and of the 50 State legislatures, and further in derogation of the rights of the American people to constitute their own civil order.

As Cornell University government professor Jeremy Rabkin has observed, although the UN charter specifies that none of its provisions "shall authorize the United Nations to intervene in matters which are essentially within the domestic jurisdiction of any State," nothing has ever been found so "essentially domestic" as to exclude UN intrusions.

The release in July 2000 of the UN Human Development Report provides unmistakable evidence of the universality of the United Nations' jurisdictional claims. Boldly proclaiming that global integration is eroding national borders, the report calls for the implementation and, if necessary, the imposition of global standards of economic and social justice by international agencies and tribunals. In a special contribution endorsing this call for the globalization of domestic policymaking, United Nations Secretary General Kofi Annan wrote, "Above all, we have committed ourselves to the idea that no individual shall have his or her human rights abused or ignored. The idea is enshrined in the charter of the United Nations. The United Nations' achievements in the area of human rights over the last 50 years are rooted in the universal acceptance of those rights enumerated in the Universal Declaration of Rights. Emerging slowly, but I believe, surely, is an international norm," and these are Annan's words, "that must and will take precedence over concerns of State sovereignty."

Although such a wholesale transfer of United States sovereignty to

132

the United Nations as envisioned by Secretary General Annan has not yet come to pass, it will, unless Congress takes action.

Mr. Speaker, H.R. 1146, the American Sovereignty Restoration Act, is my answer to this problem.

To date, Congress has attempted to curb the abuse of power of the United Nations by urging the United Nations to reform itself, threatening the nonpayment of assessments and dues allegedly owed by the United States and thereby cutting off the United Nations' major source of funds. America's problems with the United Nations will not, however, be solved by such reform measures. The threat posed by the United Nations to the sovereignty of the United States and independence is not that the United Nations is currently plagued by a bloated and irresponsible international bureaucracy. Rather, the threat arises from the United Nation's Charter which—from the beginning—was a threat to sovereignty protections in the U.S. Constitution. The American people have not, however, approved of the Charter of the United Nations which, by its nature, cannot be the supreme law of the land for it was never "made under the Authority of the U.S.," as required by Article VI.

H.R. 1146—The American Sovereignty Restoration Act of 1999 is my solution to the continued abuses of the United Nations. The U.S. Congress can remedy its earlier unconstitutional action of embracing the Charter of the United Nations by enacting H.R. 1146. The U.S. Congress, by passing H.R. 1146, and the U.S. president, by signing H.R. 1146— will heed the wise counsel of our first president, George Washington, when he advised his countrymen to "steer clear of permanent alliances with any portion of the foreign world," lest the nation's security and liberties be compromised by endless and overriding international commitments. ∎

Sitting on both the Foreign Affairs and Financial Services Committees gives me the opportunity to see where our foreign and financial polices intersect, often in danger to American taxpayers.

October 12, 2000
WARNING ABOUT FOREIGN POLICY AND MONETARY POLICY
HON. RON PAUL of TEXAS
IN THE HOUSE OF REPRESENTATIVES

Mr. Speaker, over the last three to four years, I have come to the floor on numerous occasions trying to sound a warning about both our foreign policy and our monetary policy. Today our monetary policy and our foreign policy have clashed. We see now that we face serious problems, not only in the Middle East, but in our financial markets.

Yesterday I talked a bit about what I see as a financial bubble that has developed over the past decade and made the point that a financial bubble can be financed through borrowing money, as well as inflation. A financial bubble is essentially a consequence of inflation. A lot of people talk about inflation being the mere rising of some prices, but that is not the case.

Most good economists recognize that inflation is a consequence of monetary policy; as one increases the supply of money, it inflates the currency. This distorts interest rates, and it distorts the markets. Sometimes this goes into goods and services, and other times these excessive funds will go into the marketplace and distort the value of stocks and bonds.

I believe this is what has happened for the past 10 years, Mr. Speaker. So in spite of the grand prosperity that we have had for this past decade, I believe it is an illusion in many ways, because we have not paid for it. In a true capitalist society, true wealth comes from hard work and savings.

Today the American people have a negative savings rate, which means that we get our so-called capital from a printing press—because there are no savings and no funds to invest. The Federal Reserve creates these funds to be invested. On a short term, this seems to benefit everyone.

The poor like it because they seem to get welfare benefits from it; and certainly the rich like it, because it motivates and stimulates their businesses; and politicians like it, because it takes care of deficits and it stimulates the economy.

The only problem with this is it always ends, and it always ends badly. And this is the reason that we have to meet up with a policy that seems

134

ridiculous. The economy seems to be doing quite well, but the Federal Reserve comes along and says there is a problem with economic growth. Economic growth might cause prices to go up; so, therefore, what we have to do is cut off the economic growth. If you have slower growth, the prices will not go up any longer.

They are talking about a symptom and not the cause. The cause is the Federal Reserve. The problem is that the Federal Reserve has been granted authority that is unconstitutional to counterfeit money, and until we recognize that and deal with that, we will continue to have financial problems.

We have heard that the 1990s was a different decade; it was a new era,economy—exactly what we heard throughout the decade prior to the collapse of the markets in Japan. The markets have now been down more than 50 percent in Japan for more than 10 years, and there is no sign of significant recovery there.

Also there were other times in our history when they talked about a new era economy.

Let me read a quote from Herbert Hoover in his memoirs.: "With growing optimism, they gave birth to a foolish idea called the New Economic Era. That notion spread over the whole country. We were assured that we were in a new period where the old laws of economics no longer applied."

It is an illusion to believe that the new paradigm exists. Actually, the computer industry involves five percent of the economy; 95 percent is what they called the old economy. I ascribe to old economic laws, because the truth is, we cannot change economic laws. And if inflating a currency distorts the market and the boom leads to the bust, that cannot be repelled.

If we are looking toward bad times, it is not because of current policy; it is because of previous policy, the previous policy of the last 10 years, the time when we live beyond our means. We say how did we live beyond our means? Where did the money come from? Are we not spending less in Washington? No, we are not spending less in Washington. Are not the deficits a lot less? They are less, but they are not gone.

Where did we borrow? We borrowed from overseas. We have a current account deficit that requires over a billion dollars a day that we borrow from foreigners, just to finance our current account deficit. We are now the greatest debtor in the world, and that is a problem. This is why the markets are shaky, and this is why the markets have been going down for six months. This is why in a foreign-policy crisis such as we are facing in the Middle East, we will accentuate these problems. Therefore, the foreign policy of military interventionism overseas is something that we should seriously question. ■

Here I make the point that our Middle East policy is harming our national defense.

November 15, 2000
OUR FOOLISH WAR IN THE MIDDLE EAST
HON. RON PAUL of TEXAS
IN THE HOUSE OF REPRESENTATIVES

The West has been at war with the Muslim world for over a thousand years. In this century, the British led the charge prior to World War II. Since that time it has been the United States. Although the British remain close allies of ours in intimidating the Muslim world, it is the military strength of the United States that assumes the burden of responsibility for the policy. It is justified by claiming a right and need to protect "our" oil.

For over a thousand years the West has dominated the Middle East. During these thousand years, resentment has continued, but for obvious reasons it is now being directed toward America. No one should be surprised when our ships become vulnerable and are actually blown up in the Middle East.

If the U.S. understood the history of this region, it would see the total folly of anchoring a war vessel in an enemy port. This lack of understanding of history and respect for religious beliefs of the area, in combination with our foreign policy of aggression and empire-building, leads to arrogant foreign military intervention, not only in the Middle East, but around the world as well.

It is clear that we are not in the Middle East for national security reasons, but instead to protect powerful commercial interests. This assures that we protect oil supplies for the West, and provides us with an excuse to keep the military-industrial complex active.

To put this in a proper perspective, consider how Americans, or especially Texans, would feel if the Gulf of Mexico were patrolled and protected by warships of a foreign power, say the Russians. What would we then think if that same power patrolling the Gulf built air bases in Texas and Florida with our government's complicity, with the argument that this was necessary to protect "their" oil and with our government's complicity? This would anger many Americans, and this anger would be directed to

136

both the foreign occupiers of our territorial waters and our own government that permitted it. Yet this is exactly what has been happening in the Persian Gulf region. For religious, historic and sovereignty reasons, the Muslim people harbor great resentment toward us.

As a consequence of the USS Cole incident, our Navy has recognized the great danger we face in this region. This has forced us to avoid sending any more naval vessels through the Suez Canal. The ongoing conflict cannot end peacefully as long as we pursue this policy of folly.

The Cole disaster was needless and preventable. The loss of this vessel and the senseless deaths of 17 Americans were a consequence of a policy that has led to a lack of military readiness for our country, while increasing the danger to all Americans, and in particular our servicemen in that region. It's positively amazing that, with a military budget of $300 billion, we do not have the ability to protect ourselves against a rubber raft, which destroyed a $1 billion vessel. Our sentries on duty had rifles without bullets and were prohibited from firing on any enemy targets. This policy is absurd, if not insane. It is obvious that our Navy lacks the military intelligence to warn and prevent such an event. It is incapable even of investigating the incident, since the FBI was required to try to figure out what happened. This further intrusion has only served to increase the resentment of the people of Yemen toward all Americans.

But the Yemenis never will cooperate with our CIA and FBI agents, many who already have been forced to retreat and return to the States. Our insistence on invading Yemen to search for all those involved will only make our precarious situation in the Middle East worse.

Our policy in the Middle East cannot possibly be successful. It's obvious there will be an inevitable conflict between our support for the moderate Arabs—which antagonizes the Islamic fundamentalists of this region—and our special treatment for Israel. It is clear that the powerful financial interests of this country want to use our military force to protect their commercial and oil interests in this region, while there will always remain powerful U.S. political support for the State of Israel. The two sides never will be reconciled by our attempt to balance our support by giving help to both sides. This is exactly opposite of being neutral and friends with both sides. The one reason why this confrontation is going to continue is that 75 percent of known oil reserves are now owned by Muslims around the world.

Our current foreign policy does nothing more than stir the flames of hatred of both sides, clearly evident as we witness the daily fighting between the Palestinians and the Israelis. Growing influence of the radical Islamic

137

fundamentalists will allow them one day to overthrow the secular moderate puppet regimes supported by our government.

As the world becomes less stable due to currency, trade and other economic reasons, this region will become even more volatile. We should expect higher oil prices. Hatred toward America will continue to escalate, and United States security will continue to be diminished due to the threat of terrorist attacks. All the anti-ballistic missiles in the world will not be able to protect us against attacks such as the Cole suffered or from the nuclear and biological weapons that can be brought into this country in a suitcase.

The greatest threat to our national security is our own bad policy. Our policy has continued to permit our own military technology, developed by our taxpayers, to get into the hands of our so-called allies, as well as our potential enemies like China.

The turmoil in the Middle East is now spilling over into Indonesia, a country made up of 17,000 islands and very vulnerable to political instability, especially since its currency and financial crisis of a few years ago. Indonesia is the world's fourth largest nation, with the largest Muslim population of any country. Hatred toward the West, and especially America, due to the Middle East policy, has led to Christian persecution in Indonesia. The embassy is now closed, and American Ambassador Robert Gelbard has been recalled after his life was threatened.

Our many failures in the last 50 years should prompt us to reassess our entire foreign policy of interventionism. The notion that, since we are the only superpower left, we have an obligation to tell everybody else how to live should come to an end. Our failure in Korea, Vietnam, Somalia, and the Middle East, and our failure yet to come in Bosnia and Kosovo, should alert all Americans to this great danger. But, no, we instead continue to expand our intervention by further involving ourselves in yet another sovereign nation. This time it's Columbia. By sending more weapons into the region, we continue to stir up this 30-year-old civil conflict. And just recently this conflict has spilled over into Venezuela, a major force in South America, due to its oil reserves. The Foreign Minister of Venezuela, angered by U.S. actions, recently warned, "Any ship or boat which enters the Gulf of Venezuela, of whatever nationality it may be, will be expelled." Our intervention in many of these regions, and especially in South America, has been done in the name of the drug war. But the truth is it's serving the interests of the companies who own the oil rights in this region, as well as those who produce the weapons that get sent into these regions. ∎

"Criticism in a time of war is essential to the maintenance of any kind of democratic government. "—Sen. Robert Taft, (R) Ohio

CHAPTER 12

In my last significant foreign policy statement prior to 9/11, I suggested that our foreign policy was leading us toward a significant and potentially disastrous violent conflict.

February 8, 2001
POTENTIAL FOR WAR
HON. RON PAUL of TEXAS
IN THE HOUSE OF REPRESENTATIVES

Mr. Speaker, I have asked for this special order today to express my concerns for our foreign policy of interventionism that we have essentially followed throughout the 20th Century.

Mr. Speaker, foreign military interventionism, a policy the U.S. has followed for over 100 years, encourages war and undermines peace. Even with the good intentions of many who support this policy, it serves the interests of powerful commercial entities.

Perpetual conflicts stimulate military spending. Minimal and small wars too often get out of control and cause more tragedy than originally anticipated. Small wars, like the Persian Gulf War, are more easily tolerated, but the foolishness of an out-of-control war like Vietnam is met with resistance from a justifiably aroused nation.

But both types of conflicts result from the same flawed foreign policy of foreign interventionism. Both types of conflict can be prevented. National security is usually cited to justify our foreign involvement, but this excuse distracts from the real reason we venture so far from home. Influential commercial interests dictate policy of when and where we go. Persian Gulf oil obviously got more attention than genocide in Rwanda.

If one were truly concerned about our security and enhancing peace, one would always opt for a less militaristic policy. It is not a coincidence that U.S. territory and U.S. citizens are the most vulnerable in the world to terrorist attacks.

Escalation of the war on terrorism and not understanding its causes is a dangerous temptation. Not only does foreign interventionism undermine chances for peace and prosperity, it undermines personal liberty. War and preparing for war must always be undertaken at someone's expense. Someone must pay the bills with higher taxes, and someone has to be available to pay with their lives.

It is never the political and industrial leaders who promote the policy who pay. They are the ones who reap the benefits, while at the same time arguing for the policy they claim is designed to protect freedom and prosperity for the very ones being victimized.

Many reasons given for our willingness to police the world sound reasonable: we need to protect our oil; we need to stop cocaine production in Colombia; we need to bring peace in the Middle East; we need to punish our adversaries; we must respond because we are the sole superpower, and it is our responsibility to maintain world order; it is our moral obligation to settle disputes; we must follow up on our dollar diplomacy after sending foreign aid throughout the world. In the old days it was, we need to stop the spread of communism.

The excuses are endless. But it is rarely mentioned that the lobbyists and the proponents of foreign intervention are the weapons manufacturers, the oil companies, and the recipients of huge contracts for building infrastructures in whatever far corners of the Earth we send our troops. Financial interests have a lot at stake, and it is important for them that the United States maintains its empire.

Not infrequently, ethnic groups will influence foreign policy for reasons other than preserving our security. This type of political pressure can, at times, be substantial and emotional. We often try to please too many, and by doing so support both sides of conflicts that have raged for centuries. In the end, our effort can end up unifying our adversaries while alienating our friends.

Over the past 50 years, Congress has allowed our presidents to usurp the prerogatives the Constitution explicitly gave only to the Congress. **The term "foreign policy" is never mentioned in the Constitution, and it was never intended to be monopolized by the president. Going to war was to be strictly a legislative function, not an executive one.** Operating foreign policy by executive orders and invoking unratified treaties is a slap in the face to the rule of law and our republican form of government. But that is the way it is currently being done. U.S. policy over the past 50 years has led to endless illegal military interventions, from Korea to our ongoing war with Iraq and military occupation in the Balkans. Many Americans have died. and many others have been wounded or injured, or have just simply been forgotten.

Numerous innocent victims living in foreign lands have died, as well, from the bombings and the blockades we have imposed. They have been people with whom we have had no fight but who were trapped between the bad policy of their own leaders and our eagerness to demonstrate our prowess in the world. Over 500,000 Iraqi children have reportedly died as a consequence of our bombing and denying food and medicine by our embargo.

For over 50 years, there has been a precise move towards one-world government at the expense of our own sovereignty. Our presidents claim that our authority to wage wars comes from the United Nations or NATO resolution, in contradiction to our Constitution and everything our Founding Fathers believed.

U.S. troops are now required to serve under foreign commanders and wear UN insignias. Refusal to do so prompts court-martial.

The past president, before leaving office, signed the 1998 UN-Rome treaty indicating our willingness to establish an international criminal court. This gives the UN authority to enforce global laws against Americans if ratified by the Senate. But even without ratification, we have gotten to the point where treaties of this sort can be imposed on non-participating nations. Presidents have, by executive orders, been willing to follow unratified treaties in the past. This is a very dangerous precedent. We already accept the international trade court, the WTO. Trade wars are fought with the court's supervision, and we are only too ready to rewrite our tax laws as the WTO dictates.

The only portion of the major tax bill at the end of the last Congress to be rushed through for the president's signature was the foreign sales corporation changes dictated to us by the WTO.

For years the U.S. has accepted the international financial and currency management of the IMF, another arm of one-world government.

The World Bank serves as the distributor of international welfare, of which the U.S. taxpayer is the biggest donor. This organization helps carry out a policy of taking money from poor Americans and giving it to rich foreign leaders, with kickbacks to some of our international corporations.

Support for the World Bank, the IMF, the international criminal court, always comes from the elites and almost never from the common man. These programs, run by the international institutions, are supposed to help the poor, but they never do. It is all a charade. If left unchecked, they will bankrupt us and encourage more world government mischief.

It is the responsibility of Congress to curtail this trend by reestablishing the principles of the U.S. Constitution and our national sovereignty. It is time for the United States to give up its membership in all these international organizations.

Our foreign policy has led to an incestuous relationship between our military and Hollywood. In December, our Secretary of Defense used $295,000 of taxpayers' money to host a party in Los Angeles for Hollywood bigwigs. Pentagon spokesman Kenneth Bacon said it was well worth it. The purpose was to thank the movie industry for putting the military in a good light.

A similar relationship has been reported with TV stations licensed by the U.S. government. They have been willing to accept suggestions from the government to place political messages in their programming. This is a dangerous trend, mixing government and the media. Here is where real separation is needed.

Our policy should change for several reasons. It is wrong for our foreign policy to serve any special interest, whether it is for financial benefits, ethnic pressures, or some contrived moral imperative. Too often the policy leads to an unintended consequence, and more people are killed and more property damaged than was intended.

Controlling world events is never easy. It is better to avoid the chance of one bad decision leading to another. The best way to do that is to follow the advice of the Founders and avoid all entangling alliances, and pursue a policy designed solely to protect U.S. national security interests.

The two areas in the world that currently present the greatest danger to the United States are Colombia and the Middle East. For decades we have been engulfed in the ancient wars of the Middle East by subsidizing and supporting both sides. This policy is destined to fail. We are in great danger of becoming involved in a vicious war for oil, as well as being drawn into a religious war that will not end in our lifetime.

The potential for war in this region is great, and the next one could make the Persian Gulf War look small. Only a reassessment of our entire policy will keep us from being involved in a needless and dangerous war in this region.

It will be difficult to separate any involvement in the Balkans from a major conflict that breaks out in the Middle East. It is impossible for us to maintain a policy that both supports Israel and provides security for Western-leaning secular Arab leaders, while at the same time taunting the Islamic fundamentalists. Push will come to shove, and when that happens in the midst of an economic crisis, our resources will be stretched beyond the limit. This must be prevented.

Our involvement in Colombia could easily escalate into a regional war. For over 100 years, we have been involved in the affairs of Central America, but the recent escalation of our presence in Colombia is inviting trouble for us. Although the justification for our enhanced presence is the war on drugs, protecting U.S. oil interests and selling helicopters are the real reasons for the last year's $1.3 billion emergency funding.

Already neighboring countries have expressed concern about our presence in Colombia. The U.S. policymakers gave their usual response by promising more money and support to the neighboring countries that feel threatened.

Venezuela, rich in oil, is quite nervous about our enhanced presence in the region. Their foreign minister stated that if any of our ships enter the Gulf of Venezuela, they will be expelled. This statement was prompted by an overly aggressive U.S. Coast Guard vessel's intrusion into Venezuela's territorial waters on a drug expedition. I know of no one who believes this expanded and insane drug war will do anything to dampen drug usage in the United States, yet it will cost us plenty.

Too bad our political leaders cannot take a hint. The war effort in Colombia is small now, but under current conditions, it will surely escalate. This is a 30-year-old civil war being fought in the jungles of South America. We are unwelcome by many, and we ought to have enough sense to stay out of it.

Recently, new policy has led to the spraying of herbicides to destroy the coca fields. It has already been reported that the legal crops in the nearby fields have been destroyed, as well. This is no way to win friends around the world.

There are many other areas of the world where we ought to take a second look and then come home. Instead of bullying the European Union for wanting to have their own rapid deployment force, we should praise them and bring our troops home. **World War II has been over for 55 years.**

It is time we look at Korea and ask why we have to broker, with the use of American dollars and American soldiers, the final settlement between North and South Korea. Taiwan and China are now trading and investing in each other's countries. Travel restrictions have been recently liberalized. It is time for us to let the two of them settle their own border dispute.

We continue to support Turkey with dollars and weapons. We once supported Iraq with the same. Now, we permit Turkey, armed with American weapons, to kill Kurds in Iraq, while we bomb the Iraqis if they do the same. It makes no sense.

Selling weapons to both factions of almost all the major conflicts of the past 50 years reveals that our involvement is more about selling weapons than spreading the message of freedom. That message can never be delivered through force to others over their objection. Only a policy of peace, friendship, trade, and our setting a good example can inspire others to look to what once was the American tradition of liberty and justice for all. Entangling alliances will not do it. It is time for Congress and the American people to wake up.

The political system of interventionism always leads to social discord. Interventionism is based on relative rights, majorityism, and disrespect for the Constitution. Degenerating moral standards of the people encourages and feeds on this system of special-interest favoritism, all of which contribute to the friction.

Thomas Jefferson was worried that future generations might one day squander the liberties the American Revolution secured. Writing about future generations, Jefferson wondered if, in the enjoyment of plenty, they would lose the memory of freedom. He believed material abundance without character is the path to destruction.

The challenge to America today is clearly evident. We lack character. And we also suffer from the loss of respect, understanding, and faith in the liberty that offers so much. The American Republic has been transformed and only a remnant remains. It appears that, in the midst of plenty, we have forgotten about freedom. ∎

After our being attacked on 9/11, there was no alternative other than to respond. Yet I felt it important to make the point that even necessary conflict must be entered into with a sense of apprehension.

September 14, 2001
CONGRESSIONAL AUTHORIZATION OF THE USE OF FORCE
HON. RON PAUL of TEXAS
IN THE HOUSE OF REPRESENTATIVES

Mr. Speaker, sadly we find ourselves today dealing with our responsibility to provide national security under the most difficult of circumstances.

To declare war against a group that is not a country makes the clear declaration of war more complex.

The best tool the Framers of the Constitution provided under these circumstances was the power of Congress to grant letters of marque and reprisal, in order to narrow the retaliation to only the guilty parties. The complexity of the issue, the vagueness of the enemy, and the political pressure to respond immediately limit our choices. The proposed resolution is the only option we're offered and doing nothing is unthinkable.

There are a couple of serious points I'd like to make.

For the critics of our policy of foreign interventionism in the affairs of others, the attack on New York and Washington was not a surprise; many have warned of its inevitability.

It, so far, has been inappropriate to ask why the U.S. was the target and not some other Western country. But **for us to pursue a war against our enemies, it's crucial to understand why we were attacked, which then will tell us by whom we were attacked.**

Without this knowledge, striking out at six or eight, or even ten different countries could well expand this war of which we wanted no part. Without defining the enemy, there is no way to know our precise goal or to know when the war is over. Inadvertent or casual acceptance of civilian deaths by us as part of this war, I'm certain, will prolong the agony and increase the chances of even more American casualties. We must guard against this if at all possible.

Too often over the last several decades we have supported both sides of many wars, only to find ourselves needlessly entrenched in conflicts unrelated to our national security. It is not unheard of that the weapons and support we send to foreign nations have ended up being used against us. The current crisis may well be another example of such a mishap.

Although we now must fight to preserve our national security, we should not forget that the Founders of this great nation advised that for, our own sake, we should stay out of entangling alliances and the affairs of other nations.

We are placing tremendous trust in our president to pursue our enemies as our commander-in-chief, but Congress must remain vigilant to not allow our civil liberties here at home to be eroded. The temptation will be great to sacrifice our freedoms for what may seem to be more security. We must resist this temptation.

Mr. Speaker, we must rally behind our president, pray for him to make wise decisions, and hope that this crisis is resolved a lot sooner than is now anticipated. ■

Once the conflict had begun, it was time to recall what sort of policies had set the stage for the current situation. This restatement of principle was my first extended comment on our foreign policy after the outbreak of hostilities.

September 25, 2001
FOREIGN INTERVENTIONISM IS DETRIMENTAL TO OUR SECURITY
HON. RON PAUL of TEXAS
IN THE HOUSE OF REPRESENTATIVES

Mr. Speaker, last week was a bad week for all Americans. The best we can say is that the events have rallied the American spirit of shared love and generosity. Partisanship was put on hold, as it well should have been. We now, as a free people, must deal with this tragedy in the best way possible. Punishment and prevention is mandatory. We must not, however, sacrifice our liberties at the hand of an irrational urgency. Calm deliberation in our effort to restore normalcy is crucial. Cries for dropping nuclear bombs on an enemy not yet identified cannot possibly help in achieving this goal.

Mr. Speaker, I returned to Congress five years ago out of deep concern about our foreign policy of international interventionism, and a monetary and fiscal policy I believed would lead to a financial and dollar crisis. Over the past five years, I have frequently expressed my views on these issues and why I believed our policies should be changed.

This deep concern prompted me to seek and receive seats on the Financial Services and International Relations Committees. I sought to thwart some of the dangers I saw coming, but as the horrific attacks show, these efforts were to no avail. As concerned as I was, the enormity of the two-prong crisis that we now face came with a ferocity no one ever wanted to imagine. Now we must deal with what we have and do our best to restore our country to a more normal status.

I do not believe this can happen if we ignore the truth. We cannot close our eyes to the recent history that has brought us to this international crisis. **We should guard against emotionally driven demands to kill many bystanders in an effort to liquidate our enemy.** These efforts could well fail to punish the perpetrators, while only expanding the war and making things worse by killing innocent non-combatants and further radicalizing Muslim peoples.

It is obviously no easy task to destroy an almost invisible, ubiquitous enemy spread throughout the world, without expanding the war or infringing on our liberties here at home. But above all else, that is our mandate and our key constitutional responsibility—protecting liberty and providing for national security. My strong belief is that in the past, efforts in the US Congress to do much more than this, have diverted our attention and hence led to our neglect of these responsibilities.

Following the September 11th disasters, a militant Islamic group in Pakistan held up a sign for the entire world to see. It said: AMERICANS, THINK! WHY YOU ARE HATED ALL OVER THE WORLD. We abhor the messenger, but we should not ignore the message.

Here at home we are told that the only reason for the suicidal mass killing we experienced on September 11th is that we are hated because we are free and prosperous. If these two conflicting views are not reconciled, we cannot wisely fight nor win the war in which we now find ourselves. We must understand why the hatred is directed toward Americans and not other Western countries.

In studying history, I, as many others, have come to the conclusion that war is most often fought for economic reasons. But economic wars are driven by moral and emotional overtones.

Our own Revolution was fought to escape from excessive taxation, but was inspired and driven by our desire to protect our God-given right to liberty.

The War between the States, fought primarily over tariffs, was nonetheless inspired by the abhorrence of slavery. It is this moral inspiration that drives people to fight to the death, as so many Americans did between 1861 and 1865.

Both economic and moral causes of war must be understood. Ignoring the importance of each is dangerous. We should not casually ignore the root causes of our current fight, nor pursue this fight by merely accepting the explanation that they terrorize us out of jealously.

It has already been written that Islamic militants are fighting a "holy war"—a jihad. This drives them to commit acts that to us are beyond comprehension. It seems that they have no concern for economic issues, since they have no regard even for their own lives. But an economic issue does exist in this war: OIL!

When the conflict broke out between Iraq and Iran in the early 1980s, and we helped to finance and arm Iraq, Anwar Sadat of Egypt profoundly stated: "This is the beginning of the war for oil." Our crisis today is part of this long-lasting war over oil.

Osama bin Laden, a wealthy man, left Saudi Arabia in 1979 to join American-sponsored so-called freedom fighters in Afghanistan. He received financial assistance, weapons and training from our CIA, just as his allies in Kosovo continue to receive the same from us today.

Unbelievably, to this day our foreign aid continues to flow into Afghanistan, even as we prepare to go to war against her. My suggestion is, not only should we stop this aid immediately, but we should never have started it in the first place.

It is during this time bin Laden learned to practice terror, tragically, with money from the U.S. taxpayers. But it wasn't until 1991, during what we refer to as the Persian Gulf War, that he turned fully against the United States. It was this war, said to protect our oil, that brought out the worst in him.

Of course, it isn't our oil. The oil, in fact, belongs to the Arabs and other Muslim nations of the Persian Gulf. Our military presence in Saudi Arabia is what most Muslims believe to be a sacred violation of holy land. The continuous bombing and embargo of Iraq has intensified the hatred and contributed to more than over 1,000,000 deaths in Iraq. It is clear that protecting certain oil interests and our presence in the Persian Gulf help drive the holy war.

Muslims see this as an invasion and domination by a foreign enemy which inspires radicalism. This is not new. This war, from their viewpoint, has been going on since the Crusades 1000 year ago. We ignore this history at our own peril.

The radicals react as some Americans might react if China dominated the Gulf of Mexico and had air bases in Texas and Florida. Dominating the Persian Gulf is not a benign activity. It has consequences. The attack on the USS Cole was a warning we ignored.

Furthermore, our support for secular governments in the moderate Arab countries is interpreted by the radicals as more American control over their region than they want. There is no doubt that our policies that are seen by the radicals as favoring one faction over another in the long-lasting Middle East conflict add to the distrust and hatred of America.

The hatred has been suppressed, because we are a powerful economic and military force and wield a lot of influence. But this suppressed hatred is now becoming more visible, and we as Americans for the most part are not even aware of how this could be. Americans have no animosity toward a people they hardly even know. Instead, our policies have been driven by the commercial interests of a few. And now the innocent suffer.

I am hopeful that shedding light on the truth will be helpful in resolving this conflict in the very dangerous period that lies ahead. Without some understanding of the recent and past history of the Middle East and the Persian Gulf, we cannot expect to punish the evildoers without expanding the nightmare of hatred that is now sweeping the world.

Punishing the evildoers is crucial. Restoring safety and security to our country is critical. Providing for a strong defense is essential. But extricating ourselves from a holy war that we don't understand is also necessary if we expect to achieve the above-mentioned goals. Let us all hope and pray for guidance in our effort to restore the peace and tranquility we all desire.

We did a poor job in providing the security that all Americans should expect. This is our foremost responsibility. Some Members have been quick to point out the shortcomings of the FBI, the CIA and the FAA and claim more money will rectify the situation. I'm not so sure. Bureaucracies by nature are inefficient. The FBI and CIA records come up short. The FBI loses computers and guns and is careless with records. The CIA rarely provides timely intelligence. The FAA's idea of security against hijackers is asking all passengers who packed their bag.

The clamor now is to give more authority and money to these agencies. But, remember, important industries, like as our chemical plants and refineries, do not depend on government agencies for security. They build fences and hire guards with guns. The airlines have not been allowed to do the same thing. There was a time when airline pilots were allowed and did carry weapons, yet this has been prohibited by government regulation set to go into effect in November.

If the responsibility had been left with the airlines to provide safety, they may have had armed pilots or guards on the planes just as our industrial sites have. Privatizing the FAA, as other countries have, would also give airlines more leeway in providing security. My bill, HR 2896, should be passed immediately to clarify that the federal government will never place a prohibition on pilots being armed.

We face an enormous task to restore the sense of security we have taken for granted for so long. But it can be done. Destroying the evildoers while extricating ourselves from this un-holiest of wars is no small challenge. The job is somewhat like getting out of a pit filled with venomous snakes. The sooner we shoot the snakes that immediately threaten us, the sooner we can get safely away. If we're not careful, though, we'll breed more snakes, and they'll come out of every nook and cranny from around the world, and little will be resolved.

It's no easy task, but before we fight, we'd better be precise about whom we are fighting and how many there are and where they are hiding, or we'll never know when the war is over and our goals are achieved. Without this knowledge, the war can go on for a long, long time, and the war for oil has already been going on for more than 20 years. To this point, our president and his administration have displayed the necessary deliberation. This is a positive change from unauthorized and ineffective retaliatory bombings in past years that only worsened various conflicts.

If we can't or won't define the enemy, the cost to fight such a war will be endless. How many American troops are we prepared to lose? How much money are we prepared to spend? How many innocent civilians, in our nation and others, are we willing to see killed? How many American civilians will we jeopardize? How much of our civil liberties are we prepared to give up? How much prosperity will we sacrifice?

The Founders and authors of our Constitution provided an answer for the difficult tasks that we now face. When a precise declaration of war was impossible due to the vagueness of our enemy, the Congress was expected to take it upon themselves to direct the reprisal against an enemy not recognized as a government. In the early days, the concern was piracy on the high seas. Piracy was one of only three federal crimes named in the original Constitution.

Today, we have a new type of deadly piracy, in the high sky over our country. The solution the Founders came up with under these circumstances was for Congress to grant letters of marque and reprisal. This puts the responsibility in the hands of Congress to direct the president to perform a task with permission to use and reward private sources to carry out the task, such as the elimination of Osama bin Laden and his key supporters. This allows narrow targeting of the enemy. This effort would not preclude the president's other efforts to resolve the crisis, but if successful would preclude a foolish invasion of a remote country with a forbidding terrain like Afghanistan—a country that no foreign power has ever conquered throughout all of history.

Lives could be saved, billions of dollars could be saved, and escalation due to needless and senseless killing could be prevented. Mr. Speaker, we must seriously consider this option. This answer is a world apart from the potential disaster of launching nuclear weapons or endless bombing of an unseen target. "Marque and reprisal" demands the enemy be seen and precisely targeted with minimal danger to others. It should be considered and, for various reasons, is far superior to any effort that could be carried out by the CIA.

We must not sacrifice the civil liberties that generations of Americans have enjoyed and fought for over the past 225 years. Unwise decisions in response to the terror inflicted on us may well fail to destroy our enemy, while undermining our liberties here at home. That will not be a victory worth celebrating. The wise use of marque and reprisal would negate the need to undermine the privacy and rights of our citizens.

As we work through this difficult task, let us resist the temptation to invoke the most authoritarian of all notions that, not too many years ago, tore this nation apart: the military draft. The country is now unified against the enemy. The military draft does nothing to contribute to unity nor, as the Pentagon again has confirmed, does it promote an efficient military.

Precise identification of all travelers on all our air flights is a desired goal. A national ID issued by the federal government would prove to be disastrous to our civil liberties and should not be considered. This type of surveillance power should never be given to an intrusive overbearing government, no matter how well intentioned the motives.

The same results can be better achieved by the marketplace. Passenger IDs voluntarily issued by the airlines could be counterfeit-proof; and loss or theft of an ID could be immediately reported to the proper authorities. An ID, fingerprints, birth certificates, or any other information can be required without any violations of anyone's personal liberty. This delicate information would not be placed in the hands of the government agents but could be made available to law enforcement officers like any other information obtained with probable cause and a warrant.

The heat of the moment has prompted calls by some of our officials for great sacrifice of our liberties and privacy. This poses great danger to our way of life and will provide little help in dealing with our enemies. Efforts of this sort will only punish the innocent and have no effect on a would-be terrorist. We should be careful not to do something just to do something—even something harmful.

Mr. Speaker, I fear that some big mistakes could be made in the pursuit of our enemies if we do not proceed with great caution, wisdom, and deliberation. Action is necessary; inaction is unacceptable. No doubt others recognize the difficulty in targeting such an elusive enemy. This is why the principle behind "marque and reprisal" must be given serious consideration.

In retaliation, an unintended consequence of a policy of wanton destruction without benefit to our cause, could result in the overthrow of moderate Arab nations by the radicals that support bin Laden. This will not serve our interests and will surely exacerbate the threat to all Americans.

As we search for a solution to the mess we're in, it behooves us to look at how John F. Kennedy handled the Cuban missile crisis in 1962. Personally, that crisis led to a five-year tour in the US Air Force for me.

As horrible and dangerous as the present crisis is, those of us who held our breath during some very tense moments that October realized that we were on the brink of a worldwide nuclear holocaust. That crisis represented the greatest potential danger to the world in all of human history.

President Kennedy held firm and stood up to the Soviets, as he should have, and the confrontation was resolved. What was not known at the time was the reassessment of our policy that placed nuclear missiles in the Soviet's back yard, in Turkey. These missiles were quietly removed a few months later, and the world became a safer place in which to live. Eventually, we won the cold war without starting World War III.

Our enemy today, as formidable as he is, cannot compare to the armed might of the Soviet Union in the fall of 1962.

Wisdom and caution on Kennedy's part in dealing with the crisis was indeed "a profile in courage." His courage was not only in his standing up to the Soviets, but his willingness to re-examine our nuclear missile presence in Turkey, which if it had been known at the time would have been condemned as an act of cowardice.

President Bush now has the challenge to do something equally courageous and wise. This is necessary if we expect to avert a catastrophic World War III. When the president asks for patience as he and his advisors deliberate, seeking a course of action, all Americans should surely heed his request.

Mr. Speaker, I support President Bush and voted for the authority and the money to carry out his responsibility to defend this country, but the degree of death and destruction and chances of escalation must be carefully taken into consideration.

It is only with sadness that I reflect on the support, the dollars, the troops, the weapons and training provided by U.S. taxpayers that are now being used against us. Logic should tell us that intervening in all the wars of the world has been detrimental to our self-interest and should be reconsidered.

The efforts of a small minority in Congress to avoid this confrontation by voting for the foreign policy of George Washington, John Adams, Thomas Jefferson, and all the 19th Century presidents went unheeded. The unwise policy of supporting so many militants who later became our armed enemies makes little sense, whether it's bin Laden or Saddam Hussein. A policy designed to protect America is wise and frugal and, hopefully, it will once again be considered. George Washington, as we all know, advised strongly, as he departed his presidency, that we should avoid all entangling alliances with foreign nations.

The call for a non-interventionist foreign policy over past years has fallen on deaf ears. My suggestions made here today may meet the same fate. Yet, if truth is spoken, ignoring it will not negate it. In that case something will be lost. But, if something is said to be true and it is not and is ignored, nothing is lost. My goal is to contribute to the truth and to the security of this nation.

What I have said today is different from what is said and accepted in Washington as conventional wisdom, but it is not in conflict with our history or our Constitution. It's a policy that has, whenever tried, generated more peace and prosperity than any other policy for dealing with foreign affairs. The authors of the Constitution clearly understood this. Since the light of truth shines brightest in the darkness of evil and ignorance, we should all strive to shine that light. ■

War often brings about bad policy that could not be enacted without hostilities. This speech was designed to warn, in more detail, against going down the wrong path as we faced protracted conflict.

October 25, 2001
A SAD STATE OF AFFAIRS
HON. RON PAUL of TEXAS
IN THE HOUSE OF REPRESENTATIVES

Mr. Speaker, it breaks my heart to see what is happening to our country today. All Americans have grieved over the losses suffered on 9/11. The grief for those who lost loved ones is beyond description. These losses have precipitated unprecedented giving to help the families left behind. Unless one has suffered directly, it is difficult to fully comprehend the tragic and sudden loss of close friends and family.

There are some who, in addition to feeling this huge sense of personal loss that all Americans share, grieve for other serious and profound reasons. For instance, many thoughtful Americans are convinced that the tragedy of 9/11 was preventable. Since that might be true, this provokes a tragic sadness, especially for those who understand how the events of 9/11 needlessly came about.

The reason why this is so sad and should be thoroughly understood is that so often the ones who suggest how our policies may have played a role in evoking the attacks are demonized as unpatriotic and are harshly dismissed as belonging to the "blame America crowd."

Those who are so anxious to condemn do not realize that the policies of the American government, designed by politicians and bureaucrats, are not always synonymous with American ideals. The country is not the same as the government. The spirit of America is hardly something for which the government holds a monopoly on defining.

America's heart and soul is more embedded in our love of liberty, self-reliance, and tolerance than by our foreign policy, driven by powerful special interests with little regard for the Constitution.

Throughout our early history, a policy of minding our own business and avoiding entangling alliances, as George Washington admonished, was more representative of American ideals than those we have pursued for the past 50 years. **Some sincere Americans have suggested that our modern interventionist policy set the stage for the attacks of 9/11, and for this, they are condemned as being unpatriotic**.

154

This compounds the sadness and heartbreak that some Americans are feeling. Threats, loss of jobs, censorship and public mockery have been heaped upon those who have made this suggestion. Freedom of expression and thought, the bedrock of the American Republic, is now too often condemned as something viciously evil. This should cause freedom-loving Americans to weep from broken hearts.

Another reason the hearts of many Americans are heavy with grief is because they dread what might come from the many new and broad powers the government is demanding in the name of providing security. Daniel Webster once warned, "Human beings will generally exercise power when they can get it, and they will exercise it most undoubtedly in popular governments under pretense of public safety."

A strong case can be made that the government regulations, along with a lack of private property responsibility, contributed to this tragedy, but what is proposed? More regulations, and even a takeover of all airport security by the government.

We are not even considering restoring the rights of pilots to carry weapons for self-defense as one of the solutions. Even though pilots once carried guns to protect the mail, and armored truck drivers can still carry guns to protect money, protecting passengers with guns is prohibited on commercial flights. The U.S. Air Force can shoot down a wayward aircraft, but a pilot cannot shoot down an armed terrorist.

It will be difficult to solve our problems with this attitude toward airport security.

Civil liberties are sure to suffer under today's tensions, with the people demanding that the politicians do something, anything. Should those who object to the rapid move toward massively increasing the size and scope of the federal government in local law enforcement be considered un-American because they defend the principles they truly understand to be American?

Any talk of spending restraint is now a thing of the past. We had one anthrax death, and we are asked the next day for a billion-dollar appropriation to deal with the problem.

And a lot more will be appropriated before it is all over. What about the 40,000 deaths per year on government-run highways and the needless deaths associated with the foolish and misdirected war on drugs? Why should anyone be criticized for trying to put this in proper perspective? Countless groups are now descending on Washington with their hands

155

out. As usual with any disaster, this disaster is being parlayed into an "opportunity," as one former Member of the Congress phrased it. The economic crisis that started a long time before 9/11 has contributed to the number of those now demanding federal handouts.

But there is one business that we need not fear will go into a slump: the Washington lobbying industry. Last year it spent $1.6 billion lobbying Congress. This year it will spend much more. **The bigger the disaster, the greater the number of vultures who descend on Washington.** When I see this happening, it breaks my heart, because liberty and America suffer, and it is all done in the name of justice, equality and security.

Emotions are running high in our nation's capital, and in politics emotions are more powerful tools than reason and the rule of law. The use of force to serve special interests and help anyone who claims to be in need, unfortunately, is an acceptable practice. Obeying the restraints placed in the Constitution is seen as archaic and insensitive to the people's needs. But far too often the claims of those responding to human tragedies are nothing more than politics as usual. While one group supports bailing out the corporations, another wants to prop up wages and jobs. One group supports federalizing tens of thousands of airport jobs to increase union membership, while another says we should subsidize corporate interests and keep the jobs private.

Envy and power drive both sides—the special interests of big business and the demands of the welfare/redistribution crowd.

There are many other reasons to be sad about all that is going on today. In spite of the fact that our government has done such a poor job protecting us and has no intention of changing the policy of meddling overseas (which has contributed to our problems), the people are more dependent on and more satisfied with government than they have been in decades—while demanding even more government control and intrusion in their daily lives.

It is aggravating to listen to the daily rhetoric regarding liberty and the Constitution while the same people participate in their destruction. It is aggravating to see all the money spent and civil liberties abused while the pilot's right to carry guns in self-defense is denied. It is even more aggravating to see our government rely on foreign AWACS aircraft to provide security to U.S. territory. A $325 billion military budget—and we cannot even patrol our own shores. This, of course, is just another sign of how little we are concerned about U.S. sovereignty and how willing we are to submit to international government.

It is certainly disappointing that our congressional leaders and administration have not considered using letters of marque and reprisal as an additional tool to root out those who participated in the 9/11 attacks. The difficulty in finding bin Laden and his supporters make marque and reprisal quite an appropriate option in this effort.

We already hear of plans to install and guarantee the next government of Afghanistan. Getting bin Laden and his gang is one thing; nation building is quite another. Some of our trouble in the Middle East started years ago when our CIA put the Shah in charge of Iran.

It was 25 years before he was overthrown, and the hatred toward America continues to this day. Those who suffer from our intervention have long memories.

Our support for the less-than-ethical government of Saudi Arabia, with our troops occupying what most Muslims consider sacred land, is hardly the way to bring peace to the Middle East. A policy driven by our fear of losing control over the oil fields in the Middle East has not contributed to American security. Too many powerful special interests drive our policy in this region, and this does little to help us preserve security for Americans here at home.

As we bomb Afghanistan, we continue to send foreign aid to feed the people suffering from the war. I strongly doubt if our food will get them to love us or even be our friends. There is no evidence that the starving receive the food. And too often it is revealed that it ends up in the hands of the military forces we are fighting. While we bomb Afghanistan and feed the victims, we lay plans to install the next government and pay for rebuilding the country. Quite possibly, the new faction we support will be no more trustworthy than the Taliban, to which we sent plenty of aid and weapons in the 1980s. That intervention in Afghanistan did not do much to win reliable friends in the region.

It just may be that Afghanistan would be best managed by several tribal factions, without any strong centralized government and without any outside influence, certainly not by the UN But then again, some claim that the proposed Western financed pipeline through northern Afghanistan can only happen after a strong centralized pro-Western government is put in place.

It is both annoying and sad that there is so little interest by anyone in Washington in free-market solutions to the world's economic problems. True private ownership of property without regulation and abusive taxation is a thing of the past. Few understand how the Federal Reserve monetary policy causes the booms and the busts that, when severe, as they are now, only serve to enhance the prestige of the money managers—while most politicians and Wall Streeters demand that the Fed inflate the currency at an even more rapid rate. Today's conditions give license to the politicians to spend our way out of recession, they hope.

One thing for sure, as a consequence of the recession and the 9/11 tragedy, is that big spending and deficits are alive and well. Even though we are currently adding to the national debt at the rate of $150 billion per year, most politicians still claim that Social Security is sound and has not been touched. At least the majority of American citizens are now wise enough to know better.

There is plenty of reason to feel heartbroken over current events. It is certainly not a surprise or illogical for people working in Washington to overreact to the anthrax scare. The feelings of despondency are understandable, whether due to the loss of lives, loss of property, fear of the next attack, or concern that our own frantic efforts to enhance security will achieve little. But broken or sad hearts need not break our spirits, nor impede our reasoning.

I happen to believe that winning this battle against the current crop of terrorists is quite achievable in a relatively short period of time. But winning the war over the long term is a much different situation. This cannot be achieved without a better understanding of the enemy and the geopolitics that drive this war. **Even if relative peace is achieved with a battle victory over Osama bin Laden and his followers, other terrorists will appear from all corners of the world for an indefinite period of time if we do not understand the issues.**

Changing our current foreign policy with wise diplomacy is crucial if we are to really win the war and restore the sense of tranquility to our land that now seems to be so far in our distant past. Our widespread efforts at peacekeeping and nation building will only contribute to the resentment that drives the fanatics. Devotion to internationalism and a one-world government only exacerbates regional rivalries. Denying that our economic interests drive so much of what the West does against the East impedes any efforts to diffuse the world crisis that already has a number of Americans demanding nuclear bombs to be used to achieve victory. A victory based on this type of aggressive policy would be a hollow victory indeed.

I would like to draw analogy between the drug war and the war against terrorism. In the last 30 years, we have spent hundreds of billions of dollars on a failed war on drugs. This war has been used as an excuse to attack our liberties and privacy. It has been an excuse to undermine our financial privacy, while promoting illegal searches and seizures with many innocent people losing their lives and property. Seizure and forfeiture have harmed a great number of innocent American citizens.

Another result of this unwise war has been the corruption of many law-enforcement officials. It is well known that, with the profit incentives so high, we are not even able to keep drugs out of our armed prisons. Making our whole society a prison would not bring success to this floundering war on drugs. Sinister motives of the profiteers and gangsters, along with prevailing public ignorance, keeps this futile war going.

Illegal and artificially high-priced drugs drive the underworld to produce, sell and profit from this social depravity. Failure to recognize that drug addiction, like alcoholism, is a disease rather than a crime, encourage the drug warriors in efforts that have not and will not ever work. We learned the hard way about alcohol prohibition and crime, but we have not yet seriously considered it in the ongoing drug war.

Corruption associated with the drug dealers is endless. It has involved our police, the military, border guards and the judicial system. It has affected government policy and our own CIA. The artificially high profits from illegal drugs provide easy access to funds for rogue groups involved in fighting civil wars throughout the world.

Ironically, opium sales by the Taliban and artificially high prices helped to finance their war against us. In spite of the incongruity, we rewarded the Taliban this spring with a huge cash payment for promises to eradicate some poppy fields. Sure!

For the first 140 years of our history, we had essentially no federal war on drugs, and far fewer problems with drug addiction and related crimes as a consequence. In the past 30 years, even with the hundreds of millions of dollars spent on the drug war, little good has come of it. We have vacillated from efforts to stop the drugs at the source to severely punishing the users, yet nothing has improved.

This war has been behind most big-government police powers of the last 30 years, with continual undermining of our civil liberties and personal privacy. Those who support the IRS's efforts to collect maximum revenues and root out the underground economy, have welcomed this intrusion, even if the drug underworld grows in size and influence.

The drug war encourages violence. Government violence against nonviolent users is notorious and has led to the unnecessary prison overpopulation. Innocent taxpayers are forced to pay for all this so-called justice. Our drug eradication project (using spraying) around the world, from Colombia to Afghanistan, breeds resentment because normal crops and good land can be severely damaged. Local populations perceive that the efforts and the profiteering remain somehow beneficial to our own agenda in these various countries.

Drug dealers and drug gangs are a consequence of our unwise approach to drug usage. Many innocent people are killed in the crossfire by the mob justice that this war generates. But just because the laws are unwise and have had unintended consequences, no excuses can ever be made for the monster who would kill and maim innocent people for illegal profits. As the violent killers are removed from society, reconsideration of our drug laws ought to occur.

A similar approach should be applied to our war on those who would terrorize and kill our people for political reasons. If the drug laws, and the policies that incite hatred against the United States, are not clearly understood and, therefore, never changed, the number of drug criminals and terrorists will only multiply.

Although this unwise war on drugs generates criminal violence, the violence can never be tolerated. Even if repeal of drug laws would decrease the motivation for drug-dealer violence, this can never be an excuse to condone the violence. In the short term, those who kill must be punished, imprisoned, or killed. Long term though, a better understanding of how drug laws have unintended consequences is required if we want to significantly improve the situation and actually reduce the great harms drugs are doing to our society.

The same is true in dealing with those who so passionately hate us that suicide becomes a just and noble cause in their effort to kill and terrorize us. Without some understanding of what has brought us to the brink of a worldwide conflict, and reconsideration of our policies around the globe, we will be no more successful in making our land secure and free than the drug war has been in removing drug violence from our cities and towns. **Without an understanding of why terrorism is directed towards the United States, we may well build a prison for ourselves with something called homeland security, while doing nothing to combat the root causes of terrorism.** Let us hope we figure this out soon.

We have promoted a foolish and very expensive domestic war on drugs for more than 30 years. It has done no good whatsoever. I doubt our Republic can survive a 30-year period of trying to figure out how to win this guerilla war against terrorism. Hopefully, we will all seek the answers in these trying times with an open mind and understanding. ■

160

As the first session of Congress after 9/11 began to come to a close, we had seen a rash of law-making that was certain to reduce American liberty than to secure the nation from attacks. It was becoming increasingly important to attempt to refocus our efforts.

November 29, 2001
KEEP YOUR EYE ON THE TARGET
HON. RON PAUL of TEXAS
IN THE HOUSE OF REPRESENTATIVES

Mr. Speaker, we have been told on numerous occasions to expect a long and protracted war. This is not necessary if one can identify the target, the enemy, and then stay focused on that target. It's impossible to keep one's eye on a target and hit it if one does not precisely understand it and identify it. In pursuing any military undertaking, it's the responsibility of Congress to know exactly why it appropriates the funding. Today, unlike any time in our history, the enemy and its location remain vague and pervasive. In the undeclared wars of Vietnam and Korea, the enemy was known and clearly defined, even though our policies were confused and contradictory. Today our policies relating to the growth of terrorism are also confused and contradictory; however, the precise enemy and its location are not known by anyone. Until the enemy is defined and understood, it cannot be accurately targeted or vanquished.

The terrorist enemy is no more an entity than the "mob" or some international criminal gang. It certainly is not a country, nor is it the Afghan people. The Taliban is obviously a strong sympathizer with bin Laden and his henchmen, but how much more so than the government of Saudi Arabia, or even Pakistan? Probably not much.

Ulterior motives have always played a part in the foreign policy of almost every nation throughout history. Economic gain and geographic expansion, or even just the desires for more political power, too often drive the militarism of all nations. Unfortunately, in recent years, we have not been exempt. If expansionism, economic interests, desire for hegemony, and influential allies affect our policies and they, in turn, incite mob attacks against us, they obviously cannot be ignored. The target will be illusive and ever-enlarging, rather than vanquished.

We do know a lot about the terrorists who spilled the blood of nearly 4,000 innocent civilians. There were 19 of them, 15 from Saudi Arabia, and they have paid a high price. They're all dead. So those most responsible for the attack have been permanently taken care of. If one encounters a single suicide bomber who takes his own life along with others without the help of anyone else, no further punishment is possible. The only question that can be raised under that circumstance is why did it happen and how can we change the conditions that drove an individual to perform such a heinous act.

The terrorist attacks on New York and Washington are not quite so simple, but they are similar. These attacks required funding, planning and inspiration from others. But the total number of people directly involved had to be relatively small in order to have kept the plans thoroughly concealed. Twenty accomplices, or even a hundred could have done it. But there's no way thousands of people knew and participated in the planning and carrying out of this attack. Moral support expressed by those who find our policies offensive is a different matter and difficult to discover. Those who enjoyed seeing the U.S. hit are too numerous to count and impossible to identify. To target and wage war against all of them is like declaring war against an idea or sin.

The predominant nationality of the terrorists was Saudi Arabian. Yet for political and economic reasons, even with the lack of cooperation from the Saudi government, we have ignored that country in placing blame. The Afghan people did nothing to deserve another war. The Taliban, of course, is closely tied to bin Laden and al-Qaeda, but so are the Pakistanis and the Saudis. Even the United States was a supporter of the Taliban's rise to power, and as recently as August of 2001, we talked oil pipeline politics with them.

The recent French publication of *bin Laden, The Forbidden Truth* revealed our most recent effort to secure control over Caspian Sea oil in collaboration with the Taliban. According to the two authors, the economic conditions demanded by the U.S. were turned down and led to U.S. military threats against the Taliban.

It has been known for years that Unocal, a U.S. company, has been anxious to build a pipeline through northern Afghanistan, but it has not been possible due to the weak Afghan central government. We should not be surprised now that many contend that the plan for the UN to "nation build" in Afghanistan is a logical and important consequence of this desire. The crisis has merely given those interested in this project an excuse to replace the government of Afghanistan. Since we don't even know if bin Laden is in Afghanistan, and since other countries are equally supportive of him, our concentration on this Taliban "target" remains suspect by many.

Former FBI Deputy Director John O'Neill resigned in July over duplicitous dealings with the Taliban and our oil interests. O'Neill then took a job as head of the World Trade Center security and ironically was killed in the 9/11 attack. The charges made by these authors in their recent publication deserve close scrutiny and congressional oversight investigation—and not just for the historical record.

To understand world sentiment on this subject, one might note a comment in *The Hindu,* India's national newspaper—not necessarily to agree with the paper's sentiment, but to help us better understand what is being thought about us around the world in contrast to the spin put on the war by our five major TV news networks.

This quote comes from an article written by Sitaram Yechury on October 13, 2001:

The world today is being asked to side with the U.S. in a fight against global terrorism. This is only a cover. The world is being asked today, in reality, to side with the U.S. as it seeks to strengthen its economic hegemony. This is neither acceptable nor will it be allowed. We must forge together to state that we are neither with the terrorists nor with the United States.

The need to define our target is ever so necessary if we're going to avoid letting this war get out of control.

It's important to note that in the same article, the author quoted Michael Klare, an expert on Caspian Sea oil reserves, from an interview on Radio Free Europe: "We (the U.S.) view oil as a security consideration and we have to protect it by any means necessary, regardless of other considerations, other values." This, of course, was a clearly stated position of our administration in 1990 as our country was being prepared to fight the Persian Gulf War. Saddam Hussein and his weapons of mass destruction only became the issue later on.

For various reasons, the enemy with whom we're now at war remains vague and illusive. Those who commit violent terrorist acts should be targeted with a rifle or hemlock—not with vague declarations, with some claiming we must root out terrorism in as many as 60 countries. If we're not precise in identifying our enemy, it's sure going to be hard to keep our eye on the target. Without this identification, the war will spread and be needlessly prolonged.

Why is this definition so crucial? Because without it, the special interests and the ill-advised will clamor for all kinds of expansive militarism. **Planning to expand and fight a never-ending war in 60 countries against**

163

worldwide terrorist conflicts with the notion that, at most, only a few hundred ever knew of the plans to attack the World Trade Center and the Pentagon. The pervasive and indefinable enemy—terrorism—cannot be conquered with weapons and UN nation building, only a more sensible pro-American foreign policy will accomplish this. This must occur if we are to avoid a cataclysmic expansion of the current hostilities.

It was said that our efforts were to be directed toward the terrorists responsible for the attacks, and overthrowing and instituting new governments were not to be part of the agenda. Already we have clearly taken our eyes off that target and diverted it toward building a pro-Western, UN-sanctioned government in Afghanistan. But if bin Laden can hit us in New York and DC, what should one expect to happen once the U.S./UN establishes a new government in Afghanistan with occupying troops. It seems that would be an easy target for the likes of al Qaeda.

Since we don't know in which cave or even in which country bin Laden is hiding, we hear the clamor of many for us to overthrow our next villain—Saddam Hussein—guilty or not. On the short list of countries to be attacked are North Korea, Libya, Syria, Iran, and the Sudan, just for starters. But this jingoistic talk is foolhardy and dangerous. The war against terrorism cannot be won in this manner.

The drumbeat for attacking Baghdad grows louder every day, with Paul Wolfowitz, Bill Kristol, Richard Perle, and Bill Bennett leading the charge. In a recent interview, U.S. Deputy Defense Secretary Paul Wolfowitz, made it clear: "We are going to continue pursuing the entire al Qaeda network which is in 60 countries, not just Afghanistan." Fortunately, President Bush and Colin Powell so far have resisted the pressure to expand the war into other countries. Let us hope and pray that they do not yield to the clamor of the special interests that want us to take on Iraq.

The argument that we need to do so because Hussein is producing weapons of mass destruction is the reddest of all herrings. I sincerely doubt that he has developed significant weapons of mass destruction. However, if that is the argument, we should plan to attack all those countries that have similar weapons or plans to build them—countries like China, North Korea, Israel, Pakistan, and India. Iraq has been uncooperative with the UN World Order and remains independent of Western control of its oil reserves, unlike Saudi Arabia and Kuwait. This is why she has been bombed steadily for 11 years by the U.S. and Britain. My guess is that in

164

the not-too-distant future, so-called proof will be provided that Saddam Hussein was somehow partially responsible for the attack in the United States, and it will be irresistible then for the U.S. to retaliate against him. This will greatly and dangerously expand the war and provoke even greater hatred toward the United States, and it's all so unnecessary.

It's just so hard for many Americans to understand how we inadvertently provoke the Arab/Muslim people, and I'm not talking about the likes of bin Laden and his al Qaeda gang. I'm talking about the Arab/Muslim masses.

In 1996, after five years of sanctions against Iraq and persistent bombings, CBS reporter Lesley Stahl asked our Ambassador to the United Nations, Madeline Albright, a simple question: "We have heard that a half million children have died (as a consequence of our policy against Iraq). Is the price worth it?" Albright's response was "We think the price is worth it." Although this interview won an Emmy award, it was rarely shown in the U.S. but widely circulated in the Middle East. Some still wonder why America is despised in this region of the world!

Former President George W. Bush has been criticized for not marching on to Baghdad at the end of the Persian Gulf War. He gave then, and stands by his explanation today, a superb answer of why it was ill-advised to attempt to remove Saddam Hussein from power there were strategic and tactical, as well as humanitarian, arguments against it. But the important and clinching argument against annihilating Baghdad was political. The coalition, in no uncertain terms, let it be known they wanted no part of it. Besides, the UN only authorized the removal of Saddam Hussein from Kuwait. The UN has never sanctioned the continued U.S. and British bombing of Iraq, a source of much hatred directed toward the United States.

But placing U.S. troops on what is seen as Muslim holy land in Saudi Arabia seems to have done exactly what the former president was trying to avoid, the breakup of the coalition. The coalition has hung together by a thread, but internal dissention among the secular and religious Arab/Muslim nations within individual countries has intensified. Even today, the current crisis threatens the overthrow of every puppet pro-Western Arab leader from Egypt to Saudi Arabia and Kuwait.

Many of the same advisors from the first Bush presidency are now urging the current president to finish off Hussein. However, every reason given 11 years ago for not leveling Baghdad still holds true today, if not more so.

It has been argued that we needed to maintain a presence in Saudi Arabia after the Persian Gulf War to protect the Saudi government from Iraqi attack. Others argued that it was only a cynical excuse to justify keeping troops there to protect what our officials declared were "our" oil supplies. Some have even suggested that our expanded presence in Saudi Arabia was prompted by a need to keep King Fahd in power and to thwart any effort by Saudi fundamentalists to overthrow his regime.

Expanding the war by taking on Iraq at this time may well please some allies, but it will lead to unbelievable chaos in the region and throughout the world. It will incite even more anti-American sentiment and expose us to even greater dangers. It could prove to be an unmitigated disaster. Iran and Russia will not be pleased with this move.

It is not our job to remove Saddam Hussein; that is the job of the Iraqi people. It is not our job to remove the Taliban; that is the business of the Afghan people. It is not our job to insist that the next government in Afghanistan include women, no matter how good an idea it is. If this really is an issue, why don't we insist that our friends in Saudi Arabia and Kuwait do the same thing, as well as impose our will on them? Talk about hypocrisy! The mere thought that we fight wars for affirmative action in a country 6,000 miles from home, with no cultural similarities, should insult us all. Of course it does distract us from the issue of an oil pipeline through northern Afghanistan. We need to keep our eye on the target and not be so easily distracted.

Assume for a minute that bin Laden is not in Afghanistan. Would any of our military efforts in that region be justified? Since none of it would be related to American security, it would be difficult to justify.

Assume for a minute that bin Laden is as ill, as I believe he is, with serious renal disease. Would he not do everything conceivable for his cause by provoking us into expanding the war and alienating as many Muslims as possible?

Remember that, to bin Laden, martyrdom is a noble calling, and he just may be more powerful in death than he is in life. An American invasion of Iraq would please bin Laden, because it would rally his troops against any moderate Arab leader who appears to be supporting the United States. It would prove his point that America is up to no good; that oil and Arab infidels are the source of all the Muslims' problems.

We have recently been reminded of Admiral Yamamoto's quote after the bombing of Pearl Harbor in expressing his fear that the event "awakened a sleeping giant." Almost everyone agrees with the prophetic wisdom of that comment. But I question the accuracy of drawing an analogy between the Pearl Harbor event and the World Trade Center attack. We are hardly the same nation we were in 1941. Today we're anything but a sleeping giant. There's no contest for our status as the world's only economic, political and military super power. A "sleeping giant" would not have troops in 141 countries throughout the world and be engaged in every conceivable conflict, with 250,000 troops stationed abroad.

The fear I have is that our policies, along with those of Britain, the UN, and NATO since World War II, have inspired and now awakened a long-forgotten sleeping giant—Islamic fundamentalism.

Let's hope for all our sakes that Iraq is not made the target in this complex war.

The president, in the 2000 presidential campaign, argued against nation building, and he was right to do so. He also said, "If we're an arrogant nation, they'll resent us." He wisely argued for humility and a policy that promotes peace. Attacking Baghdad or declaring war against Saddam Hussein, or even continuing the illegal bombing of Iraq, is hardly a policy of humility designed to promote peace.

As we continue our bombing of Afghanistan, plans are made to install a new government sympathetic to the West and under UN control. The persuasive argument, as always, is money. We were able to gain Pakistan's support, although it continually wavers, in this manner. Appropriations are already being prepared in the Congress to rebuild all that we destroy in Afghanistan, and then some, even before the bombing has stopped.

Rumsfeld's plan, as reported in Turkey's *Hurriyet* newspaper, outlines the plan for the next Iraqi government. Turkey's support is crucial, so the plan is to give Turkey oil from the northern Iraq Karkuk field. The United States has also promised a pipeline running from Iraq through Turkey. How can the Turks resist such a generous offer? Since we subsidize Turkey and they bomb the Kurds, while we punish the Iraqis for the same, this plan to divvy up wealth in the land of the Kurds is hardly a surprise.

It seems that Washington never learns. Our foolish foreign interventions continually get us into more trouble than we have bargained for—and the spending is endless. I am not optimistic that this Congress will anytime soon come to its senses. I am afraid that we will never treat the taxpayers with respect. National bankruptcy is a more likely scenario than Congress adopting a frugal and wise spending policy.

Mr. Speaker, we must make every effort to precisely define our target in this war and keep our eye on it.

It is safe to assume that the number of people directly involved in the 9/11 attacks is closer to several hundred than the millions we are now talking about targeting with our planned shotgun approach to terrorism.

One commentator pointed out that when the mafia commits violence, no one suggests we bomb Sicily. Today it seems we are, in a symbolic way, not only bombing "Sicily," but are thinking about bombing "Athens" (Iraq).

If a corrupt city or state government does business with a drug cartel or organized crime and violence results, we don't bomb city hall or the state capital—we limit the targets to those directly guilty and punish them. Could we not learn a lesson from these examples?

It is difficult for everyone to put the 9/11 attacks in a proper perspective, because any attempt to do so is construed as diminishing the utter horror of the events of that day. We must remember, though, that the 3,900 deaths incurred in the World Trade Center attacks are just slightly more than the deaths that occur on our nation's highways each month. Could it be that the sense of personal vulnerability we survivors feel motivates us in meting out justice, rather than the concern for the victims of the attacks? Otherwise, the numbers don't add up to the proper response. If we lose sight of the target and unwisely broaden the war, the tragedy of 9/11 may pale in the death and destruction that could lie ahead.

As Members of Congress, we have a profound responsibility to mete out justice, provide security for our nation, and protect the liberties of all the people, without senselessly expanding the war at the urging of narrow political and economic special interests. The price is too high, and the danger too great. We must not lose our focus on the real target and inadvertently create new enemies for ourselves.

We have not done any better keeping our eye on the terrorist target on the home front than we have overseas. Not only has Congress come up short in picking the right target, it has directed all its energies in the wrong direction. The target of our efforts has sadly been the liberties all Americans enjoy. With all the new power we have given to the administration, none has truly improved the chances of catching the terrorists who were responsible for the 9/11 attacks. All Americans will soon feel the consequences of this new legislation.

Just as the crisis provided an opportunity for some to promote a special-interest agenda in our foreign policy efforts, many have seen the crisis as a chance to achieve changes in our domestic laws, changes which, up until now, were seen as dangerous and unfair to American citizens.

Granting bailouts is not new for Congress, but current conditions have prompted many takers to line up for handouts. There has always been a large constituency for expanding federal power for whatever reason, and these groups have been energized. The military-industrial complex is out in full force and is optimistic. Union power is pleased with recent events and has not missed the opportunity to increase membership rolls. Federal policing powers, already in a bull market, received a super shot in the arm. The IRS, which detests financial privacy, gloats—while all the big spenders in Washington applaud the tools made available to crack down on tax dodgers. The drug warriors and anti-gun zealots love the new powers that now can be used to watch every move of our citizens. "Extremists" who talk of the Constitution, promote right-to-life, form citizen militias, or participate in non-mainstream religious practices now can be monitored much more effectively by those who find their views offensive. **Laws recently passed by the Congress apply to all Americans, not just terrorists. We should remember that if the terrorists are known and identified, existing laws would have been quite adequate to deal with them.**

Even before the passage of the recent draconian legislation, hundreds had already been arrested under suspicion, and millions of dollars of al Qaeda funds had been frozen. None of these new laws will deal with uncooperative foreign entities like the Saudi government, which chose not to relinquish evidence pertaining to exactly who financed the terrorists' operations. Unfortunately, the laws will affect all innocent Americans, yet will do nothing to thwart terrorism.

The laws recently passed in Congress in response to the terrorist attacks can be compared to the effort by anti-gun fanatics, who jump at every chance to undermine the Second Amendment. When crimes are committed with the use of guns, it's argued that we must remove guns from society, or at least register them and make it difficult to buy them. The counter argument made by Second Amendment supporters correctly explains that this would only undermine the freedom of law-abiding citizens and do nothing to keep guns out of the hands of criminals or to reduce crime.

Now we hear a similar argument that a certain amount of privacy and personal liberty of law-abiding citizens must be sacrificed in order to root out possible terrorists. This will result only in liberties being lost and will not serve to preempt any terrorist act. The criminals, just as they know how to get guns even when they are illegal, will still be able to circumvent anti-terrorist laws. To believe otherwise is to endorse a Faustian bargain, but that is what I believe the Congress has done.

We know from the ongoing drug war that federal drug police frequently make mistakes, break down the wrong doors and destroy property. Abuses of seizure and forfeiture laws are numerous. Yet the new laws will encourage even more mistakes by federal law-enforcement agencies. It has long been forgotten that law enforcement in the United States was supposed to be a state and local government responsibility, not that of the federal government. The federal government's policing powers have just gotten a giant boost in scope and authority through both new legislation and executive orders.

Before the 9/11 attack, Attorney General Ashcroft let his position be known regarding privacy and government secrecy. Executive Order 13223 made it much more difficult for researchers to gain access to presidential documents from previous administrations—now a "need to know" has to be demonstrated. This was a direct hit at efforts to demand openness in government, even if only for analysis and writing of history. Ashcroft's position is that presidential records ought to remain secret, even after an administration has left office. He argues that government deserves privacy while ignoring the 4th Amendment protections of the people's privacy. He argues his case by absurdly claiming he must "protect" the privacy of the individuals who might be involved, a non-problem that could easily be resolved without closing public records to the public.

It is estimated that approximately 1,200 men have been arrested as a consequence of 9/11, yet their names and the charges are not available, and according to Ashcroft, will not be made available. Once again, he uses the argument that he's protecting the privacy of those charged. Unbelievable! Due process for the detainees has been denied. Secret government is winning out over open government. This is the largest number of people to be locked up under these conditions since FDR's internment of Japanese-Americans during World War II. Information regarding these arrests is a must, in a constitutional republic. If they're terrorists or accomplices, just let the public know and pursue their prosecution. But secret arrests and silence are not acceptable in a society that professes to be free. Curtailing freedom is not the answer to protecting freedom under adverse circumstances.

The administration has severely curtailed briefings regarding the military operation in Afghanistan for congressional leaders, ignoring a long-time tradition in this country. One person or one branch of government should never control military operations. Our system of government has always required a shared-power arrangement.

The Anti-Terrorism Bill did little to restrain the growth of Big Government. **In the name of patriotism, the Congress did some very unpatriotic things. Instead of concentrating on the persons or groups that committed the attacks on 9/11, our efforts have unfortunately undermined the liberties of all Americans.**

"Know Your Customer" type banking regulations, resisted by most Americans for years, have now been put in place in an expanded fashion. Not only will the regulations affect banks, thrifts and credit unions, but all businesses will also be required to file suspicious transaction reports if cash is used with the total transaction reaching $10,000. Retail stores will be required to spy on all their customers and send reports to the U.S. government. Financial services consultants are convinced that this new regulation will affect literally millions of law-abiding American citizens. The odds that this additional paperwork will catch a terrorist are remote. The sad part is that the regulations have been sought after by federal law-enforcement agencies for years. The 9/11 attacks have served as an opportunity to get them by the Congress and the American people.

Only now are the American people hearing about the onerous portions of the anti-terrorism legislation, and they are not pleased.

It's easy for elected officials in Washington to tell the American people that the government will do whatever it takes to defeat terrorism. Such assurances inevitably are followed by proposals either to restrict the constitutional liberties of the American people or to spend vast sums of money from the federal treasury. The history of the 20th Century shows that the Congress violates our Constitution most often during times of crisis. Accordingly, most of our worst unconstitutional agencies and programs began during the two World Wars and the Depression. Ironically, the Constitution itself was conceived in a time of great crisis. The Founders intended its provision to place severe restrictions on the federal government, even in times of great distress. America must guard against current calls for government to sacrifice the Constitution in the name of law enforcement.

The "anti-terrorism" legislation recently passed by Congress demonstrates how well-meaning politicians make shortsighted mistakes in a rush to respond to a crisis. Most of its provisions were never carefully studied by Congress, nor was sufficient time taken to debate the bill despite its importance. No testimony was heard from privacy experts or from other fields outside of law enforcement. Normal congressional committee and hearing processes were suspended. In fact, the final version of the bill was not even made available to Members before the vote! The American public should not tolerate these political games, especially when our precious freedoms are at stake.

Almost all of the new laws focus on American citizens rather than potential foreign terrorists. For example, the definition of "terrorism," for federal criminal purposes, has been greatly expanded. A person could now be considered a terrorist by belonging to a pro-Constitution group, a citizen militia, or a pro-life organization. Legitimate protests against the government could place tens of thousands of other Americans under federal surveillance. Similarly, internet use can be monitored without a user's knowledge, and internet providers can be forced to hand over user information to law-enforcement officials without a warrant or subpoena.

The bill also greatly expands the use of traditional surveillance tools, including wiretaps, search warrants, and subpoenas. Probable-cause standards for these tools are relaxed, or even eliminated in some circumstances. Warrants become easier to obtain and can be executed without notification. Wiretaps can be placed without a court order. In fact, the FBI and CIA now can tap phones or computers nationwide, without demonstrating that a criminal suspect is using a particular phone or computer.

The biggest problem with these new law-enforcement powers is that they bear little relationship to fighting terrorism. Surveillance powers are greatly expanded, while checks and balances on government are greatly reduced. Most of the provisions have been sought by domestic law-enforcement agencies for years, not to fight terrorism, but rather to increase their police power over the American people. There is no evidence that our previously held civil liberties posed a barrier to the effective tracking or prosecution of terrorists. The federal government has made no showing that it failed to detect or prevent the recent terrorist strikes because of the civil liberties that will be compromised by this new legislation.

In his speech to the joint session of Congress following the September 11th attacks, President Bush reminded all of us that the United States outlasted and defeated Soviet totalitarianism in the last century. The numerous internal problems in the former Soviet Union—its centralized economic planning and lack of free markets, its repression of human liberty and its excessive militarization—all led to its inevitable collapse. We must be vigilant to resist the rush toward ever-increasing state control of our society, so that our own government does not become a greater threat to our freedoms than any foreign terrorist.

The executive order that has gotten the most attention by those who are concerned that our response to 9/11 is overreaching and dangerous to our liberties is the one authorizing military justice, in secret. Nazi war criminals were tried in public, but plans now are laid to carry out the trials and punishment, including possibly the death penalty, outside the eyes and ears of the legislative and judicial branches of government and the American public. Since such a process threatens national security and the Constitution, it cannot be used as a justification for their protection.

Some have claimed this military tribunal has been in the planning stages for five years. If so, what would have been its justification?

The argument that FDR did it and, therefore, it must be OK is a rather weak justification. Roosevelt was hardly one that went by the rule book, the Constitution. But the situation then was quite different from today. There was a declared war by Congress against a precise enemy, the Germans, who sent eight saboteurs into our country. Convictions were unanimous, not 2/3 of the panel, and appeals were permitted. That's not what's being offered today. Furthermore, the previous military tribunals expired when the war ended. Since this war will go on indefinitely, so too will the courts.

The real outrage is that such a usurpation of power can be accomplished with the stroke of a pen. It may be that we have come to that stage in our history when an executive order is "the law of the land," but it's not "kinda cool," as one member of the previous administration bragged. It's a process that is unacceptable, even in this professed time of crisis.

There are well-documented histories of secret military tribunals. Up until now, the United States has consistently condemned them. The fact that a two-thirds majority can sentence a person to death in secrecy in the United States is scary. With no appeals available, and no defense attorneys of choice being permitted, fairness should compel us to reject such a system outright.

Those who favor these trials claim they are necessary to halt terrorism in its tracks. We are told that only terrorists will be brought before these tribunals. This means that the so-called suspects must be tried and convicted before they are assigned to this type of "trial" without due process. They will be deemed guilty by hearsay, in contrast to the traditional American system of justice where all are innocent until proven guilty. This turns the justice system on its head.

One cannot be reassured by believing these courts will only apply to foreigners who are terrorists. Sloppiness in convicting criminals is a slippery slope. We should not forget that the Davidians at Waco were "convicted" and demonized and slaughtered outside our judicial system, and they were, for the most part, American citizens. Randy Weaver's family fared no better.

It has been said that the best way for us to spread our message of freedom, justice and prosperity throughout the world is through example and persuasion, not through force of arms. We have drifted a long way from that concept. Military courts will be another bad example for the world. **We were outraged in 1996 when Lori Berenson, an American citizen, was tried, convicted, and sentenced to life by a Peruvian military court. Instead of setting an example, now we are following the lead of a Peruvian dictator.**

The ongoing debate regarding the use of torture in rounding up the criminals involved in the 9/11 attacks is too casual. This can hardly represent progress in the cause of liberty and justice. Once government becomes more secretive, it is more likely this tool will be abused. Hopefully the Congress will not endorse or turn a blind eye to this barbaric proposal. For every proposal made to circumvent the justice system, it's intended that we visualize that these infractions of the law and the Constitution will apply only to terrorists and never involve innocent U.S. citizens. This is impossible, because someone has to determine exactly who to bring before the tribunal, and that involves all of us. That is too much arbitrary power for anyone to be given in a representative government and is more characteristic of a totalitarian government.

Many throughout the world, especially those in Muslim countries, will be convinced by the secretive process that the real reason for military courts is that the U.S. lacks sufficient evidence to convict in an open court. Should we be fighting so strenuously the war against terrorism and carelessly sacrifice our traditions of American justice? If we do, the war will be for naught and we will lose, even if we win.

Congress has a profound responsibility in all of this and should never concede this power to a president or an attorney general. Congressional oversight powers must be used to their fullest to curtail this unconstitutional assumption of power.

The planned use of military personnel to patrol our streets and airports is another challenge of great importance that should not go uncontested. For years, many in Washington have advocated a national approach to all policing activity. This current crisis has given them a tremendous boost. Believe me, this is no panacea and is a dangerous move. The Constitution never intended that the federal government assume this power. This concept

174

was codified in the Posse Comitatus Act of 1878. This act prohibits the military from carrying out law-enforcement duties such as searching or arresting people in the United States, the argument being that the military is only used for this type of purpose in a police state. Interestingly, it was the violation of these principles that prompted the Texas Revolution against Mexico. The military under the Mexican Constitution at that time was prohibited from enforcing civil laws, and when Santa Anna ignored this prohibition, the revolution broke out. We should not so readily concede the principle that has been fought for on more than one occasion in this country.

The threats to liberty seem endless. It seems we have forgotten to target the enemy. Instead we have inadvertently targeted the rights of American citizens. The crisis has offered a good opportunity for those who have argued all along for bigger government.

For instance, the military draft is the ultimate insult to those who love personal liberty. The Pentagon, even with the ongoing crisis, has argued against the reinstatement of the draft. Yet the clamor for its reinstatement grows louder daily by those who wanted a return to the draft all along. I see the draft as the ultimate abuse of liberty. Morally it cannot be distinguished from slavery. All the arguments for drafting 18-year old men and women and sending them off to foreign wars are couched in terms of noble service to the country and benefits to the draftees. The need-for-discipline argument is the most common reason given, after the call for service in an effort to make the world safe for democracy. There can be no worse substitute for the lack of parental guidance of teenagers than the federal government's domineering control by forcing them to fight an enemy they don't even know in a country they can't even identify.

Now it's argued that since the federal government has taken over the entire job of homeland security, all kinds of jobs can be found for the draftees to serve the state, even for those who are conscientious objectors.

The proponents of the draft call it "mandatory service." Slavery, too, was mandatory, but few believed it was a service. They claim that every 18-year old owes at least two years of his life to his country. Let's hope the American people don't fall for this "need to serve" argument. The Congress should refuse to even consider such a proposal. Better yet, what we need to do is abolish the Selective Service altogether.

However, if we get to the point of returning to the draft, I have a proposal. **Every news commentator, every Hollywood star, every newspaper editorialist, and every Member of Congress under the**

age of 65 who has never served in the military and who demands that the draft be reinstated, should be drafted first—the 18-year olds last. Since the Pentagon says they don't need draftees, these new recruits can be the first to march to the orders of the general in charge of homeland security. For those less robust individuals, they can do the hospital and cooking chores for the rest of the newly formed domestic army. After all, someone middle-aged owes a lot more to his country than an 18-year old.

I'm certain that this provision would mute the loud demands for the return of the military draft.

I see good reason for American citizens to be concerned, not only about another terrorist attack, but for their own personal freedoms as the Congress deals with the crisis. Personal freedom is the element of the human condition that has made America great and unique and something we all cherish. Even those who are more willing to sacrifice a little freedom for security do it with the firm conviction that they are acting in the best interest of freedom and justice. However, good intentions can never suffice for sound judgment in the defense of liberty.

I do not challenge the dedication and sincerity of those who disagree with the freedom philosophy and confidently promote government solutions for all our ills. I am just absolutely convinced that the best formula for giving us peace and preserving the American way of life is freedom, limited government, and minding our own business overseas.

Henry Grady Weaver, author of a classic book on freedom, *The Mainspring of Human Progress*, years ago warned us that good intentions in politics are not good enough and actually are dangerous to the cause. Weaver stated:

> *Most of the major ills of the world have been caused by well-meaning people who ignored the principle of individual freedom, except as applied to themselves, and who were obsessed with fanatical zeal to improve the lot of mankind-in-the-mass through some pet formula of their own. The harm done by ordinary criminals, murderers, gangsters, and thieves is negligible in comparison with the agony inflicted upon human beings by the professional do-gooders, who attempt to set themselves up as gods on earth and who would ruthlessly force their views on all others—with the abiding assurance that the end justifies the means. This message is one we should all ponder.* ■

If intervention in the Middle East is the problem, then the solution is neutrality. I have often believed that we would do more good for the peace and security of Middle Eastern nations, and our own, if we renewed our commitment to this traditional American policy.

December 5, 2001
ONGOING VIOLENCE IN ISRAEL AND PALESTINE —THE CASE FOR NEUTRALITY
HON. RON PAUL of TEXAS
IN THE HOUSE OF REPRESENTATIVES

Mr. Speaker, I rise in opposition to the resolution and not, obviously, because it condemns violence. We all condemn the violence. There is more to this resolution than just condemning the violence. I have a problem with most resolutions like this, because they endorse a foreign policy that I do not endorse and by putting on unnecessary demands. So the demands part of this resolution is the part that I object to, not the condemnation of violence.

By doing this, we serve to antagonize. **We hear today talk about having solidarity with Israel. Others get up and try in their best way to defend the Palestinians and the Arabs. So it is sort of a contest: should we be pro-Israel or pro-Arab, or anti-Israel or anti-Arab, and how are we perceived in doing this? It is pretty important.**

But I think there is a third option to this that we so often forget about. Why can we not be pro-American? What is in the best interests of the United States? We have not even heard that yet.

I believe that it is in the best interests of the United States not to get into a fight, a fight that we do not have the wisdom to figure out.

Now, I would like to have neutrality. That has been the tradition for America, at least a century ago, to be friends with everybody, trade with everybody, and to be neutral, unless somebody declares war against us— but not to demand that we pick sides in every fight in the world. Yet this is what we are doing. I think our perceptions are in error, because it is not intended that we make the problem worse. Obviously, the authors of the resolution do not want to make the problem worse. But we have to realize, perceptions are pretty important. So the perceptions are, yes, we have solidarity with Israel. What is the opposite of solidarity? It is hostility. So if we have solidarity with Israel, then we have hostility to the Palestinians.

I have a proposal and a suggestion which I think fits the American

177

tradition. We should treat both sides equally, but in a different way. Today we treat both sides equally by giving both sides money and telling them what to do. Not $1 million here or there, not $100 million here or there, but tens of billions of dollars over decades to both sides, always trying to buy peace.

My argument is that it generally does not work, that there are unintended consequences. These things backfire. They come back to haunt us. We should start off by defunding—defunding both sides. I am just not for giving all of this money, because every time there are civilians killed on the Israeli side or civilians killed on the Palestinian side, we can be assured that either our money was used directly or indirectly to do that killing.

So we are, in a way, an accomplice on all of this killing because we fund both sides. So I would argue we should consider neutrality, to consider friendship with both sides, and not to pretend that we are all so wise that we know exactly with whom to have solidarity. I think that is basically our problem. We have a policy that is doomed to fail in the Middle East; and it fails slowly and persistently, always drawing us in, always demanding more money.

With the Arabs, we cannot tell the Arabs to get lost. The Arabs are important. They have a lot of oil under their control. We cannot flaunt the Arabs and say, get lost. We must protect our oil. It is called "our oil." At the same time, there is a strong constituency for never offending Israel.

I think that we cannot buy peace under these circumstances. I think we can contribute by being more neutral. I think we can contribute a whole lot by being friends with both sides. But I believe the money is wasted, it is spent unwisely, and it actually does not serve the interests of the American people.

First, it costs us money. That means that we have to take this money from the American taxpayer.

Second, it does not achieve the peace that we all hope to have.

Therefore, the policy of foreign nonintervention—where the United States is not the bully and does not come in and tell everybody exactly what to do by putting demands on them—I think if we did not do that, yes, we could still have some moral authority to condemn violence.

But **should we not condemn violence equally? Could it be true that only innocent civilians have died on one side and not the other? I do not believe that to be the case. I believe that it happens on both sides, and on both sides they use our money to do it.**

I urge a No vote on this resolution.

178

Mr. Speaker, like most Americans, I was appalled by the suicide bombings in Israel over the weekend. I am appalled by all acts of violence targeting noncombatants. The ongoing cycle of violence in the Middle East is robbing generations of their hopes and dreams and freedom. The cycle of violence ensures economic ruin and encourages political extremism; it punishes, most of all, the innocent.

The people of the Middle East must find a way to break this cycle of violence. As Secretary of State Colin Powell told the House International Relations Committee in October, "You have got to find a way not to find justifications for what we are doing, but to get out of what we are doing to break the cycle."

Mr. Speaker, I agree with our Secretary of State. The Secretary also said that we need to move beyond seeing the two sides there as "just enemies." I agree with that too. I don't think this piece of legislation moves us any closer to that important goal. While it rightly condemns the senseless acts of violence against the innocent, it unfortunately goes much further than that—and that is where I regrettably must part company with this bill. Rather than stopping at condemning terrorism, this bill makes specific demands on Israel and the Palestinian areas regarding internal policy, and specifically the apprehension and treatment of suspected terrorists. I don't think that is our job here in Congress.

Further, it recommends that the president suspend all relations with Yasir Arafat and the Palestinian Authority if they do not abide by the demands of this piece of legislation. I don't think this is a very helpful approach to the problem. Ceasing relations with one side in the conflict is, in effect, picking sides in the conflict. I don't think that has been our policy, nor is it in our best interest, be it in the Middle East, Central Asia, or anywhere else. The people of the United States contribute a substantial amount of money to both Israel and to the Palestinian people. We have made it clear in our policy and with our financial assistance that we are not taking sides in the conflict, but rather seeking a lasting peace in the region. Even with the recent, terrible attack. I don't think this is the time for Congress to attempt to subvert our government's policy on the Israeli-Palestinian conflict.

Finally, the bill makes an attempt to join together our own fight against those who have attacked the Untied States on September 11 and Israel's ongoing dispute with the Palestinians. I don't think that is necessary. We are currently engaged in a very difficult and costly effort to seek out and bring to justice those who have attacked us and those who supported them, "wherever they may be," as the president has said. Today's reports of the possible loss of at least two of our servicemen in Afghanistan drives that point home very poignantly. As far as I know, none of those who attacked us had ties to Palestine or were harbored there. Mr. Speaker, I think we can all condemn terrorism, wherever it may be, without committing the United States to joining endless ongoing conflicts across the globe. ∎

The next to last floor vote of the year in 2001 was on a resolution offered by Lindsay Graham. This legislation moved us closer to war in the name of promoting the UN agenda. Little attention has been paid to the fact that much of the long march to war in Iraq was done in promotion of UN resolutions.

December 19, 2001
STATEMENT IN OPPOSITION TO
THE HOUSE RESOLUTION ON IRAQ
HON. RON PAUL of TEXAS
IN THE HOUSE OF REPRESENTATIVES

Mr. Speaker, I strongly oppose House Joint Resolution 75, because it solves none of our problems and only creates new ones. Though the legislation before us today does wisely excise the most objectionable part of the original text of H.J. Res. 75—the resolution's clause stating that by not obeying a UN resolution Iraqi dictator Saddam Hussein has been committing an "act of aggression" against the United States—what remains in the legislation only serves to divert our attention from what should be our number one priority at this time: finding and bringing to justice those who attacked the United States on September 11, 2001.

Saddam Hussein is a ruthless dictator. The Iraqi people would no doubt be better off without him and his despotic rule. But the call in some quarters for the United States to intervene to change Iraq's government is a voice that offers little in the way of a real solution to our problems in the Middle East, many of which were caused by our interventionism in the first place. **Secretary of State Colin Powell underscored recently this lack of planning on Iraq, saying, "I never saw a plan that was going to take [Saddam] out. It was just some ideas coming from various quarters about 'let's go bomb.'"**

Mr. Speaker, House Joint Resolution 64, passed on September 14 just after the terrorist attack, states:

180

The president is authorized to use all necessary and appropriate force against those nations, organizations or persons he determines planned, authorized, committed or aided the terrorist attacks that occurred on Sept. 11, 2001, or harbored such organizations or persons.

From all that we know at present, Iraq appears to have had no such role. Indeed, we have seen "evidence" of Iraqi involvement in the attacks on the United States proven false over the past couple of weeks. Just this week, for example, the "smoking gun" of Iraqi involvement in the attack seems to have been debunked. The *New York Times* reported: "the Prague meeting (allegedly between al-Qaeda terrorist Mohammed Atta and an Iraqi intelligence agent) has emerged as an object lesson in the limits of intelligence reports rather than the cornerstone of the case against Iraq." The *Times* goes on to suggest that the "Mohammed Atta," who was in the Czech Republic this summer, seems to have been a Pakistani national who happened to have the same name. It appears that this meeting never took place, or at least not in the way it has been reported. This conclusion has also been drawn by the Czech media and is reviewed in a report on Radio Free Europe's "Newsline." Even those asserting Iraqi involvement in the anthrax scare in the United States, a theory forwarded most aggressively by Iraqi defector Khidir Hamza and former CIA director James Woolsey, have, with the revelation that the anthrax is domestic, had their arguments silenced by the facts.

Absent Iraqi involvement in the attack on the United States, I can only wonder why so many in Congress seek to divert resources away from our efforts to bring those who did attack us to justice. That hardly seems a prudent move. Many will argue that it doesn't matter whether Iraq had a role in the attack on us; Iraq is a threat to the United States and therefore must be dealt with. Some on this committee have made this very argument. Mr. Speaker, most of us here have never been to Iraq; however, those who have, like former UN Chief Arms Inspector Scott Ritter—who led some thirty inspection missions to Iraq—come to different conclusions on the country. Asked in November on Fox News Channel by John Kasich, sitting in for Bill O'Reilly, about how much of a threat Saddam Hussein poses to the United States, former Chief Inspector Ritter said, "In terms of military threat, absolutely nothing. Diplomatically, politically, Saddam's a little bit of a threat. In terms of real national security threat to the United States, no, none." Mr. Speaker, shouldn't we even stop for a moment to consider what some of these experts are saying before we move further down the road toward military confrontation?

The rationale for this legislation is suspect, not the least because it employs a revisionist view of recent Middle East history. **This legislation brings up, as part of its indictment against Iraq, that Iraq attacked Iran some 20 years ago. What the legislation fails to mention is that at that time Iraq was an ally of the United States, and counted on technical and military support from the United States in its war on Iran.** Similarly, the legislation mentions Iraq's invasion of Kuwait more than 10 years ago. But at that time, U.S. foreign policy was sending Saddam Hussein mixed messages, as Iraq's dispute with Kuwait simmered. At the time, U.S. Ambassador April Glaspie was reported in the *New York Times* giving very ambiguous signals to Saddam Hussein regarding Kuwait, allegedly telling Hussein that the United States had no interest in Arab-Arab disputes.

We must also consider the damage a military invasion of Iraq will do to our alliance in this fight against terrorism. An attack on Iraq could destroy that international coalition against terrorism. Most of our European allies, critical in maintaining this coalition, have explicitly stated their opposition to any attack on Iraq. German Foreign Minister Joschka Fischer warned recently that Europe was "completely united" in opposition to any attack on Iraq. Russian president Vladimir Putin cautioned recently against American military action in Iraq. Mr. Putin urged the next step to be centered around cutting off the financial resources of terrorists worldwide. As for Iraq, the Russian president said, "So far I have no confirmation, no evidence that Iraq is financing the terrorists that we are fighting against." Relations with our European allies would suffer should we continue down this path toward military conflict with Iraq.

Likewise, U.S. relations with the Gulf States like Saudi Arabia could collapse should the United States initiate an attack on Iraq. Not only would our Saudi allies deny us the use of their territory to launch the attack, but a certain backlash from all Gulf and Arab states could well produce even an oil embargo against the United States. Egypt, a key ally in our fight against terrorism, has also warned against any attack on Iraq. Egyptian Foreign Minister Ahmed Maher said recently of the coalition, "If we want to keep consensus, we should not resort, after Afghanistan, to military means."

Mr. Speaker, I do not understand this push to seek out another country to bomb next. Media and various politicians and pundits seem to delight in predicting from week to week which country should be next on our bombing list. Is military action now the foreign policy of first resort for the

182

United States? When it comes to other countries and warring disputes, the United States counsels dialogue without exception. **We urge the Catholics and Protestants to talk to each other; we urge the Israelis and Palestinians to talk to each other. Even at the height of the Cold War, when the Soviet Union had missiles pointed at us from 90 miles away in Cuba, we solved the dispute through dialogue and diplomacy. Why is it, in this post-Cold War era, that the United States seems to turn first to the military to solve its foreign policy problems? Is diplomacy dead?**

In conclusion, Mr. Speaker, this legislation, even in its watered-down form, moves us closer to conflict with Iraq. This is not in our interest at this time. It also, ironically enough, could serve to further Osama bin Laden's twisted plans for a clash of civilizations between Islam and the West. Invading Iraq, with the massive loss of lives on both sides, would only forward bin Laden's hateful plan. I think we need to look at our priorities here. We are still seeking those most responsible for the attacks on the United States. Now hardly seems the time to go out in search of new battles. ■

"The Constitution vests the power of declaring war in Congress; therefore no offensive expedition of importance can be undertaken until after they shall have deliberated upon the subject and authorized such a measure."—George Washington

CHAPTER 13

As the new legislative session began and the President would give his first post-9/11 State of the Union Address, it was time to reflect upon recent events and also to restate the case for a policy dedicated to defending the USA.

January 24, 2002
THE CASE FOR DEFENDING AMERICA
HON. RON PAUL of TEXAS
IN THE HOUSE OF REPRESENTATIVES

As we begin this new legislative session, we cannot avoid reflecting on this past year. All Americans will remember the moment and place when tragedy hit us on September 11th. We also all know that a good philosophy to follow is to turn adversity into something positive if at all possible. Although we have suffered for years from a flawed foreign policy and were already in a recession before the attacks, the severity of these events has forced many of us to reassess our foreign and domestic policies. Hopefully, positive changes will come of this.

It is just as well that the economy was already in recession for six months prior to the September attacks. Otherwise, the temptation would have been too great to blame the attacks for the weak economy rather than look for the government policies responsible for the recession. Terrorist attacks alone, no matter how disruptive, could never be the sole source of a significant economic downturn.

A major debate over foreign policy has naturally resulted from this crisis. Dealing with the shortcomings of our policies of the past is essential. We were spending $40 billion a year on intelligence gathering that, we must admit, failed. This tells us a problem exists. There are shortcomings with our $320 billion DOD budget that did not provide the protection Americans expect.

Obviously a proper response to the terrorists requires sound judgment in order to prevent further suffering of the innocent or to foolishly bring about a worldwide conflict.

One of the key responsibilities of the federal government in providing for national defense is protection of liberty here at home. Unwisely responding to the attacks could undermine our national defense while threatening our liberties. What we have done so far since last September is not very reassuring. What we do here in the Congress in the coming months may well determine the survival of our Republic. Fear and insecurity must not drive our policies. Sacrificing personal liberty should never be an option.

Involving ourselves in every complex conflict around the globe hardly enhances our national security. The special interests that were already lined up at the public trough should not be permitted to use the ongoing crisis as an opportunity to demand even more benefits. Let us all remember why the U.S. Congress was established, what our responsibilities are and what our oath of office means.

It's been reported that since the 9/11 attacks, big-government answers have gained in popularity, and people, fearful for their security, have looked to the federal government for help. Polls indicate that acceptance of government solutions to our problems is at its highest level in decades. That may be true to some degree, or it may merely reflect the sentiments of the moment, or even the way the questions were asked. Only time will tell. Since the welfare state is no more viable in the long run than a Communist or fascist state, most Americans will eventually realize the fallacy of depending on the government for economic security and know that personal liberty should not be sacrificed out of fear.

Even with this massive rush to embrace all the bailouts offered up by

Washington, a growing number of Americans are rightfully offended by the enormity of it all and annoyed that powerful and wealthy special interests seem to be getting the bulk of the benefits. In one area, though, a very healthy reaction has occurred. Almost all Americans—especially those still flying commercial airlines—now know that they have a personal responsibility to react to any threat on any flight. Passengers have responded magnificently. Most people recognize that armed citizens best protect our homes, because it is impossible for the police to be everywhere and prevent crimes from happening. A homeowner's ability to defend himself serves as a strong deterrent.

Our government's ridiculous policy regarding airline safety and prohibiting guns on airplanes had indoctrinated us all—pilots, passengers and airline owners—to believe we should never resist hijackers. This set up the perfect conditions for terrorists to take over domestic flights, just as they did on September 11th.

The people of this country now realize, more than ever, their own responsibility for personal self-defense, using guns if necessary. The anti-gun fanatics have been very quiet since 9/11, and more Americans are ready to assume responsibility for their own safety than ever before. This is all good.

But sadly, the Congress went in the opposite direction in providing safety on commercial flights. Pilots are not carrying guns, and security has been socialized—in spite of the fact that security procedures authorized by the FAA prior to 9/11 were not compromised. The problem did not come from *failure to follow* FAA rules; the problem resulted from *precisely* following FAA rules. No wonder so many Americans are wisely assuming they'd better be ready to protect theirselves when necessary!

This attitude is healthy, practical and legal under the Constitution. Unfortunately, too many people who have come to this conclusion still cling to the notion that economic security is a responsibility of the U.S. government. That's the reason we have a $2 trillion annual budget and a growing $6 trillion national debt.

Another positive result of last year's attacks was the uniting of many Americans in an effort to deal with the problems the country faced. This applies more to the people who reflect true patriotism than it does to some of the politicians and special interests who took advantage of the situation. If this renewed energy and sense of unity could be channeled correctly, much good could come of it. If misdirected, actual harm will result.

I give less credit to the Washington politicians who sing the songs of patriotism, but use the crisis to pursue their endless personal goal to gain more political power. But the greatest condemnation should be directed toward the special-interest lobbyists, who finance the politicians in order to secure their power, while using patriotism as a cover and the crisis as a golden opportunity. Indeed, those who are using the crisis to promote their own agenda are many.

There is no doubt, as many have pointed out, our country changed dramatically with the horror that hit us on 9/11. The changes obviously are a result of something other than the tragic loss of over 3,900 people. We kill that many people every month on our government highways. We lost 60,000 young people in the Vietnam War, yet the sense of fear in our country then was not the same as it is today. The major difference is that last year's attacks made us feel vulnerable, because it was clear that our federal government had failed in its responsibility to provide defense against such an assault. And the anthrax scare certainly didn't help to diminish that fear.

Giving up our civil liberties has made us feel even less safe from our own government's intrusion in our lives. The two seem to be in conflict. How can we be safer from outside threats while making ourselves more exposed to our own government's threat to our liberty?

The most significant and dangerous result of last year's attacks has been the bold expansion of the federal police state and our enhanced international role as the world's policeman.

Although most of the legislation pushing the enhanced domestic and international role for our government passed by huge majorities, I'm convinced that the people's support for much of it is less enthusiastic than Washington politicians believe. As time progresses, the full impact of Homeland Security, and the unintended consequences of our growing overseas commitments, will become apparent. And a large majority of Americans will appropriately ask, "Why did the Congress do it?"

Unless we precisely understand the proper role of government in a free society, our problems will not be solved without sacrificing liberty. The wonderful thing is that our problems can be easily solved when protecting individual liberty becomes our goal, rather than the erroneous assumption that solutions must always be in conflict with liberty and that sacrificing some liberty is to be expected during trying times. This is not necessary.

Our Attorney General established a standard for disloyalty to the U.S. government by claiming that those who talk of "lost liberty"

serve to "erode our national unity" and "give ammunition to America's enemies" and "only aid terrorists."

The dangerous assumption is that, in the eyes of our top law-enforcement official, perceived disloyalty or even criticism of the government is approximating an act of terrorism. The grand irony is that this criticism is being directed toward those who, heaven forbid, are expressing concern for losing our cherished liberties here at home. This, of course, is what the whole war on terrorism is supposed to be about, protecting liberty, and that includes the right of free expression.

Our government leaders have threatened foreign countries by claiming that if they "are not with us, they are against us," which leaves no room for the neutrality that has been practiced by some nations for centuries. This position could easily result in perpetual conflicts with dozens of nations around the world.

Could it ever come to a point where those who dissent at home against our military operations overseas will be considered too sympathetic to the enemy? The Attorney General's comments suggest just that, and it has happened here in our past. We indeed live in dangerous times. We are unable to guarantee protection from outside threats and may be approaching a time when our own government poses a threat to our liberties.

No matter how sincere and well-motivated, the effort to fight terrorism and provide for homeland security, if ill-advised, will result neither in vanquishing terrorism nor in preserving our liberties. I am fearful that, here in Washington, there's little understanding of the real cause of the terrorist attacks on us, little remembrance of the grand purpose of the American experiment with liberty, or even how our Constitution was written to strictly limit government officials in all that they do.

The military operation against the Taliban has gone well. The Taliban has been removed from power, and our government, with the help of the UN, is well along the way toward establishing a new Afghan government. We weren't supposed to be in the business of nation building, but I guess 9/11 changed all that. The one problem is that the actual number of al-Qaida members captured or killed is uncertain. Also the number of Taliban officials that had any direct contact or knowledge of the attacks on us is purely speculative. Since this war is carried out in secrecy, we'll probably not know the details of what went on for years to come.

I wonder how many civilians have been killed so far. I know a lot of Members could care less, remembering innocent American civilians who were slaughtered in New York and Washington. But a policy that shows

189

no concern for the innocent will magnify our problems, rather than lessen them. The hard part to understand in all of this is that Saudi Arabia probably had more to do with these attacks than did Afghanistan.

But then again, who wants to offend our oil partners?

Our sterile approach to the bombing, with minimal loss of American life, is to be commended, but it may generate outrage toward us by this lopsided killing of persons totally unaware of the events of September 11th.

Our president wisely has not been anxious to send large numbers of occupying forces into Afghanistan. This also guarantees chaos among the warring tribal factions. The odds of a stable Afghan government evolving out of this mess are *remote*. The odds of our investing large sums of money to buy support for years to come are *great*.

Unfortunately, it has been seen only as an opportunity for Pakistan and India to resume their warring ways, placing us in a dangerous situation. This could easily get out of control, since China will not allow a clear-cut Indian victory over Pakistan. The danger of a nuclear confrontation is real. Even the British have spoken sympathetically about Pakistan's interests over India. The tragedy is that we have helped both India and Pakistan financially, and, therefore, the American taxpayer has indirectly contributed funds for the weapons on both sides. Our troops in this region are potential targets of either or both countries.

Fortunately, due to the many probable repercussions, a swift attack on Iraq now seems less likely. Our surrogate army, organized by the Iraqi national congress, is now known to be a charade, prompting our administration to stop all funding of this organization. Relying on the Kurds to help remove Hussein defies logic, as the U.S.-funded Turkish army continues its war on the Kurds. There is just no coalition in the Persian Gulf to take on Iraq, and, fortunately, our Secretary of State knows it.

Our terrorist enemy is vague and elusive. Our plans to expand our current military operations into many other countries are fraught with great risks, risks of making our problems worse. Not dealing with the people actually responsible for the attacks and ignoring the root causes of the terrorism will needlessly perpetuate and expand a war that will do nothing to enhance the security and safety of the American people.

Since Iraq is now less likely to be hit, it looks like another poverty-ridden, rudderless nation, possibly Somalia, will be the next target. No good can come of this process. It will provide more fodder for the radicals' claim that the war is about America against Islam. Somalia poses no threat to the United States, but bombing Somalia as we have Afghanistan, and

Iraq for 12 years, will only incite more hatred toward the U.S. and increase the odds of our someday getting hit again by some frustrated, vengeful, radicalized Muslim.

Our presence in the Persian Gulf is not necessary to provide for America's defense. Our presence in the region makes all Americans more vulnerable to attacks and defending America much more difficult.

The real reason for our presence in the Persian Gulf, as well as our eagerness to assist in building a new Afghan government under UN authority, should be apparent to us all.

Stewart Eizenstat, Undersecretary of Economics, Business, and Agricultural Affairs for the previous administration, succinctly stated U.S. policy for Afghanistan, testifying before the Senate Foreign Relations "Trade" Subcommittee on October 13, 1997:

> *[One of] five main foreign policy interests in the Caspian region [is] continued support for U.S. companies" [and] "the least progress has been made in Afghanistan, where gas and oil pipeline proposals designed to carry central Asian energy to world markets have been delayed indefinitely pending establishment of a broad-based multi-ethnic government.*

This was a rather blunt acknowledgment of our intentions

It is apparent that our policy has not changed with this administration. Our new special envoy to Afghanistan, Zalmay Khalilzad, was at one time a lobbyist for the Taliban and worked for Unocal, the American oil company seeking rights to build oil and gas pipelines through northern Afghanistan. During his stint as a lobbyist, he urged approval of the Taliban and defended them in the U.S. press. He now, of course, sings a different tune with respect to the Taliban, but I am sure his views on the pipeline by U.S. companies have not changed.

Born in Afghanistan, Khalilzad is a controversial figure, to say the least, due to his close relationship with the oil industry and previously with the Taliban. His appointment to the national Security Council very conveniently did not require confirmation by the Senate. Khalilzad also is a close ally of the Secretary of Defense, Paul Wolfowitz, in promoting early and swift military action against Iraq.

The point being, of course, that it may be good to have a new Afghan government, but the question is whether that is *our responsibility* and whether we *should be doing it* under the constraints of our Constitution. There's a real question of whether it will serve our best interests in the long-term.

CIA support for the Shah of Iran for 25 years led to the long-term serious problems with that nation that persist even to this day. Could oil be the reason we have concentrated on bombing Afghanistan while ignoring Saudi Arabia, even though we have never found Osama bin Laden? Obviously, Saudi Arabia is culpable in these terrorist attacks in the United States, yet little is done about it.

There are quite a few unintended consequences that might occur if our worldwide commitment to fighting terrorism is unrestrained.

Russia's interests in the Afghan region are much more intense than Putin would have us believe, and Russia's active involvement in a spreading regional conflict should be expected.

An alliance between Iraq and Iran against the U.S. is a more likely possibility now than ever before. Iraqi Foreign Minister Naji Sabri is optimistically working on bringing the two nations together in a military alliance. His hope is that this would be activated if we attacked Iraq. The two nations have already exchanged prisoners of war as a step in that direction.

U.S. military planners are making preparations for our troops to stay in Central Asia for a long time. *A long time* could mean 50 years! We have been in Korea for that long, and have been in Japan and Europe even longer, but the time will come when we will wear out our welcome and have to leave these areas. The Vietnam War met with more resistance, and we left relatively quickly in humiliating defeat. Similarly, episodes of a more minor nature occurred in Somalia and Lebanon.

Why look for more of these kinds of problems when it does not serve our interests? Jeopardizing our security violates the spirit of our Constitution and inevitably costs us more than we can afford.

Our permanent air bases built in Saudi Arabia are totally unessential to our security, contributed to the turmoil in the Middle East, and continue to do so.

We're building a giant new air base in Kyrgyzstan, a country once part of the Soviet Union and close to Russia. China, also a neighbor, with whom we eagerly seek a close relationship as a trading partner, will not ignore our military buildup in this region.

Islamic fundamentalists may overthrow the current government of Saudi Arabia, a fear that drives her to cooperate openly with the terrorists while flaunting her relationship with the United States. *The Wall Street Journal* has editorialized that the solution ought to be our forcibly seizing the Saudi Arabian oil fields and replacing the current government with an even more pro-Western government. All along I thought we condemned regimes that took over their neighbors' oil fields!

The editorial, unbelievably explicit, concluded by saying: "Finally, we must be prepared to seize the Saudi oil fields and administer them for the greater good." *The greater good?* I just wonder whose greater good?

If the jingoism of the *Wall Street Journal* prevails, and the warmongers in the Congress and the administration carry the day, we can assume with certainty that these efforts being made will precipitate an uncontrollable breakout of hostilities in the region that could lead to World War III.

How a major publication can actually print an article that openly supports such aggression as a serious proposal is difficult to comprehend! Two countries armed with nuclear weapons, on the verge of war in the region, and we're being urged to dig a deeper hole for ourselves by seizing the Saudi oil fields?

Already the presence of our troops in the Muslim holy land of Saudi Arabia has inflamed the hatred that drove the terrorists to carry out their tragic acts of 9/11. Pursuing such an aggressive policy would only further undermine our ability to defend the American people and will compound the economic problems we face.

Something, anything, regardless of its effectiveness, had to be done, since the American people expected it, and Congress and the Administration willed it. An effort to get the terrorists and their supporters is obviously in order, and hopefully that has been achieved. But a never-ending commitment to end all terrorism in the world, whether it is related to the attack on September 11th or not, is neither a legitimate nor wise policy.

HJ RES 64 gives the president authority to pursue only those guilty of the attack on us, not every terrorist in the entire world. Let there be no doubt: for every *terrorist* identified, others will see only a *freedom fighter*.

When we aided Osama bin Laden in the 1980s, he was a member of the Mujahidien, and they were the *freedom fighters* waging a *just* war against the Soviet Army. A broad definition of terrorism outside the understanding of "those who attack the United States" opens Pandora's box in our foreign policy commitments.

If we concentrate on searching for all terrorists throughout the world and bombing dozens of countries, but forget to deal with the important contributing factors that drove those who killed our fellow citizens, we will only make ourselves more vulnerable to new attacks.

How can we forever fail to address the provocative nature of U.S.

taxpayer money being used to suppress and kill Palestinians and ignore the affront to the Islamic people that our military presence on their holy land of Saudi Arabia causes, not to mention the persistent 12 years of bombing Iraq?

I'm fearful that an unlimited worldwide war against all terrorism will distract from the serious consideration that must be given to our policy of foreign interventionism, driven by the powerful commercial interests and a desire to promote world government. This is done while ignoring our principle responsibility of protecting national security and liberty here at home.

There is a serious problem with a policy that has allowed a successful attack on our homeland. It cannot be written off as a result of irrational yet efficient evildoers who are merely jealous of our success and despise our freedoms.

We've had enemies throughout our history, but never before have we suffered such an attack that has made us feel so vulnerable. The cause of this crisis is much more profound and requires looking inward, as well as outward, at our own policies as well as those of others.

The Founders of this country were precise in their beliefs regarding foreign policy. Our Constitution reflects these beliefs, and all of our early presidents endorsed these views. It was not until the 20th Century that our nation went off to far away places looking for dragons to slay. This past century reflects the new and less-traditional American policy of foreign interventionism. Our economic and military power, a result of our domestic freedoms, has permitted us to survive and even thrive while dangerously expanding our worldwide influence.

There's no historic precedent that such a policy can be continued forever. All empires and great nations throughout history have ended when they stretched their commitments overseas too far and abused their financial system at home. The over-commitment of a country's military forces when faced with budgetary constraints can only lead to a lower standard of living for its citizens. That has already started to happen here in the United States. Who today is confident the government and our private retirement systems are sound and the benefits guaranteed?

The unfortunate complicating factor that all great powers suffer is the buildup of animosity toward the nation currently at the top of the heap, which is aggravated by arrogance and domination over the weaker nations. We are beginning to see this, and the *Wall Street Journal* editorial clearly symbolizes this arrogance.

194

The traditional American foreign policy of the Founders and our presidents for the first 145 years of our history entailed three points:

Friendship with all nations desiring of such;

As much free trade and travel with those countries as possible;

Avoiding entangling alliances.

This is still good advice. The Framers also understood that the important powers for dealing with other countries and the issue of war were to be placed in the hands of the Congress. This principle has essentially been forgotten.

The executive branch now has much more power than does the Congress. Congress continues to allow its authority to be transferred to the executive branch, as well as to international agencies, such as the UN, NAFTA, IMF, and the WTO. Through executive orders, our presidents routinely use powers once jealously guarded and held by the Congress.

Today, through altering aid and sanctions, we buy and sell our "friendship" with all kinds of threats and bribes in our effort to spread our influence around the world. To most people in Washington, free trade means international managed trade, with subsidies and support for the WTO, where influential corporations can seek sanctions against their competitors. Our alliances, too numerous to count, have committed our dollars and our troops to such an extent that, under today's circumstances, there's not a border war or civil disturbance in the world in which we do not have a stake. And more than likely, we have a stake—foreign aid—in *both* sides of each military conflict.

After the demise of our nemesis, the Soviet Union, many believed that we could safely withdraw from some of our worldwide commitments. It was hoped we would start minding our own business, save some money, and reduce the threat to our military personnel. But the opposite has happened. Without any international competition for super-power status, our commitments have grown and spread, so that today we provide better military protection to Taiwan and South Korea and Saudi Arabia than we do for our own cities of New York and Washington.

I am certain that national security and defense of our own cities can never be adequately provided unless we reconsider our policy of foreign interventionism.

Conventional wisdom in Washington today is that we have *no choice* but to play the role of the world's only superpower. Recently we had to cancel flights of our own Air Force over our cities because of spending constraints, and we rely on foreign AWACS aircraft to patrol our airspace.

The American people are not in sync with the assumption that we must commit ourselves endlessly to being the world's policemen. If we do not wisely step back and reassess our worldwide commitments and our endless entanglements as we march toward world government, economic law will one day force us to do so anyway under undesirable circumstances. In the meantime, we can expect plenty more military confrontations around the world while becoming even more vulnerable to attack by terrorists here at home. ■

By February of 2002, we had heard the President identify an "axis of evil" and the march toward war in Iraq demanded even more focus.

February 26, 2002
BEFORE WE BOMB IRAQ...
HON. RON PAUL of TEXAS
IN THE HOUSE OF REPRESENTATIVES

The war drums are beating, louder and louder. Iraq, Iran and North Korea have been forewarned. Plans have been laid and, for all we know, already initiated, for the overthrow and assassination of Saddam Hussein.

There's been talk of sabotage, psychological warfare, arming domestic rebels, killing Hussein, and even an outright invasion of Iraq with hundreds of thousands of US troops. All we hear about in the biased media is the need to eliminate Saddam Hussein, with little regard for how this, in itself, might totally destabilize the entire Middle East and Central Asia. It could, in fact, make the Iraq "problem" much worse.

The assumption is that, with our success in Afghanistan, we should now pursue this same policy against any country we choose, no matter how flimsy the justification. It hardly can be argued that it is because authoritarian governments deserve our wrath, considering the number of current and past such governments that we have not only tolerated but subsidized.

Protestations from our Arab allies are silenced by dumping more American taxpayer dollars upon them.

European criticism that the United States is now following a unilateral approach is brushed off, which only causes more apprehension in the European community. Widespread support from the eager media pumps the public to support the warmongers in the administration.

The pros and cons of how dangerous Saddam Hussein actually is are legitimate. However, it is rarely pointed out that the CIA has found no evidence whatsoever that Iraq was involved in the terrorist attacks of 9/11.

Rarely do we hear that Iraq has never committed any aggression against the United States. No one in the media questions our aggression against Iraq for the past 12 years by continuous bombing and imposed sanctions responsible for the deaths of hundreds of thousands of children.

Iraq's defense of her homeland can hardly be characterized as aggression against those who rain bombs down on them. We had to go over 6,000 miles to pick this fight against a third-world nation with little ability to defend itself.

Our policies have actually served to generate support for Saddam Hussein, in spite of his brutal control of the Iraq people. He is as strong today—if not stronger—as he was prior to the Persian Gulf War 12 years ago.

Even today, our jingoism ironically is driving a closer alliance between Iraq and Iran, two long-time bitter enemies.

While we trade with, and subsidize to the hilt, the questionable government of China, we place sanctions on and refuse to trade with Iran and Iraq, which only causes greater antagonism. But if the warmongers' goal is to have a war, regardless of international law and the Constitution, current policy serves their interests.

Could it be that only through war and removal of certain governments we can maintain control of the oil in this region? Could it be all about oil, and have nothing to do with U.S. national security?

Too **often when we dictate who will lead another country, we only replace one group of thugs with another**—as we just did in Afghanistan—with the only difference being that the thugs we support are expected to be puppet-like and remain loyal to the U.S., or else.

Although bits and pieces of the administration's plans to wage war against Iraq, and possibly Iran and North Korea, are discussed, we never hear any mention of the authority to do so. It seems that Tony Blair's approval is more important than the approval of the American people!

Congress never complains about its lost prerogative to be the sole declarer of war. Astoundingly, Congress is only too eager to give war power to our presidents through the back door, by the use of some fuzzy resolution that the president can use as his justification. And once the hostilities begin, the money always follows, because Congress fears criticism for not "supporting the troops." But putting soldiers in harm's way without proper authority, and unnecessarily, can hardly be the way to "support the troops."

Let it be clearly understood: there is no authority to wage war

against Iraq without Congress passing a Declaration of War. HJ RES 65, passed in the aftermath of 9/11, does not even suggest that this authority exists. A UN Resolution authorizing an invasion of Iraq, even if it were to come, cannot replace the legal process for the United States going to war as precisely defined in the Constitution. We must remember that a covert war is no more justifiable, and is even more reprehensible.

Only tyrants can take a nation to war without the consent of the people. The planned war against Iraq without a Declaration of War is illegal. It is unwise because of many unforeseen consequences that are likely to result. It is immoral and unjust, because it has nothing to do with U.S. security, and because Iraq has not initiated aggression against us.

We must understand that the American people become less secure when we risk a major conflict driven by commercial interests and not constitutionally authorized by Congress. Victory under these circumstances is always elusive, and unintended consequences are inevitable. ■

As meddling in the Middle East moved us toward war, meddling in Europe threatened to further overextend our country and embroil us in other problems.

March 20, 2002
STATEMENT AGAINST MEDDLING IN DOMESTIC UKRAINIAN POLITICS
HON. RON PAUL of TEXAS
IN THE HOUSE OF REPRESENTATIVES

Mr. Speaker, I strongly oppose H. Res. 339, a bill by the United States Congress that seeks to tell a sovereign nation how to hold its own elections. It seems the height of arrogance for us to sit here and lecture the people and government of Ukraine on what they should do and should not do in their own election process. One would have thought after our own election debacle in November 2000, that we would have learned how counterproductive and hypocritical it is to lecture other democratic countries on their electoral processes. **How would Members of this body, or any American, react if countries like the Ukraine demanded that our elections here in the United States conform to their criteria?** I think we can guess how Ukrainians feel about this piece of legislation.

Mr. Speaker, Ukraine has been the recipient of hundreds of millions of dollars in foreign aid from the United States. In fiscal year 2002 alone,

Ukraine was provided $154 million. Yet after all this money, which we were told was to promote democracy, and more than ten years after the end of the Soviet Union, we are told in this legislation that Ukraine has made little if any progress in establishing a democratic political system.

Far from getting more involved in Ukraine's electoral process, which is where this legislation leads us, the United States is already much too involved in the Ukrainian elections. The U.S. government has sent some $4.7 million dollars to Ukraine for monitoring and assistance programs, including training their electoral commission members and domestic monitoring organizations. There have been numerous reports of U.S.-funded non-governmental organizations in Ukraine being involved in pushing one or another political party. This makes it look like the United States is taking sides in the Ukrainian elections.

The legislation calls for the full access of Organization for Security and Cooperation in Europe (OSCE) monitors to all aspects of the parliamentary elections, but that organization has time and time again, from Slovakia to Russia and elsewhere, shown itself to be unreliable and politically biased. Yet the United States continues to fund and participate in OSCE activities. As British writer John Laughland observed this week in *The Guardian* newspaper, "Western election monitoring has become the political equivalent of an Arthur Andersen audit. This supposedly technical process is now so corrupted by political bias that it would be better to abandon it. Only then will countries be able to elect their leaders freely." Mr. Speaker, I think this is advice we would be wise to heed.

Other aspects of this bill are likewise troubling. This bill seeks, from thousands of miles away and without any of the facts, to demand that the Ukrainian government solve crimes within Ukraine that have absolutely nothing to do with the United States. No one knows what happened to journalist Heorhiy Gongadze or any of the alleged murdered Ukrainian journalists, yet by adding it to this ill-advised piece of legislation, we are sitting here suggesting that the government has something to do with the alleged murders. This meddling in the Ukrainian judicial system is inappropriate and counter-productive.

Mr. Speaker, we are legislators in the United States Congress. We are not in Ukraine. We have no right to interfere in the internal affairs of that country and no business telling them how to conduct their elections. A far better policy toward Ukraine would be to eliminate any U.S.-government imposed barrier to free trade between Americans and Ukrainians. ■

Different people opposed the war in Iraq for different reasons, when I was asked to state mine, here is what I had to say.

March 20, 2002
WHY INITIATE WAR ON IRAQ?
HON. RON PAUL of TEXAS
IN THE HOUSE OF REPRESENTATIVES

I was recently asked why I thought it was a bad idea for the president to initiate a war against Iraq. I responded by saying that I could easily give a half a dozen reasons why; and if I took a minute, I could give a full dozen. For starters, here are a half a dozen:

Number One, Congress has not given the president the legal authority to wage war against Iraq as directed by the Constitution, nor does he have UN authority to do so. Even if he did, it would not satisfy the rule of law laid down by the Framers of the Constitution.

Number Two, Iraq has not initiated aggression against the United States. Invading Iraq and deposing Saddam Hussein, no matter how evil a dictator he may be, has nothing to do with our national security. Iraq does not have a single airplane in its air force and is a poverty-ridden, third-world nation, hardly a threat to U.S. security. Stirring up a major conflict in this region will actually jeopardize our security.

Number Three, a war against Iraq initiated by the United States cannot be morally justified. The argument that someday in the future Saddam Hussein might pose a threat to us means that any nation, any place in the world is subject to an American invasion without cause. This would be comparable to the impossibility of proving a negative.

Number Four, initiating a war against Iraq will surely antagonize all neighboring Arab and Muslim nations, as well as the Russians, the Chinese, and the European Union, if not the whole world. Even the English people are reluctant to support Tony Blair's prodding of our president to invade Iraq. There is no practical benefit for such action. Iraq could end up in even more dangerous lands like Iran.

Number Five, an attack on Iraq will not likely be confined to Iraq alone. Spreading the war to Israel and rallying all Arab nations against her may well end up jeopardizing the very existence of Israel. The president has already likened the current international crisis more to that of World War II than the more localized Vietnam War. The law of unintended consequences applies to international affairs every bit as much as to domestic interventions, yet the consequences of such are much more dangerous.

Number Six, **the cost of a war against Iraq would be prohibitive. We paid a heavy economic price for the Vietnam War in direct cost, debt and inflation. This coming war could be a lot more expensive.** Our national debt is growing at a rate greater than $250 billion per year. This will certainly accelerate. The dollar cost will be the least of our concerns, compared to the potential loss of innocent lives, both theirs and ours. The systematic attack on civil liberties that accompanies all wars cannot be ignored. Already we hear cries for resurrecting the authoritarian program of constriction in the name of patriotism, of course.

Could any benefit come from all this warmongering? Possibly. Let us hope and pray so. It should be evident that big government is anathema to individual liberty. In a free society, the role of government is to protect the individual's right to life and liberty. The biggest government of all, the UN, consistently threatens personal liberties and U.S. sovereignty. But our recent move toward unilateralism hopefully will inadvertently weaken the United Nations. Our participation more often than not lately is conditioned on following the international rules and courts and trade agreements only when they please us, flaunting the consensus, without rejecting internationalism on principle, as we should.

The way these international events will eventually play out is unknown, and in the process we expose ourselves to great danger. Instead of replacing today's international government, (the United Nations, the IMF, the World Bank, the WTO, the international criminal court) with free and independent republics, it is more likely that we will see a rise of militant nationalism with a penchant for solving problems with arms and protectionism rather than free trade and peaceful negotiations.

The last thing this world needs is the development of more nuclear weapons, as is now being planned in a pretense for ensuring the peace. We would need more than an office of strategic information to convince the world of that.

What do we need? We need a clear understanding and belief in a free society, a true republic that protects individual liberty, private property, free markets, voluntary exchange and private solutions to social problems, placing strict restraints on government meddling in the internal affairs of others.

Indeed, we live in challenging and dangerous times. ∎

Here I sought to point out that our entanglements in the Middle East are hardly one-sided, consistent, or even rational.

April 10, 2002
AMERICA'S ENTANGLING ALLIANCES
IN THE MIDDLE EAST
HON. RON PAUL of TEXAS
IN THE HOUSE OF REPRESENTATIVES

We were warned, and in the early years of our Republic, we heeded that warning. Today, though, we are entangled in everyone's affairs throughout the world, and we are less safe as a result. The current Middle-East crisis is one that we helped create, and it is typical of how foreign intervention fails to serve our interests. Now we find ourselves smack-dab in the middle of a fight that will not soon end. No matter what the outcome, we lose.

By trying to support both sides we, in the end, will alienate both sides. We are forced, by domestic politics here at home, to support Israel at all costs, with billions of dollars of aid, sophisticated weapons, and a guarantee that America will do whatever is necessary for Israel's security.

Political pressure compels us to support Israel, but it is oil that prompts us to guarantee security for the Western puppet governments of the oil-rich Arab nations.

Since the Israeli-Arab fight will not soon be resolved, our policy of involving ourselves in a conflict unrelated to our security guarantees that we will suffer the consequences.

What a choice! We must choose between the character of Arafat versus that of Sharon.

The information the average American gets from the major media outlets, with their obvious bias, only makes the problem worse. Who would ever guess that the side that loses *seven* people to every *one* on the other side is portrayed as the sole aggressor and condemned as terrorist? We should remember that Palestinian deaths are seen by most Arabs as being American-inspired, since our weapons are being used against them, and they're the ones whose land has been continuously taken from them.

Yet there are still some in this country who can't understand why many in the Arab/Muslim world hate America.

Is it any wonder that the grassroots people in Arab nations, even in Kuwait, threaten their own governments that are totally dominated by

202

American power and money?

The arguments against foreign intervention are many. The chaos in the current Middle-East crisis should be evidence enough for all Americans to reconsider our extensive role overseas and reaffirm the foreign policy of our early leaders, a policy that kept us out of the affairs of others.

But here we are in the middle of a war that has no end and serves only to divide us here at home, while the unbalanced slaughter continues with tanks and aircraft tearing up a country that does not even have an army.

It is amazing that the clamor of support for Israel here at home comes from men of deep religious conviction in the Christian faith who are convinced they are doing the Lord's work. That, quite frankly, is difficult for me as a Christian to comprehend. We need to remember the young people who will be on the front lines when the big war starts, which is something so many in this body seem intent on provoking.

Ironically, the biggest frustration in Washington, for those who eagerly resort to war to resolve differences, is that the violence in the Middle East has delayed plans for starting another war against Iraq.

Current policy prompts our government on one day to give the go-ahead to Sharon to do what he needs to do to combat terrorism (a term that now has little or no meaning); on the next day, however, our government tells him to quit, for fear that we may overly aggravate our oil pals in the Arab nations and jeopardize our oil supplies. This is an impossible policy that will inevitably lead to chaos.

Foreign interventionism is bad for America. Special interests control our policies, while true national security is ignored. **Real defense needs, the defense of our borders, are ignored, and the financial interests of corporations, bankers, and the military-industrial complex gain control, and the American people lose.**

It's costly, to say the least. Already our military budget has sapped domestic spending and caused the deficit to explode. But the greatest danger is that one day these contained conflicts will get out of control. Certainly the stage is set for that to happen in the Middle East and south central Asia. A world war is a possibility that should not be ignored. Our policy of subsidizing both sides is ludicrous. We support Arabs and Jews, Pakistanis and Indians, Chinese and Russians. We have troops in 140 countries around the world just looking for trouble. Our policies have led us to support Al Qaeda in Kosovo and bomb their Serb adversaries. We have, in the past, allied ourselves with bin Laden, as well as Saddam Hussein, only to find out later the seriousness of our mistake. Will this foolishness ever end?

A non-interventionist foreign policy has a lot to say for itself, especially when one looks at the danger and inconsistency of our current policy in the Middle East. ■

After we returned from summer recess in 2002, it seemed obvious that we would take the disastrous plunge in Iraq, and just as obvious that it was essential to once again restate the reasons for my objections to this policy.

September 4, 2002
ARGUMENTS AGAINST A WAR IN IRAQ
HON. RON PAUL of TEXAS
IN THE HOUSE OF REPRESENTATIVES

Mr. Speaker, I rise to urge the Congress to think twice before thrusting this nation into a war without merit, one fraught with the danger of escalating into something no American will be pleased with.

Thomas Jefferson once said: "Never was so much false arithmetic employed on any subject as that which has been employed to persuade nations that it is in their interests to go to war."

We have for months now heard plenty of false arithmetic and lame excuses for why we must pursue a preemptive war of aggression against an impoverished, third-world nation 6,000 miles from our shores that doesn't even possess a navy or air force, on the pretense that it must be done for national security reasons.

For some reason, such an attack makes me feel much less secure, while our country is made more vulnerable.

Congress must consider the fact that those with military experience advocate a "go slow" policy, while those without military experience are the ones demanding this war.

We cannot ignore the fact that all of Iraq's neighbors oppose this attack, and our European allies object as well.

If the military and diplomatic reasons for a policy of restraint make no sense to those who want a war, I advise they consider the $100 billion cost that will surely compound our serious budget and economic problems we face here at home. We need no more false arithmetic on our budget or false reasons for pursuing this new adventure into preemptive war and worldwide nation building.

Mr. Speaker, allow me to offer another quote from Jefferson. Jefferson said: "No country perhaps was ever so thoroughly against war as ours. These dispositions pervade every description of its citizens, whether in or out of office. We love and we value peace, we know its blessings from experience."

We need this sentiment renewed in this Congress in order to avoid a needless war that offers us nothing but trouble. Congress must deal with this serious matter of whether or not we go to war. I believe it would be a mistake with the information that is available to us today. I do not see any reason whatsoever to take young men and young women and send them 6,000 miles away to attack a country that has not committed any aggression against this country. Many American now share my belief that it would be a serious mistake.

First, there is a practical reason to oppose a war in Iraq. Our military now has been weakened over the last decade, and when we go into Iraq we will clearly dilute our ability to defend our country. We do not enhance our national defense by initiating this war. Besides, it is impractical because of unintended consequences which none of us know about. We do not know exactly how long this will last. It could be a six-day war, a six-month war, six years or even longer.

There is a military reason for not going to war. We ought to listen to the generals and other military experts, including Colin Powell, Brent Scowcroft, Anthony Zinni, and Norman Schwarzkopf, who are now advising us NOT to go to war. Some have even cautioned against the possibility of starting World War III. They understand that our troops have been spread too thin around the world, and it is dangerous from a purely military standpoint to go to war today.

There is a constitutional argument and a constitutional mistake that could be made. If we once again go to war, as we have done on so many occasions since World War II, without a clear declaration of war by Congress, we blatantly violate the Constitution. I fear we will once again go to war in a haphazard way, by executive order, or even by begging permission from the rotten, anti-American United Nations. This haphazard approach, combined with lack of a clearly defined goal for victory, makes it almost inevitable that true victory will not come. So we should look at this from a constitutional perspective. Congress should assume its responsibility, because war is declared by Congress, not by a president and not by the UN

This is a very important matter, and I am delighted to hear that there will be congressional hearings and discussion. I certainly believe we should have a balanced approach. We have already had some hearings in the other body, where we heard only one side of the issue. If we want to have real hearings, we should have a debate and hear evidence on *both* sides, rather than just hearing pro-war interests arguing for war.

There are even good political reasons for not initiating this conflict. War is not popular. It may seem popular in the short run, when there appears to be an immediate victory and everyone is gloating, but war is not popular. People get killed, and body bags end up coming back. War is very unpopular, and it is not the politically smart thing to do.

There are economic reasons to avoid this war. We can do serious damage to our economy. It is estimated that this venture in Iraq may well cost over a hundred billion dollars. Our national debt right now is increasing at a rate of over $450 billion yearly, and we are talking about spending another hundred billion dollars on an adventure when we do not know what the outcome will be and how long it will last? What will happen to oil prices? What will happen to the recession that we are in? What will happen to the deficit? We must expect all kinds of economic ramifications.

There are countless diplomatic reasons for not going. All the Arab nations near Iraq object to and do not endorse our plan, and none of our European allies are anxious for this to happen. So diplomatically we make a serious mistake by doing this. I hope we have second thoughts and are very cautious in what we do.

There are philosophical reasons for those who believe in limited government to oppose this war. "War is the health of the state," as the saying goes. War necessarily means more power is given to the state. This additional power always results in a loss of liberty. Many of the worst government programs of the 20th Century began during wartime "emergencies" and were never abolished. War and big government go hand in hand, but we should be striving for peace and freedom.

Finally, there is a compelling moral argument against war in Iraq. Military force is justified only in self-defense; naked aggression is the province of dictators and rogue states. This is the danger of a new "preemptive first strike" doctrine. America is the most moral nation on earth, founded on moral principles, and we must apply moral principles when deciding to use military force. ■

Since I was against the foreign policy that was leading us into war once again, I needed to be something more than a mere critic; I also needed to state once again what the alternative was. Here I make the case for a new approach by outlining what exactly we support in the way of foreign affairs.

September 5, 2002
A FOREIGN POLICY FOR PEACE, PROSPERITY AND LIBERTY
HON. RON PAUL of TEXAS
IN THE HOUSE OF REPRESENTATIVES

Mr. Speaker, Thomas Jefferson spoke for the Founders and all our early presidents when he stated: "peace, commerce, and honest friendship with all nations, entangling alliances with none..." which is, "one of the essential principles of our government." The question is: whatever happened to this principle and should it be restored?

We find the 20th Century was wracked with war, peace was turned asunder, and our liberties were steadily eroded. Foreign alliances and meddling in the internal affairs of other nations became commonplace. On many occasions, involvement in military action occurred through UN resolutions or a presidential executive order, despite the fact that the war power was explicitly placed in the hands of Congress.

Since World War II, nearly 100,000 deaths and over a quarter million wounded (not counting the many thousands that have been affected by Agent Orange and the Persian Gulf War Syndrome) **have all occurred without a declaration of war and without a clear-cut victory.** The entire 20th Century was indeed costly, with over 600,000 killed in battle and an additional million wounded.

If liberty had been truly enhanced during that time, less could be said about the imperfections of the policy. The evidence, however, is clear that we as a people are less free, and the prosperity we still enjoy may be more illusionary than many realize. The innocent victims who have suffered at the hands of our militarism abroad are rarely considered by our government. Yet they may well be a major factor in the hatred now being directed toward America. It is not currently popular to question corporate and banking influence over a foreign policy that replaced the wisdom of Washington and Jefferson. Questioning foreign government influence on our policies, although known about for years, is not acceptable in the politically correct environment in which we live.

There's little doubt that our role in the world dramatically changed in the 20th Century, inexorably evolving from that of strict non-interventionism to that of sole superpower, with the assumption that we were destined to be the world policeman. By the end of the 20th Century, in fact, this occurred. We have totally forgotten that for well over a hundred years, we followed the advice of the Founders by meticulously avoiding overseas conflicts. Instead we now find ourselves in charge of an American hegemony spread to the four corners of the earth.

Now we have entered the 21st Century, and there is not a country in the world that does not either depend on the U.S. for protection, or fear her wrath if they refuse to do her bidding. As the 20th Century progressed, American taxpayers were required to finance, with great sacrifices to their pocketbooks and their liberty, the buying of loyalty through foreign aid and intimidation of those countries that did not cooperate.

The question remains, however: Has this change been beneficial to freedom and prosperity here at home, and has it promoted peace and trade throughout the world? Those who justify our interventionist policies abroad argue that the violation of the rule of law is not a problem, considering the *benefits* we receive for maintaining the American empire. But has this really taken into consideration the cost in lives lost, the damage to long-term prosperity, as well as the dollar cost and freedoms we have lost? What about the future? Has this policy of foreign intervention set the stage for radically changing America—and the world—in ways not yet seen? Were the Founders completely off track because they lived in different times, or was the foreign policy they advised based on an *essential principle* of lasting value? Choosing the wrong answer to this question could very well be deadly to the grand experiment in liberty begun in 1776.

THE SLIPPERY ROAD TO WORLD POLICEMAN

The transition from non-interventionism to our current role as world arbiter in all conflicts was insidious and fortuitous. In the early part of the 20th Century, the collapse of the British Empire left a vacuum, which was steadily filled by a US presence. In the latter part of the century, the results of World War II and the collapse of the Soviet system propelled us into our current role. Throughout most of the 20th Century, it was our competition with the Soviets that prompted our ever-expanded presence around the world. We are where we are today almost by default. But does that justify interventionism or prove it is in our best interest?

Disregarding for the moment the moral and constitutional arguments against foreign intervention, a strong case can be made against it for other reasons. It is clear that one intervention begets another. The first problem is rarely solved, and new ones are created. Indeed, in foreign affairs a slippery slope exists. In recent years, we too often slipped into war through the back door, with the purpose rarely defined or understood and the need for victory ignored.

A restrained effort of intervention frequently explodes into something that we did not foresee. Policies end up doing the opposite of their intended purpose, with unintended consequences. The result is that the action taken turns out to actually be detrimental to our national security interests. Yet no effort is made to challenge the fundamental principle behind our foreign policy. It is this failure to adhere to a set of principles that has allowed us to slip into this role, and if unchallenged, could well undo the liberties we all cherish.

Throughout history, there has always been a great temptation for rulers to spread their influence and pursue empire over liberty. Few resist this temptation to power. There always seems to be a natural inclination to yield to this historic human passion. Could it be that progress and civilization and promoting freedom require ignoring this impulse to control others, as the Founders of this great nation advised?

Historically, the driving force behind world domination is usually an effort to control wealth. The Europeans were searching for gold when they came to the Americas. Now it's our turn to seek control over the black gold that drives much of what we do today in foreign affairs. Competing with the Soviet Union prompted our involvement in areas of the world where the struggle for the balance of power was the sole motivating force.

The foreign policy of the 20th Century replaced the policy endorsed by all the early presidents. This permitted our steadily growing involvement overseas in an effort to control the world's commercial interests, with a special emphasis on oil.

Our influence in the Middle East evolved out of concern for the newly created state of Israel in 1947, and our desire to secure control over the flow of oil in that region. Israel's needs and Arab oil have influenced our foreign policy for more than a half a century.

In the 1950s, the CIA installed the Shah in Iran. It was not until the hostage crisis of the late 1970s that the unintended consequences of this became apparent. This generated Iranian hatred of America and led to the takeover by the reactionary Khoumini and the Islamic fundamentalists. It caused greater regional instability than we anticipated. Our meddling in the internal affairs of Iran was of no benefit to us and set the stage for our failed policy in dealing with Iraq.

We allied ourselves in the 1980s with Iraq in its war with Iran, and assisted Saddam Hussein in his rise to power. As recent reports reconfirm, we did nothing to stop Hussein's development of chemical and biological weapons and, at least indirectly, assisted in their development. Now, as a consequence of that needless intervention, we're planning a risky war to remove him from power. As usual, the probable result of such an effort will be something our government does not anticipate, like a takeover by someone much worse. As bad as Hussein is, he's an enemy of the Al Qaeda, and someone new may well be a close ally of the Islamic radicals.

Although our puppet dictatorship in Saudi Arabia has lasted for many decades, it's becoming shakier every day. The Saudi people are not exactly friendly toward us, and our military presence on their holy soil is greatly resented. This contributes to the radical fundamentalist hatred directed toward us. Another unfavorable consequence to America, such as a regime change not to our liking, could soon occur in Saudi Arabia. It is not merely a coincidence that 15 of the 9/11 terrorists are Saudis.

The Persian Gulf War, fought without a declaration of war, is in reality still going on. It looks now like 9/11 may well have been a battle in that war, perpetrated by fanatical guerillas. It indicates how seriously flawed our foreign policy is. In the 1980s, we got involved in the Soviet/Afghan war and actually sided with the forces of Osama bin Laden, helping him gain power. This obviously was an alliance of no benefit to the United States, and it has now come back to haunt us. Our policy for years was to encourage Saudi Arabia to oppose communism by financing and promoting Islamic fundamentalism. Surely the shortcomings of that policy are now evident to everyone.

Clinton's bombing of Sudan and Afghanistan on the eve of his indictment over Monica Lewinsky shattered a Taliban plan to expel Osama bin Laden from Afghanistan. Clinton's bombing of Baghdad on the eve of his impeachment hardly won any converts to our cause or reassured Muslim people in the Middle East of a balanced American policy.

The continued bombing of Iraq over these past 12 years, along with the deadly sanctions resulting in hundreds of thousands of

needless Iraqi civilian deaths, has not been beneficial to our security. And it has been used as one of the excuses for recruiting fanatics ready to sacrifice their lives in demonstrating their hatred toward us.

Essentially all Muslims see our policy in the Israeli-Palestinian conflict as openly favorable toward Israel and in opposition to the Palestinians. It is for this reason they hold us responsible for Palestinian deaths, since all the Israeli weapons are from the United States. Since the Palestinians don't even have an army and must live in refugee camps, one should understand why the animosity builds, even if our pro-Israeli position can be explained.

There is no end in sight. Since 9/11, our involvement in the Middle East and Saudi Arabia has grown significantly. Though we can badger those countries—whose leaders depend upon us to keep them in power—to stay loyal to the United States, the common people of the region become more alienated. Our cozy relationship with the Russians may not be as long-lasting as our current administration hopes, considering the $40 billion trade deal recently made between Russia and Saddam Hussein. It's more than a bit ironic that we find the Russians now promoting free trade as a solution to a difficult situation, while we're promoting war.

This continuous escalation of our involvement overseas has been widespread. We've been in Korea for more than 50 years. We have promised to never back away from the China-Taiwan conflict over territorial disputes. Fifty-seven years after World War II, we still find our military spread throughout Europe and Asia.

And now, the debate rages over whether our national security requires that we, for the first time, escalate this policy of intervention to include "anticipatory self-defense and preemptive war." If our interventions of the 20th Century led to needless deaths, unwinable wars, and continuous unintended consequences, imagine what this new doctrine is about to unleash on the world.

Our policy has prompted us to announce that our CIA will assassinate Saddam Hussein whenever it gets the chance and that the government of Iraq is to be replaced. Evidence now has surfaced that the United Nations inspection teams in the 1990s definitely included American CIA agents who were collecting information on how to undermine the Iraqi government and continue with the routine bombing missions. Why should there be a question of why Saddam Hussein might not readily accept UN inspectors without some type of assurances? **Does anybody doubt that control of Iraqi oil supplies, second only to Saudi Arabia, is the reason U.S.**

policy is belligerent toward Saddam Hussein? If our goal is honestly to remove dictators around the world, then this is the beginning of an endless task.

In the transition from the original American foreign policy of peace, trade, and neutrality to that of world policeman, we have sacrificed our sovereignty to world government organizations, such as the UN, the IMF, the World Bank, and the WTO. To further confuse and undermine our position, we currently have embarked on a policy of unilateralism within these world organizations. This means we accept the principle of globalized government when it pleases us, but when it does not, we ignore it for the sake of our own interests.

Acting in our own interest is to be applauded, but what we're getting is not a good alternative to a one-world government. We don't get our sovereignty back, yet we continue to subject ourselves to a great potential financial burden and loss of liberty as we shift from a national government, with constitutional protection of our rights, to an international government, where our citizens' rights are threatened by treaties we haven't ratified, like the Kyoto and International Criminal Court treaties. We cannot depend on controlling the world government at some later date, even if we seem to be able to do that now.

The unilateralist approach of dominating world leaders and arbitrarily ignoring certain mandates—something we can do with impunity because of our intimidating power—serves only to further undermine our prestige and acceptability throughout the world. And this includes the Muslim countries as well as our European friends. This merely sets the stage for both our enemies and current friends to act in concert against our interests when the time comes. This is especially true if we become financially strapped and our dollar is sharply weakened and we are in a much more vulnerable bargaining position.

Unilateralism within a globalist approach to government is the worst of all choices. It ignores national sovereignty, dignifies one-world government, and places us in the position of demanding dictatorial powers over the world community. Demanding the right to set all policy and exclude ourselves from jurisdictional restraints sows the seeds of future discontent and hostility.

The downside is we get all the bills, risk the lives of our people without cause, and make ourselves the target for every event that goes badly. We get blamed for the unintended, unforeseen consequences and become the target of terrorists that evolve from the radicalized fringes.

Long-term, foreign interventionism does not serve our interests. Tinkering on the edges of our current policy will not help. An announced policy of support for globalist government, assuming the financial and military role of world policeman, maintaining an American world empire, while flaunting unilateralism, is a recipe for disaster. U.S. unilateralism is a far cry from the non-intervention that the founders advised.

THE PRINCIPLE BEHIND FOREIGN POLICY

The term "foreign policy" does not exist in the Constitution. All members of the federal government have sworn to uphold the Constitution, and should do only those things that are clearly authorized. Careful reading of the Constitution reveals Congress has a lot more responsibility than the president in dealing with foreign affairs. The president is the Commander-in-Chief, but can't declare war or finance military action without explicit congressional approval. A good starting point would be for Congress to assume the responsibility given it and to make sure the executive branch does not usurp any authority explicitly granted to Congress.

A proper foreign policy of non-intervention is built on friendship with other nations, free trade, and open travel, maximizing the exchanges of goods and services and ideas. Nations that trade with each other are definitely less likely to fight against each other. Unnecessary bellicosity and jingoism is detrimental to peace and prosperity, and incites unnecessary confrontation. And yet, today, that's about all we hear coming from the politicians and the media pundits who are so anxious for this war against Iraq.

We should avoid entangling alliances and stop meddling in the internal affairs of other nations, no matter how many special interests demand otherwise. The entangling alliances that we should avoid include the complex alliances in the UN, the IMF, the World Bank, and the WTO. One-world government goals are anathema to non-intervention and free trade. The temptation to settle disputes and install better governments abroad is fraught with great danger and many uncertainties.

Protecting our national sovereignty and guaranteeing constitutional protection of our citizens' rights are crucial. Respecting the sovereignty of other nations, even when we're in disagreement with some of their policies, is also necessary. Changing others then becomes a job of persuasion and example—not force and intimidation—just as it is in trying to improve personal moral behavior of our fellow citizens here at home.

Defending our country from outside attack is legitimate and is of the highest priority. Protecting individual liberty should be our goal. This does not mean, however, that our troops should follow our citizens or their investments throughout the world. While foreign visitors should be welcomed, no tax-supported services should be provided. Citizenship should be given with caution, and not automatically by merely stepping over a national boundary for the purpose of giving birth.

A successful and prosperous society comes from such policies and is impossible without a sound free-market economy, one not controlled by a central bank. Avoiding trade wars, devaluations, inflations, deflations, and disruption of free trade with protectionist legislation is impossible under a system of international trade dependent on fluctuating fiat currencies controlled by world central banks and influenced by powerful financial interests. Instability in trade is one of the prime causes of creating conditions that lead to war.

The basic moral principle underpinning a non-interventionist foreign policy is that of rejecting the initiation of force against others. It is based on non-violence and friendship unless attacked, self-determination, and self-defense while avoiding confrontation, even when we disagree with the way other countries run their affairs. It simply means that we should mind our own business and not be influenced by special interests that have an ax to grind or benefits to gain by controlling our foreign policy. Manipulating our country into conflicts that are none of our business and unrelated to national security provides no benefits to us, while exposing us to great risks financially and militarily.

WHAT WOULD A FOREIGN POLICY
FOR PEACE LOOK LIKE?

Our troops would be brought home, systematically but soon. Being in Europe and Japan for over 50 years is long enough. The failure in Vietnam resulted in no occupation and a more westernized country now doing business with the United States. There's no evidence that the military approach in Vietnam was superior to that of trade and friendship. The lack of trade and the imposition of sanctions have not served us well in Cuba or in the Middle East. The mission for our Coast Guard would change if our foreign policy became non-interventionist. They, too, would come home, protect our coast, and stop being the enforcers of bureaucratic laws that either should not exist or should be a state function.

All foreign aid would be discontinued. Most evidence shows that this money rarely helps the poor, but instead solidifies power in the hands of dictators. There's no moral argument that can justify taxing poor people in this country to help rich people in poor countries. Much of the foreign aid, when spent, is channeled back to weapons manufacturers and other special interests in the United States who are the strong promoters of these foreign-aid expenditures. Yet it's all done in the name of humanitarian causes.

A foreign policy of freedom and peace would prompt us to give ample notice before permanently withdrawing from international organizations that have entangled us for over a half a century. US membership in world government was hardly what the Founders envisioned when writing the Constitution. The principle of marque and reprisal would be revived, and specific problems such as terrorist threats would be dealt with on a contract basis incorporating private resources to more accurately target our enemies and reduce the chances of needless and endless war. This would help prevent a continual expansion of conflicts into areas not relating to any immediate threat. By narrowing the target, there's less opportunity for special interests to manipulate our foreign policy to serve the financial needs of the oil and military-weapon industries.

The Logan Act would be repealed, thus allowing maximum freedom of our citizens to volunteer to support their war of choice. This would help diminish the enthusiasm for wars the proponents have used to justify our world policies and diminish the perceived need for a military draft.

If we followed a constitutional policy of non-intervention, we would never have to entertain the aggressive notion of preemptive war based on speculation of what a country might do at some future date. Political pressure by other countries to alter our foreign policy for their benefit would never be a consideration. Commercial interests and our citizens investing overseas could not expect our armies to follow them and protect their profits. A non-interventionist foreign policy would not condone subsidies to our corporations through programs like the Export/ Import Bank and the Overseas Private Investment Corporation. These programs guarantee against losses, while the risk takers want our military to protect their investments from political threats. This current flawed policy removes the tough decisions of when to invest in foreign countries and diminishes the pressure on those particular countries to clean up their political acts in order to entice foreign capital to move into their country. Today's foreign policy encourages bad investments. Ironically this is all done in the name of free trade and capitalism, but it does more to export jobs and businesses than promote free trade. Yet when it fails, capitalism and freedom are blamed.

A non-interventionist foreign policy would go a long way toward preventing 9/11 type attacks. The Department of Homeland Security would be unnecessary, and the military, along with less bureaucracy in our intelligence-gathering agencies, could instead provide the security the new department is supposed to provide. A renewed respect for gun ownership and responsibility for defending one's property would provide additional protection against potential terrorists.

CONCLUSION

There are many reasons why a policy of peace is superior to a policy of war. The principle that we do not have the moral authority to forcibly change governments in foreign lands just because we don't approve of their shortcomings should be our strongest argument, but rarely today is a moral argument in politics worth much.

The practical argument against intervention, because of its record of failure, should certainly prompt all thoughtful people to reconsider what we have been doing for the past many decades.

We should all be aware that war is a failure of relationships between foreign powers. Since this is such a serious matter, our American tradition as established by the Founders made certain that the executive is subservient to the more democratically responsive legislative branch on the issue of war. Therefore, no war is ever to be the prerogative of a president through his unconstitutional use of executive orders, nor should it ever be something where the legal authority comes from an international body, such as NATO or the United Nations. Up until 50 years ago, this had been the American tradition.

Non-intervention prevents the unexpected and unintended consequences that inevitably result from well-intended meddling in the affairs of others.

Countries like Switzerland and Sweden who promote neutrality and non-intervention have benefited, for the most part, by remaining secure and free of war over the centuries. Non-intervention consumes a lot less of the nation's wealth, and with fewer wars, a higher standard of living for all citizens results. But this, of course, is not attractive to the military-industrial complex, which enjoys a higher standard of living at the expense of the taxpayer when a policy of intervention and constant war preparation is carried out.

216

Wisdom, morality, and the Constitution are very unlikely to invade the minds of the policy makers that control our foreign affairs. We have institutionalized foreign intervention over the past 100 years through the teachings of all our major universities and the propaganda that the media spews out. The powerful influence over our policy, both domestic and foreign, is not soon going to go away.

I'm convinced, however, that eventually restraint in our interventions overseas will be guided by a more reasonable constitutional policy. Economic reality will dictate it. Although political pressure in times of severe economic downturn and domestic strife encourage planned distractions overseas, these adventures always cause economic harm due to the economic costs. When the particular country or empire involved overreaches, as we are currently doing, national bankruptcy and a severely weakened currency call the whole process to a halt.

The Soviet system armed with an aggressive plan to spread its empire worldwide collapsed, not because we attacked it militarily, but for financial and economic reasons. They no longer could afford it, and the resources and wealth that it drained finally turned the people against its authoritarian rule.

Maintaining an overseas empire is incompatible with the American tradition of liberty and prosperity. The financial drain and the antagonism that it causes with our enemies, and even our friends, will finally force the American people to reject the policy outright. There will be no choice. Gorbachev just walked away and Yeltsin walked in, with barely a ripple. A non-violent revolution of unbelievable historic magnitude occurred and the Cold War ended. We are not immune from such a similar change.

This Soviet collapse ushered in the age of unparalleled American dominance over the entire world, and along with it allowed the new expanded hot war between the West and the Muslim East. All the hostility directed toward the West built up over the centuries between the two factions is now directed toward the United States. We are now the only power capable of paying for and literally controlling the Middle East and its cherished wealth, and we have not hesitated. Iraq, with its oil and water and agricultural land, is a prime target of our desire to further expand our dominion. The battle is growing tenser with our acceptance and desire to control the Caspian Sea oil riches. But Russia, now licking its wounds and once again accumulating wealth, will not sit idly by and watch the American empire engulf this region. When time runs out for us, we can be sure Russia will once again be ready to fight for control of all those resources in countries adjacent to her borders. And expect the same for China and India. Who knows? Maybe one day even Japan will return to the ancient art of using force to occupy the cherished territories in her region of the world.

The most we can hope for will be, once the errors of our ways are acknowledged and we can no longer afford our militarism, to reestablish the moral principle that underpins the policy of "peace, commerce and honest friendship with all nations, entangling alliances with none." Our modern-day war hawks do not respect this American principle, nor do they understand how the love of liberty drove the Founders in their great battle against tyranny.

We must prepare for the day when our financial bankruptcy and the failure of our effort at world domination are apparent. The solution to such a crisis can be easily found in our Constitution and in our traditions. But ultimately, the love of liberty can only come from a change in the hearts and minds of the people and with an answered prayer for the blessings of divine intervention. ■

This statement, which is really simply a list of questions, became rather popular on the internet. A number of the questions look on our foreign policy in general, as well as the need to make war in a way that accords with our oath of office to uphold the Constitution.

September 10, 2002
QUESTIONS THAT WON'T BE ASKED ABOUT IRAQ
HON. RON PAUL of TEXAS
IN THE HOUSE OF REPRESENTATIVES

Mr. Speaker, soon we hope to have hearings on the pending war with Iraq. I am concerned there are some questions that won't be asked, and maybe will not even be allowed to be asked. Here are some questions I would like answered by those who are urging us to start this war.

1. Is it not true that the reason we did not bomb the Soviet Union at the height of the Cold War was because we knew they *could* retaliate?

2. Is it not also true that we are willing to bomb Iraq now because we know it *cannot* retaliate, which just confirms that there is *no real threat*?

3. Is it not true that those who argue that even *with* inspections, we cannot be sure that Hussein might be hiding weapons, at the same time imply that we can be surer that weapons exist *in the absence of* inspections?

4. Is it not true that the UN's International Atomic Energy Agency was able to complete its yearly verification mission to Iraq just this year with Iraqi cooperation?

5. Is it not true that the intelligence community has been unable to develop a case tying Iraq to global terrorism at all, much less the attacks on the United States last year? Does anyone remember that 15 of the 19 hijackers came from Saudi Arabia and that none came from Iraq?

6. Was former CIA counter-terrorism chief Vincent Cannistraro wrong when he recently said there is no confirmed evidence of Iraq's links to terrorism?

7. Is it not true that the CIA has concluded that there is no evidence that a Prague meeting between 9/11 hijacker Atta and Iraqi intelligence took place?

8. Is it not true that northern Iraq, where the administration claimed al-Qaeda was hiding out, is in the control of our "allies," the Kurds?

9. Is it not true that the vast majority of al-Qaeda leaders who escaped appear to have safely made their way to Pakistan, another of our so-called allies?

10. Has anyone noticed that Afghanistan is rapidly sinking into total chaos, with bombings and assassinations becoming daily occurrences, and that according to a recent UN report the al-Qaeda "is, by all accounts, alive and well and poised to strike again, how, when, and where it chooses"?

11. Why are we taking precious military and intelligence resources away from tracking down those who did attack the United States—and who may again attack the United States—and using them to invade countries that have not attacked the United States?

12. Would an attack on Iraq not just confirm the Arab world's worst suspicions about the US, and isn't this what bin Laden wanted?

13. How can Hussein be compared to Hitler when he has no navy or air force, and now has an army one-fifth the size of twelve years ago, which even then proved totally inept at defending the country?

14. Is it not true that the constitutional power to declare war is exclusively that of the Congress? Should presidents, contrary to the Constitution, allow Congress to concur only when pressured by public opinion? Are presidents permitted to rely on the UN for permission to go to war?

15. Are you aware of a Pentagon report studying charges that thousands of Kurds in one village were gassed by the Iraqis, which found no conclusive evidence that Iraq was responsible, that Iran occupied the

very city involved, and that evidence indicated the type of gas used was more likely controlled by Iran not Iraq?

16. Is it not true that anywhere between 100,000 and 300,000 US soldiers have suffered from Persian Gulf War Syndrome from the first Gulf War, and that thousands may have died?

17. Are we prepared for possibly thousands of American casualties in a war against a country that does not have the capacity to attack the United States?

18. Are we willing to bear the economic burden of a 100 billion dollar war against Iraq, with oil prices expected to skyrocket and further rattle an already shaky American economy? How about an estimated 30 years occupation of Iraq that some have deemed necessary to "build democracy" there?

19. Iraq's alleged violations of UN resolutions are given as reason to initiate an attack, yet is it not true that hundreds of UN Resolutions have been ignored by various countries without penalty?

20. Did former president Bush not cite the UN Resolution of 1990 as the reason he could *not* march into Baghdad, while supporters of a new attack assert that it is the very reason we *can* march into Baghdad?

21. Is it not true that, contrary to current claims, the no-fly zones were set up by Britain and the United States without specific approval from the United Nations?

22. If we claim membership in the international community and conform to its rules only when it pleases us, does this not serve to undermine our position, directing animosity toward us by both friend and foe?

23. How can our declared goal of bringing democracy to Iraq be believable when we prop up dictators throughout the Middle East and support military tyrants like Musharaf in Pakistan, who overthrew a democratically-elected president?

24. Are you familiar with the 1994 Senate Hearings that revealed the U.S. knowingly supplied chemical and biological materials to Iraq during the Iran-Iraq war and as late as 1992, including *after* the alleged Iraqi gas attack on a Kurdish village?

25. Did we not assist Saddam Hussein's rise to power by supporting and encouraging his invasion of Iran? Is it honest to criticize Saddam now for his invasion of Iran, which at the time we actively supported?

26. Is it not true that preventive war is synonymous with an act of aggression, and has never been considered a moral or legitimate U.S. policy?

27. Why do the oil company executives strongly support this war if oil is not the real reason we plan to take over Iraq?

28. Why is it that those who never wore a uniform and are confident that they won't have to personally fight this war are more anxious for this war than our generals?

29. What is the moral argument for attacking a nation that has not initiated aggression against us, and could not if it wanted?

30. Where does the Constitution grant us permission to wage war for any reason other than self-defense?

31. Is it not true that a war against Iraq rejects the sentiments of the time-honored Treaty of Westphalia, nearly 400 years ago, that countries should never go into another for the purpose of regime change?

32. Is it not true that the more civilized a society, the less likely disagreements will be settled by war?

33. Is it not true that, since World War II, Congress has not declared war, and (not coincidentally) we have not since then had a clear-cut victory?

34. Is it not true that Pakistan, especially through its intelligence services, was an active supporter and key organizer of the Taliban?

35. Why don't those who want war bring a formal declaration of war resolution to the floor of Congress? ■

Political considerations often drive the decision making in Washington. I tried here to warn that the impending war decision would upset the Republican majorities in Washington.

September 18, 2002
WAR IS A POLITICAL MISTAKE
HON. RON PAUL of TEXAS
IN THE HOUSE OF REPRESENTATIVES

Mr. Speaker, I have for years advocated a moral and constitutional approach to our foreign policy. This has been done in the sincerest belief that a policy of peace, trade, and friendship with all nations is far superior in all respects to a policy of war, protectionism and confrontation. But in the Congress I find, with regards to foreign affairs, no interest in following the precepts of the Constitution and the advice of our early presidents.

Interventionism, internationalism, inflationism, protectionism, jingoism, and bellicosity are much more popular in our nation's capital than a policy of restraint. I have heard all the arguments on why we must immediately invade and occupy Iraq and have observed that there are only a few hardy souls left in the Congress who are trying to stop this needless, senseless and dangerous war. They have adequately refuted every one of the excuses for this war of aggression; but, obviously, either no one listens, or the unspoken motives for this invasion silence those tempted to dissent.

But the tragic and most irresponsible excuse for the war rhetoric is now emerging in the political discourse. We now hear rumblings that the vote is all about politics, the November elections, and the control of the U.S. Congress, that is, the main concern is political power. Can one imagine delaying the declaration of war against Japan after Pearl Harbor for political reasons? Or can one imagine forcing a vote on the issue of war before an election for political gain? Can anyone believe there are those who would foment war rhetoric for political gain at the expense of those who are called to fight and might even die if the war does not go as planned?

I do not want to believe it is possible, but rumors are rampant that looking weak on the war issue is considered to be unpatriotic and a risky political position to take before the November elections. Taking pleasure in the fact that this might place many politicians in a difficult position is a sobering thought indeed.

There is a bit of irony over all of this political posturing on a vote to condone a war of aggression and force some Members into a tough vote. Guess what: **contrary to conventional wisdom, war is never politically beneficial to the politicians who promote it.** Presidents Wilson and Roosevelt were reelected by promising to stay out of war. Remember, the party in power during the Korean War was routed in 1952 by a general who promised to stop the bloodshed. Vietnam, which started with overwhelming support and hype and jingoistic fervor, ended President Johnson's political career in disgrace and humiliation. The most significant plight on the short term of President Kennedy was his effort at regime change in Cuba and the fate he met at the Bay of Pigs. Even Persian Gulf War I, thought at the time to be a tremendous victory, with its aftermath still lingering, did not serve President Bush, Sr.'s reelection efforts in 1992.

War is not politically beneficial for two reasons: innocent people die, and the economy is always damaged. These two things, after the dust settles from the hype and the propaganda, always make the people unhappy. **The euphoria associated with the dreams of grandiose and painless victories is replaced by the stark reality of death, destruction, and economic pain.** Instead of euphoria, we end up with heartache as we did after the Bay of Pigs, Korea, Vietnam, Somalia, and Lebanon.

Since no one wants to hear any more of morality and constitutionality and justice, possibly some will listen to the politics of war, since that is what drives so many. A token victory at the polls this fall by using a vote on the war as a lever will be to little avail. It may not even work in the short run. Surely, history shows that war is never a winner, especially when the people who have to pay, fight, and die for it come to realize that the war was not even necessary and had nothing to do with national security or fighting for freedom, but was promoted by special interests who stood to gain from taking over a sovereign country.

Mr. Speaker, peace is always superior to war; it is also a political winner. ■

War costs the precious blood of our soldiers but also has cost our national treasure. War always makes government bigger and more expensive. When people suggest war will pay for itself, this must always be challenged.

September 24, 2002
CAN WE AFFORD THIS WAR?
HON. RON PAUL of TEXAS
IN THE HOUSE OF REPRESENTATIVES

Mr. Speaker, a casual analysis of the world economy shows it rapidly deteriorating into recession, with a possible depression on the horizon. Unemployment is sharply rising with price inflation rampant, despite official government inflationary reports. The world's stock markets continue to collapse, even after trillions of dollars in losses have been recorded in the past two years. These losses already have set historic records.

With government revenues shrinking at all levels, we find deficits exploding. Our national debt is currently rising at $450 billion per year. Confidence in corporate America has shrunk to levels usually reserved for governments alone.

Government spending in all areas is skyrocketing, much of it out of the control of the politicians, who show little concern. Yet we are expected to believe our government leaders who say that we are experiencing a recovery and that a return to grand prosperity is just around the corner. The absence of capital formation, savings, and corporate profits are totally ignored.

Evidence abounds that our $350 billion DOD budget and the $40 billion spent on intelligence gathering and our immigration policies have failed miserably in protecting our homeland. In spite of the rhetoric and new legislation attacking our civil liberties, we are as vulnerable to outside attack as before.

Our military is drastically smaller than a decade ago, and we are spread around the world and involved in world conflicts more than we have ever been before.

We have run a huge current account deficit for 15 years and massively expanded our money supply. No one should be surprised that the dollar is weakening and the commodity, natural resources, and precious metal prices are rising.

Oil prices are over $31 a barrel, and predictions are that they can easily go up another $15 to $20 if international tensions grow.

But the only talk here in the nation's capitol is about when, not if, we must initiate a war that even the administration admits could cost $200 billion. Some are not even embarrassed to gloat about the political benefits for those who preach war over those who prefer negotiations, diplomacy and containment. The fact that the Arab nations are overwhelmingly opposed to an attack on Iraq and are joined by the European Community is of no concern to those who demand war regardless of any circumstance.

Eighty percent of the American people now report they believe that a war with Iraq will increase the chances of our suffering from a new terrorist attack. If this is true, we become less secure with an attack on Iraq, since little has been done to correct the deficiencies in the intelligence gathering agencies and our immigration policies.

No credible evidence has been produced that Iraq has or is close to having nuclear weapons. No evidence exists to show that Iraq harbors al Qaeda terrorists. Quite to the contrary, experts on this region recognize Hussein as an enemy of the al Qaeda and a foe to Islamic fundamentalism. Many other nations pose much greater threats to world peace. Yet no one is clamoring for war against them. Saddam Hussein is now weaker than ever.

Reports are now appearing that we are negotiating with allies to share in the oil bounty once Iraq is occupied in order to get support for our invasion from various countries around the world.

Our national debt is over $6 trillion and is increasing by nearly half a trillion dollars a year. Since Social Security funds are all placed in the general revenues and spent and all funds are fungible, honest accounting, of which there has been a shortage lately, dictates that a $200 billion war must jeopardize Social Security funding. This is something the American

224

people deserve to know.

Since there are limits to borrowing and taxing, but no limits to the Fed printing money to cover our deficit, we can be assured this will occur. This guarantees that Social Security checks will never stop coming, but it also guarantees that the dollars that all retired people receive will buy less. We have already seen this happening in providing medical services. A cheap dollar, that is, an inflated dollar, is a sinister and deceitful way of cutting benefits.

Rest assured, a $200 billion hit on the economy will have economic consequences, and the elderly retirees on fixed incomes, and especially Social Security beneficiaries, will suffer the greatest burden of policy, reflecting a belief that our country is so rich that it can afford both guns and butter. Remember, we have tried that before.

The tragedy is that once the flaw in policy is discovered, it is too late to prevent the pain and suffering, and only finger pointing occurs. Now is the only time we can give serious attention to the true cost of assuming the burden of an endless task of being the world's policeman and starting wars that have nothing to do with defense or national security.

A nation suffering from recession can ill afford a foreign policy that encourages unnecessary military action that will run up huge deficits. Congress ought to pause a moment, and carefully contemplate the consequences of the decisions we are about to make in the coming days. ■

In the House International Relations Committee I introduced a resolution calling for a Declaration of War against Iraq, to point out that it is the constitutional duty of Congress to make these decisions, rather than giving them to the President. Nobody voted for the resolution despite an overwhelming number favoring war. The debate shows that Congress is not accidentally neglecting its duty in this area, instead it is purposely relinquishing its constitutional responsibility.

October 2, 2002
AMENDMENT TO H.J. RESOLUTION 114
HON. RON PAUL of TEXAS
IN THE HOUSE OF REPRESENTATIVES

Chairman HYDE. The Clerk will report the amendment of Mr. Paul.

Ms. RUSH. Amendment offered by Mr. Paul: Strike all after the Resolving clause and insert the following:

Mr. PAUL. I ask unanimous consent that it be considered as read and that the three amendments be considered as one.

Chairman HYDE. Without objection, so ordered. The gentleman is recognized for 5 minutes.

Mr. PAUL. Five or ten?

Chairman HYDE. I guess 10. I tried to get away with something.

Mr. PAUL. Thank you, Mr. Chairman. Mr. Chairman, this is a substitute amendment and it is a simple, clear-cut, straightforward, front-door declaration of war. No back door to war, it is the front door. I am depending on you, Mr. Chairman, to make sure it doesn't pass.

Chairman HYDE. A very wise move.

Mr. LANTOS. You may count on me, too.

Mr. PAUL. Mr. Chairman, I will be voting with you and the Administration on this bill, on this particular substitute. But nevertheless, I consider what I am doing here very important and not frivolous, because this is a declaration of war. As I mentioned before, in the resolution that we have before us, we never mention war. We never mention article I, section 8. We only talk about transferring the power and the authority to the president to wage war when he pleases. I consider that unconstitutional.

Of course, we cite the UN 25 times as back-up evidence for what we are doing, so I think it is appropriate for us to think about our oath of office and the Constitution, what America is all about. Because, quite frankly, I think we have suffered tremendously over the last 50 or 60 years, since World War II, since we have rejected the constitutional process of Congress declaring war, because we don't win wars but men die. One hundred thousand men have died in that period of time, and many hundreds of thousands wounded, and many ignored. The Persian Gulf syndrome ignored, yet over 100,000 may be suffering from that.

I see this as very important that we should be up front with the American people, because, if not, we can well slip into war once again. And that, to me, is not what we are supposed to be doing. We are supposed to be very up-front in doing this as we have been obligated to do.

I would like to read a quote from a former President of a few years back. He had something to do with the Constitution. He speaks for that time. Of course, most people believe today that the Constitution is a living, ever-changing document, that the truth is not everlasting and that the Founders are irrelevant. But we still have the law on the book. We haven't changed the law. And this quote emphasizes how they looked at foreign policy and the separation of powers, because at the time of our Revolution they had firsthand experience of what happened in Europe when the King or one leader has the authority and the power to go to war.

So it was strongly emphasized by those who were writing the Constitution of where this war power would reside. It was put into the legislative branch of government, which was closest to the people. That is very important, because our failure to win wars is one of the strongest motivations on my part to address this subject.

Quite frankly, I believe that the Persian Gulf War, one, never ended. We are just dealing with one more segment of a war that is perpetual because it was not declared. We half-heartedly committed, we had the restraints of the United Nations, we did not go for the right reasons, and we didn't win. Therefore, we didn't do the job that should have been done in 1990 if we had declared war.

The same thing could have been said about Korea and Vietnam. It is time we address the process just as emphatically as we address the pros and cons of whether this country should go to war.

Now, let me quote from James Madison. Madison said in 1798:
The Constitution supposes what the history of all governments demonstrate, that the Executive is the branch of power most interested in war and most prone to it. It has accordingly, with studied care, vested the question of war in the legislature.

We have now just carelessly over the years, and today once again, easily given this up.

You say, no, this doesn't necessarily mean that, and we have done before. We have allowed our Presidents to do this. But if the President can go to war, this is the permission that we are giving.

It is interesting to note that in the United Nations Charter, you do not have a provision that says well, when you want to declare war, here you come, and these are the procedures. When the United Nations gets involved, we are always declaring the use of force for peace. But it gets difficult and it gets muddied, and it is murky under today's conditions because there is no war going on in Iraq. Yet we have not exhausted the vehicle of negotiations and other things that could be done.

So, this is why, unfortunately, I have very little faith and confidence this will be the solution to solve the problem in Iraq and the Middle East. As a matter of fact, if that happens, this is a dramatic reversal of 60 years of history. It is not going to happen.

We have not dealt with the unintended consequences, what we are dealing with today in the sense that the wars continue, but the unintended consequences. And I disagree with the previous speaker who said that

227

this resolution is not dealing with preemptive strikes. That is what the whole thing is about, **allowing the President the authority to do a preemptive strike against a nation that has not committed aggression against us.** This is the whole issue.

So I would say that this is the time that we ought to not only think about the issue of the pros and cons of war, but the issue of how much of our sovereignty we give away to the United Nations and how many restraints will be placed on us, not only now as we try to satisfy everybody in the United Nations, but later on as well.

It was said we didn't finish the war in 1990 because of the resolution not permitting us to do this, and therefore it wasn't done, but we were following the rules. Of course, that is why you need—if you commit the country and commit the young people and commit the taxpayer to war— you need to call it war.

So those of you who are for war, vote for this. Those who are opposed to it should vote against the war, because we don't believe it is necessary to go to war right now. If you are honest with yourself, this is what you should do. Otherwise you are perpetuating a fraud on the American people, perpetuating a system that has not worked, perpetuating a system that ends too often in chaos.

I just don't think that is good. I really don't. I think we should think about this very carefully and make sure that we follow the process as well as our best judgments on war.

Some have argued that in this case what you are saying is we would tie the hands of the President. We would tie the hands of the President. Well, that sounds a little strong. But you know what? That is what was intended in the Constitution. That is what Madison is talking about, tying the hands of one person to make the decision to go to war. Therefore, I think—I want and desire so much to think more seriously, because if there is a declaration of war, we will fight to win it and it won't drag on and be endless and lead to another one.

At this time, I reserve the balance of my time.

Mr. DELAHUNT. Will the gentleman yield?

If the gentleman will yield, much of what you say truly resonates, because I do concur. I do believe this is about a doctrine of preemption. I think we all feel uneasy about it. I am not denying that inherent in a Nation State, if there is a real clear, convincing threat, that that doctrine does not apply. I think it should apply.

But what concerns me is that the standards that are being set by the underlying resolution here are so low that it could very well create a new concept in the international order that, as you described, will give other states, the most obvious examples being India and Pakistan, the right to say to the international community we are going to launch a nuclear strike, when it ought not to be an option.

I mean, there are many rogue nations, if you will. We have discussed them here today: Iran, North Korea. There is a long litany of nations that possess weapons of mass destruction.

Mr. PAUL. Excuse me, if I might. I would like to reserve a few minutes of my time. Thank you.

Chairman HYDE. You have 3 seconds left, Mr. Paul.

Mr. PAUL. I allow you to finish my time. Mr. Chairman, you were watching closely.

Chairman HYDE. Yes, with great interest. Are you through?

Mr. DELAHUNT. I yield.

Chairman HYDE. All right. The Chair yields himself the 10 minutes in opposition to this.

It is fascinating to go back in history and see how our Constitution was drafted and what it means. **There are things in the Constitution that have been overtaken by events, by time. Declaration of war is one. Letters of mark and reprisal are others. There are things no longer relevant to a modern society.**

The problem with a declaration of war is that is a formal step taken by a nation. And when you do that, you kick in other laws. Enemy aliens—people suddenly become who are of German extraction or Saudi extraction, depending on whom you are declaring war against, suddenly become enemy aliens. Trading with the enemy becomes effective. Therefore, if a country is trading with your enemy, they are your enemy.

Most importantly and psychologically, if you declare war, if we had declared war on Vietnam, China would have had to declare war on us, and then the Soviet Union, not to be outdone fraternally, would have had to declare war on us. And you start a chain of events. That is the last thing you want to do. You want to isolate these conflicts. You don't want them to metastasize.

Declaration of war metastasizes conflict.

Insurance policies are invalidated in time of war. There are so many consequences, criminal statutes. So there are laws affecting military personnel in time of war and in time of peace.

Now, the Congress always has the last word in war and peace because we control the purse strings. We could introduce a bill and rush it through that would say no funds appropriated herein may be used to pay for an expedition to France or to the Caribbean. Congress always has the last word because we control the purse strings. But now this resolution we are dealing with today does not declare war. It does not approach war. War may never happen. If we mean what we say and we say what we mean and we have a reasonably tough posture, we may avoid war.

Why declare war if you don't have to? We are saying to the President, use your judgment. We know you have tried to have inspections work. We have tried the UN, they have been made a fool of for 11 years now. The League of Nations was muscular compared to the UN That is the situation we are in now.

So to demand that we declare war is to strengthen something to death. You have got a hammerlock on this situation, and it is not called for. Inappropriate, anachronistic, it isn't done anymore because it has the effect of pyramiding when what you want to do is to isolate.

So with great respect for the gentleman's knowledge of political science, I suggest this is inappropriate, and I would hope it would be defeated.

Mr. Green wants to say something.

Mr. GREEN. In many ways, our colleague Dr. Paul is the constitutional conscience of the House, and I appreciate it. But one thing I wanted not to leave unchallenged.

He said in his remarks that Iraq is a country which has committed no acts of aggression against the U.S. There are many people who would disagree with that, not the least of whom would be the pilots in the no-fly zone, who are routinely fired upon. I think we have to be a little bit careful in our remarks.

Chairman HYDE. Mr. Lantos.

Mr. LANTOS. Thank you, Mr. Chairman.

I think you handled, as you always do, the issue perfectly, but I would like to just add a footnote. I have great affection for my friend from Texas, but I detect a touch of frivolity and mischief in his amendment, because I do not believe—I do not believe he is serious about this amendment, not only because of all the reasons you have cited, but because the resolution we are considering is aimed at avoiding war. It is geared to having unfettered, unlimited, foolproof inspections, and not a war.

The possibility of using force is the only mechanism of potentially persuading Saddam Hussein to allow inspections, to have the destruction

230

of weapons of mass destruction be brought about by nonviolent means. So I think, while at one level it is a frivolous proposal, which I strongly urge my colleagues to reject, at a more profound level, it totally misunderstands or deliberately misinterprets the underlying resolution.

It is our hope that we can move to inspections which will achieve the goal of finding and destroying Iraq's weapons of mass destruction without a single shot being fired. That is my earnest hope, that is the earnest hope of, I take it, all of us who support the resolution.

Thank you, Mr. Chairman.

Chairman HYDE. Thank you.

Mr. Royce.

Mr. ROYCE. Thank you, Mr. Chairman.

And I think a formal declaration of war, as opposed to an authorization to use force should Iraq not disarm, is going to have consequences under domestic law, but it is also going to have consequences under international law. And I think for those of us here in Congress we have got to contemplate the fact that it is going to have the effect of transferring power, conferring power to the president and to the Attorney General and to the Pentagon that they cannot otherwise exercise. One of those powers is going to be the power to wiretap, notwithstanding what we do in Congress, once there is a declaration of war, they are automatically going to be able to wiretap.

Another concern would be what we would do to insurance contracts, because once you have a declaration of war, you bring into effect an exclusionary clause in the contracts that are out there. I think also you have to consider the fact that we are moving away from our joint objective here, which is to leverage Iraq to disarm, to have a credible threat against that regime, the threat of use of force. And instead we are abandoning that, if we go with a formal declaration of war, we then take on these international and domestic changes under our Constitution.

And I wanted to ask the author if he contemplated those changes. Should we actually pass this initiative? What do we do about them?

Mr. PAUL. Would the gentleman yield?

Yes, I certainly did. But that emphasizes and makes my point how serious this is, because you are ignoring how serious war is. And then we know that is what we are talking about here today. No matter what you call it, we are talking about a resolution that permits the President to wage war.

Mr. ROYCE. It permits the president to wage war, and the reason we are going through this exercise is to present a credible threat to the

Iraqi regime so that they do disarm.

And you move us off of that strategy on a completely different track, a completely different track with this particular amendment. And that is why I oppose the amendment.

I thank you.

Chairman HYDE. The question occurs on the amendment offered by the gentleman from Texas. All those in favor, say aye.

Opposed, nay.

Mr. PAUL. I ask for a recorded vote. ■

The Constitution rests war-making authority with Congress in an artful way, and with good reason. Here I point toward the folly of ignoring that art, which is also the highest law of our land.

October 3, 2002
IS CONGRESS RELEVANT WITH REGARDS TO WAR?
HON. RON PAUL of TEXAS
IN THE HOUSE OF REPRESENTATIVES

The last time Congress declared war was on December 11, 1941, against Germany in response to its formal declaration of war against the United States. This was accomplished with wording that took less than one-third of a page, without any nitpicking arguments over precise language. Yet it was a clear declaration of who the enemy was and what had to be done. And in three-and-a-half hours, this was accomplished. A similar resolve came from the declaration of war against Japan three days earlier. Likewise, a clear-cut victory was achieved against Japan.

Many Americans have been forced into war since that time on numerous occasions, with no congressional declaration of war and with essentially no victories. Today's world political condition is as chaotic as ever. We're still in Korea and we're still fighting the Persian Gulf War that started in 1990.

The process by which we've entered wars over the past 57 years, and the inconclusive results of each war since that time are obviously related to Congress' abdication of its responsibility regarding war, given to it by Article I Section 8 of the Constitution.

Congress has either ignored its responsibility entirely over these years, or transferred the war power to the executive branch by a near majority vote of its Members, without consideration of it by the states as an amendment required by the Constitution.

Congress is about to circumvent the Constitution and avoid the tough decision of whether war should be declared by transferring this monumental decision-making power regarding war to the president. Once again, the process is being abused. Odds are, since a clear-cut decision and commitment by the people through their representatives are not being made, the results will be as murky as before. We will be required to follow the confusing dictates of the UN, since that is where the ultimate authority to invade Iraq is coming from—rather than from the American people and the U.S. Constitution.

Controversial language is being hotly debated in an effort to satisfy political constituencies and for Congress to avoid responsibility of whether to go to war. So far the proposed resolution never mentions war, only empowering the president to use force at his will to bring about peace. Rather strange language indeed!

A declaration of war limits the presidential powers, narrows the focus, and implies a precise end point to the conflict. A declaration of war makes Congress assume the responsibilities directed by the Constitution for this very important decision, rather than assume that if the major decision is left to the president and a poor result occurs, it will be his fault, not that of Congress. Hiding behind the transfer of the war power to the executive through the War Powers Resolution of 1973 will hardly suffice.

However, the modern way we go to war is even more complex and deceptive. We must also write language that satisfies the UN and all our allies. Congress gladly transfers the legislative prerogatives to declare war to the president, and the legislative and the executive branch both acquiesce in transferring our sovereign rights to the UN, an un-elected international government. No wonder the language of the resolution grows in length and incorporates justification for starting this war by citing UN Resolutions.

In order to get more of what we want from the United Nations, we rejoined UNESCO, which Ronald Reagan had bravely gotten us out of, and promised millions of dollars of U.S. taxpayer support to run this international agency started by Sir Julian Huxley. In addition, we read of promises by our administration that once we control Iraqi oil, it will be available for allies like France and Russia, who have been reluctant to join our efforts.

What a difference from the days when a declaration of war was clean and precise and accomplished by a responsible Congress and an informed people!

A great irony of all this is that the United Nations Charter doesn't permit declaring war, especially against a nation that has been in a state of peace for 12 years. The UN can only declare peace. Remember, it wasn't a war in Korea; it was only a police action to bring about peace. But at least in Korea and Vietnam, there was fighting going on, so it was a bit easier to stretch the language than it is today regarding Iraq. Since Iraq doesn't even have an air force or a navy, is incapable of waging a war, and remains defenseless against the overwhelming powers of the United States and the British, it's difficult to claim that we're going into Iraq to restore peace.

History will eventually show that, if we launch this attack, the real victims will be the innocent Iraqi civilians who despise Saddam Hussein and are terrified of the coming bombs that will destroy their cities.

The greatest beneficiaries of the attack may well be Osama bin Laden and the al Qaeda. Some in the media have already suggested that the al Qaeda may be encouraging the whole event. Unintended consequences will occur—what will come from this attack is still entirely unknown.

It's a well-known fact that the al Qaeda are not allies of Saddam Hussein, and despise the secularization and partial westernization of Iraqi culture. They would welcome the chaos that's about to come. This will give them a chance to influence post-Saddam Hussein Iraq. The attack, many believe, will confirm to the Arab world that indeed the Christian West has once again attacked the Muslim East, providing radical fundamentalists a tremendous boost for recruitment.

An up or down vote on declaring war against Iraq would not pass the Congress, and the president has no intention of asking for it. This is unfortunate, because if the process were carried out in a constitutional fashion, the American people and the U.S. Congress would vote "No" on assuming responsibility for this war.

Transferring authority to wage war, calling it permission to use force to fight for peace in order to satisfy the UN Charter, which replaces the Article I, Section 8 war power provision, is about as close to 1984 "newspeak" as we will ever get in the real world.

Not only is it sad that we have gone so far astray from our Constitution, but it's also dangerous for world peace and threatens our liberties here at home. ■

Congress would debate an "authorization to use force" instead of a declaration of war. Not only was this unconstitutional, it was the kind of political cowardice that dishonors the courage of our service members.

October 8, 2002
STATEMENT OPPOSING THE USE OF MILITARY FORCE AGAINST IRAQ
HON. RON PAUL of TEXAS
IN THE HOUSE OF REPRESENTATIVES

Madam Speaker, I rise in opposition to this resolution. The wisdom of the war is one issue, but the process and the philosophy behind our foreign policy are important issues as well. I have come to the conclusion that I see no threat to our national security. There is no convincing evidence that Iraq is capable of threatening the security of this country, and, therefore, very little reason, if any, to pursue a war.

But I am very interested also in the process that we are pursuing. This is not a resolution to declare war. We know that. This is a resolution that does something much different. This resolution transfers the responsibility, the authority, and the power of the Congress to the president so he can declare war when, and if, he wants to. He has not even indicated that he wants to go to war or has to go to war; but he will make the full decision, not the Congress, not the people through the Congress of this country in that manner.

It does something else, though. One-half of the resolution delivers this power to the president, but it also instructs him to enforce UN resolutions. I happen to think I would rather listen to the president when he talks about unilateralism and national security interests, than accept this responsibility to follow all of the rules and the dictates of the United Nations. That is what this resolution does. It instructs him to follow all of the resolutions.

But an important aspect of the philosophy and the policy we are endorsing here is the preemption doctrine. This should not be passed off lightly. It has been done to some degree in the past, but never been put into law that we will preemptively strike another nation that has not attacked us. No matter what the arguments may be, this policy is new—and it will have ramifications for our future, and it will have ramifications for the future of the world because other countries will adopt this same philosophy.

I also want to mention very briefly something that has essentially never been brought up. **For more than a thousand years, there has been a doctrine and Christian definition of what a just war is all about. I think this effort and this plan to go to war comes up short of that doctrine.** First, it says that there has to be an act of aggression; and there has not been an act of aggression against the United States. We are 6,000 miles from their shores.

Also, it says that all efforts at negotiations must be exhausted. I do not believe that is the case. It seems to me like the opposition, the enemy, right now is begging for more negotiations.

Also, the Christian doctrine says that the proper authority must be responsible for initiating the war. I do not believe that proper authority can be transferred to the president or to the United Nations.

But a very practical reason why I have a great deal of reservation has to do with the issue of no-win wars that we have been involved in for so long. Once we give up our responsibilities from here in the House and the Senate to make these decisions, it seems that we depend on the United Nations for our instructions; and that is why, as a Member earlier indicated, essentially we are already at war. That is correct. We are still in the Persian Gulf War. We have been bombing for 12 years, and the reason President Bush, Sr., did not go all the way? He said the UN did not give him permission to.

My argument is when we go to war through the back door, we are more likely to have the wars last longer and not have resolution of the wars, such as we had in Korea and Vietnam. We ought to consider this very seriously.

Also it is said we are wrong about the act of aggression. There has been an act of aggression against us because Saddam Hussein has shot at our airplanes. The fact that he has missed every single airplane for 12 years, and tens of thousands of sorties have been flown, indicates the strength of our enemy, an impoverished, Third World nation that does not have an air force, anti-aircraft weapons, or a navy.

But the indication is because he shot at us, therefore, it is an act of aggression. However, what is cited as the reason for us flying over the no-fly zone comes from UN Resolution 688, which instructs us to contribute to humanitarian relief in the Kurdish and the Shiite areas. It says nothing about no-fly zones, and it says nothing about bombing missions over Iraq.

So to declare that we have been attacked, I do not believe for a minute that this fulfills the requirement that we are retaliating against aggression by this country. There is a need for us to assume responsibility for the declaration of war, and also to prepare the American people for the taxes that will be raised and the possibility of a military draft which may well come.

I must oppose this resolution which, regardless of what many have tried to claim, will lead us into war with Iraq. This resolution is not a declaration of war, however, and that is an important point; this resolution transfers the constitutionally-mandated congressional authority to declare wars to the executive branch. This resolution tells the president that he alone has the authority to determine when, where, why, and how war will be declared. It merely asks the president to pay us a courtesy call a couple of days after the bombing starts to let us know what is going on. This is exactly what our Founding Fathers cautioned against when crafting our form of government: most had just left behind a monarchy where the power to declare war rested in one individual. It is this they most wished to avoid.

As James Madison wrote in 1798, "The Constitution supposes what the history of all governments demonstrates, that the executive is the branch of power most interested in war, and most prone to it. It has, accordingly, with studied care, vested the question of war in the legislature."

Some—even some in this body—have claimed that this constitutional requirement is an anachronism, and that those who insist on following the founding legal document of this country are just being frivolous. I could not disagree more.

Mr. Speaker, for more than the dozen years I have spent as a federal legislator, I have taken a particular interest in foreign affairs and especially the politics of the Middle East. From my seat on the international relations committee, I have had the opportunity to review dozens of documents and to sit through numerous hearings and mark-up sessions regarding the issues of both Iraq and international terrorism.

Back in 1997 and 1998, I publicly spoke out against the actions of the Clinton administration, which I believed was moving us once again toward war with Iraq. I believe the genesis of our current policy was unfortunately being set at that time. Indeed, many of the same voices who then demanded that the Clinton administration attack Iraq are now demanding that the Bush administration attack Iraq. It is unfortunate that these individuals are using the tragedy of September 11, 2001, as cover to force their long-standing desire to see an American invasion of Iraq. Despite all of the information to which I have access, I remain very skeptical that the nation of Iraq poses a serious and imminent terrorist threat to the United States. If I were convinced of such a threat, I would support going to war, as I did when I supported President Bush by voting to give him both the authority and the necessary funding to fight the war on terror.

Mr. Speaker, consider some of the following claims presented by supporters of this resolution, and contrast them with the following facts:

Claim: Iraq has consistently demonstrated its willingness to use force against the U.S. through its firing on our planes patrolling the UN-established "no-fly zones."

Reality: The "no-fly zones" were never authorized by the United Nations, nor was their 12-year patrol by American and British fighter planes sanctioned by the United Nations. Under UN Security Council Resolution 688 (April, 1991), Iraq's repression of the Kurds and Shiites was condemned, but there was no authorization for "no-fly zones," much less air strikes. The resolution only calls for member states to "contribute to humanitarian relief" in the Kurd and Shiite areas. Yet the British and the U.S. have been bombing Iraq in the "no-fly zones" for 12 years. While one can only condemn any country firing on our pilots, isn't the real argument whether we should continue to bomb Iraq relentlessly? Just since 1998, some 40,000 sorties have been flown over Iraq.

Claim: Iraq is an international sponsor of terrorism.

Reality: According to the latest edition of the State Department's "Patterns of Global Terrorism," Iraq sponsors several minor Palestinian groups, the Mujahedin-e-Khalq (MEK), and the Kurdistan Workers' Party (PKK). None of these carries out attacks against the United States. As a matter of fact, the MEK (an Iranian organization located in Iraq) has enjoyed broad congressional support over the years. According to last year's "Patterns of Global Terrorism," Iraq has not been involved in terrorist activity against the West since 1993—the alleged attempt against former President Bush.

Claim: Iraq tried to assassinate President Bush in 1993.

Reality: It is far from certain that Iraq was behind the attack. News reports at the time were skeptical about Kuwaiti assertions that the attack was planned by Iraq against former President Bush. Following is an interesting quote from Seymour Hersh's article from November 1993:

Three years ago, during Iraq's six-month occupation of Kuwait, there had been an outcry when a teen-age Kuwaiti girl testified eloquently and effectively before Congress about Iraqi atrocities involving newborn infants. The girl turned *out to be the **daughter of the Kuwaiti Ambassador to Washington, Sheikh Saud** Nasir al-Sabah, and her account of Iraqi soldiers flinging babies out of incubators was challenged as exaggerated both by journalists and by human-rights groups. (**Sheikh Saud was subsequently named Minister of Information in Kuwait, and he was the government official in charge of briefing the international press on the alleged assassination attempt against George Bush.**) In a second incident, in August of 1991, Kuwait provoked a special session of the United Nations Security Council by claiming that twelve Iraqi vessels, including a speedboat, had been involved in an attempt to assault Bubiyan Island, long-disputed territory that was then under Kuwaiti control. The Security Council eventually concluded that, while the Iraqis had been provocative, there had been no Iraqi military raid, and that the Kuwaiti government knew there hadn't. What did take place was nothing more than a smuggler-versus-smuggler dispute over war booty in a nearby demilitarized zone that had emerged, after the Gulf War, as an illegal marketplace for alcohol, ammunition, and livestock.*

This establishes that, on several occasions, Kuwait has lied about the threat from Iraq. Hersh goes on to point out in the article numerous other times the Kuwaitis lied to the U.S. and the UN about Iraq. Here is another good quote from Hersh:

*The president was not alone in his caution. Janet Reno, the Attorney General, also had her doubts. "The A.G. remains skeptical of certain aspects of the case," a senior Justice Department official told me in late July, a month after the bombs were dropped on Baghdad...Two weeks later, what amounted to open warfare broke out among various factions in the government on the issue of who had done what in Kuwait. Someone gave a Boston Globe reporter access to a classified C.I.A. study that was highly skeptical of the Kuwaiti claims of an Iraqi assassination attempt. **The study, prepared by the C.I.A.'s Counter Terrorism Center, suggested that Kuwait might have "cooked the books" on the alleged plot in an effort to play up the "continuing Iraqi threat" to Western interests in the Persian Gulf.** Neither the* Times *nor the* Post *made any significant mention of the* Globe Dispatch, *which had been written by a Washington correspondent named Paul Quinn-Judge, although the story cited specific paragraphs from the C.I.A. assessment. The two major American newspapers had been driven by their sources to the other side of the debate.*

At the very least, the case against Iraq for the alleged bomb threat is not conclusive.

Claim: Saddam Hussein will use weapons of mass destruction against us—he has already used them against his own people (the Kurds in 1988 in the village of Halabja).

Reality: It is far from certain that Iraq used chemical weapons against the Kurds. It may be accepted as conventional wisdom in these times, but back when it was first claimed, there was great skepticism. The evidence is far from conclusive. A 1990 study by the Strategic Studies Institute of the U.S. Army War College cast great doubts on the claim that Iraq used chemical weapons on the Kurds. Following are the two gassing incidents as described in the report:

*In September 1988, however—a month after the war (between Iran and Iraq) had ended—the State Department abruptly, and in what many viewed as a sensational manner, condemned Iraq for allegedly using chemicals against its Kurdish population. The incident cannot be understood without some background of Iraq's relations with the Kurds…throughout the war Iraq effectively faced two enemies —Iran and elements of its own Kurdish minority. Significant numbers of the Kurds had launched a revolt against Baghdad and in the process teamed up with Tehran. As soon as the war with Iran ended, Iraq announced its determination to crush the Kurdish insurrection. It sent Republican Guards to the Kurdish area, and in the course of the operation—according to the U.S. State Department—gas was used, with the result that numerous Kurdish civilians were killed. The Iraqi government denied that any such gassing had occurred. Nonetheless, Secretary of State Schultz stood by U.S. accusations, and the U.S. Congress, acting on its own, sought to impose economic sanctions on Baghdad as a violator of the Kurds' human rights….**Having looked at all the evidence that was available to us, we find it impossible to confirm the State Department's claim that gas was used in this instance. To begin with, there were never any victims produced.** International relief organizations who examined the Kurds—in Turkey where they had gone for asylum—failed to discover any. Nor were there ever any found inside Iraq. **The claim rests solely on testimony*** *of the Kurds who had crossed the border into Turkey, where they were interviewed by staffers of the Senate Foreign Relations Committee...*

It appears that in seeking to punish Iraq, the Congress was influenced by another incident that occurred five months earlier in another Iraqi-Kurdish city, Halabjah. In March 1988, the Kurds at Halabjah were bombarded with chemical weapons, producing many deaths. Photographs of the Kurdish victims were widely disseminated in the international media. Iraq was blamed for the Halabjah attack, even though it was subsequently brought out that Iran too had used chemicals in this operation and it seemed likely that it was the Iranian bombardment that had actually killed the Kurds....

Thus, in our view, the Congress acted more on the basis of emotionalism than factual information, and without sufficient thought for the adverse diplomatic effects of its action.

Claim: Iraq must be attacked because it has ignored UN Security Council resolutions—these resolutions must be backed up by the use of force.

Reality: Iraq is but one of the many countries that have not complied with UN Security Council resolutions. In addition to the dozen or so resolutions currently being violated by Iraq, a conservative estimate reveals that there are an additional 91 Security Council resolutions by countries other than Iraq that are also currently being violated. Adding in older resolutions that were violated would mean easily more than 200 UN Security Council resolutions have been violated with total impunity. Countries currently in violation include: Israel, Turkey, Morocco, Croatia, Armenia, Russia, Sudan, Turkey-controlled Cyprus, India, Pakistan, Indonesia. None of these countries have been threatened with force over their violations.

Claim: Iraq has anthrax and other chemical and biological agents.

Reality: That may be true. However, according to UNSCOM's chief weapons inspector, 90-95 percent of Iraq's chemical and biological weapons and capabilities were destroyed by 1998; those that remained have likely degraded in the intervening four years and are likely useless. A 1994 Senate Banking Committee hearing revealed some 74 shipments of deadly chemical and biological agents from the U.S. to Iraq in the 1980s. As one recent press report stated:

One 1986 shipment from the Virginia-based American Type Culture Collection included three strains of anthrax, six strains of the bacteria that make botulinum toxin and three strains of the bacteria that cause gas gangrene. **Iraq later admitted to the United Nations that it had made weapons out of all three...**

The **CDC, meanwhile, sent shipments of germs** *to the Iraqi Atomic Energy Commission and other agencies involved in Iraq's weapons of mass destruction programs. It sent samples in 1986 of botulinum toxin and botulinum toxoid—used to make vaccines against botulinum toxin—directly to the Iraqi chemical and biological weapons complex at al-Muthanna, the records show.*

These were sent while the United States was supporting Iraq covertly in its war against Iran. U.S. assistance to Iraq in that war also included covertly delivered intelligence on Iranian troop movements and other assistance. This is just another example of our policy of interventionism in affairs that do not concern us—and how this interventionism nearly always ends up causing harm to the United States.

Claim: The president claimed last night: "Iraq possesses ballistic missiles with a likely range of hundreds of miles, far enough to strike Saudi Arabia, Israel, Turkey and other nations in a region where more than 135,000 American civilians and service members live and work."

Reality: Then why is only Israel talking about the need for the U.S. to attack Iraq? None of the other countries seem concerned at all. Also, the fact that some 135,000 Americans in the area are under threat from these alleged missiles just makes the point that it is time to bring our troops home to defend our own country.

Claim: Iraq harbors al-Qaeda and other terrorists.

Reality: The administration has claimed that some al-Qaeda elements have been present in Northern Iraq. This is territory controlled by the Kurds—who are our allies—and is patrolled by U.S. and British fighter aircraft. Moreover, dozens of countries—including Iran and the United States—are said to have al-Qaeda members in their territory. Other terrorists allegedly harbored by Iraq, all are affiliated with Palestinian causes and do not attack the United States.

Claim: President Bush said in his speech on October 7, 2002: "Many people have asked how close Saddam Hussein is to developing a nuclear weapon. *Well, we don't know exactly, and that's the problem...*"

Reality: An admission of a *lack* of information is justification for an attack? ■

"Remember that a government big enough to give you everything you want is also big enough to take away everything you have."
—Davy Crockett

CHAPTER 14

I gave a "State of the Republic" speech in 2003 focusing on the fact that democracy had replaced republicanism with disastrous results. Excerpts relative to foreign policy follow.

January 29, 2003
SORRY, MR. FRANKLIN,
"WE'RE ALL *DEMOCRATS* NOW"
FOREIGN AFFAIRS AND DEMOCRACY
HON. RON PAUL of TEXAS
IN THE HOUSE OF REPRESENTATIVES

The dramatic shift away from republicanism that occurred in 1913, as expected, led to a bold change of purpose in foreign affairs. The goal of "making the world safe for democracy" was forcefully put forth by president Wilson. Protecting national security had become too narrow a goal and selfish in purpose. An obligation for spreading democracy became a noble obligation backed by a moral commitment, every bit as utopian as striving for economic equality in an egalitarian society here at home.

With the growing affection for democracy, it was no giant leap to assume that majority opinion should mold personal behavior. It was no mere coincidence that the 18th Amendment—alcohol prohibition—was passed in 1919.

Ever since 1913, all our presidents have endorsed meddling in the internal affairs of other nations and have given generous support to the notion that a world government would facilitate the goals of democratic welfare or socialism. On a daily basis, we hear that we must be prepared to spend our money and use our young people to police the entire world in order to spread democracy. Whether in Venezuela or Columbia, Afghanistan or Pakistan, Iraq or Iran, Korea or Vietnam, our intervention is always justified with a tone of moral arrogance that "it's for their own good."

Our policymakers promote democracy as a cure-all for the various complex problems of the world. Unfortunately, the propaganda machine is able to hide the real reasons for our empire building. **"Promoting democracy" overseas merely becomes a slogan for doing things that the powerful and influential strive to do for their own benefit.** To get authority for these overseas pursuits, all that is required of the government is that the majority be satisfied with the stated goals—no matter how self-serving they may be. The rule of law, that is, constitutional restraint, is ignored. But as successful as the policy may be on the short run and as noble as it may be portrayed, it is a major contributing factor to the violence and chaos that eventually come from pure democracy.

There is abundant evidence that the pretense of spreading democracy contradicts the very policies we are pursuing. We preach about democratic elections, but we are only too willing to accept some for-the-moment friendly dictator who actually overthrew a democratically elected leader or to interfere in some foreign election.

This is the case with Pakistan's Mushariff. For a temporary alliance, he reaps hundreds of millions of dollars, even though strong evidence exists that the Pakistanis have harbored and trained al Qaeda terrorists, that they have traded weapons with North Korea, and that they possess weapons of mass destruction. No one should be surprised that the Arabs are confused by our overtures of friendship. We have just recently promised $28 billion to Turkey to buy their support for Persian Gulf War II.

Our support of Saudi Arabia, in spite of its ties to al Qaeda through financing and training, is totally ignored by those obsessed with going to war against Iraq. Saudi Arabia is the furthest thing from a democracy. As a matter of fact, if democratic elections were permitted, the Saudi government would be overthrown by a bin Laden ally.

Those who constantly preach global government and democracy ought to consider the outcome of their philosophy in a hypothetical Mid-East regional government. If these people were asked which country in this region possesses weapons of mass destruction, has a policy of oppressive occupation, and constantly defies UN Security council resolutions, the vast majority would overwhelmingly name Israel. Is this ludicrous? No, this is what democracy is all about and what can come from a one-man, one-vote philosophy.

U.S. policy supports the overthrow of the democratically elected Chavez government in Venezuela, because we don't like the economic policy it pursues. We support a military takeover as long as the new dictator will do as we tell him.

There is no creditability in our contention that we really want to impose democracy on other nations. Yet promoting democracy is the public justification for our foreign intervention. It sounds so much nicer than saying we're going to risk the lives of our young people and massively tax our citizens to secure the giant oil reserves in Iraq.

After we take over Iraq, how long would one expect it to take until there are authentic nationwide elections in that country? The odds of that happening in even a hundred years are remote. It's virtually impossible to imagine a time when democratic elections would ever occur for the election of leaders in a constitutional Republic dedicated for protection of liberty any place in the region.

FOREIGN POLICY, WELFARE, AND 9/11

The tragedy of 9/11 and its aftermath dramatize so clearly how a flawed foreign policy has served to encourage the majoritarians determined to run everyone's life.

Due to its natural inefficiencies and tremendous costs, a failing welfare state requires an ever-expanding authoritarian approach to enforce mandates, collect the necessary revenues, and keep afloat an unworkable system. Once the people grow to depend on government subsistence, they demand its continuation.

Excessive meddling in the internal affairs of other nations and involving ourselves in every conflict around the globe has not endeared the United States to the oppressed of the world. The Japanese are tired of us. The South Koreans are tired of us. The Europeans are tired of us. The Central Americans are tired of us. The Filipinos are tired of us. And above all, the

245

Arab Muslims are tired of us.

Angry and frustrated by our persistent bullying and disgusted with having their own government bought and controlled by the United States, joining a radical Islamic movement was a natural and predictable consequence for Muslims.

We believe bin Laden when he takes credit for an attack on the West, and we believe him when he warns us of an impending attack. But we refuse to listen to his explanation of why he and his allies are at war with us.

Bin Laden's claims are straightforward. The U.S. defiles Islam with military bases on holy land in Saudi Arabia, its initiation of war against Iraq, with 12 years of persistent bombing, and its dollars and weapons being used against the Palestinians as the Palestinian territory shrinks and Israel's occupation expands. There will be no peace in the world for the next 50 years or longer if we refuse to believe why those who are attacking us do it.

To dismiss terrorism as the result of Muslims hating us because we're rich and free is one of the greatest foreign-policy frauds ever perpetrated on the American people. Because the propaganda machine, the media, and the government have restated this so many times, the majority now accept it at face value. And the administration gets the political cover it needs to pursue a "holy" war for democracy against the infidels who hate us for our goodness.

Polling on the matter is followed closely and, unfortunately, is far more important than the rule of law. Do we hear the pundits talk of constitutional restraints on the Congress and the administration? No, all we ever hear are reassurances that the majority supports the president; therefore it must be all right.

The terrorists' attacks on us, though never justified, are related to our severely flawed foreign policy of intervention. They also reflect the shortcomings of a bureaucracy that is already big enough to know everything it needs to know about any impending attack but too cumbersome to do anything about it. Bureaucratic weaknesses within a fragile welfare state provide a prime opportunity for those whom we antagonize through our domination over world affairs and global wealth to take advantage of our vulnerability.

But what has been our answer to the shortcomings of policies driven by majority opinion manipulated by the powerful elite? We have responded by massively increasing the federal government's policing activity to hold American citizens in check and make sure we are well behaved and pose no threat, while massively expanding our aggressive presence around the world. There is no possible way these moves can make us more secure against terrorism, yet they will accelerate our march toward national bankruptcy with a currency collapse.

Relying on authoritarian democracy and domestic and international meddling only move us sharply *away* from a constitutional republic and the rule of law and *toward* the turbulence of a decaying democracy, about which Madison and others had warned.

Once the goal of liberty is replaced by a preconceived notion of the benefits and the moral justifications of a democracy, a trend toward internationalism and world government follows.

We certainly witnessed this throughout the 20th Century. Since World War II, we have failed to follow the Constitution in taking this country to war, but instead have deferred to the collective democratic wisdom of the United Nations.

Once it's recognized that ultimate authority comes from an international body, whether the United Nations, NATO, the WTO, the World Bank, or the IMF, the contest becomes a matter of who holds the reins of power and is able to dictate what is perceived as the will of the people (of the world). In the name of democracy, just as it is done in Washington, powerful nations with the most money will control UN policy. Bribery, threats, and intimidation are common practices used to achieve a "democratic" consensus-no matter how controversial and short-lived the benefits.

Can one imagine what it might be like if a true worldwide democracy existed and the United Nations were controlled by a worldwide, one man/one vote philosophy? The masses of China and India could vote themselves whatever they needed from the more prosperous western countries. How long would a world system last based on this absurdity? Yet this is the principle that we're working so hard to impose on ourselves and others around the world.

In spite of the great strides made toward one-world government based on egalitarianism, I'm optimistic that this utopian nightmare will never come to fruition. I have already made the case that here at home powerful special interests take over controlling majority opinion, making sure fairness in distribution is never achieved. This fact causes resentment and becomes so expensive that the entire system becomes unstable and eventually collapses.

The same will occur internationally, even if it miraculously did not cause conflict among the groups demanding the loot confiscated from the producing individuals (or countries). Democratic socialism is so destructive to production of wealth that it must fail, just as socialism failed under Soviet communism. We have a long way to go before old-fashioned nationalism is dead and buried. In the meantime, the determination of those promoting democratic socialism will cause great harm to many people before its chaotic end and we rediscover the basic principle responsible for all of human progress. ∎

As mentioned, the UN cannot be absolved of its role in these wars, and the U.S. can only expect long-term commitments (often beyond any acknowledged at the start of the war) to result.

February 26, 2003
ANOTHER UNITED NATIONS WAR?
HON. RON PAUL of TEXAS
IN THE HOUSE OF REPRESENTATIVES

President Bush, Sr. proudly spoke of "The New World Order," a term used by those who promote one-world government under the United Nations. In going to war in 1991, he sought and received UN authority to push Iraqi forces out of Kuwait. He forcefully stated that this UN authority was adequate, and that although a congressional resolution was acceptable, it was entirely unnecessary and he would proceed regardless. At that time, there was no discussion regarding a congressional declaration of war. The first Persian Gulf War, therefore, was clearly a UN, political war fought within UN guidelines, not for U.S. security—and it was not fought through to victory. The bombings, sanctions, and harassment of the Iraqi people have never stopped. We are now about to resume the active fighting. Although this is referred to as the second Persian Gulf War, it's merely a continuation of a war started long ago, and is likely to continue for a long time, even after Saddam Hussein is removed from power.

Our attitude toward the United Nations is quite different today compared to 1991. I have argued for years against our membership in the United Nations because it compromises our sovereignty. The U.S. has always been expected to pay an unfair percentage of UN expenses. I contend that membership in the United Nations has led to impractical military conflicts that were highly costly both in lives and dollars, and that were rarely resolved.

Our 58 years in Korea have seen 33,000 lives lost, 100,000 casualties, and over a trillion dollars in today's dollars spent. Korea is the most outrageous example of our fighting a UN war without a declaration from the U.S. Congress. And where are we today? On the verge of a nuclear confrontation with a North Korean regime nearly out of control. And to compound the irony, the South Koreans are intervening in hopes of diminishing the tensions that exist between the United States and North Korea!

As bad as the Vietnam nightmare was, at least we left and the UN was not involved. We left in defeat and Vietnam remained a unified Communist country. The results have been much more salutary. Vietnam is now essentially non-Communist, and trade with the West is routine. We didn't disarm Vietnam, we never counted their weapons, and so far no one cares. Peaceful relations have developed between our two countries, not by force of arms, but through trade and friendship. No United Nations, no war, and no inspections served us well—even after many decades of war and a million deaths inflicted on the Vietnamese in an effort by both the French and the United States to force them into compliance with Western demands.

But in this new battle with Iraq, our relationship with the United Nations and our allies is drawing a lot of attention. The administration now says it would be nice to have UN support, but it's not necessary. The president argues that a unilateralist approach is permissible with his understanding of national sovereignty. But no mention is made of the fact that the authority to go to war is not a UN prerogative, and that such authority can only come from the U.S. Congress.

Although the argument that the United Nations cannot dictate to us what is in our best interest is correct, and we do have a right to pursue foreign policy unilaterally, it's ironic that we're making this declaration in order to pursue an unpopular war that very few people or governments throughout the world support.

But the argument for unilateralism and national sovereignty cannot be made for the purpose of enforcing UN Security Council resolutions. That doesn't make any sense. If one wants to enforce UN Security Council resolutions, authority can only come from the United Nations itself. We end up with the worst of both worlds: hated for our unilateralism, but still lending credibility to the UN.

The Constitution makes it clear that if we must counter a threat to our security, that authority must come from the U.S. Congress. Those who believe, and many sincerely do, that the United Nations serves a useful function, argue that ignoring the United Nations at this juncture will surely make it irrelevant. Even with my opposition to the United Nations, I can hardly be pleased that its irrelevancy might come about because of our rush to war against a nation that has not aggressed against us nor poses any threat to us.

From my viewpoint, the worst scenario would be for the United Nations to sanction this war, which may well occur if we offer enough U.S. taxpayer money and Iraqi oil to the reluctant countries. If that happens, we could be looking at another 58-year occupation, expanded Middle East chaos, or a dangerous spread of hostilities to all of Asia or even further.

With regard to foreign affairs, the best advice comes from our Founders and the Constitution. It is better to promote peace and commerce with all nations, and exclude ourselves from the entangling, dangerous, complex, and unworkable alliances that come with our membership in the United Nations. ■

March 19, 2003
NOTES FROM A PERSONAL DIARY

In 8 ½ hours, Saddam Hussein's 48 hours will be up (he was ordered to leave town by President Bush). The bombs will fall shortly thereafter. Baghdad will be hit with more bombs (possibly) than any other city in the history of the world. According to our president, this will be done in the name of peace and liberation. More likely, this will unleash a war of gigantic proportions—even if the actual battle to eliminate Saddam Hussein and seize Iraq's oil goes well and ends quickly. To claim this pre-emptive strike will bring greater peace for both the U.S. and the world is the height of naiveté and arrogance.

The numerous excuses for starting this war against Iraq are deeply flawed. The superficial excuse is absurd. Promoters of the war argue that United Nations security resolutions demanding disarmament of Iraq must be enforced. Over 100 other UN resolutions, mostly directed against Israel, have gone unenforced and no one cares. The UN itself is not enforcing these resolutions in Iraq; explicit authority to use force was considered and denied. But the U.S. unilaterally takes it upon itself to enforce a resolution written by the United Nations. History surely will recognize this as bizarre and disingenuous.

Not only is there no UN authority to initiate this war against Iraq, there is no *congressional* authority—no declaration of war as required by our Constitution. This is a presidential war plain and simple. Congress acquiesces, and the inept, useless world government body—the United

Nations—can't do anything about it. So the neoconservative advisors who control our foreign policy and the president will have their war.

This strike is a major event! It has implications far beyond anything the sponsors can imagine. Those who agitated for this takeover of Iraq for almost 12 years see only smooth sailing with no downside. When the history of this period is written, many will shake their heads in disbelief about the reasons given for the takeover and occupation of Iraq. The sacrifice of our liberties that will accompany this war adventure (and the "permanent" conflict between the Christian West and Muslim East) surely will surpass anything anticipated by those who succumbed to the propaganda that our efforts were noble and success would be easy.

With this huge escalation of the war (we've been bombing Iraq for more than 12 years), dissent has been squelched in the United States. A large majority now sees being pro-peace as being un-American and deserving of contempt. The propaganda machine has been effective for the masses; the internet, however, provides a sensational haven for those who oppose war and chose to demonstrate against it. Propaganda and the destruction of truth in time of war are hardly new, and the government always wins the public opinion battle at home. But internationally the success of the pro-war propaganda has been limited. This is an American war and we're king of the hill: militarily, politically, and economically our power has been insurmountable. But the people in the street in almost all countries of the world could not be influenced by the feeble excuses of their own governments to support American imperialism and hegemonic efforts. Thus, it's now the United States against the world—even though Saddam Hussein is a tyrant deserving of removal from office.

If friendship with our allies depends only on dollars or intimidation, as it seems, our arrogance in dealing with them over the past year guarantees a souring of relations that will not improve anytime soon.

Bewilderment is the only way to describe sentiments regarding our policy toward Iraq and the world. It's surreal! It's almost as though our policies are controlled by an external force, and not a good one. The war has been inevitable for years. The pretense of inspectors looking for weapons and satisfying UN rules were a mere charade to justify what seemed ordained from the beginning. The neoconservative takeover of the administration guaranteed a war to occupy Iraq and eliminate Saddam Hussein. Although perhaps only a relative few were the original true believers, their placement in the media, think tanks, and government was enough to brainwash many Americans into believing this war was needed for national security and because of 9/11. Yet the opposite was the case.

They—the war promoters—never asked and never answered the obvious questions: What did the Iraqis ever do to the United States or her citizens to justify this assault on tens of thousands of innocent Iraqi citizens? Why must this be done, even if weapons of mass destruction did exist, since our attack would only endanger innocent life, American, Iraqi, and in particular Israeli? We obviously are much more cautious with North Korea because we know it possesses nuclear weapons. Why initiate a war of aggression in the name of Christian morality, when most Christian denominations object based on "just war" doctrine? How can some Christian leaders preach war and yet claim an understanding of the love that Christ taught?

This determination to go to war is best described as an obsession, more like the Salem witch trials than a justified war of defense. That bad leaders exist does not justify initiating wars of occupation and regime change. Not only is this morally reprehensible, it's fraught with great danger to our troops, to innocent Iraqis, and to all American citizens, as this surely will serve to inspire more radical terrorist attacks against us.

As despicable as 9/11 and other terrorist attacks against us are, the terrorists are nevertheless rational and predictable. Many acts are explicitly a blowback reaction to the seriously flawed foreign policy pursued by our leaders for 100 years, but much more so since World War II. The intensity of this hatred, which we help to create, obviously has escalated since we firmly placed ourselves on Arab territory in the Middle East in 1990. The insanity of spending hundreds of billions of dollars each year to protect "our oil" costs us dearly at home, making our oil more expensive, not less. And in time it will make the flow of oil less certain due to the resulting instability. Yet the cost—through taxes, inflation, and a tottering economy—will surpass the going price. Nothing we say will ever change the belief of most Muslims worldwide that this is a religious war against them, designed to control their oil.

Most Muslims do not believe Bush's argument that it's a war to liberate the Iraqi people. They see this as a religious war, with the Christian capitalist West allied with Zionists who are determined to steal Muslim oil wealth. Although there is support for the war at home, the motivation is more complex considering the aggressive mentality of the neoconservatives. Muslims throughout the world will have their worst fears, as claimed by Osama bin Laden, confirmed: This is a western war against all Muslims, whether they are in Indonesia, the Philippines, the Middle East, or anywhere else in the world. This tragic conclusion is unavoidable.

March 20, 2003

The Persian Gulf War has escalated, modestly so far—just more of what we have been doing for the past 12 years. But the huge escalation will begin soon. George Bush will have his war, the neocons will gloat, and Rupert Murdoch will achieve his immediate goal of getting this war heated up. The outcome is far from certain. The warmongers will not win in the end. Already they have practically destroyed the United Nations. This is not a bad idea in itself, but their goal, I'm sure, is a strong UN controlled by neoconservatives. Long-term alliances have been severely fractured—the realignments throughout the world as governments react to American expansionism and neo-colonialism are yet to come. Before it's all over the U.S. will go broke, which means the dollar will be rejected and our free ride will end. The nearly $500 billion annual cash inflow that finances our current account deficit will not be sustained. Even with temporary military victories, the economic consequences of world domination will dictate our policies.

Policy makers in Congress and the administration don't have the foggiest notion about the cause of the business cycle, and the costs incurred by trusting Allen Greenspan to keep the economy together. Most people trust the Fed's money and banking cartel, and believe manipulating interest rates can save the economy. The magic props up the stock market and the dollar, and of course prevents price inflation. Not only do politicians lie to the public, they lie to themselves. Economic truth would paralyze them, while clinging to clichés and myths sustain them in their plans to dominate the world.

In economics it's called "pretense of knowledge." In foreign affairs it's arrogance of power.

As we watch the war erupt, the most offensive lesson is that presidents have too much power. Congress is like Tony Blair, a puppy dog that tags along and wags its tail when told what to do. But the amount of power the president has didn't come overnight. It gradually was ceded to successive presidents over many decades. This president, for whatever reason, has relished his omnipotence. Probably the worst thing that can be said about George W. Bush is that he sleeps well at night, without remorse and without concern for the death and destruction he causes. He's doing the Lord's work. He is on a holy crusade—a term he used after 9/11, but was told since to avoid since it's too descriptive of what this administration is actually doing. He risks initiating World War III, yet is convinced he is duty bound to pursue this Christian-Zionist-oil crusade against the infidels. He's purely good, they are purely evil. I too like to see things in black and white. Yet history will prove that Bush is politically colorblind. Only a dictator can assume that what he says defines a war crime—a crime against humanity deserving international criminal prosecution and execution—such as burning an oil well to defend against an invading force.

The first goal in this war is to "rescue" the oil wells. And the warmongers still claim and will always claim it has nothing to do with oil. Only the French care about oil, we are told. At least France and Russia have valid contracts for that oil, contracts the U.S. will void. Oil rights then will be given to British and U.S. companies. But still we are assured it's not about oil. Only time will tell how successful this plan will be.

This is truly an historic event. Yes, we have flaunted the rules for engaging in war and ignored the advice of our Founders regarding an interventionist foreign policy. But this pre-emptive strike far surpasses any previous military strike by the United States in sheer arrogance. At least in the past we picked sides and chose allies in ongoing wars. We're *starting* this war, and will set a standard for all the world to follow. Attack anyone we disapprove of, anyone who *might* have weapons, and anyone who *might* strike us at a later date. We are opening a Pandora's Box, and can be certain that others will use it as a justification to strike—maybe even against the U.S., since we have let the world know that this attack on Iraq is only the beginning. Several other nations have been forewarned about a potential U.S. strike. Others will view our actions as a Pearl Harbor type attack against a nation unable to defend itself, that has not committed aggression against us. Iraq's crime is they are too slow in following UN resolutions, while we ignore the will of the UN when it pleases us.

The world is about to get a lot more dangerous, and it's all so unnecessary. The inexplicable need to go abroad seeking monsters to destroy has prompted us to accept a foreign policy better suited to a tyrant than a constitutional republic.

The odds of a worldwide conflict involving many nations have risen, as the chaos from this naked act of aggression materializes. The consequences of this assault will be unpredictable and horrendous.

I'm sure Osama bin Laden is pleased with our reaction. Hatred for the United States surely will escalate, greatly increasing the odds of terrorist attacks against us for years to come. Guerrilla warfare is the only option for terrorists against a giant military power.

We're suppose to believe that our effort to destroy the current Iraqi government and kill its supporters in the name of Christianity is part of a plan to create peace, justice, and democracy. Peace is war! Democracy is freedom! Stealing oil is humanitarian! Killing is a holy duty! Aggression is good! War dissent is un-American!

The propaganda machine not surprisingly has won a tremendous victory. The imperial presidency has gained even more ground. Constitutional restraints on war power are now quaint history, as Congress willfully acquiesces in transferring its responsibilities to the executive branch without a whimper. The UN can be used when it pleases the designers of this brave new world, but unilateralism and nationalism are cited when the votes go against us in the Security Council or the General Assembly. War is the main tool to bring about the new world, and the UN can go along or be swept aside.

The Constitution, our rule of law, is now an anachronism according to Henry Hyde. Congress need not declare war. Even those who believe in the international rule of law under the United Nations now realize that it too does not restrain the tyrants who preach war in order to remake the world.

Of course *our* wars are wars of liberation, waged in the name of peace. James Baker and others claim that all U.S. wars are sacrificial, motivated by noble purposes. According to Baker, we fight, "at great cost in treasure and blood—to protect others and win their freedom, not to gain land or resources." That's the party line and the moral justification given to the masses, who accept it at face value. I wish it were so: that the greedy beneficiaries and special interests weren't really in charge of our foreign policy. But even if their claim had some legitimacy, and U.S. policy was noble in its desire to promote freedom abroad, it could not be achieved without using force against the taxpayers of the United States. The good intentions they claim motivate them cannot justify immoral force against U.S. citizens and the subsequent loss of liberty and life.

But I don't believe for a minute that our policies are based on good intentions. A lust for power, religious fanaticism, and seriously flawed thinking drive our leaders. The only war involving America that comes close to being morally justified by a noble cause, where the survivors actually ended up with more freedom, was our revolution against England.

War is too often fought for pure economic gain. For the most part, wars are promoted by politicians, bureaucrats, misfits, demagogues, and immoral thugs. Wars are fought, however, by others: those who are naïve and easily influenced by the warmongers who claim the cause is just. The poor too often pay the price in blood or poverty, as the war plays havoc with the economy. The beneficiaries of aggressive wars, meanwhile, rarely are identified.

Almost all wars waged for plunder and wealth are promoted by appeals to higher ideals. This pacifies those who fight, die, and pay for the war. We must stamp out slavery, make the world safe for democracy, bring peace and freedom to Iraq, and so on. It's never admitted that the desire to control a region or seize wealth is the real motivation. And of course the claim that God is on our side is the clincher for any doubters. Goodness and mercy, peace and freedom, always promoted by those ordained by God, march off on a crusade that prohibits dissent. Instead, dissenters are condemned for a lack of patriotism or humanitarian concern for their fellow man.

The so called neoconservatives, who are in fact not in any way conservative, have tried to distance themselves from what has become an unpopular war, but their pernicious influence is beyond question.

July 10, 2003
NEO-CONNED!
HON. RON PAUL of TEXAS
IN THE HOUSE OF REPRESENTATIVES

The modern-day limited-government movement has been co-opted. The conservatives have failed in their effort to shrink the size of government. There has not been, nor will there soon be, a conservative revolution in Washington. Party control of the federal government has changed, but the inexorable growth in the size and scope of government has continued unabated. The liberal arguments for limited government in personal affairs and foreign military adventurism were never seriously considered as part of this revolution.

Since the change of the political party in charge has not made a difference, who's really in charge? If the particular party in power makes little difference, whose policy is it that permits expanded government programs, increased spending, huge deficits, nation building and the pervasive invasion of our privacy, with fewer Fourth Amendment protections than ever before?

Someone is responsible, and it's important that those of us who love liberty, and resent Big-Brother government, identify the philosophic supporters who have the most to say about the direction our country is going. If they're wrong—and I believe they are—we need to show it, alert the American people, and offer a more positive approach to government. However, this depends on whether the American people desire to live in a free society and reject the dangerous notion that we need a strong central government to take care of us from the cradle to the grave. Do the American people really believe it's the government's responsibility to make us morally better and economically equal? **Do we have a responsibility to police the world, while imposing our vision of good government on everyone else in the world with some form of utopian nation building?** If not, and the contemporary enemies of liberty are exposed and rejected, then it behooves us to present an alternative philosophy that is morally superior and economically sound and provides a guide to world affairs to enhance peace and commerce.

One thing is certain: conservatives who worked and voted for less government in the Reagan years and welcomed the takeover of the U.S. Congress and the presidency in the 1990s and early 2000s were deceived. Soon they will realize that the goal of limited government has been dashed and that their views no longer matter.

The so-called conservative revolution of the past two decades has given us massive growth in government size, spending and regulations. Deficits are exploding and the national debt is now rising at greater than $500 billion dollars per year. Taxes do not go down—even if we vote to lower them. They can't, as long as spending is increased, since all spending must be paid for one way or another. Both Presidents Reagan and the elder George Bush raised taxes directly. With this administration, so far, direct taxes have been reduced—and they certainly should have been— but it means little if spending increases and deficits rise.

When taxes are not raised to accommodate higher spending, the bills must be paid by either borrowing or "printing" new money. This is one reason why we conveniently have a generous Federal Reserve chairman who is willing to accommodate the Congress. With borrowing and inflating, the "tax" is delayed and distributed in a way that makes it difficult for those paying the tax to identify it. Like future generations and those on fixed incomes who suffer from rising prices, and those who lose jobs, they certainly feel the consequences of economic dislocation that this process causes. Government spending is always a "tax" burden on the American people and is never equally

257

or fairly distributed. The poor and low-middle income workers always suffer the most from the deceitful tax of inflation and borrowing.

Many present-day conservatives, who generally argue for less government and who supported the Reagan/Gingrich/Bush takeover of the federal government, are now justifiably disillusioned. Although not a monolithic group, they wanted to shrink the size of government.

Early in our history, the advocates of limited, constitutional government recognized two important principles: the rule of law was crucial, and a constitutional government must derive "just powers from the consent of the governed." It was understood that an explicit transfer of power to government could only occur with power rightfully and naturally endowed to each individual as a God-given right. Therefore, the powers that could be transferred would be limited to the purpose of protecting liberty. Unfortunately, in the last 100 years, the defense of liberty has been fragmented and shared by various groups, with some protecting civil liberties, others economic freedom, and a small diverse group arguing for a foreign policy of nonintervention.

The philosophy of freedom has had a tough go of it. It was hoped that the renewed interest in limited government of the past two decades would revive an interest in reconstituting the freedom philosophy into something more consistent. Those who worked for the goal of limited government power believed the rhetoric of politicians who promised smaller government. Sometimes it was just plain sloppy thinking on their part, but at other times, they fell victim to a deliberate distortion of a concise limited-government philosophy by politicians who misled many into believing that we would see a rollback on government intrusiveness.

Yes, there was always a remnant who long for truly limited government and maintain a belief in the rule of law, combined with a deep conviction that free people and a government bound by a Constitution are the most advantageous form of government. They recognized it as the only practical way for prosperity to be spread to the maximum number of people while promoting peace and security.

That remnant—imperfect as it may have been—was heard from in the elections of 1980 and 1994 and then achieved major victories in 2000 and 2002, when professed limited-government proponents took over the White House, the Senate and the House. However, the true believers in limited government are now shunned and laughed at. At the very least, they are ignored—except when they are used by the new leaders of the right, the new conservatives now in charge of the U.S. government.

The remnant's instincts were correct, and the politicians placated them with talk of free markets, limited government, and a humble, non-nation-building foreign policy. However, little concern for civil liberties was expressed in this recent quest for less government. Yet, for an ultimate victory of achieving freedom, this must change. Interest in personal privacy and choices has generally remained outside the concern of many conservatives—especially with the great harm done by their support of the drug war. Even though some confusion has emerged over our foreign policy since the breakdown of the Soviet empire, it's been a net benefit in getting some conservatives back on track with a less militaristic, interventionist foreign policy. Unfortunately, after 9/11, the cause of liberty suffered a setback. As a result, millions of Americans voted for the less-than-perfect conservative revolution because they believed in the promises of the politicians.

Now there's mounting evidence to indicate exactly what happened to the revolution. Government is bigger than ever, and future commitments are overwhelming. Millions will soon become disenchanted with the new status quo delivered to the American people by the advocates of limited government and will find it to be just more of the old status quo. Victories for limited government have turned out to be hollow indeed.

Since the national debt is increasing at a rate greater than half a trillion dollars per year, the debt limit was recently increased by an astounding $984 billion dollars. **Total U.S. government obligations are $43 trillion, while the total net worth of U.S. households is about $40.6 trillion. The country is broke, but no one in Washington seems to notice or care.** The philosophic and political commitment for both guns and butter—and especially the expanding American empire—must be challenged. This is crucial for our survival.

In spite of the floundering economy, Congress and the administration continue to take on new commitments in foreign aid, education, farming, medicine, multiple efforts at nation building, and preemptive wars around the world. Already we're entrenched in Iraq and Afghanistan, with plans to soon add new trophies to our conquest. War talk abounds as to when Syria, Iran and North Korea will be attacked.

How did all this transpire? Why did the government do it? Why haven't the people objected? How long will it go on before something is done? Does anyone care?

Will the euphoria of grand military victories—against non-enemies—ever be mellowed? Someday, we as a legislative body must face the reality

259

of the dire situation in which we have allowed ourselves to become enmeshed. Hopefully, it will be soon!

We got here because ideas do have consequences. Bad ideas have bad consequences, and even the best of intentions have unintended consequences. We need to know exactly what the philosophic ideas were that drove us to this point; then, hopefully, reject them and decide on another set of intellectual parameters.

There is abundant evidence exposing those who drive our foreign policy justifying preemptive war. Those who scheme are proud of the achievements in usurping control over foreign policy. These are the neoconservatives of recent fame. Granted, they are talented and achieved a political victory that all policymakers must admire. But can freedom and the Republic survive this takeover? That question should concern us.

Neoconservatives are obviously in positions of influence and are well placed throughout our government and the media. An apathetic Congress put up little resistance and abdicated its responsibilities over foreign affairs. The electorate was easily influenced to join in the patriotic fervor supporting the military adventurism advocated by the neoconservatives.

The numbers of those who still hope for truly limited government diminished and had their concerns ignored these past 22 months, during the aftermath of 9/11. Members of Congress were easily influenced to publicly support any domestic policy or foreign military adventure that was supposed to help reduce the threat of a terrorist attack. Believers in limited government were harder to find. Political money, as usual, played a role in pressing Congress into supporting almost any proposal suggested by the neocons. This process—where campaign dollars and lobbying efforts affect policy—is hardly the domain of any single political party, and unfortunately, is the way of life in Washington.

There are many reasons why government continues to grow. It would be naïve for anyone to expect otherwise. Since 9/11, protection of privacy, whether medical, personal or financial, has vanished. Free speech and the Fourth Amendment have been under constant attack. Higher welfare expenditures are endorsed by the leadership of both parties. Policing the world and nation-building issues are popular campaign targets, yet they are now standard operating procedures. There's no sign that these programs will be slowed or reversed until either we are stopped by force overseas (which won't be soon) or we go broke and can no longer afford these grandiose plans for a world empire (which will probably come sooner than later.)

None of this happened by accident or coincidence. Precise philosophic ideas prompted certain individuals to gain influence to implement these plans. The neoconservatives—a name they gave themselves—diligently worked their way into positions of power and influence. They documented their goals, strategy and moral justification for all they hoped to accomplish. Above all else, they were not and are not conservatives dedicated to limited, constitutional government.

Neo-conservatism has been around for decades and, strangely, has connections to past generations as far back as Machiavelli. Modern-day neo-conservatism was introduced to us in the 1960s. It entails both a detailed strategy as well as a philosophy of government. The ideas of Teddy Roosevelt, and certainly Woodrow Wilson, were quite similar to many of the views of present-day neocons. Neocon spokesman Max Boot brags that what he advocates is "hard Wilsonianism." In many ways, there's nothing "neo" about their views, and certainly nothing conservative. Yet they have been able to co-opt the conservative movement by advertising themselves as a new or modern form of conservatism.

More recently, the modern-day neocons have come from the far left, a group historically identified as former Trotskyites. Liberal Christopher Hitchens, has recently officially joined the neocons, and it has been reported that he has already been to the White House as an ad hoc consultant. Many neocons now in positions of influence in Washington can trace their status back to Professor Leo Strauss of the University of Chicago. One of Strauss' books was *Thoughts on Machiavelli*. This book was not a condemnation of Machiavelli's philosophy. Paul Wolfowitz actually got his PhD under Strauss. Others closely associated with these views are Richard Perle, Eliot Abrams, Robert Kagan, and William Kristol. All are key players in designing our new strategy of preemptive war. Others include: Michael Ledeen of the American Enterprise Institute; former CIA Director James Woolsey; Bill Bennett of *Book of Virtues* fame; Frank Gaffney; Dick Cheney; and Donald Rumsfeld. There are just too many to mention who are philosophically or politically connected to the neocon philosophy in some varying degree.

The godfather of modern-day neo-conservatism is considered to be Irving Kristol, father of Bill Kristol, who set the stage in 1983 with his publication *Reflections of a Neoconservative*. In this book, Kristol also defends the traditional liberal position on welfare.

More important than the names of people affiliated with neo-conservatism are the views they adhere to. Here is a brief summary of the general understanding of what neocons believe:

1. They agree with Trotsky on permanent revolution, violent as well as intellectual.
2. They are for redrawing the map of the Middle East and are willing to use force to do so.
3. They believe in preemptive war to achieve desired ends.
4. They accept the notion that the ends justify the means—that hardball politics is a moral necessity.
5. They express no opposition to the welfare state.
6. They are not bashful about an American empire; instead they strongly endorse it.
7. They believe lying is necessary for the state to survive.
8. They believe a powerful federal government is a benefit.
9. They believe pertinent facts about how a society should be run should be held by the elite and withheld
from those who do not have the courage to deal with it.
10. They believe neutrality in foreign affairs is ill advised.
11. They hold Leo Strauss in high esteem.
12. They believe imperialism, if progressive in nature, is appropriate.
13. Using American might to force American ideals on others is acceptable. Force should not be limited to the defense of our country.
14. 9/11 resulted from the lack of foreign entanglements, not from too many.
15. They dislike and despise libertarians (therefore, the same applies to all strict constitutionalists.)
16. They endorse attacks on civil liberties, such as those found in the Patriot Act, as being necessary.
17. They unconditionally support Israel and have a close alliance with the Likud Party.

Various organizations and publications over the last 30 years have played a significant role in the rise to power of the neoconservatives. It took plenty of money and commitment to produce the intellectual arguments needed to convince the many participants in the movement of its respectability.

It is no secret—especially after the rash of research and articles written about the neocons since our invasion of Iraq—how they gained influence and what organizations were used to promote their cause. Although for decades, they agitated for their beliefs through publications like *The National Review, The Weekly Standard, The Public Interest, The Wall*

Street Journal, *Commentary*, and the *New York Post*, their views only gained momentum in the 1990s following the first Persian Gulf War—which still has not ended even with removal of Saddam Hussein. They became convinced that a much more militant approach to resolving all the conflicts in the Middle East was an absolute necessity, and they were determined to implement that policy.

In addition to publications, multiple think tanks and projects were created to promote their agenda. A product of the Bradley Foundation, the American Enterprise Institute (AEI) led the neocon charge, but the real push for war came from the Project for a New American Century (PNAC) another organization helped by the Bradley Foundation. This occurred in 1998 and was chaired by *Weekly Standard* editor Bill Kristol. They urged early on for war against Iraq, but were disappointed with the Clinton administration, which never followed through with its periodic bombings. Obviously, these bombings were motivated more by Clinton's personal and political problems than a belief in the neocon agenda.

The election of 2000 changed all that. **The Defense Policy Board, chaired by Richard Perle, played no small role in coordinating the various projects and think tanks, all determined to take us into war against Iraq.** It wasn't too long before the dream of empire was brought closer to reality by the election of 2000 with Paul Wolfowitz, Richard Cheney, and Donald Rumsfeld playing key roles in this accomplishment. The plan to promote an "American greatness" imperialistic foreign policy was now a distinct possibility. Iraq offered a great opportunity to prove their long-held theories. This opportunity was a consequence of the 9/11 disaster.

The money and views of Rupert Murdoch also played a key role in promoting the neocon views, as well as rallying support by the general population, through his News Corporation, which owns Fox News Network, the *New York Post*, and *Weekly Standard*. This powerful and influential media empire did more to galvanize public support for the Iraqi invasion than one might imagine. This facilitated the Rumsfeld/Cheney policy as their plans to attack Iraq came to fruition. It would have been difficult for the neocons to usurp foreign policy from the restraints of Colin Powell's State Department without the successful agitation of the Rupert Murdoch empire. Max Boot was satisfied, as he explained: "Neoconservatives believe in using American might to promote American ideals abroad." This attitude is a far cry from the advice of the Founders, who advocated no entangling alliances and neutrality as the proper goal of American foreign policy.

Let there be no doubt, those in the neocon camp had been anxious to go to war against Iraq for a decade. They justified the use of force to accomplish their goals, even if it required preemptive war. If anyone doubts this assertion, they need only to read of their strategy in "A Clean Break: a New Strategy for Securing the Realm." Although they felt morally justified in changing the government in Iraq, they knew that public support was important, and justification had to be given to pursue the war. Of course, a threat to us had to exist before the people and the Congress would go along with war. The majority of Americans became convinced of this threat, which, in actuality, never really existed. Now we have the ongoing debate over the location of weapons of mass destruction. Where was the danger? Was all this killing and spending necessary? How long will this nation building and dying go on? When will we become more concerned about the needs of our own citizens than the problems we sought in Iraq and Afghanistan? Who knows where we'll go next—Iran, Syria or North Korea?

At the end of the Cold War, the neoconservatives realized a rearrangement of the world was occurring and that our superior economic and military power offered them a perfect opportunity to control the process of remaking the Middle East.

It was recognized that a new era was upon us, and the neocons welcomed Frances Fukuyama's "end of history" declaration. To them, the debate was over. The West won; the Soviets lost. Old-fashioned communism was dead. Long live the new era of neoconservatism. The struggle may not be over, but the West won the intellectual fight, they reasoned. The only problem is that the neocons decided to define the philosophy of the victors. They have been amazingly successful in their efforts to control the debate over what Western values are and by what methods they will be spread throughout the world.

Communism surely lost a lot with the breakup of the Soviet Empire, but this can hardly be declared a victory for American liberty, as the Founders understood it. **Neoconservatism is not the philosophy of free markets and a wise foreign policy. Instead, it represents big-government welfare at home and a program of using our military might to spread their version of American values throughout the world.** Since neoconservatives dominate the way the U.S. government now operates, it behooves us all to understand their beliefs and goals. The breakup of the Soviet system may well have been an epic event, but to say that the views of the neocons are the unchallenged victors and that all we need do is wait for their implementation is a capitulation to controlling the forces of history that many Americans are not yet ready to concede. There is surely no need to do so.

There is now a recognized philosophic connection between modern-day neoconservatives and Irving Kristol, Leo Strauss, and Machiavelli. This is important in understanding that today's policies and the subsequent problems will be with us for years to come if these policies are not reversed.

Not only did Leo Strauss write favorably of Machiavelli, Michael Ledeen, a current leader of the neoconservative movement, did the same in 1999 in his book with the title, *Machiavelli on Modern Leadership,* and subtitled: *Why Machiavelli's iron rules are as timely and important today as five centuries ago.* Ledeen is indeed an influential neocon theorist whose views get lots of attention today in Washington. His book on Machiavelli, interestingly enough, was passed out to Members of Congress attending a political strategy meeting shortly after its publication and at just about the time *A Clean Break* was issued.

In Ledeen's most recent publication, *The War Against the Terror Masters*, he reiterates his beliefs outlined in this 1999 Machaivelli book. He specifically praises: "Creative destruction...both within our own society and abroad...(foreigners) seeing America undo traditional societies may fear us, for they do not wish to be undone." Amazingly, Ledeen concludes: "They must attack us in order to survive, just as we must destroy them to advance our historic mission."

If those words don't scare you, nothing will. If they are not a clear warning, I don't know what could be. It sounds like both sides of each disagreement in the world will be following the principle of preemptive war. The world is certainly a less safe place for it.

In *Machiavelli on Modern Leadership*, Ledeen praises a business leader for correctly understanding Machiavelli: "There are no absolute solutions. It all depends. What is right and what is wrong depends on what needs to be done and how." This is a clear endorsement of situational ethics and is not coming from the traditional left. It reminds me of: "It depends on what the definition of the word 'is' is."

Ledeen quotes Machiavelli approvingly on what makes a great leader. "A prince must have no other objectives or other thoughts or take anything for his craft, except war." To Ledeen, this meant: "...the virtue of the warrior are those of great leaders of any successful organization." Yet it's obvious that war is not coincidental to neocon philosophy, but an integral part. The intellectuals justify it, and the politicians carry it out. There's a precise reason to argue for war over peace according to Ledeen, for "...peace increases our peril by making discipline less urgent, encouraging some of our worst instincts, in depriving us of some of our best leaders." Peace, he claims, is a dream and not even a pleasant one, for it would cause indolence and would undermine the power of the state. Although I concede the history of the world is a history of frequent war, to capitulate and give up even striving for peace—believing peace is not a benefit to mankind—is a frightening thought that condemns the world to perpetual war and justifies it as a benefit and necessity. These are dangerous ideas, from which no good can come.

The conflict of the ages has been between the state and the individual: central power versus liberty. The more restrained the state and the more emphasis on individual liberty, the greater has been the advancement of civilization and general prosperity. Just as man's condition was not locked in place by the times and wars of old and improved with liberty and free markets, there's no reason to believe a new stage for man might not be achieved by believing and working for conditions of peace. The inevitability and so-called need for preemptive war should never be intellectually justified as being a benefit. Such an attitude guarantees the backsliding of civilization. Neocons, unfortunately, claim that war is in man's nature and that we can't do much about it, so let's use it to our advantage by promoting our goodness around the world through force of arms. That view is anathema to the cause of liberty and the preservation of the Constitution. If it is not loudly refuted, our future will be dire indeed.

Ledeen believes man is basically evil and cannot be left to his own desires. Therefore, he must have proper and strong leadership, just as Machiavelli argued. Only then can man achieve good, as Ledeen explains: "In order to achieve the most noble accomplishments, the leader may have to 'enter into evil.' This is the chilling insight that has made Machiavelli so feared, admired and challenging...we are rotten," argues Ledeen. "It's true that we can achieve greatness if, and only if, we are properly led." In other words, man is so depraved that individuals are incapable of moral, ethical and spiritual greatness; and achieving excellence and virtue can only come from a powerful authoritarian leader. What depraved ideas are these to now be influencing our leaders in Washington? The question Ledeen doesn't answer is: "Why do the political leaders not suffer from the same shortcomings and where do they obtain their monopoly on wisdom?"

Once this trust is placed in the hands of a powerful leader, this neocon argues that certain tools are permissible to use. For instance: "Lying is central to the survival of nations and to the success of great enterprises, because if our enemies can count on the reliability of everything you say, your vulnerability is enormously increased." What about the effects of lying on one's own people? Who cares if a leader can fool the enemy? Does calling it "strategic deception" make lying morally justifiable? Ledeen and Machiavelli argue that it does, as long as the survivability of the state is at stake. Preserving the state is their goal, even if the personal liberty of all individuals has to be suspended or canceled.

Ledeen makes it clear that war is necessary to establish national boundaries—because that's the way it's always been done. Who needs progress of the human race! He explains:

Look at the map of the world: national boundaries have not been drawn by peaceful men leading lives of spiritual contemplation. National boundaries have been established by war, and national character has been shaped by struggle, most often bloody struggle.

Yes, but who is to lead the charge and decide which borders we are to fight for? What about borders 6,000 miles away, unrelated to our own contiguous borders and our own national security? Stating a relative truism regarding the frequency of war throughout history should hardly be the moral justification for expanding the concept of war to settle man's disputes. How can one call this progress?

Machiavelli, Ledeen and the neocons recognized a need to generate a religious zeal for promoting the state. This, he claims, is especially necessary when force is used to promote an agenda. It's been true throughout history and remains true today; each side of major conflicts invokes God's approval. Our side refers to a "crusade;" theirs to a "holy Jihad." Too often wars boil down to their god against our God. It seems this principle is more a cynical effort to gain approval from the masses, especially those most likely to be killed for the sake of the war promoters on both sides who have power, prestige and wealth at stake.

Ledeen explains why God must always be on the side of advocates of war: "Without fear of God, no state can last long, for the dread of eternal damnation keeps men in line, causes them to honor their promises, and inspires them to risk their lives for the common good." It seems dying for the common good has gained a higher moral status than eternal salvation of one's soul. Ledeen adds:

Without fear of punishment, men will not obey laws that force them to act contrary to their passions. Without fear of arms, the state cannot enforce

267

the laws...to this end, Machiavelli wants leaders to make the state spectacular.

It's of interest to note that some large Christian denominations have joined the neoconservatives in promoting preemptive war, while completely ignoring the Christian doctrine of a Just War. The neocons sought and openly welcomed their support.

I'd like someone to glean anything from what the Founders said or placed in the Constitution that agrees with this now-professed doctrine of a "spectacular" state promoted by those who now have so much influence on our policies here at home and abroad. Ledeen argues that this religious element, this fear of God, is needed for discipline of those who may be hesitant to sacrifice their lives for the good of the "spectacular state."

He explains in eerie terms: "Dying for one's country doesn't come naturally. Modern armies, raised from the populace, must be inspired, motivated, indoctrinated. Religion is central to the military enterprise, for men are more likely to risk their lives if they believe they will be rewarded forever after for serving their country." This is an admonition that might just as well have been given by Osama bin Laden, in rallying his troops to sacrifice their lives to kill the invading infidels, as by our intellectuals at the AEI, who greatly influence our foreign policy.

Neocons—anxious for the U.S. to use force to realign the boundaries and change regimes in the Middle East—clearly understand the benefit of a galvanizing and emotional event to rally the people to their cause. Without a special event, they realized the difficulty in selling their policy of preemptive war where our own military personnel would be killed. Whether it was the Lusitania, Pearl Harbor, the Gulf of Tonkin, or the Maine, all served their purpose in promoting a war that was sought by our leaders.
Ledeen writes of a fortuitous event (1999):

> ...*of course, we can always get lucky. Stunning events from outside can providentially awaken the enterprise from its growing torpor, and demonstrate the need for reversal, as the devastating Japanese attack on Pearl Harbor in 1941 so effectively aroused the U.S. from its soothing dreams of permanent neutrality.*

Amazingly, Ledeen calls Pearl Harbor a "lucky" event. The Project for a New American Century, as recently as September 2000, likewise, foresaw the need for "a Pearl Harbor event" that would galvanize the American people to support their ambitious plans to ensure political and economic domination of the world, while strangling any potential "rival."

Recognizing a "need" for a Pearl Harbor event, and referring to Pearl Harbor as being "lucky" are not identical to support and knowledge of such an event, but this sympathy for a galvanizing event, as 9/11 turned out to be, was used to promote an agenda that strict constitutionalists and devotees of the Founders of this nation find appalling is indeed disturbing. After 9/11, Rumsfeld and others argued for an immediate attack on Iraq, even though it was not implicated in the attacks.

The fact that neoconservatives ridicule those who firmly believe that U.S. interests and world peace would best be served by a policy of neutrality and avoiding foreign entanglements should not go unchallenged. Not to do so is to condone their grandiose plans for American world hegemony.

The current attention given neocons is usually done in the context of foreign policy. But there's more to what's going on today than just the tremendous influence the neocons have on our new policy of preemptive war with a goal of empire. Our government is now being moved by several ideas that come together in what I call "neoconism." The foreign policy is being openly debated, even if its implications are not fully understood by many who support it. Washington is now driven by old views brought together in a new package.

We know those who lead us—both in the administration and in Congress—show no appetite to challenge the tax or monetary systems that do so much damage to our economy. The IRS and the federal Reserve are off limits for criticism or reform. There's no resistance to spending, either domestic or foreign. Debt is not seen as a problem. The supply-siders won on this issue, and now many conservatives readily endorse deficit spending.

There's no serious opposition to the expanding welfare state, with rapid growth of the education, agriculture and medical-care bureaucracy. Support for labor unions and protectionism are not uncommon. Civil liberties are easily sacrificed in the post-9/11 atmosphere prevailing in Washington. Privacy issues are of little concern, except for a few Members of Congress. Foreign aid and internationalism—in spite of some healthy criticism of the UN and growing concerns for our national sovereignty— are championed on both sides of the aisle. Lip service is given to the free market and free trade, yet the entire economy is run by special-interest legislation favoring big business, big labor and, especially, big money.

Instead of the "end of history," we are now experiencing the end of a vocal limited-government movement in our nation's capital.

269

While most conservatives no longer defend balanced budgets and reduced spending, most liberals have grown lazy in defending civil liberties and now are approving wars that we initiate. The so-called "third way" has arrived and, sadly, it has taken the worst of what the conservatives and liberals have to offer. The people are less well off for it, while liberty languishes as a result.

Neocons enthusiastically embrace the Department of Education and national testing. Both parties overwhelmingly support the huge commitment to a new prescription drug program. Their devotion to the new approach called "compassionate conservatism" has lured many conservatives into supporting programs for expanding the federal role in welfare and in church charities. The faith-based initiative is a neocon project, yet it only repackages and expands the liberal notion of welfare. The intellectuals who promoted these initiatives were neocons, but there's nothing conservative about expanding the federal government's role in welfare.

The supply-siders' policy of low-marginal tax rates has been incorporated into neoconism, as well as their support for easy money and generous monetary inflation. Neoconservatives are disinterested in the gold standard and even ignore the supply-siders' argument for a phony gold standard.

Is it any wonder that federal government spending is growing at a rate faster than in any time in the past 35 years?

Power, politics and privilege prevail over the rule of law, liberty, justice and peace. But it does not need to be that way. Neoconism has brought together many old ideas about how government should rule the people. It may have modernized its appeal and packaging, but authoritarian rule is authoritarian rule, regardless of the humanitarian overtones. A solution can only come after the current ideology driving our government policies is replaced with a more positive one. In a historical context, liberty is a modern idea and must once again regain the high moral ground for civilization to advance. Restating the old justifications for war, people control and a benevolent state will not suffice. It cannot eliminate the shortcomings that always occur when the state assumes authority over others and when the will of one nation is forced on another—whether or not it is done with good intentions.

I realize that all conservatives are not neoconservatives, and all neocons don't necessarily agree on all points—which mean that, in spite of their tremendous influence, most Members of Congress and those in the administration do not necessarily take their marching orders from the AEI or Richard Perle. But to use this as a reason to ignore what neoconservative leaders believe, write about it and agitate for—with amazing success I might point out—would be at our own peril. This country still allows open discourse—though less everyday—and we who disagree should push the discussion and expose those who drive our policies. It is getting more difficult to get fair and balanced discussion on the issues, because it has become routine for the hegemons to label those who object to preemptive war and domestic surveillance as traitors, unpatriotic and un-American. The uniformity of support for our current foreign policy by major and cable-news networks should concern every American. We should all be thankful for CSPAN and the internet.

Michael Ledeen and other neoconservatives are already lobbying for war against Iran. Ledeen is pretty nasty to those who call for a calmer, reasoned approach by calling those who are not ready for war "cowards and appeasers of tyrants." Because some urge a less militaristic approach to dealing with Iran, he claims they are betraying America's best "traditions." I wonder where he learned early American history! It's obvious that Ledeen doesn't consider the Founders and the Constitution part of our best traditions. We were hardly encouraged by the American revolutionaries to pursue an American empire. We were, however, urged to keep the Republic they so painstakingly designed.

If the neoconservatives retain control of the conservative, limited-government movement in Washington, the ideas, once championed by conservatives, of limiting the size and scope of government will be a long-forgotten dream.

The believers in liberty ought not to deceive themselves. Who should be satisfied? Certainly not conservatives, for there is no conservative movement left. How could liberals be satisfied? They are pleased with the centralization of education and medical programs in Washington and support many of the administration's proposals. But none should be pleased with the steady attack on the civil liberties of all American citizens and the now-accepted consensus that preemptive war—for almost any reason—is an acceptable policy for dealing with all the conflicts and problems of the world.

In spite of the deteriorating conditions in Washington—with loss of personal liberty, a weak economy, exploding deficits, and perpetual war, followed by nation building—there are still quite a number of us who would relish the opportunity to improve things, in one way or another. Certainly, a growing number of frustrated Americans, from both the right and the

271

left, are getting anxious to see this Congress do a better job. But first, Congress must stop doing a bad job.

We're at the point where we need a call to arms, both here in Washington and across the country. I'm not talking about firearms. Those of us who care need to raise both arms and face our palms out and begin waving and shouting: Stop! Enough is enough! It should include liberals, conservatives and independents. We're all getting a bum rap from politicians who are pushed by polls and controlled by special-interest money.

One thing is certain: no matter how morally justified the programs and policies seem, the ability to finance all the guns and butter being promised is limited, and those limits are becoming more apparent every day.

Spending, borrowing and printing money cannot be the road to prosperity. It hasn't worked in Japan, and it isn't working here either. As a matter of fact, it's never worked anytime throughout history. A point is always reached where government planning, spending and inflation run out of steam. Instead of these old tools reviving an economy, as they do in the early stages of economic interventionism, they eventually become the problem. Both sides of the political spectrum must one day realize that limitless government intrusion in the economy, in our personal lives and in the affairs of other nations cannot serve the best interests of America. This is not a conservative problem, nor is it a liberal problem—it's a government intrusion problem that comes from both groups, albeit for different reasons. The problems emanate from both camps that champion different programs for different reasons. The solution will come when both groups realize that it's not merely a single-party problem, or just a liberal or just a conservative problem.

Once enough of us decide we've had enough of all these so-called good things that the government is always promising—or more likely, when the country is broke and the government is unable to fulfill its promises to the people—we can start a serious discussion on the proper role for government in a free society. Unfortunately, it will be some time before Congress gets the message that the people are demanding true reform. This requires that those responsible for today's problems are exposed and their philosophy of pervasive government intrusion is rejected.

Let it not be said that no one cared, that no one objected once it's realized that our liberties and wealth are in jeopardy. A few have, and others will continue to do so, but too many—both in and out of government—close their eyes to the issue of personal liberty and ignore the fact that endless borrowing to finance endless demands cannot be

272

sustained. True prosperity can only come from a healthy economy and sound money. That can only be achieved in a free society. ■

Truth is always a casualty of war, never more so than with regard to the lead-up to the current conflict.

July 21, 2003
THE JUSTIFICATIONS FOR WAR (PROVEN FALSE)
HON. RON PAUL of TEXAS
IN THE HOUSE OF REPRESENTATIVES

Madam Speaker, the truth about whether or not Saddam Hussein sought to buy uranium from Niger has dominated the news for the past several weeks. Many of those challenging the administration on this issue are motivated more by politics than by policy. Some of today's critics were strongly in favor of going to war against Iraq when doing so appeared politically popular, but now are chagrined that the war is not going as smoothly as was hoped.

I am sure once the alleged attempt to buy uranium is thoroughly debunked, the other excuses for going to war will be examined with a great deal of scrutiny as well. It is obvious that the evidence used to justify going to war is now less than convincing. The charge that Saddam Hussein had aluminum tubes used in manufacturing nuclear weapons was in error. A fleet of unmanned aerial vehicles capable of dispensing chemical and biological weapons did not exist.

The 63,000 liters of anthrax and botulism have not been found, nor have any of the mobile germ labs. There are no signs of the one million pounds of sarin, mustard, and VX gasses alleged to exist.

No evidence has been revealed to indicate Iraq was a threat to the security of any nation, let alone America.

The charge that Saddam Hussein was connected to the al Qaeda was wrong. Saddam Hussein's violations the UN resolutions regarding weapons of mass destruction remain unproven.

How could so many errors have occurred? Some say it was incompetence, while others claim outright deception and lies. Some say it was selective use of intelligence to promote a particular policy already decided upon. This debate, I am sure, will rage on for a long time, and since motivations are subjective and hard to prove, resolving the controversy will be difficult. However, this should not diminish the importance of sorting out truth from fiction, errors from malice.

One question, though, I hope gets asked: Why should we use intelligence cited by a foreign government as justification for going to war? One would think the billions we spend would produce reliable intelligence-gathering agencies.

Since we lack a coherent foreign policy, we see support for war from different groups depending on circumstances unrelated to national defense. For instance, those who strenuously objected to Kosovo promoted war in Iraq. And those who objected to Iraq are now anxious to send troops to Liberia. For some, UN permission is important and necessary. For others, the UN is helpful provided it endorses the war they want.

Only a few correctly look to the Constitution and to Congress to sort out the pros and cons of each conflict, and decide whether or not a declaration of war is warranted.

The sad fact is that we have lost our way. A legitimate threat to national security is no longer a litmus test for sending troops hither and yon, and the American people no longer require Congress to declare the wars we fight. Hopefully, some day this will change.

The raging debate over whether or not Saddam Hussein tried to buy uranium, as important as it is, distracts from the much more important strategic issue of the proper foreign policy in a Republic.

Hopefully, we will soon seriously consider the foreign policy approach advocated by our Founding Fathers, a policy of nonintervention in the affairs of other nations. Avoiding entangling alliances and staying out of the internal affairs of other nations is the policy most conducive to peace and prosperity. Policing the world and nation building are not proper for our constitutional republic. ■

Moves toward sanctions against nations like Syria tend to be another direct result of war. This policy restricts economic freedom and serves only to widen tensions.

October 16, 2003
STATE OPPOSING TRADE SANCTIONS AGAINST SYRIA
HON. RON PAUL of TEXAS
IN THE HOUSE OF REPRESENTATIVES

Mr. Speaker, I would like to express my strong opposition to this ill-conceived and ill-timed legislation.

This bill will impose what is effectively a trade embargo against Syria and will force the severance of diplomatic and business ties between the United States and Syria. It will also significantly impede travel between the United States and Syria. Worse yet, the bill also provides essentially an open-ended authorization for the president to send U.S. taxpayer money to Syria should that country do what we are demanding in this bill.

This bill cites Syria's alleged support for Hamas, Hizballah, Palestine Islamic Jihad, the Popular Front for the Liberation of Palestine, and other terrorist groups as evidence that Syria is posing a threat to the United States. Not since the Hizballah bombing of a U.S. Marine barracks in Lebanon in 1983, have any of these organizations attacked the United States. After that attack on our Marines, who were sent to Beirut to intervene in a conflict that had nothing to do with the United States, President Ronald Reagan wisely ordered their withdrawal from that volatile area. Despite what the interventionists constantly warn, the world did not come to an end back in 1983 when the president decided to withdraw from Beirut and leave the problems there to be worked out by those countries most closely involved.

What troubles me greatly about this bill is that, although the named, admittedly bad, terrorist organizations do not target the United States at present, we are basically declaring our intention to pick a fight with them. **We are declaring that we will take pre-emptive actions against organizations that apparently have no quarrel with us.** Is this wise, particularly considering their capacity to carry out violent acts against those with whom they are in conflict? Is this not inviting trouble by stirring up a hornet's nest? Is there anything to be gained in this?

This bill imposes an embargo on Syria for, among other reasons, the Syrian government's inability to halt fighters crossing the Syrian border into Iraq. While I agree that any foreign fighters coming into Iraq to attack American troops is totally unacceptable, I wonder just how much control Syria has over its borders—particularly over the chaotic border with Iraq. If Syria has no control over its borders, is it valid to impose sanctions on the country for its inability to halt clandestine border crossings? **I find it a bit ironic to be imposing** a trade embargo on Syria for failing to control its borders when we do not have control of our own borders. Scores cross illegally into the United States each year—potentially including those who cross over with the intent to do us harm—yet very little is done to secure our own borders. Perhaps this is because our resources are too engaged guarding the borders of countless countries overseas. But there is no consistency in our policy. Look at the border between Pakistan and Afghanistan: while we continue to maintain friendly relations and deliver generous foreign aid to Pakistan, it is clear that Pakistan does not control its border with Afghanistan. In all likelihood, Osama bin Laden himself has crossed over the Afghan border into Pakistan. No one proposes an embargo on Pakistan. On the contrary: the supplemental budget request we are taking up this week includes another $200 million in loan guarantees to Pakistan.

I am also concerned about the timing of this bill. As we continue to pursue Al-Qaeda—some of which escaped and continue to operate—it seems to me we need all the help we can get in tracking these criminals down and holding them to account for the attack on the United States. As the AP reported recently:

So, too, are Syria's claims, supported by U.S. intelligence, that Damascus has provided the United States with valuable assistance in countering terror. ...The Syrians have in custody Mohammed Haydar Zammer, believed to have recruited some of the Sept. 11 hijackers, and several high-level Iraqis who were connected to the Saddam Hussein government have turned up in U.S. custody.

Numerous other press reports detail important assistance Syria has given the US after 9/11. If Syria is providing assistance to the U.S. in tracking these people down—any assistance—passing this bill can only be considered an extremely counterproductive development. Does anyone here care to guess how much assistance Syria will be providing us once this bill is passed? Can we afford to turn our back on Syria's assistance, even if it is not as complete as it could be?

That is the problem with this approach. Imposing sanctions and cutting off relations with a country is ineffective and counterproductive. It is only a half step short of war and very often leads to war. This bill may well even completely eliminate any trade between the two countries. It will almost completely shut the door on diplomatic relations. It sends a strong message to Syria and the Syrian people that we no longer wish to engage you. This cannot be in our best interest.

This bill may even go further than that. In a disturbing bit of déjà vu, the bill makes references to "Syria's acquisition of weapons of mass destruction (WMD)" and threatens to "impede" Syrian weapons ambitions. This was the justification for our intervention in Iraq, yet after more than a thousand inspectors have spent months and some $300 million, none have

276

been found. Will this bill's unproven claims that Syria has WMD be later used to demand military action against that country?

Mr. Speaker, history is replete with examples of the futility of sanctions and embargoes and travel bans. More than 40 years of embargo against Cuba have not produced the desired change there. Sadly, embargoes and sanctions most often hurt those least responsible. A trade embargo against Syria will hurt American businesses and will cost American jobs. It will make life more difficult for the average Syrian, with whom we have no quarrel. Making life painful for the population is not the best way to win over hearts and minds. I strongly urge my colleagues to reject this counterproductive bill. ■

Economic liberty is not the only likely victim of war, the most egregious threat to personal liberty is conscription. The specter of a draft accompanies war, especially when it is unpopular and not properly declared.

November 21, 2003
CONSCRIPTION—THE TERRIBLE PRICE OF WAR
HON. RON PAUL of TEXAS
IN THE HOUSE OF REPRESENTATIVES

The ultimate cost of war is almost always the loss of liberty. True defensive wars and revolutionary wars against tyrants may preserve or establish a free society, as did our war against the British. But these wars are rare. Most wars are unnecessary, dangerous, and cause senseless suffering with little being gained. The result of most conflicts throughout the ages has been loss of liberty and life on both sides. **The current war in which we find ourselves clearly qualifies as one of those unnecessary and dangerous wars. To get the people to support ill-conceived wars, the nation's leaders employ grand schemes of deception.**

Woodrow Wilson orchestrated our entry into World War I by first promising during the election of 1916 to keep us out of the European conflict, then a few months later pressuring and maneuvering Congress into declaring war against Germany. Whether it was the Spanish American War before that, or all the wars since, U.S. presidents have deceived the people to gain popular support for ill-conceived military ventures. Wilson wanted the war and immediately demanded conscription to fight it. He didn't have the guts even to name the program a military draft; instead in a speech before Congress calling for war he advised the army should be "chosen upon the principle of universal liability to service." Most Americans at the time of the declaration didn't believe actual combat troops would be sent. What a dramatic change from this early perception, when the people endorsed the war, to the carnage that followed—and the later disillusionment with Wilson and his grand scheme for world government under the League of Nations. The American people rejected this gross new entanglement, a reflection of a somewhat healthier age than the one we find ourselves in today.

But when it comes to war, the principle of deception lives on. The plan for "universal liability to serve" once again is raising its ugly head. The dollar cost of the current war is already staggering, yet plans are being made to drastically expand the human cost by forcing conscription on the young men (and maybe women) who have no ax to grind with the Iraqi people and want no part of this fight.

Hundreds of Americans have already been killed, and thousands more wounded and crippled, while thousands of others will experience new and deadly war-related illnesses not yet identified.

We were told we had to support this pre-emptive war against Iraq because Saddam Hussein had weapons of mass destruction (and to confront al Qaeda). It was said our national security depended on it. But all these dangers were found not to exist in Iraq. It was implied that lack of support for this Iraqi invasion was un-American and unpatriotic.

Since the original reasons for the war never existed, it is now claimed that we're there to make Iraq a Western-style democracy and to spread Western values. And besides, it's argued, it's nice that Saddam Hussein has been removed from power. But **does the mere existence of evil somewhere in the world justify preemptive war at the expense of the American people? Utopian dreams, fulfilled by autocratic means, hardly qualify as being morally justifiable.**

These after-the-fact excuses for invasion and occupation of a sovereign nation direct attention away from the charge that the military-industrial complex encouraged this war. It was encouraged by war profiteering, a desire to control natural resources (oil), and a neo-con agenda of American hegemony with the goal of redrawing the borders of the countries of the Middle East.

The inevitable failure of such a seriously flawed foreign policy cannot be contemplated by those who have put so much energy into this occupation. The current quagmire prompts calls from many for escalation, with more troops being sent to Iraq. Many of our reservists and National Guardsmen cannot wait to get out and have no plans to re-enlist. The odds are that our policy of foreign intervention, which has been with us for many decades, is not likely to soon change. The dilemma of how to win an un-winnable war is the issue begging for an answer.

To get more troops, the draft will likely be reinstated. The implicit prohibition of "involuntary servitude" under the 13th Amendment to the Constitution has already been ignored many times, so few will challenge the constitutionality of the coming draft.

Unpopular wars invite conscription. Volunteers disappear, as well they should. A truly defensive just war prompts popular support. A conscripted, unhappy soldier is better off in the long run than the slaves of old since the "enslavement" is only temporary. But in the short run, the draft may well turn out to be more deadly and degrading, as one is forced to commit life and limb to a less than worthy cause—like teaching democracy to unwilling and angry Arabs. Slaves were safer in that their owners had an economic interest in protecting their lives. Endangering the lives of our soldiers is acceptable policy, and that's why they are needed. Too often, though, our men and women who are exposed to the hostilities of war and welcomed initially are easily forgotten after the fighting ends. Soon afterward, the injured and the sick are ignored and forgotten.

It is said we go about the world waging war to promote peace, yet the price paid is rarely weighed against the failed efforts to make the world a better place. **Justifying conscription to promote the cause of liberty is one of the most bizarre notions ever conceived by man! Forced servitude, with the risk of death and serious injury as a price to live free, makes no sense.** What right does anyone have to sacrifice the lives of others for some cause of questionable value? Even if well motivated, it can't justify using force on uninterested persons.

It's said that the 18-year-old owes it to his country. Hogwash! It just as easily could be argued that a 50-year-old chicken-hawk, who promotes war and places the danger on innocent young people, owes a heck of a lot more to the country than the 18-year-old being denied his liberty for a cause that has no justification.

All drafts are unfair. All 18- and 19-year-olds are never drafted. By its very nature, a draft must be discriminatory. All drafts hit the most vulnerable young people, as the elites learn quickly how to avoid the risks of combat.

The dollar cost of war and the economic hardship is great in all wars and cannot be minimized. War is never economically beneficial, except for those in position to profit from war expenditures. The great tragedy of war is the careless disregard for civil liberties of our own people. Abuses of German and Japanese Americans in World War I and World War II are well known.

But the real sacrifice comes with conscription—forcing a small number of young vulnerable citizens to fight the wars that older men and women—who seek glory in military victory without themselves being exposed to danger—promote. These are wars with neither purpose nor moral justification, and too often not even declared by the Congress.

Without conscription, unpopular wars are much more difficult to fight. Once the draft was undermined in the 1960s and early 1970s, the Vietnam War came to an end. But most importantly, liberty cannot be preserved by tyranny. A free society must always resort to volunteers. Tyrants think nothing of forcing men to fight and serve in wrongheaded wars; a true fight for survival and defense of America would elicit, I'm sure, the assistance of every able-bodied man and woman. This is not the case for wars of mischief far away from home in which we so often have found ourselves in the past century.

One of the worst votes that an elected official could ever cast would be to institute a military draft to fight an illegal war, if that individual himself maneuvered to avoid military service. But avoiding the draft on principle qualifies oneself to work hard to avoid all unnecessary war and oppose the draft for all others.

A government that is willing to enslave a portion of its people to fight an unjust war can never be trusted to protect the liberties of its own citizens. The ends can never justify the means, no matter what the Neo-cons say. ∎

"Of all tyrannies, a tyranny exercised 'for the good of its victims' may be the most oppressive."—C. S. Lewis

CHAPTER 15

As the politics heated up, Congress wanted to absolve itself of blame for an unpopular war. I wanted to remind my colleagues that when this business started they had a chance to make a difference and consciously chose inaction.

February 4, 2004
CONGRESS ABANDONED ITS DUTY TO DEBATE AND DECLARE WAR
HON. RON PAUL of TEXAS
IN THE HOUSE OF REPRESENTATIVES

There is plenty of blame to go around for the mistakes made by going to war in Iraq, especially now that it is common knowledge Saddam Hussein told the truth about having no weapons of mass destruction, and that al Qaida and 9/11 were in no way related to the Iraqi government.

Our intelligence agencies failed for whatever reason this time, but their frequent failures should raise the question of whether or not secretly spending forty billion taxpayer dollars annually gathering bad information is a good investment. The administration certainly failed us by making the decision to sacrifice so much in life and limb, by plunging us into this Persian Gulf quagmire that surely will last for years to come.

But before Congress gets too carried away with condemning the administration or the intelligence gathering agencies, it ought to look to itself. A proper investigation and debate by this Congress—as we're now scrambling to accomplish—clearly was warranted prior to any decision to go to war. An open and detailed debate on a proper declaration of war certainly would have revealed that U.S. national security was not threatened—and the whole war could have been avoided. Because Congress did not do that, it deserves the greatest criticism for its dereliction of duty.

There was a precise reason why the most serious decision made by a country—the decision to go to war—was assigned in our Constitution to the body closest to the people. If we followed this charge I'm certain fewer wars would be fought, wide support would be achieved for just defensive wars, there would be less political finger-pointing if events went badly, and blame could not be placed on one individual or agency. This process would more likely achieve victory, which has eluded us in recent decades.

The president reluctantly has agreed to support an independent commission to review our intelligence gathering failures, and that is good. Cynics said nothing much would be achieved by studying pre-9/11 intelligence failures, but it looks like some objective criticisms will emerge from that inquiry. We can hope for the best from this newly appointed commission.

But already we hear the inquiry will be deliberately delayed, limited to investigating only the failures of the intelligence agencies themselves, and may divert its focus to studying intelligence gathering related to North Korea and elsewhere. If the commission avoids the central controversy— whether or not there was selective use of information or undue pressure put on the CIA to support a foregone conclusion to go to war by the administration—the commission will appear a sham.

Regardless of the results, the process of the inquiry is missing the most important point—the failure of Congress to meet its responsibility on the decision to go, or not go, to war. The current mess was predictable from the beginning. Unfortunately, Congress voluntarily gave up its prerogative over war and illegally transferred this power to the president in October of 2002. The debate we are having now should have occurred here in the halls of Congress then. We should have debated a declaration of war resolution. Instead, Congress chose to transfer this decision-making power to the president to avoid the responsibility of making the hard choice of sending our young people into harms way, against a weak, third world country. This the president did on his own, with congressional acquiescence. The blame game has emerged only now that we are in the political season. Sadly, the call for and the appointment of the commission is all part of this political process.

It is truly disturbing to see many who abdicated their congressional responsibility to declare or reject war, who timidly voted to give the president the power he wanted, now posturing as his harshest critics. ■

The problems in Iraq are not new, nor the result of "mismanagement," rather, they represent the result of a bad policy long pursued.

June 3, 2004
THE SAME OLD FAILED POLICIES IN IRAQ
HON. RON PAUL of TEXAS
IN THE HOUSE OF REPRESENTATIVES

Mr. Speaker, the more things change, the more they stay the same. Our allegiances to our allies and friends change constantly. For a decade, exiled Iraqi Ahmed Chalabi was our chosen leader-to-be in a new Iraq. Championed by Pentagon neocons and objected to by the State Department, Mr. Chalabi received more than 100 million U.S. taxpayer dollars as our man designated to be leader of a new Iraqi government.

But something happened on the way to the coronation. The State Department finally won out in its struggle with the Pentagon to dump Chalabi and his Iraqi National Congress, delivering Iraq to a competing exiled group, Dr. Iyad Allawi's Iraqi national Accord. But never fear, both groups were CIA supported and both would be expected to govern as an American puppet. And that's the problem. Under the conditions that currently exist in Iraq, American sponsorship of a government, or even United Nations approval, for that matter, will be rejected by a nationalistic Iraqi people.

We never seem to learn, and the Muslim Middle East never forgets. Our support for the Shah of Iran and Saddam Hussein's war against Iran has never endeared us to the Iranians. We're supposed to be surprised to discover that our close confidant Ahmed Chalabi turns out to be a cozy pragmatic friend of Iran. The CIA may have questioned the authenticity of Iranian intelligence passed on to the U.S. by Chalabi, yet still this intelligence was used eagerly to promote the pro-war propaganda that so many in Congress and the nation bought into. And now it looks like the intelligence fed to Chalabi by Iran was deliberately falsified, but because it fit in so neatly with the neocon's determination to remake the entire Middle East, starting with a preemptive war against Iraq, it was received enthusiastically.

Inadvertently we served the interests of both Iran and Osama bin Laden by eliminating the very enemy they despised—Saddam Hussein. To the Iranians delight, it was payback time for our allegiance with Saddam Hussein against Iran in the 1980s.

The serious concern is that valuable and top-secret U.S. intelligence may well have gone in the other direction: to Iran with the help of Chalabi.

These serious concerns led to the dumping of the heir apparent Chalabi, the arrest of his colleagues, and the raid on his home and headquarters to seize important documents. The connection between Chalabi and the UN food-for-oil scandal is yet to be determined.

What a mess! But no one should be surprised. Regime change plans—whether by CIA operations or by preemptive war—almost always go badly. American involvement in installing the Shah of Iran in the fifties, killing Diem in South Vietnam in the sixties, helping Osama bin Laden against the Soviets in the eighties, assisting Saddam Hussein against Iran in the eighties, propping up dictators in many Arab countries, and supporting the destruction of the Palestinian people all have had serious repercussions on American interests including the loss of American life. We have wasted hundreds of billions of dollars while the old wounds in the Middle East continue to fester.

How many times have our friends become our enemies and our enemies our friends, making it difficult to determine which is which? Our relationship with Kadafi in Libya is an example of the silliness of our policy. Does his recent "conversion" to our side qualify him for U.S. assistance? No one can possibly predict what our relationship with Kadafi will be in a year or two from now. My guess is that he too has a long memory. And even if he becomes a U.S. stooge, it will only foment antagonism from his own people for his cozy relationship with the United States. Long term, interference in the internal affairs of other nations doesn't help us or those we support.

Those who strongly argue behind the scenes that we must protect "our oil" surely should have second thoughts, as oil prices soar over $40 with our current policy of military interventionism.

The real tragedy is that even those with good intentions who argue the case for our military presence around the world never achiever their stated goals. Not only do the efforts fall short, the unintended consequences in life and limb and dollars spent are always much greater than ever anticipated. The blow-back effects literally go on for decades.

The invisible economic costs are enormous but generally ignored. A policy of militarism and constant war has huge dollar costs, which contribute to the huge deficits, higher interest rates, inflation, and economic dislocations. War cannot raise the standard of living for the average American. Participants in the military-industrial complex do benefit, however. Now the grand scheme of physically rebuilding Iraq using American corporations may well prove profitable to the select few with political connections.

The clear failure of the policy of foreign interventionism followed by our leaders for more than a hundred years should prompt a reassessment of our philosophy. Tactical changes, or relying more on the UN, will not solve these problems. Either way the burden will fall on the American taxpayer and the American soldier.

The day is fast approaching when we no longer will be able to afford this burden. For now foreign governments are willing to loan us the money needed to finance our current account deficit, and indirectly the cost of our worldwide military operations. It may seem possible for the moment because we have been afforded the historically unique privilege of printing the world's reserve currency. Foreigners have been only too willing to take our depreciating dollars for their goods. **Economic law eventually will limit our ability to live off others by credit creation. Eventually trust in the dollar will be diminished, if not destroyed.** Those who hold these trillion plus dollars can hold us hostage if it's ever in their interest. It may be that economic law and hostility toward the United States will combine to precipitate an emotionally charged rejection of the dollar.

That's when the true wealth of the country will become self-evident and we will no longer be able to afford the extravagant expense of pursuing an American empire. No nation has ever been able to finance excessive foreign entanglements and domestic entitlements through printing press money and borrowing from abroad.

It's time we reconsider the advice of the Founding Fathers and the guidelines of the Constitution, which counsel a foreign policy of non-intervention and strategic independence. Setting a good example is a far better way to spread American ideals than through force of arms. Trading with nations, without interference by international government regulators, is far better than sanctions and tariffs that too often plant the seeds of war.

The principle of self-determination should be permitted for all nations and all demographically defined groups. The world tolerated the breakup of the ruthless Soviet and Yugoslavian systems rather well, even as certain national and ethnic groups demanded self-determination and independence.

This principle is the source of the solution for Iraq. We should suggest and encourage each of the three groups—the Sunnis, the Shiites, and the Kurds—to seek self-government and choose voluntarily whether they want to associate with a central government.

Instead of the incessant chant about us forcing democracy on others, why not read our history and see how thirteen nations joined together to form a loose-knit republic with emphasis on local self-government. Part of the problem with our effort to re-order Iraq is that the best solution is something we have essentially rejected here in the United States. It would make a lot more sense to concentrate on rebuilding our Republic, emphasizing the principles of private property, free markets, trade, and personal liberty here at home rather then pursuing war abroad. If this were done, we would not be a militaristic state spending ourselves into bankruptcy, and government benefits to the untold thousands of corporations and special interest would be denied.

True defense is diminished when money and energy are consumed by activities outside the scope of specifically protecting our national security. **Diverting resources away from defense and the protection of our borders while antagonizing so many around the world actually serves to expose us to greater danger from more determined enemies.**

A policy of non-intervention and strategic independence is the course we should take if we're serious about peace and prosperity. Liberty works! ∎

Just as we saw in Iraq, the ground begins to be laid for war with Iran.

May 6, 2004
DON'T START A WAR WITH IRAN!
HON. RON PAUL of TEXAS
IN THE HOUSE OF REPRESENTATIVES

Mr. Speaker, I rise in strong opposition to this ill-conceived and ill-timed legislation. Let's not fool ourselves: this concurrent resolution leads us down the road to war against Iran. It creates a precedent for future escalation, as did similar legislation endorsing "regime change" in Iraq back in 1998.

I find it incomprehensible that as the failure of our Iraq policy becomes more evident—even to its most determined advocates—we here are approving the same kind of policy toward Iran. With Iraq becoming more of a problem daily, the solution as envisioned by this legislation is to look for yet another fight. And we should not fool ourselves: this legislation sets the stage for direct conflict with Iran. The resolution "calls upon all State Parties to the Treaty on the Non-Proliferation of Nuclear Weapons (NPT), including the United States, to use all appropriate means to deter, dissuade, and prevent Iran from acquiring nuclear weapons…" Note the phrase "…use all appropriate means…."

Additionally, this legislation calls for yet more and stricter sanctions on Iran, including a demand that other countries also impose sanctions on Iran. As we know, sanctions are unmistakably a move toward war, particularly when, as in this legislation, a demand is made that the other nations of the world similarly isolate and blockade the country. Those who wish for a regime change in Iran should especially reject sanctions—just look at how our Cuba policy has allowed Fidel Castro to maintain his hold on power for decades. **Sanctions do not hurt political leaders, as we know most recently from our sanctions against Iraq, but rather sow misery among the poorest and most vulnerable segments of society. Dictators do not go hungry when sanctions are imposed.**

It is somewhat ironic that we are again meddling in Iranian affairs. Students of history will recall that the U.S. government's ill-advised coup against Iranian leader Mohammed Mossadegh in 1953 and its subsequent installation of the Shah as the supreme ruler led to intense hatred of the United States and eventually to the radical Islamic revolution of 1979. One can only wonder what our relations would be with Iran if not for the decades of meddling in that country's internal affairs. We likely would not be considering resolutions such as this. Yet the solution to all the difficulties created by our meddling foreign policy always seems to always be yet more meddling. Will Congress ever learn?

I urge my colleagues to reject this move toward war with Iran, to reject the failed policies of regime-change and nation building, and to return to the wise and consistent policy of non-interventionism in the affairs of other sovereign nations. ■

*Resolutions commending, absolving or condemning service members
usually have language designed to support bad policy as well. Seldom
do such resolutions look at our policy errors and so often they are
designed to give political cover to House Members.*

May 6, 2004
STATEMENT ON THE ABUSE OF PRISONERS IN IRAQ
HON. RON PAUL of TEXAS
IN THE HOUSE OF REPRESENTATIVES

Mr. Speaker, I rise in opposition to this resolution as written. Like so
many resolutions we have seen here on the Iraq war, this one is not at all
what it purports to be. Were this really a resolution condemning abuse of
prisoners and other detainees, I doubt anyone here would oppose it. Clearly
the abuse and humiliation of those in custody is deplorable, and the pictures
we have all seen over the past week are truly horrific.

But why are we condemning a small group of low-level service
members when we do not yet know the full story? Why are we rushing to
insert ourselves into an ongoing investigation, pretending that we already
know the conclusions when we have yet to even ask all the questions? As
revolting as the pictures we have seen are, they are all we have to go by,
and we are reacting to these pictures alone. We do not and cannot know
the full story at this point, yet we jump to condemn those who have not
even yet had the benefit of a trial. We appear to be operating on the
principle of guilty until proven innocent. It seems convenient and perhaps
politically expedient to blame a small group of "bad apples" for what may
well turn out to be something completely different—as the continuously
widening investigation increasingly suggests.

Some of the soldiers in the photographs claim that their superior officers
and the civilian contractors in charge of the interrogations forced them to
pose this way. We cannot say with certainty what took place in Iraq's
prisons based on a few photographs. We have heard that some of those
soldiers put in charge of prisons in Iraq were woefully unprepared for the
task at hand. We have heard that they were thrown into a terribly confusing,
stressful, and dangerous situation with little training and little understanding
of the rules and responsibilities. What additional stresses and psychological
pressures were applied by those in charge of interrogations? We don't
know. Does this excuse what appears to be reprehensible behavior? Not
in the slightest, but it does suggest that we need to get all the facts before

we draw conclusions. It is more than a little disturbing that this resolution does not even mention the scores of civilian contractors operating in these prisons at whom numerous fingers are being pointed as instigators of these activities. While these individuals seem to operate with impunity, this legislation before us all but convicts without trial those lowest in the chain of command.

But this resolution is only partly about the alleged abuses of detainees in Iraq. Though this is the pretext for the legislation, this resolution is really just an enthusiastic endorsement of our nation-building activities in Iraq. This resolution "expresses the continuing solidarity and support of the House of Representatives...with the Iraqi people in building a viable Iraqi government and a secure nation." Also this resolution praises the "mission to rebuild and rehabilitate a proud nation after liberating it..." At least the resolution is honest in admitting that our current presence in Iraq is nothing more than a nation-building exercise.

Further, this resolution explicitly endorses what is clearly a failed policy in Iraq. I wonder whether anyone remembers that we did not go to war against Iraq to build a better nation, or to bring about "improvements in...water, sewage, power, infrastructure, transportation, telecommunications, and food security   " as this resolution touts. Nor did those who urged this war claim at the time that the goals were to "significantly improve...food availability, health service, and educational opportunities" in Iraq, as this legislation also references. No, the war was essential, they claimed, to stop a nation poised to use weapons of mass destruction to inflict unspeakable harm against the United States. Now, **historical revisionists are pointing out how wonderful our nation building is going in Iraq, as if that justifies the loss of countless American and Iraqi civilian lives.**

This resolution decries the fact that the administration had not informed Congress of these abuses and that the administration has not kept Congress in the information loop. Yet, Congress made it clear to the administration from the very beginning that Congress wanted no responsibility for the war in Iraq. If Congress wanted to be kept in the loop it should have vigorously exercised its responsibilities from the very beginning. This means, first and foremost, that Congress should have voted on a declaration of war as required in the Constitution. Congress, after abrogating this responsibility in October 2002, now is complaining that it is in the dark. Indeed, who is to say that the legal ambiguity created by the congressional refusal to declare war may not have contributed to the notion that detainees need not be treated in accordance with the Geneva Convention, that governs the treatment of prisoners during a time of war? Until Congress takes up its constitutional responsibilities, complaints that the administration is not sufficiently forthcoming with information ring hollow.

This resolution calls on the administration to keep Congress better informed. But Congress has the power—and the obligation—to keep itself better informed! If Congress is truly interested in being informed, it should hold hearings—exercising its subpoena power if necessary. Depending on the administration to fulfill what is our own constitutional responsibility is once again passing the buck. Isn't this what has gotten us into this trouble in the first place?

I urge my colleagues to oppose this resolution. ■

The 9/11 commission largely offered "more of the same." Until we question our foreign entanglements, we will not search for the right answers.

April 22, 2004
THE LESSONS OF 9/11
HON. RON PAUL of TEXAS
IN THE HOUSE OF REPRESENTATIVES

We are constantly admonished to remember the lessons of 9/11. Of course the real issue is not remembering, but rather knowing what the pertinent lesson of that sad day is.

The 9/11 Commission soon will release its report after months of fanfare by those whose reputations are at stake. The many hours and dollars spent on the investigation may well reveal little we don't already know, while ignoring the most important lessons that should be learned from this egregious attack on our homeland. Common sense already tells us the tens of billions of dollars spent by government agencies, whose job it is to provide security and intelligence for our country, failed.

A full-fledged investigation into the bureaucracy may help us in the future, but one should never pretend that government bureaucracies can be made efficient. It is the very nature of bureaucracies to be inefficient. Spending an inordinate amount of time finger pointing will distract from the real lessons of 9/11. Which agency, which department, or which individual receives the most blame should not be the main purpose of the investigation.

Despite our serious failure to prevent the attacks, it's disturbing to see how politicized the whole investigation has become. Which political party receives the greatest blame is a high stakes election-year event, and distracts from the real lessons ignored by both sides.

Everyone on the Commission assumes that 9/11 resulted from a lack of government action. No one in Washington has raised the question of whether our shortcomings, brought to light by 9/11, could have been a result of too much government. Possibly in the final report we will discuss this, but to date no one has questioned the assumption that we need more government and, of course—though elusive—a more efficient one.

The failure to understand the nature of the enemy who attacked us on 9/11, along with a pre-determined decision to initiate a pre-emptive war against Iraq, prompted our government to deceive the people into believing that Saddam Hussein had something to do with the attacks on New York and Washington. The majority of the American people still contend the war against Iraq was justified because of the events of 9/11. These misinterpretations have led to many U.S. military deaths and casualties, prompting a growing number of Americans to question the wisdom of our presence and purpose in a strange foreign land 6,000 miles from our shores.

The neoconservative defenders of our policy in Iraq speak of the benefits that we have brought to the Iraqi people: removal of a violent dictator, liberation, democracy, and prosperity. If all this were true, the resistance against our occupation would not be growing. We ought to admit we have not been welcomed as liberators as was promised by the proponents of the war.

Though we hear much about the so-called "benefits" we have delivered to the Iraqi people and the Middle East, we hear little talk of the cost to the American people: lives lost, soldiers maimed for life, uncounted thousands sent home with diseased bodies and minds, billions of dollars consumed, and a major cloud placed over U.S. markets and the economy. Sharp political divisions, reminiscent of the 1960s, are arising at home.

Failing to understand why 9/11 happened and looking for a bureaucratic screw-up to explain the whole thing—while using the event to start an unprovoked war unrelated to 9/11—have dramatically compounded the problems all Americans and the world face. Evidence has shown that there was no connection between Saddam Hussein and the guerilla attacks on New York and Washington, and since no weapons of mass destruction were found, other reasons are given for invading Iraq. The real reasons are either denied or ignored: oil, neoconservative empire building, and our support for Israel over the Palestinians.

The proponents of the Iraqi war do not hesitate to impugn the character of those who point out the shortcomings of current policy, calling them unpatriotic and appeasers of terrorism. It is said that they are responsible for the growing armed resistance, and for the killing of American soldiers. It's conveniently ignored that had the opponents of the current policy prevailed, not one single American would have died nor would tens of thousands of Iraqi civilians have suffered the same fate.

Al Qaeda and many new militant groups would not be enjoying a rapid growth in their ranks. By denying that our sanctions and bombs brought havoc to Iraq, it's easy to play the patriot card and find a scapegoat to blame. We are never at fault and never responsible for bad outcomes of what many believe is, albeit well intentioned, interference in the affairs of others 6,000 miles from our shores.

Pursuing our policy has boiled down to "testing our resolve." It is said by many—even some who did not support the war—that now we have no choice but to "stay the course." They argue that it's a noble gesture to be courageous and continue no matter how difficult. But that should not be the issue. It is not a question of resolve, but rather a question of wise policy. If the policy is flawed and the world and our people are less safe for it, unshakable resolve is the opposite of what we need. Staying the course only makes sense when the difficult tasks are designed to protect our country and to thwart those who pose a direct threat to us. Wilsonian idealism of self-sacrifice to "make the world safe for democracy" should never be an excuse to wage preemptive war—especially since it almost never produces the desired results. There are always too many unintended consequences.

In our effort to change the political structure of Iraq, we continue alliances with dictators and even develop new ones with countries that are anything but democracies. We have a close alliance with Pakistan, Saudi Arabia, many other Arab dictatorships, and a new one with Kadafi of Libya. This should raise questions about the credibility of our commitment to promoting democracy in Iraq—which even our own government wouldn't tolerate.

Show me one neo-con that would accept a national election that put the radical Shiites in charge. As Secretary Rumsfeld said, it's not going to happen. These same people are condemning the recent democratic decisions made in Spain. We should remember that since World War II, in 35 U.S. attempts to promote democracy around the world none have succeeded.

Promoters of war too often fail to contemplate the unintended consequences of an aggressive foreign policy. So far, the anti-war forces have not been surprised with the chaos that has now become Iraq, or Iran's participation—but even they cannot know all the long-term shortcomings of such a policy.

In an eagerness to march on Baghdad, the neo-cons gloated—and I heard them—of the "shock and awe" that was about to hit the Iraqi people. It turns out that the real shock and awe is that we're further from peace in Iraq than we were a year ago—and Secretary Rumsfeld admits his own surprise.

The only policy now offered is to escalate the war and avenge the deaths of American soldiers—if they kill 10 of our troops, we'll kill 100 of theirs. Up until now, announcing the number of Iraqi deaths has been avoided purposely, but the new policy announces our success by the number of Iraqis killed. But the more we kill, the greater the incitement of the radical Islamic militants. The harder we try to impose our will on them, the greater the resistance becomes.

Amazingly, our occupation has done what was at one time thought to be impossible—it has united the Sunnis and Shiites against our presence. Although this is probably temporary, it is real and has deepened our problems in securing Iraq. The results are an escalation of the conflict and the requirement for more troops. This acceleration of the killing is called "pacification"—a bit of 1984 newspeak.

The removal of Saddam Hussein has created a stark irony. The willingness and intensity of the Iraqi people to fight for their homeland has increased many times over. Under Saddam Hussein, essentially no resistance occurred. Instead of jubilation and parades for the liberators, we face much greater and unified efforts to throw out all foreigners than when Saddam Hussein was in charge.

It's not whether the Commission investigation of the causes of 9/11 is unwarranted; since the Commissioners are looking in the wrong places for answers, it's whether much will be achieved.

I'm sure we will hear that the bureaucracy failed, whether it was the FBI, the CIA, the NSC, or all of them for failure to communicate with each other. This will not answer the question of why we were attacked and why our defenses were so poor. Even though $40 billion are spent on intelligence gathering each year, the process failed us. It's likely to be said that what we need is more money and more efficiency. Yet, that approach fails to recognize that depending on government agencies to be efficient is a risky assumption.

We should support efforts to make the intelligence agencies more effective, but one thing is certain: more money won't help. Of the $40 billion spent annually for intelligence, too much is spent on nation building and activities unrelated to justified surveillance.

There are two other lessons that must be learned if we hope to benefit by studying and trying to explain the disaster that hit us on 9/11. If we fail to learn them, we cannot be made safer and the opposite is more likely to occur.

The first point is to understand who assumes most of the responsibility for the security of our homes and businesses in a free society. It's not the police. There are too few of them, and it's not their job to stand guard outside our houses or places of business. More crime occurs in the inner city, where there are not only more police, but more restrictions on property owners' rights to bear and use weapons if invaded by hoodlums. In safer rural areas, where every home has a gun and someone in it who is willing to use it is, there is no false dependency on the police protecting them, but full reliance on the owners' responsibility to deal with any property violators. This understanding works rather well—at least better than in the inner cities where the understanding is totally different.

How does this apply to the 9/11 tragedies? The airline owners accepted the rules of the inner city rather than those of rural America. They all assumed that the government was in charge of airline security—and unfortunately, by law, it was. Not only were the airlines complacent about security, but the FAA dictated all the rules relating to potential hijacking. Chemical plants or armored truck companies that carry money make the opposite assumption, and private guns do a reasonably good job in providing security. Evidently we think more of our money and chemical plants than we do our passengers on airplanes.

The complacency of the airlines is one thing, but the intrusiveness of the FAA is another. Two specific regulations proved to be disastrous for dealing with the thugs who, without even a single gun, took over four airliners and created the havoc of 9/11. Both the prohibition against guns in cockpits and precise instructions that crews not resist hijackers contributed immensely to the horrors of 9/11.

Instead of immediately legalizing a natural right of personal self-defense guaranteed by an explicit Second Amendment freedom, we still do not have armed pilots in the sky. Instead of more responsibility being given to the airlines, the government has taken over the entire process. This has been encouraged by the airline owners, who seek subsidies and insurance protection. Of course, the nonsense of never resisting has been forever vetoed by all passengers.

Unfortunately, the biggest failure of our government will be ignored. I'm sure the Commission will not connect our foreign policy of interventionism—practiced by both major parties for over a hundred years—as an important reason 9/11 occurred. Instead, the claims will stand that the motivation behind 9/11 was our freedom, prosperity, and way of life. If this error persists, all the tinkering and money to improve the intelligence agencies will bear little fruit.

Over the years, the entire psychology of national defense has been completely twisted. Very little attention had been directed toward protecting our national borders and providing homeland security.

Our attention, all too often, was and still is directed outward toward distant lands. Now a significant number of our troops are engaged in Afghanistan and Iraq. We've kept troops in Korea for over 50 years, and thousands of troops remain in Europe and in over 130 other countries. This twisted philosophy of ignoring national borders while pursuing an empire created a situation where Seoul, Korea, was better protected than Washington, DC, on 9/11. These priorities must change, but I'm certain the 9/11 Commission will not address this issue.

This misdirected policy has prompted the current protracted war in Iraq, which has gone on for 13 years with no end in sight. The al Qaeda attacks should not be used to justify more intervention; instead they should be seen as a guerilla attacks against us for what the Arabs and Muslim world see as our invasion and interference in their homelands. This cycle of escalation is rapidly spreading the confrontation worldwide between the Christian West and the Muslim East. With each escalation, the world becomes more dangerous. It is especially made worse when we retaliate against Muslims and Arabs who had nothing to do with 9/11—as we have in Iraq—further confirming the suspicions of the Muslim masses that our goals are more about oil and occupation than they are about punishing those responsible for 9/11.

Those who claim that Iraq is another Vietnam are wrong. They can't be the same. There are too many differences in time, place, and circumstance. But that doesn't mean the Iraqi conflict cannot last longer, spread throughout the region and throughout the world—making it potentially much worse than what we suffered in Vietnam. **In the first 6 years we were in Vietnam, we lost less than 500 troops. Over 700 have been killed in Iraq in just over a year.**

Our failure to pursue al Qaeda and bin Laden in Pakistan and Afghanistan—and diverting resources to Iraq—have seriously compromised our ability to maintain a favorable world opinion of support and cooperation in this effort.

Instead, we have chaos in Iraq while the Islamists are being financed by a booming drug business from U.S.-occupied Afghanistan.

Continuing to deny that the attacks against us are related to our overall policy of foreign meddling through many years and many administrations, makes a victory over our enemies nearly impossible. Not understanding the true nature and motivation of those who have and will commit deadly attacks against us prevents a sensible policy from being pursued. Guerilla warriors, who are willing to risk and sacrifice everything as part of a war they see as defensive, are a far cry, philosophically, from a band of renegades who out of unprovoked hate seek to destroy us and kill themselves in the process. How we fight back depends on understanding these differences.

Of course, changing our foreign policy to one of no pre-emptive war, no nation building, no entangling alliances, no interference in the internal affairs of other nations, and trade and friendship with all who seek it, is no easy task.

The real obstacle, though, is to understand the motives behind our current policy of perpetual meddling in the affairs of others for more than a hundred years.

Understanding why both political parties agree on the principle of continuous foreign intervention is crucial. Those reasons are multiple and varied. They range from the persistent Wilsonian idealism of making the world safe for democracy to the belief that we must protect "our" oil.

Also contributing to this bipartisan, foreign policy view is the notion that promoting world government is worthwhile. This involves support for the United Nations, NATO, control of the world's resources through the IMF, the World Bank, the WTO, NAFTA, FTAA, and the Law of the Sea Treaty—all of which gain the support of those sympathetic to the poor and socialism, while too often the benefits accrue to the well-connected international corporations and bankers sympathetic to economic fascism.

Sadly, in the process the people are forgotten, especially those who pay the taxes, those whose lives are sacrificed in no-win undeclared wars, and the unemployed and poor as the economic consequences of financing our foreign entanglements evolve.

Regardless of one's enthusiasm or lack thereof for the war and the general policy of maintaining American troops in more than 130 countries, one cold fact soon must be recognized by all of us in Congress. The American people cannot afford it; and when the market finally recognizes the over-commitment we've made, the results will not be pleasing to anyone.

A "guns and butter" policy was flawed in the 60s, and gave us interest rates of 21% in the 70s with high inflation rates. The current "guns and butter" policy is even more intense, and our economic infrastructure is more fragile than it was back then. These facts dictate our inability to continue this policy both internationally and domestically. It is true, an unshakable resolve to stay the course in Iraq, or any other hot spot, can be pursued for years. But when a country is adding to its future indebtedness by over $700 billion per year, it can only be done with great economic harm to all our citizens.

Huge deficits, financed by borrowing and Federal Reserve monetization, are an unsustainable policy and always lead to higher price inflation, higher interest rates, a continued erosion of the dollar's value, and a faltering economy. Economic law dictates that the standard of living then must go down for all Americans—except for the privileged few who have an inside track on government largess—if this policy of profligate spending continues. Ultimately, the American people, especially the younger generation, will have to decide whether to languish with current policy or reject the notion that perpetual warfare and continued growth in entitlements should be pursued indefinitely.

CONCLUSION

I'm sure the Commission will not deal with the flaw in the foreign policy endorsed by both parties for these many decades. I hope the Commission tells us why members of the bin Laden family were permitted, immediately after 9/11, to leave the United States without interrogation, when no other commercial or private flights were allowed. That event should have been thoroughly studied and explained to the American people. We actually had a lot more reason to invade Saudi Arabia than we did Iraq in connection with 9/11, but that country, obviously no friend of democracy, remains an unchallenged ally of the United States with few questions asked.

I'm afraid the Commission will answer only a few questions while raising many new ones. Overall, though, the Commission has been beneficial and provides some reassurance to those who believe we operate in a much too closed society. Fortunately, any administration, under the current system, still must respond to reasonable inquiries. ■

Once again, resolutions to support our troops are often designed to reinforce bad policy. These resolutions are rushed to the floor, without committee review, for purely political purposes.

March 17, 2004
OPPOSE A FLAWED POLICY OF PREEMPTIVE WAR
HON. RON PAUL of TEXAS
IN THE HOUSE OF REPRESENTATIVES

Mr. Speaker, today during the floor debate on H. Res. 557 (the Iraq resolution), I unfortunately was denied time to express my dissent on the policy of preemptive war in Iraq—even though I am a member of the International Relations committee. The fact that the committee held no hearings and did not mark up the resolution further challenges the fairness of the process.

I wish to express my opposition to H. Res. 557, obviously not because our armed forces do not deserve praise, but rather because our policy in the Persian Gulf is seriously flawed. **A resolution commending our forces should not be used to rubber-stamp a policy of folly. To do so is disingenuous. Though the resolution may have political benefits, it will prove to be historically incorrect.**

Justifying preemption is not an answer to avoiding appeasement. Very few wars are necessary. Very few wars are good wars. And this one does not qualify. Most wars are costly beyond measure, in life and limb and economic hardship. In this regard, this war does qualify: 566 deaths, 10,000 casualties, and hundreds of billions of dollars for a victory requiring self-deception.

Rather than bragging about victory, we should recognize that the war raging on between the Muslim East and the Christian West has intensified and spread, leaving our allies and our own people less safe. Denying we have an interest in oil, and denying that occupying an Islamic country is an affront to the sensitivities of most Arabs and Muslims, is foolhardy.

Reasserting UN Security Council resolutions as a justification for the war further emphasizes our sacrifice of sovereignty, and only underscores how Congress has reneged its constitutional responsibility over war.

This resolution dramatizes how we have forgotten that for too long we were staunch military and economic allies of Saddam Hussein, confirming the folly of our policy of foreign meddling over many decades. From the days of installing the Shah of Iran to the current worldwide spread of hostilities and hatred, our unnecessary involvement shows so clearly how unintended consequences come back to haunt generation after generation.

Someday our leaders ought to ask why Switzerland, Sweden, Canada, Mexico, and many others are not potential targets of an Islamic attack. Falsely believing that al Qaeda was aligned with Saddam Hussein has resulted in al Qaeda now having a strong presence and influence in Iraq. Falsely believing that Iraq had a supply of weapons of mass destruction has resulted in a dramatic loss of U.S. credibility, as anti-Americanism spreads around the world. Al Qaeda recruitment, sadly, has been dramatically increased.

We all praise our troops and support them. Challenging one's patriotism for not supporting this resolution and/or policy in the Persian Gulf is not legitimate. We should all be cautious about endorsing and financing a policy that unfortunately expands the war rather than ends it. ■

"When goods don't cross borders, soldiers will."—Fredric Bastiat

CHAPTER 16

Asking "what if" is an approach from which our overall foreign policy and our current war effort could benefit. A properly functioning Congress would constantly take this approach.

January 26, 2005
WHAT IF IT WAS ALL A BIG MISTAKE?
HON. RON PAUL of TEXAS
IN THE HOUSE OF REPRESENTATIVES

America's policy of foreign intervention, while still debated in the early 20th Century, is today accepted as conventional wisdom by both political parties. But what if the overall policy is a colossal mistake, a major error in judgment? Not just bad judgment regarding when and where to impose ourselves, but the entire premise that we have a moral right to meddle in the affairs of others? Think of the untold harm done by years of fighting— hundreds of thousands of American casualties, hundreds of thousands of foreign civilian casualties, and unbelievable human and economic costs. What if it was all needlessly borne by the American people? If we do conclude that grave foreign policy errors have been made, a very serious question must be asked: What would it take to change our policy to one more compatible with a true republic's goal of peace, commerce, and friendship with all nations? Is it not possible that Washington's admonition to avoid entangling alliances is sound advice, even today?

In medicine mistakes are made—man is fallible. Misdiagnoses are made, incorrect treatments are given, and experimental trials of medicines are advocated. A good physician understands the imperfections in medical care, advises close follow-ups, and double-checks the diagnosis, treatment, and medication. Adjustments are made to assure the best results. But what if a doctor never checks the success or failure of a treatment, or ignores bad results and assumes his omnipotence—refusing to concede that the initial course of treatment was a mistake? Let me assure you, the results would not be good. Litigation and the loss of reputation in the medical community place restraints on this type of bullheaded behavior.

Sadly, though, when governments, politicians, and bureaucrats make mistakes and refuse to reexamine them, there is little the victims can do to correct things. Since the bully pulpit and the media propaganda machine are instrumental in government cover-ups and deception, the final truth emerges slowly, and only after much suffering. The arrogance of some politicians, regulators, and diplomats actually causes them to become even more aggressive and more determined to prove themselves right, to prove their power is *not to be messed with* by never admitting a mistake. Truly, power corrupts!

The unwillingness to ever reconsider our policy of foreign intervention, despite obvious failures and shortcomings over the last 50 years, has brought great harm to our country and our liberty. Historically, financial realities are the ultimate check on nations bent on empire. Economic laws ultimately prevail over bad judgment. But tragically, the greater the wealth of a country, the longer the flawed policy lasts. We'll probably not be any different.

We are still a wealthy nation, and our currency is still trusted by the world, yet we are vulnerable to some harsh realities about our true wealth and the burden of our future commitments. Overwhelming debt and the precarious nature of the dollar should serve to restrain our determined leaders, yet they show little concern for deficits. Rest assured, though, the limitations of our endless foreign adventurism and spending will become apparent to everyone at some point in time.

Since 9/11, a lot of energy and money have gone into efforts ostensibly designed to make us safer. Many laws have been passed and many dollars have been spent. Whether or not we're better off is another question.

Today we occupy two countries in the Middle East. We have suffered over 20,000 casualties, and caused possibly 100,000 civilian casualties in

Iraq. We have spent over $200 billion in these occupations, as well as hundreds of billions of dollars here at home hoping to be safer. We've created the Department of Homeland Security, passed the Patriot Act, and created a new super CIA agency.

Our government now is permitted to monitor the Internet, to read our mail, to search us without proper search warrants, to develop a national ID card, and to investigate what people are reading in libraries. Ironically, illegal aliens flow into our country and qualify for driving licenses and welfare benefits with little restraint.

These issues are discussed, but nothing has been as highly visible to us as the authoritarianism we accept at the airport. The creation of the Transportation Security Administration (TSA) has intruded on the privacy of all airline travelers, and there is little evidence that we are safer for it. Driven by fear, we have succumbed to the age-old temptation to sacrifice liberty on the pretense of obtaining security. Love of security, unfortunately, all too often vanquishes love of liberty.

Unchecked fear of another 9/11-type attack constantly preoccupies our leaders and most of our citizens, and drives the legislative attack on our civil liberties. It's frightening to see us doing to ourselves what even bin Laden never dreamed he could accomplish with his suicide bombers.

We don't understand the difference between a vague threat of terrorism and the danger of a guerilla war. One prompts us to expand and nationalize domestic law enforcement while limiting the freedoms of all Americans. The other deals with understanding terrorists like bin Laden, who declared war against us in 1998. Not understanding the difference makes it virtually impossible to deal with the real threats. We are obsessed with passing new laws to make our country safe from a terrorist attack. This confusion about the cause of the 9/11 attacks, the fear they engendered, and the willingness to sacrifice liberty prompts many to declare their satisfaction with the inconveniences and even humiliation at our nation's airports.

There are always those in government who are anxious to increase its power and authority over the people. Strict adherence to personal privacy annoys those who promote a centralized state.

It's no surprise to learn that many of the new laws passed in the aftermath of 9/11 had been proposed long before that date. The attacks merely provided an excuse to do many things previously proposed by dedicated statists.

All too often, government acts perversely, professing to advance liberty while actually doing the opposite. Dozens of new bills passed since 9/11 promise to protect our freedoms and our security. In time we will realize there is little chance our security will be enhanced or our liberties protected.

The powerful and intrusive TSA certainly will not solve our problems. Without a full discussion, greater understanding, and ultimately a change in the foreign policy that incites those who declared war against us, no amount of pat-downs at airports will suffice. Imagine the harm done, the staggering costs, and the loss of liberty if the next 20 years pass and airplanes are never employed by terrorists. Even if there is a possibility that airplanes will be used to terrorize us, TSA's bullying will do little to prevent it. Patting down old women and little kids in airports cannot possibly make us safer!

TSA cannot protect us from another attack and it is not the solution. It serves only to make us all more obedient and complacent toward government intrusions into our lives.

The airport mess has been compounded by other problems, which we fail to recognize. Most assume the government has the greatest responsibility for making private aircraft travel safe. But this assumption only ignores mistakes made before 9/11, when the government taught us to not resist, taught us that airline personnel could not carry guns, and that the government would be in charge of security. Airline owners became complacent and dependent upon the government.

After 9/11 we moved in the wrong direction by allowing total government control and a political takeover by the TSA—which was completely contrary to the proposition that private owners have the ultimate responsibility to protect their customers.

Discrimination laws passed during the last 40 years ostensibly fuel the Transportation Secretary's near obsession with avoiding the appearance of discrimination toward young Muslim males. Instead TSA seemingly targets white children and old women. We have failed to recognize that a safety policy by a private airline is quite a different thing from government agents blindly obeying anti-discrimination laws.

Governments do not have a right to use blanket discrimination, such as that which led to incarceration of Japanese Americans in World War II. However, local law-enforcement agencies should be able to target their searches if the description of a suspect is narrowed by sex, race, or religion.

We are dealing with an entirely different matter when it comes to safety on airplanes. The federal government should not be involved in local law enforcement, and has no right to discriminate. Airlines, on the other hand, should be permitted to do whatever is necessary to provide safety. Private firms—long denied the right—should have a right to discriminate. Fine restaurants, for example, can require that shoes and shirts be worn for service in their establishments. The logic of this remaining property right should permit more sensible security checks at airports. The airlines should be responsible for the safety of their property, and liable for it as well. This is not only the responsibility of the airlines, but it is a civil right that has long been denied them and other private companies.

The present situation requires the government to punish some by targeting those individuals who clearly offer no threat. Any airline that tries to make travel safer and happens to question a larger number of young Muslim males than the government deems appropriate can be assessed huge fines. To add insult to injury, the fines collected from airlines are used for forced sensitivity training of pilots who do their very best, under the circumstances, to make flying safer by restricting the travel of some individuals. We have embarked on a process that serves no logical purpose. While airline safety suffers, personal liberty is diminished and costs skyrocket.

If we're willing to consider a different foreign policy, we should ask ourselves a few questions:

1. *What if* the policies of foreign intervention, entangling alliances, policing the world, nation building, and spreading our values through force are deeply flawed?

2. *What if* it is true that Saddam Hussein never had weapons of mass destruction?

3. *What if* it is true that Saddam Hussein and Osama bin Laden were never allies?

4. *What if* it is true that the overthrow of Saddam Hussein did nothing to enhance our national security?

5. *What if* our current policy in the Middle East leads to the overthrow of our client oil states in the region?

6. *What if* the American people really knew that more than 20,000 American troops have suffered serious casualties or died in the Iraq war, and 9% of our forces already have been made incapable of returning to battle?

7. *What if* it turns out there are many more guerrilla fighters in Iraq than our government admits?

8. *What if* there really have been 100,000 civilian Iraqi casualties, as some claim, and what is an acceptable price for "doing good?"

9. *What if* Rumsfeld is replaced for the wrong reasons, and things

become worse under a Defense Secretary who demands more troops and an expansion of the war?

10. *What if* we discover that, when they do vote, the overwhelming majority of Iraqis support Islamic (Sharia) law over Western secular law, and want our troops removed?

11. *What if* those who correctly warned of the disaster awaiting us in Iraq are never asked for their opinion of what should be done now?

12. *What if* the only solution for Iraq is to divide the country into three separate regions, recognizing the principle of self-determination while rejecting the artificial boundaries created in 1918 by non-Iraqis?

13. *What if* it turns out radical Muslims don't hate us for our freedoms, but rather for our policies in the Middle East that directly affected Arabs and Muslims?

14. *What if* the invasion and occupation of Iraq actually distracted from pursuing and capturing Osama bin Laden?

15. *What if* we discover that democracy can't be spread with force of arms?

16. *What if* democracy is deeply flawed, and instead we should be talking about liberty, property rights, free markets, the rule of law, localized government, weak centralized government, and self-determination promoted through persuasion, not force?

17. *What if* Osama bin Laden and al Qaeda actually welcomed our invasion and occupation of Arab/Muslim Iraq as proof of their accusations against us, and it served as a magnificent recruiting tool for them?

18. *What if* our policy greatly increased and prolonged our vulnerability to terrorists and guerilla attacks both at home and abroad?

19. *What if* the Pentagon, as reported by its Defense Science Board, actually recognized the dangers of our policy before the invasion, and their warnings were ignored or denied?

20. *What if* the argument that by fighting over there, we won't have to fight here, is wrong, and the opposite is true?

21. *What if* we can never be safer by giving up some of our freedoms?

22. *What if* the principle of pre-emptive war is adopted by Russia, China, Israel, India, Pakistan, and others, "justified" by current U.S. policy?

23. *What if* pre-emptive war and pre-emptive guilt stem from the same flawed policy of authoritarianism, though we fail to recognize it?

24. *What if* Pakistan is not a trustworthy ally, and turns on us when conditions deteriorate?

25. *What if* plans are being laid to provoke Syria and/or Iran into

306

actions that would be used to justify a military response and pre-emptive war against them?

26. **What if** our policy of democratization of the Middle East fails, and ends up fueling a Russian-Chinese alliance that we regret—an alliance not achieved even at the height of the Cold War?

27. **What if** the policy forbidding profiling at our borders and airports is deeply flawed?

28. **What if** presuming the guilt of a suspected terrorist without a trial leads to the total undermining of constitutional protections for American citizens when arrested?

29. **What if** we discover the army is too small to continue policies of pre-emption and nation-building? *What if* a military draft is the only way to mobilize enough troops?

30. **What if** the "stop-loss" program is actually an egregious violation of trust and a breach of contract between the government and soldiers? *What if* it actually is a backdoor draft, leading to unbridled cynicism and rebellion against a voluntary army and generating support for a draft of both men and women? Will lying to troops lead to rebellion and anger toward the political leadership running the war?

31. **What if** the Pentagon's legal task-force opinion that the president is not bound by international or federal law regarding torture stands unchallenged, and sets a precedent which ultimately harms Americans, while totally disregarding the moral, practical, and legal arguments against such a policy?

32. **What if** the intelligence reform legislation—which gives us bigger, more expensive bureaucracy—doesn't bolster our security, and distracts us from the real problem of revamping our interventionist foreign policy?

33. **What if** we suddenly discover we are the aggressors, and we are losing an unwinnable guerrilla war?

34. **What if** we discover, too late, that we can't afford this war— and that our policies have led to a dollar collapse, rampant inflation, high interest rates, and a severe economic downturn?

Why do I believe these are such important questions? Because the #1 function of the federal government—to provide for national security—has been severely undermined. **On 9/11 we had a grand total of 14 aircraft in place to protect the entire U.S. mainland, all of which proved useless that day.** We have an annual DOD budget of over $400 billion, most of which is spent overseas in over 100 different countries. On 9/11 our Air Force was better positioned to protect Seoul, Tokyo, Berlin, and

London than it was to protect Washington D.C. and New York City.

Moreover, our ill-advised presence in the Middle East and our decade-long bombing of Iraq served only to incite the suicidal attacks of 9/11.

Before 9/11, our CIA ineptly pursued bin Laden, whom the Taliban was protecting. At the same time, the Taliban was receiving significant support from Pakistan—our "trusted ally" that received millions of dollars from the United States. We allied ourselves with both bin Laden and Hussein in the 1980s, only to regret it in the 1990s. And it's safe to say we have used billions of U.S. taxpayer dollars in the last 50 years pursuing this contradictory, irrational, foolish, costly, and very dangerous foreign policy.

Policing the world, spreading democracy by force, nation building, and frequent bombing of countries that pose no threat to us—while leaving the homeland and our borders unprotected—result from a foreign policy that is contradictory and not in our self interest.

I hardly expect anyone in Washington to pay much attention to these concerns. If I'm completely wrong in my criticisms, nothing is lost except my time and energy expended in efforts to get others to reconsider our foreign policy.

But the bigger question is:

What if I'm right, or even partially right, and we urgently need to change course in our foreign policy for the sake of our national and economic security, yet no one pays attention?

For that a price will be paid. Is it not worth talking about? ■

March 19, 2005
NOTES FROM A PERSONAL DIARY

It is now two years since the president, unilaterally and without a congressional declaration, started a war by arbitrarily invading Iraq. The lies told convinced the American people that Saddam Hussein had weapons of mass destruction, nuclear weapons, chemical weapons, and that he was a grave threat to us. It was implied that he was responsible for 9/11. Congress, instead of exerting restraint and exercising its constitutional responsibility regarding war, mostly condoned the war and encouraged the president.

On that day two years ago I wrote: "According to our president, this will be done in the name of peace and liberation. More likely, this will unleash a war of gigantic proportions—even if the actual battle to eliminate Saddam Hussein and seize Iraq's oil goes well and ends quickly. To claim this pre-emptive strike will bring greater peace for both the U.S. and the world is the height of naiveté and arrogance…This strike is a major event. It has implications for far beyond anything the promoters can imagine."

With that, it seems nothing that has happened should surprise me. The ongoing distortions are convincing fewer and fewer Americans every day, as the people begin to realize the cost and uselessness of Bush's war. Though I was prepared for the worst, and anticipated much tragedy from our policy, certain events over the past two years shock, disappoint, and scare me as I look toward the future. A few points follow:

- The Republic is long dead, and few care or understand the significance. The incessant call by the president for spreading democracy, dutifully reported and never challenged by the media, helps bury any remnants of thought regarding the nature of a true republic. Randolph Bourne, who coined, "War is the health of the state," had it right. That peace is the foundation of liberty means little today.

- As bad as it is to see Bush and his neoconservative cronies get away with needless killing and mayhem, the more disheartening and disgusting spectacle is the pro-war position of Christian leaders with their TV-financed empires. They cannot help but force all Christians to reassess their theological moorings and spiritual beliefs. Translating the bible to support aggression against a defenseless country should concern all thoughtful Christians.

- The government propaganda machine, though I recognize its long history of achievement in promoting war, was amazingly successful once again. Television, radio, newspapers, and talk show hosts lapped up the official line and regurgitated the news without seriously challenging anything the administration said. This is especially true of the "imbedded" reporters who are totally controlled by the military and government censors. No body bags, no walking wounded, only a sterile war where great things are achieved for world peace and democracy. Even the opposition party served as nothing more than a rubber stamp—just as Kerry's candidacy did in the 2004 election. According to the state propagandists, everyone was happy. No interviews with the families of the 1500 plus killed, the 15 or 20 thousand wounded, or the 100,000 Iraqi civilians slaughtered in our "humanitarian" pursuits.

We have yet to see any serious concern shown for our guns and butter policy. Congress doesn't even blink as it passes a $2.6 trillion budget, with $82 billion more in off-budget emergency spending for the war. The only argument is about how much to increase food stamps and Medicare.

The fake election in March in Iraq, and the false propaganda and arrogance of the neoconservatives—from Cheney to Perle—has been nauseating. They seem to care little about human or economic costs, as long as their empire moves forward.

Denying the truth, however, won't work forever. Soon the U.S. will become the dispensable nation, instead of the indispensable economic and military power that the neocons use to promote ugly and dangerous ideals first promoted by Lincoln and later by Wilson.

As long as we deny the truth regarding real costs, the more rapidly we move toward a dollar crisis that all the neocons put together will be powerless to stop. The real tragedy here is that all Americans will suffer, as the standard of living plunges and liberty is further threatened.

Either from total ignorance or just wishful thinking, the neoconservatives totally deny that our invasion of Iraq benefited Osama bin Laden and al Qaeda. Yet nothing could have galvanized their efforts against the West more than our occupation of two more Muslim countries. Still, no thought is given to changing our approach in the Middle East. This will go down in history as one of the greatest errors in judgment of all time.

Today, the feeding tube was removed from Terri Schiavo after 15 years in a semi-vegetative state. Virtually all "decent" Christian warmongers enjoyed the political feeding frenzy surrounding efforts to save her life. I share their concern about life, but recognize that (as usual) Congress has no authority to decide such state matters. But the most disgusting thing is their sheer hypocrisy. They show tremendous concern for Ms. Schiavo (and unborn victims of abortion), while promoting an aggressive war that kills hundreds of thousands of innocent civilians.

The neoconservatives and their fellow travelers have turned our country into a nation of torturers, a champion of aggression, and the world's bully. As one would predict, the world is less safe and we're less free. Over 20,000 American families have suffered tragic losses from this war.

The general acceptance of the dictatorial policies of the Bush administration is astounding, but it helps explain how the German people allowed Hitler's rise to power. The propagandists have made "support the troops" synonymous with support for evil policies. Those who object are easily smeared as un-American and unpatriotic. Irrational and excessive nationalism—a tool of the neo-cons—is winning out over common sense, commerce, and concern for peace. It certainly would be in bad taste to suggest that our obsession with satisfying Israel's every demand, and the desire to protect "our" oil, has something to do with the insane sacrifice of our young soldiers, the hundreds of billions of dollars spent, and the loss of freedoms here at home. It still remains a mystery why reasonably intelligent people succumb to such evil and malevolent policies of war and hate.

It is impossible to analyze if a nation is better off "in general" without considering the various affects on specific individuals.

April 6, 2005
WHO'S BETTER OFF?
HON. RON PAUL of TEXAS
IN THE HOUSE OF REPRESENTATIVES

Whenever the administration is challenged regarding the success of the Iraq war, or regarding the false information used to justify the war, the retort is: "Aren't the people of Iraq better off?" The insinuation is that anyone who expresses any reservations about supporting the war is an apologist for Saddam Hussein and every ruthless act he ever committed. The short answer to the question of whether the Iraqis are better off is that it's too early to declare, "Mission Accomplished." But more importantly, we should be asking if the mission was ever justified or legitimate. Is it legitimate to justify an action that some claim have yielded good results, if the means used to achieve them are illegitimate? Do the ends justify the means?

The information Congress was given prior to the war was false. There were no weapons of mass destruction; the Iraqis did not participate in the 9/11 attacks; Osama bin Laden and Saddam Hussein were enemies and did not conspire against the United States; our security was not threatened; we were not welcomed by cheering Iraqi crowds as we were told; and Iraqi oil has not paid any of the bills. Congress failed to declare war, but instead passed a wishy-washy resolution citing UN resolutions as justification for our invasion. After the fact we're now told the real reason for the Iraq invasion was to spread democracy, and that the Iraqis are better off. Anyone who questions the war risks being accused of supporting Saddam Hussein, disapproving of democracy, or "supporting terrorists." It's implied that lack of enthusiasm for the war means one is not patriotic and doesn't support the troops. In other words, one must march lock step with the consensus or be ostracized.

However, conceding that the world is better off without Saddam Hussein is a far cry from endorsing the foreign policy of our own

311

government that led to the regime change. In time it will become clear to everyone that support for the policies of pre-emptive war and interventionist nation-building will have much greater significance than the removal of Saddam Hussein itself. The interventionist policy should be scrutinized more carefully than the purported benefits of Saddam Hussein's removal from power. **The real question ought to be: "Are we better off with a foreign policy that promotes regime change while justifying war with false information?"** Shifting the stated goals as events unravel should not satisfy those who believe war must be a last resort used only when our national security is threatened.

How much better off are the Iraqi people? Hundreds of thousands of former inhabitants of Falluah are not better off with their city flattened and their homes destroyed. Hundreds of thousands are not better off living with foreign soldiers patrolling their street, curfews, and the loss of basic utilities. One hundred thousand dead Iraqis, as estimated by the Lancet Medical Journal, certainly are not better off. Better to be alive under Saddam Hussein than lying in some cold grave.

Praise for the recent election in Iraq has silenced many critics of the war. Yet the election was held under martial law implemented by a foreign power, mirroring conditions we rightfully condemned as a farce when carried out in the old Soviet system and more recently in Lebanon. Why is it that what is good for the goose isn't always good for the gander?

Our government fails to recognize that legitimate elections are the *consequence* of freedom, and that an artificial election does not create freedom. In our own history we note that freedom was achieved first and elections followed—not the other way around.

One news report claimed that the Shiites actually received 56% of the vote, but such an outcome couldn't be allowed for it would preclude a coalition of the Kurds and Shiites from controlling the Sunnis and preventing a theocracy from forming. This reminds us of the statement made months ago by Secretary Rumsfeld when asked about a Shiite theocracy emerging from a majority democratic vote; he assured us that would not happen. Democracy, we know, is messy and needs tidying up a bit when we don't like the results.

Some have described Baghdad and especially the green zone, as being surrounded by unmanageable territory. The highways in and out of Baghdad are not yet secured. Many anticipate a civil war will break out sometime soon in Iraq; some claim it's already underway.

We have seen none of the promised oil production that was supposed to provide grateful Iraqis with the means to repay us for the hundreds of billions that American taxpayers have spent on the war. Some have justified our continuous presence in the Persian Gulf since 1990 because of a need to protect "our" oil. Yet now that Saddam Hussein is gone, and the occupation supposedly is a great success, gasoline at the pumps is reaching record highs approaching $3 per gallon.

Though the Iraqi election has come and gone, there still is no government in place and the next election—supposedly the real one—is not likely to take place on time. Do the American people have any idea who really won the dubious election at all?

The oil-for-food scandal under Saddam Hussein has been replaced by corruption in the distribution of U.S. funds to rebuild Iraq. Already there is an admitted $9 billion discrepancy in the accounting of these funds. The over-billing by Halliburton is no secret, but the process has not changed.

The whole process is corrupt. It just doesn't make sense to most Americans to see their tax dollars used to fight an unnecessary and unjustified war. First they see American bombs destroying a country, and then American taxpayers are required to rebuild it. Today it's easier to get funding to rebuild infrastructure in Iraq than to build a bridge in the United States. Indeed, we cut the Army Corps of Engineers' budget and operate on the cheap with our veterans as the expenditures in Iraq skyrocket.

One question the war promoters don't want to hear asked, because they don't want to face up to the answer, is this: "Are Christian Iraqis better off today since we decided to build a new Iraq through force of arms?" The answer is plainly "No."

Sure, there are only 800,000 Christians living in Iraq, but under Saddam Hussein they were free to practice their religion. Tariq Aziz, a Christian, served in Saddam Hussein's cabinet as Foreign Minister—something that would never happen in Saudi Arabia, Israel, or any other Middle Eastern country. Today, the Christian churches in Iraq are under attack and Christians are no longer safe. Many Christians have been forced to flee Iraq and migrate to Syria. **It's strange that the human rights advocates in the U.S. Congress have expressed no concern for the persecution now going on against Christians in Iraq.** Both the Sunni and the Shiite Muslims support the attacks on Christians. In fact, persecuting Christians is one of the few areas in which they agree—the other being the removal of all foreign forces from Iraqi soil.

Considering the death, destruction, and continual chaos in Iraq, it's difficult to accept the blanket statement that the Iraqis all feel much better off with the U.S. in control rather than Saddam Hussein. Security in the streets and criminal violence are not anywhere near being under control.

But there's another question that is equally important: "Are the American people better off because of the Iraq war?"

One thing for sure, the 1,500-plus dead American soldiers aren't better off. The nearly 20,000 severely injured or sickened American troops are not better off. The families, the wives, the husbands, children, parents, and friends of those who lost so much are not better off.

The families and the 40,000 troops who were forced to re-enlist against their will—a de facto draft—are not feeling better off. They believe they have been deceived by their enlistment agreements.

The American taxpayers are not better off having spent over $200 billion to pursue this war, with billions yet to be spent. The victims of the inflation that always accompanies a guns-and-butter policy are already getting a dose of what will become much worse.

Are our relationships with the rest of the world better off? I'd say no. Because of the war, our alliances with the Europeans are weaker than ever. The anti-American hatred among a growing number of Muslims around the world is greater than ever. This makes terrorist attacks more likely than they were before the invasion. Al Qaeda recruiting has accelerated. Iraq is being used as a training ground for al Qaeda terrorists, which it never was under Hussein's rule. So as our military recruitment efforts suffer, Osama bin Laden benefits by attracting more terrorist volunteers.

Oil was approximately $27 a barrel before the war, now it's more than twice that. I wonder who benefits from this?

Because of the war, fewer dollars are available for real national security and defense of this country. Military spending is up, but the way the money is spent distracts from true national defense and further undermines our credibility around the world.

The ongoing war's lack of success has played a key role in diminishing morale in our military services. Recruitment is sharply down, and most branches face shortages of troops. Many young Americans rightly fear a coming draft—which will be required if we do not reassess and change the unrealistic goals of our foreign policy.

The appropriations for the war are essentially off-budget and obscured, but contribute nonetheless to the runaway deficit and increase in the national debt. If these trends persist, inflation with economic stagnation will be the inevitable consequences of a misdirected policy.

One of the most significant consequences in times of war that we ought to be concerned about is the inevitable loss of personal liberty. Too often in the patriotic nationalism that accompanies armed conflict, regardless of the cause, there is a willingness to sacrifice personal freedoms in pursuit of victory. The real irony is that we are told we go hither and yon to fight for freedom and our Constitution, while carelessly sacrificing the very freedoms here at home we're supposed to be fighting for. It makes no sense.

This willingness to give up hard-fought personal liberties has been especially noticeable in the atmosphere of the post-September 11th war on terrorism. Security has replaced liberty as our main political goal, damaging the American spirit. Sadly, the whole process is done in the name of patriotism and in a spirit of growing militant nationalism.

These attitudes and fears surrounding the 9/11 tragedy, and our eagerness to go to war in the Middle East against countries not responsible for the attacks, have allowed a callousness to develop in our national psyche that justifies torture and rejects due process of law for those who are suspects and not convicted criminals.

We have come to accept pre-emptive war as necessary, constitutional, and morally justifiable. Starting a war without a proper declaration is now of no concern to most Americans or the U.S. Congress. Let's hope and pray the rumors of an attack on Iran in June by U.S. Armed Forces are wrong.

A large segment of the Christian community and its leadership think nothing of rationalizing war in the name of a religion that prides itself on the teachings of the Prince of Peace, who instructed us that blessed are the peacemakers—not the warmongers.

We casually accept our role as world policeman, and believe we have a moral obligation to practice nation building in our image regardless of the number of people who die in the process.

We have lost our way by rejecting the beliefs that made our country great. We no longer trust in trade, friendship, peace, the Constitution, and the principle of neutrality while avoiding entangling alliances with the rest of the world. Spreading the message of hope and freedom by setting an example for the world has been replaced by a belief that use of armed might is the only practical tool to influence the world—and we have accepted, as the only superpower, the principle of initiating war against others.

In the process, Congress and the people have endorsed a usurpation

315

of their own authority, generously delivered to the executive and judicial branches—not to mention international government bodies. The concept of national sovereignty is now seen as an issue that concerns only the fringe in our society.

Protection of life and liberty must once again become the issue that drives political thought in this country. If this goal is replaced by an effort to promote world government, use force to plan the economy, regulate the people, and police the world, against the voluntary desires of the people, it can be done only with the establishment of a totalitarian state. There's no need for that. It's up to Congress and the American people to decide our fate, and there is still time to correct our mistakes. ■

The costs of war, all the costs of war, are seldom considered, yet nothing is more important than giving such consideration.

June 14, 2005
THE HIDDEN COST OF WAR
HON. RON PAUL of TEXAS
IN THE HOUSE OF REPRESENTATIVES

The cost of war is always more than anticipated. If all the costs were known prior to the beginning of a war, fewer wars would be fought. At the beginning, optimism prevails. Denial and deception override the concern for the pain and penalties yet to come. Jingoistic patriotism and misplaced militarism too easily silence those who are cautious about the unforeseen expenses and hardships brought on by war. Conveniently forgotten are the goals never achieved by armed conflict, and the negative consequences that linger for years. Even some who recognize that the coming war will be costly easily rationalize that the cost will be worth it Others claim it's unmanly or weak to pursue a negotiated settlement of a political dispute, which helps drive the march toward armed conflict.

It has been argued by proponents of modern technological warfare in recent decades that sophisticated weapons greatly reduce the human costs by using a smaller number of troops equipped with smart weapons that minimize battle deaths and collateral damage. This belief has led some to be more willing to enter an armed conflict. The challenge will be deciding whether or not modern weapons actually make war more acceptable and less costly. So far the use of sanctions, the misjudgments of resistance to occupation, and unintended consequences reveal that fancy weapons do

316

not guarantee fancy and painless outcomes. Some old-fashioned rules relating to armed conflicts cannot be easily repealed despite the optimism of the "shock and awe" crowd. It seems that primitive explosive weapons can compete quite effectively with modern technology when the determination exists and guerrilla tactics are used. The promised efficiency and the reduced casualties cannot yet be estimated.

Costs are measured differently depending on whether or not a war is defensive or offensive in nature. Costs in each situation may be similar but are tolerated quite differently. The determination of those defending their homeland frequently is underestimated, making it difficult to calculate costs. Consider how long the Vietnamese fought and suffered before routing all foreign armies. For 85 years the Iraqis steadfastly have resisted all foreign occupation, and even their previous history indicates that meddling by Western and Christian outsiders in their country would not be tolerated. Those who fight a defensive war see the cost of the conflict differently. Defenders have the goal of surviving and preserving their homeland, religious culture, and their way of life—despite the shortcomings their prior leaders. Foreigners are seen as a threat. This willingness to defend to the last is especially strong if the society they fight for affords more stability than a war-torn country.

Hardships can be justified in defensive wars, and use of resources is more easily justified than in an unpopular far-away conflict. Motivations are stronger, especially when the cause seems to be truly just and the people are willing to sacrifice for the common goal of survival. Defensive war provides a higher moral goal, and this idealism exceeds material concerns. In all wars, however, there are profiteers and special interests looking after their own selfish interests.

Truly defensive wars never need a draft to recruit troops to fight. Large numbers voluntarily join to face the foreign threat.

In a truly defensive war, huge costs in terms of money, lives, and property are endured because so much is at stake. Total loss of one's country is the alternative.

The freer a country, where the love of liberty is alive and well, the greater the resistance. A free society provides greater economic means to fight than a tyrannical society. For this reason, truly free societies are less likely to be attacked by tyrants.

But societies that do not enjoy maximum freedom and economic prosperity still pull together to resist invaders. A spirit of nationalism brings people together when attacked, as do extreme religious beliefs. The cause of liberty or a "divine" emperor or radical Islam can inspire those willing to fight to the death to stop a foreign occupation. These motivations make the costs and risks necessary and justifiable, where a less popular offensive war will not be tolerated as long. Idealism inspires a strong defense; cynicism eventually curtails offensive wars.

The cost of offensive war over time is viewed quite differently by the people who actually pay. Offensive wars include those that are initiated by one country to seek some advantage over another without provocation. This includes needless intervention in the internal affairs of others and efforts at nation building, even when well intentioned. **Offensive war never achieves the high moral ground in spite of proclamations made by the initiators of the hostilities. Offensive wars eventually fail, but tragically only after much pain and suffering.** The cost is great, and not well accepted by the people who suffer and have nothing to gain. The early calls for patriotism and false claims generate initial support, but the people eventually tire.

At the beginning of an offensive war the people are supportive because of the justifications given by government authorities, who want the war for ulterior reasons. But the demands to sacrifice liberty at home to promote freedom and democracy abroad ring hollow after the cost and policy shortcomings become evident. Initially, the positive propaganda easily overshadows the pain of the small number who must fight and suffer injury.

Offensive wars are fought without as much determination as defensive wars. They tend to be less efficient and more political, causing them to linger and drift into stalemate or worse.

In almost all wars, governments use deception about the enemy that needs to be vanquished to gain the support of the people. In our recent history, just since 1941, our government has entirely ignored the requirement that war be fought only after a formal congressional declaration—further setting the stage for disenchantment once the war progresses poorly. Respect for the truth is easily sacrificed in order to rally the people for the war effort. Professional propagandists, by a coalition of the media and government officials, beat the war drums. The people follow out of fear of being labeled unpatriotic and weak in the defense of our nation—even when there is no national security threat at all.

Joining in support for the war are the special-interest groups that have other agendas to pursue: profits, religious beliefs, and partisan political obligations.

Ideologues use war to pursue personal ambitions unrelated to national defense, and convert the hesitant with promises of spreading democracy, freedom, and prosperity. The tools they use are unrestrained state power to force their ideals on others, no matter how unjust it seems to the unfortunate recipients of the preemptive war. For some, the more chaos the greater the opportunity to jump in and remake a country or an entire region. At times in history the opening salvo has been deliberately carried out by the ones anxious to get the war underway while blaming the opposition for the incident. The deceptions must stir passion for the war through an appeal to patriotism, nationalism, machismo, and jingoistic manliness of proving oneself in great feats of battle.

This early support, before the first costs are felt, is easily achieved. Since total victory may not come quickly, however, support by the people is gradually lost. When the war is questioned, the ill-conceived justifications for getting involved are reexamined and found to have been distorted. Frequently, the people discover they were lied to, so that politicians could gain support for a war that had nothing to do with national security.

These discoveries and disenchantments come first to those directly exposed to danger in the front lines, where soldiers die or lose their limbs. Military families and friends bear the burden of grief, while the majority of citizens still hope the war will end or never affect them directly in any way. But as the casualties grow the message of suffering spreads, and questions remain unanswered concerning the real reason an offensive war was necessary in the first place.

Just when the human tragedy becomes evident to a majority of the citizens, other costs become noticeable. Taxes are raised, deficits explode, inflation raises its ugly head and the standard of living for the average citizen is threatened. **Funds for the war, even if immediate direct taxes are not levied, must come from the domestic economy and everyone suffers. The economic consequences of the Vietnam War were felt throughout the 1970s and into the early 1980s.**

As the problems mount, the falsehoods and distortions on which the war was based become less believable and collectively resented. The government and the politicians who pursued the policy lose credibility. The tragedy, however, is that once even the majority discovers the truth, much more time is needed to change the course of events. This is the sad part.

Political leaders who needlessly dragged us into the war cannot and will not admit an error in judgment. In fact they do the opposite to prove they were right all along. Instead of winding down, the war gets a boost to prove the policy was correct and to bring the war to a victorious conclusion.

This only motivates the resistance of those fighting the defensive side of the war. More money and more troops must be sacrificed before the policy changes. Using surrogate foreign troops may seem to cut domestic troop loses in the country starting the war, but will only prolong the agony, suffering, and costs and increase the need for even more troops.

Withdrawing financial support for the effort is seen as being even more unpatriotic than not having supported the war in the first place. Support for the troops becomes equivalent to supporting the flawed policy that led to the mess.

No matter how unwise the policy and how inevitable the results, changing course becomes almost impossible for those individuals who promoted the war. This fear of being labeled unpatriotic and not supportive of the troops on the battlefield ironically drives a policy that is more harmful to the troops and costly to the folks at home. Sometimes it requires a new group of politicians, removed from the original decision makers who initiated the war, to bring about a shift in policy. Johnson couldn't do it in Vietnam, and Nixon did it slowly, awkwardly and not without first expanding the war before agreeing enough was enough.

With the seemingly inevitable delays in altering policy, the results are quite predictable. Costs escalate and the division between supporters and non-supporters widens. This adds to economic problems while further eroding domestic freedoms, as with all wars. On occasion, as we've seen in our own country, dissent invites harsh social and legal repercussions. Those who speak out in opposition will not only be ostracized, but may feel the full force of the law coming down on them. Errors in foreign affairs leading to war are hard to reverse. But even if deliberate action doesn't change the course of events, flawed policies eventually will fail as economic laws will assert themselves.

The more people have faith in and depend upon the state, the more difficult it is to keep the state from initiating wars. If the state is seen as primarily responsible for providing personal and economic security, obedience and dependency become pervasive problems. If the state is limited to protecting liberty, and encourages self-reliance and personal responsibility, there's a much better chance for limiting pro-war attitudes. The great danger of war, especially unnecessary war, is that it breeds more dependency while threatening liberty—always allowing the state to grow regardless of existing attitudes before the war. War unfortunately allows the enemies of liberty to justify the sacrifice of personal freedoms, and the people all too often carelessly sacrifice precisely what they are supposed to be fighting for: freedom. Our Revolution was a rare exception. It was one war where the people ended up with more freedom not less.

ECONOMICS AND WAR

Almost every war has an economic component, some more obvious than others. Our own Civil War dealt with slavery, but tariffs and economic oppression by the North were also major factors. Remember, only a small number of Southern soldiers personally owned slaves, yet they were enthusiastic in their opposition to the northern invasion. The battles fought in the Middle East since WWI had a lot to do with securing Arab oil fields for the benefit of Western nations. Not only are wars fought for economic reasons, wars have profound economic consequences for the countries involved, even if one side is spared massive property damage. The economic consequences of war play a major role in bringing hostilities to an end. The consequences are less tolerated by the citizens of countries whose leaders drag them into offensive and unnecessary wars. The determination to fight on can't compete with those who see their homeland threatened by foreign invaders.

IRAQ

There's essentially no one, not even among the neo-con crowd, claiming that the Iraqi war is defensive in nature for America. Early on there was an attempt to do so, and it was successful to a large degree in convincing the American people that Saddam Hussein had weapons of mass destruction and was connected to al Qaeda. Now the justification for the war is completely different and far less impressive. If the current justification had been used to rally the American people and Congress from the beginning, the war would have been rejected. The fact that we are bogged down in an offensive war makes it quite difficult to extricate ourselves from the mess. Without the enthusiasm that a defensive war generates, prolonging the Iraq war will play havoc with our economy. The insult of paying for the war in addition to the fact that the war was not truly necessary makes the hardship less tolerable. This leads to domestic turmoil, as proponents become more vocal in demanding patriotic support and opponents become angrier for the burden they must bear.

So far the American people have not yet felt the true burden of the costs of this war. Even with 1,700 deaths and 13,000 wounded, only a small percentage of Americans have suffered directly—but their pain and suffering are growing and are more noticeable every day. Taxes have not been raised to pay the bills for the current war, so annual deficits and national debt continue to grow. This helps delay the pain of paying the bills, but the consequences of this process are starting to be felt. Direct tax increases, a more honest way to finance foreign interventionism, would serve to restrain those who so cavalierly take us to war. The borrowing authority of government permits wars to be started and prolonged which otherwise would be resisted if the true cost were known to the people from the beginning.

Americans have an especially unique ability to finance our war efforts while minimizing the immediate effect. As the issuer of the world's reserve currency, we are able to finance our extravagance through inflating our dollars. We have the special privilege of printing that which the world accepts as money in lieu of gold. This is an invitation to economic disaster, permitting an ill-founded foreign policy that sets the stage for problems for years to come. A system of money that politicians and central bankers could not manipulate would restrain those with grandiose ideas of empire.

The Federal Reserve was created in 1913, and shortly thereafter the Fed accommodated the Wilsonians bent on entering WWI by inflating and deficit financing that ill-begotten involvement. Though it produced the 1921 depression and many other problems since, the process subsequently has become institutionalized in financing our militarism in the 20th Century and already in the 21st. Without the Fed's ability to create money out of thin air, our government would be severely handicapped in waging wars that do not serve our interests. The money issue and the ability of our government to wage war are intricately related. Anyone interested in curtailing wartime spending and our militarism abroad is obligated to study the monetary system, through which our government seductively and surreptitiously finances foreign adventurism without the responsibility of informing the public of its cost or collecting the revenues required to finance the effort.

Being the issuer of the world's premier currency allows for a lot more abuse than a country would have otherwise. World businesses, governments, and central banks accept our dollars as if they are as good as gold. This is a remnant of a time when the dollar *was* as good as gold. That is no longer the case. The trust is still there, but it's a misplaced trust. Since the dollar is simply a paper currency without real value, someday confidence will be lost and our goose will no longer be able to lay the golden egg. That's when reality will set in and the real cost of our extravagance, both domestic and foreign, will be felt by all Americans. We will no longer be able to finance our war machine through willing foreigners, who now gladly take our newly printed dollars for their newly produced goods and then loan them back to us at below-market interest rates to support our standard of living and our war effort.

The payment by American citizens will come as the dollar loses value, interest rates rise, and prices increase. The higher prices become the tax that a more honest government would have levied directly to pay for the war effort. An unpopular war especially needs this deception as a method of payment, hiding the true costs which are dispersed and delayed through this neat little monetary trick. The real tragedy is that this "inflation tax" is not evenly distributed among all the people, and more often than not is borne disproportionately by the poor and the middle class as a truly regressive tax in the worst sense. Politicians in Washington do not see inflation as an unfair seductive tax. Our monetary policy unfortunately is never challenged even by the proponents of low taxes who care so little about deficits, but eventually it all comes to an end because economic law overrides the politicians' deceit.

Already we are seeing signs on the horizon that this free ride for us is coming to an end. Price inflation is alive and well and much worse than government statistics show. The sluggish economy suggests that the super stimulation of easy credit over the last decades is no longer sufficient to keep the economy strong. Our personal consumption and government spending are dependent on borrowing from foreign lenders. Artificially high standards of living can mask the debt accumulation that it requires, while needed savings remain essentially nil.

This ability to print the reserve currency of the world, and the willingness of foreigners to take it, causes gross distortions in our current account deficits and total foreign indebtedness. It plays a major role in the erosion of our manufacturing base, and causes the exporting of our jobs along with our dollars. Bashing foreigners, in particularly the Chinese and the Japanese, as the cause of our dwindling manufacturing and job base is misplaced. It prevents the evaluation of our own policies—policies that undermine and increase the price of our own manufacturing goods while distorting the trade balance. Though we continue to benefit from the current circumstances, through cheap imports on borrowed money, the shaky fundamentals make our economy and financial system vulnerable to sudden and severe adjustments. **Foreigners will not finance our excessive**

standard of living and our expensive war overseas indefinitely. It will end! What we do in the meantime to prepare for that day will make all the difference in the world for the future of freedom in this country. It's the future of freedom in this country that is truly the legitimate responsibility of us as Members of Congress.

Centuries ago the notion of money introduced the world to trade and the principle of division of labor, ushering in for the first time a level of economic existence above mere subsistence. Modern fiat money with electronic transactions has given an additional boost to that prosperity. But unlike sound commodity money, fiat money—with easy credit and artificially low interest rates—causes distortions and mal-investments that require corrections. The modernization of electronic global transfers, which with sound money would be beneficial, has allowed for greater distortion and debt to be accumulated—setting the stage for a much more serious period of adjustment requiring an economic downturn, liquidation of debt, and reallocation of resources that must come from savings rather than a central bank printing press.

These economic laws will limit our ability to pursue our foreign interventions, no matter how well intentioned and "successful" they may seem. The Soviet system collapsed of its own weakness. I fear an economic collapse here at home much more than an attack by a foreign country. Above all, the greatest concern should be for the systematic undermining of our personal liberties since 9/11, which will worsen with an ongoing foreign war and the severe economic problems that are coming.

Since we are not fighting the war to defend our homeland and we abuse so many of our professed principles, we face great difficulties in resolving the growing predicament in which we find ourselves. Our options are few, and admitting errors in judgment is not likely to occur. Moral forces are against us as we find ourselves imposing our will on a people six thousand miles from our shores. **How would the American people respond if a foreign country, with people of a different color, religion, and language imposed itself on us to make us conform to their notions of justice and goodness? None of us would sit idly by.** This is why those who see themselves as defenders of their homeland and their way of life have the upper hand, regardless of the shock and awe of military power available to us. At this point, our power works perversely. The stronger and more violent we are, the greater the resistance becomes.

The neoconservatives who took us to war under false pretenses either didn't know or didn't care about the history and traditions of the Iraqi people. Surely they must have heard of an Islamic defensive jihad that is easy to promote when one's country is being attacked by foreign forces. Family members have religious obligations to avenge all killings by foreign forces, which explains why killing insurgents only causes their numbers to multiply. This family obligation to seek revenge is closely tied to achieving instant eternal martyrdom through vengeful suicide attacks. Parents of martyrs do not weep as the parents of our soldiers do; they believe the suicide bombers and their families are glorified. These religious beliefs cannot simply be changed during the war. The only thing we can do is remove the incentives we give to the religious leaders of the jihad by leaving them alone. Without our presence in the Middle East, whether on the Arabian Peninsula or in Iraq, the rallying cry for suicidal jihadists would ring hollow. Was there any fear for our national security from a domestic terrorist attack by Islamists before we put a base in Saudi Arabia?

Our freedoms here at home have served the interests of those who are hell-bent on pursuing an American empire, though this too will be limited by economic costs and the undermining of our personal liberties.

A free society produces more wealth for more people than any other. That wealth for many years can be confiscated to pay for the militarism advocated by those who promote preemptive war. But militarism and its costs undermine the very market system that provided the necessary resources to begin with. As this happens, productivity and wealth are diminished, putting pressure on authorities to ruthlessly extract even more funds from the people. For what they cannot collect through taxes, they take through currency inflation—eventually leading to an inability to finance unnecessary and questionable warfare and bringing the process to an end. It happened to the Soviets and their military machine collapsed. Hitler destroyed Germany's economy, but he financed his aggression for several years by immediately stealing the gold reserves of every country he occupied. That, too, was self-limited and he met his military defeat. For us it's less difficult since we can confiscate the wealth of American citizens and the savers of the world merely by printing more dollars to support our militarism. Though different in detail, we too must face the prospect that this system of financing is seriously flawed, and our expensive policy of worldwide interventionism will collapse. Only a profound change in attitudes regarding our foreign policy, our fiscal policy, and our monetary policy will save us from ourselves.

If we did make these changes, we would not need to become isolationists, despite what many claim. Isolationism is not the only alternative to intervention in other nations' affairs. Freedom works! Free markets supported by sound money, private property, and respect for all voluntary contracts can set an example for the world—since the resulting prosperity would be significant and distributed more widely than any socialist system. Instead of using force to make others do it our way, our influence could be through the example we set that would motivate others to emulate us. Trade, travel, exchange of ideas, and friendly relationships with all those who seek friendship are a far cry from a protectionist closed border nation that would serve no one's interest.

This type of society would be greatly enhanced with a worldwide commodity standard of money. This would prevent the imbalances that are a great burden to today's economy. Our current account deficits and total foreign indebtedness would not occur under honest non-political commodity money. Competitive devaluations and abnormally fixed exchanged rates would not be possible as tools of protectionism. We can be certain that the distortions in trade balance and the WTO trade wars that are multiplying will eventually lead to a serious challenge to worldwide trade. The tragedy of trade wars is that they frequently lead to military wars between nations, and until the wealth is consumed and young men are no longer available to fight and die, the process will cost plenty.

We must not forget that real peace and prosperity are available to us. America has a grand tradition in this regard despite her shortcomings. It's just that in recent decades, the excessive unearned wealth available to us to run our welfare/warfare state has distracted us from our important traditions—honoring liberty and emphasizing self-reliance and responsibility. Up until the 20th Century, we were much less eager to go around the world searching for dragons to slay. That tradition is a good one, and one that we must soon reconsider before the ideal of personal liberty is completely destroyed.

SUMMARY
1. The costs of war are always much more than anticipated, while the benefits are much less.
2. The cost of war is more than just the dollars spent; it includes deaths, injuries, and destruction along with the unintended consequences that go on for decades.
3. Support for offensive wars wears thin; especially when they are not ended quickly.
4. The Iraq war now has been going on for 15 years with no end in

sight.

5. Ulterior motives too often preempt national security in offensive wars.
6. Powerful nations too often forget humility in their relationships to other countries.
7. World history and religious dogmatism are too often ignored and misunderstood.
8. World government is no panacea for limiting war.
9. Most wars could be avoided with better diplomacy, a mutual understanding of minding one's own business, and respect for the right of self-determination. ■

To figure out what is wrong with the basis of a particular policy requires that we first look beyond the justifications and see the real causes motivating government action.

September 8, 2005
WHY WE FIGHT
HON. RON PAUL of TEXAS
IN THE HOUSE OF REPRESENTATIVES

Many reasons have been given for why we fight and our youth must die in Iraq. The reasons now given for why we must continue this war bear no resemblance to the reasons given to gain the support of the American people and the United States Congress prior to our invasion in March of 2003. Before the war, we were told we faced an imminent threat to our national security from Saddam Hussein. This rationale, now proven grossly mistaken, has been changed. Now we're told we must honor the fallen by "completing the mission." To do otherwise would demean the sacrifice of those who have died or been wounded. Any lack of support for "completing the mission" is said, by the promoters of the war, to be unpatriotic, un-American, and detrimental to the troops. They insist the only way one can support the troops is to never waver on the policy of nation building, no matter how ill-founded that policy may be. The obvious flaw in this argument is that the mission, of which they so reverently speak, has changed constantly from the very beginning.

Though most people think this war started in March of 2003, the seeds were sown many years before. The actual military conflict, involving U.S. troops against Iraq, began in January 1991. The prelude to this actually dates back over a hundred years, when the value of Middle East oil was recognized by the industrialized West.

Our use of troops to eject Saddam Hussein from Kuwait was the beginning of the current conflict with Muslim fundamentalists who have been, for the last decade, determined to force the removal of American troops from all Muslim countries—especially the entire Arabian Peninsula, which they consider holy. Though the strategic and historic reasons for our involvement in the Middle East are complex, the immediate reasons given in 2002 and 2003 for our invasion of Iraq were precise. The only problem is they were not based on facts.

The desire by American policymakers to engineer regime change in Iraq had been smoldering since the first Persian Gulf conflict in 1991. This reflected a dramatic shift in our policy, since in the 1980s we maintained a friendly alliance with Saddam Hussein as we assisted him in his war against our arch nemesis, the Iranian Ayatollah. Most Americans ignore that we provided assistance to this ruthless dictator with biological and chemical weapons technology. We heard no complaints in the 1980s about his treatment of the Kurds and Shiites, or the ruthless war he waged against Iran. Our policy toward Iraq played a major role in convincing Saddam Hussein he had free reign in the Middle East, and the results demonstrate the serious shortcomings of our foreign policy of interventionism that we have followed now for over a hundred years.

In 1998 Congress capitulated to the desires of the Clinton administration and overwhelmingly passed the Iraq Liberation Act, which stated quite clearly that our policy was to get rid of Saddam Hussein. This act made it official: "The policy of the United States to support efforts to remove the regime headed by Saddam Hussein." This resolution has been cited on numerous occasions by neoconservatives as justification for the pre-emptive, deliberate invasion of Iraq. When the resolution was debated, I saw it as a significant step toward a war that would bear no good fruit. No legitimate national security concerns were cited for this dramatic and serious shift in policy.

Shortly after the new administration took office in January 2001, this goal of eliminating Saddam Hussein quickly morphed into a policy of remaking the entire Middle East, starting with regime change in Iraq. This aggressive interventionist policy surprised some people, since the victorious 2000 campaign indicated we should pursue a foreign policy of humility, no nation building, reduced deployment of our forces overseas, and a rejection of the notion that we serve as world policemen. The 9/11 disaster proved a catalyst to push for invading Iraq and restructuring the entire Middle East. Though the plan had existed for years, it quickly was recognized that the fear engendered by the 9/11 attacks could be used to mobilize the American people and Congress to support this war. Nevertheless, supposedly legitimate reasons had to be given for the already planned pre-emptive war, and as we now know the "intelligence had to be fixed to the policy."

Immediately after 9/11 the American people were led to believe that Saddam Hussein somehow was responsible for the attacks. The fact that Saddam Hussein and Osama bin Laden were enemies, not friends, was kept from the public by a compliant media and a lazy Congress. Even today many Americans still are convinced of an alliance between the two. The truth is Saddam Hussein never permitted al Qaeda into Iraq out of fear that his secular government would be challenged. And yet today we find that al Qaeda is now very much present in Iraq, and causing chaos there.

The administration repeatedly pumped out alarming propaganda that Saddam Hussein was a threat to us with his weapons of mass destruction, meaning nuclear, biological, and chemical. Since we helped Saddam Hussein obtain biological and chemical weapons in the 1980s, we assumed that he had maintained a large supply— which of course turned out not to be true. The people, frightened by 9/11, easily accepted these fear-mongering charges.

Behind the scenes many were quite aware that Israel's influence on our foreign policy played a role. She had argued for years, along with the neoconservatives, for an Iraqi regime change. This support was nicely coordinated with the Christian Zionists' enthusiasm for the war.

As these reasons for the war lost credibility and support, other reasons were found for why we had to fight. As the lone superpower, we were told we had a greater responsibility to settle the problems of the world lest someone else gets involved. Maintaining and expanding our empire is a key element of the neoconservative philosophy. This notion that we must fight to spread American goodness was well received by these neo-Jacobins. They saw the war as a legitimate moral crusade, arguing that no one should be allowed to stand in our way! In their minds using force to spread democracy is legitimate and necessary.

We also were told the war was necessary for national security purposes because of the threat Saddam Hussein presented, although the evidence was fabricated. Saddam Hussein's ability to attack us was non-existent, but the American people were ripe for alarming predictions by those who wanted this war.

Of course the routine canard for our need to fight, finance, and meddle around the world ever since the Korean War was repeated incessantly: UN Resolutions had to be enforced lest the United Nations be discredited. The odd thing was that on this occasion the United Nations itself did everything possible to stop our pre-emptive attack. And as it turned out, Saddam Hussein was a lot closer to compliance than anyone dreamed. It wasn't long before concern for the threat of Saddam Hussein became nearly hysterical, drowning out any reasoned opposition to the planned war.

The one argument that was not publicly used by those who propagandized for the war may well be the most important—oil. Though the administration in 1990 hinted briefly that we had to eject Saddam Hussein from Kuwait because of oil, the stated reasons for that conflict soon transformed into stopping a potential Hitler and enforcing UN resolutions.

Publicly oil is not talked about very much, but behind the scenes many acknowledge this is the real reason we fight. Not only the politicians say this. American consumers have always enjoyed cheap gasoline and want it kept that way. The real irony is that the war has reduced Iraqi oil production by one-half million barrels per day and prices are soaring—demonstrating another unintended economic consequence of war.

Oil in the Middle East has been a big issue since the industrial revolution, when it was realized that the black substance bubbling out of the ground in places like Iraq had great value. It's interesting to note that in the early 20th century Germany, fully aware of oil's importance, allied itself with the Turkish Ottoman Empire and secured the earliest rights to drill Iraqi oil. They built the Anatalia railroad between Baghdad and Basra, and obtained oil and mineral rights on twenty kilometers on each side of this right-of-way. World War I changed all this, allowing the French and the British to divide the oil wealth of the entire Middle East.

The Versailles Treaty created the artificial nation of Iraq, and it wasn't long before American oil companies were drilling and struggling to participate in the control of Middle East oil. But it was never smooth sailing for any occupying force in Iraq. After WWI, the British generals upon arriving to secure "their" oil said: "Our armies do not come into your cities and lands as conquerors or enemies, but as liberators." Not long afterward, a jihad was declared against Britain and eventually they were forced to leave. The more things change, the more they stay the same! Too bad we are not better at studying history.

After World War II, the U.S. emerged as the #1 world power, and moved to assume what some believed was our responsibility to control Middle East oil in competition with the Soviets. This role prompted us to use our CIA, along with the help of the British, to oust democratically elected Mohammed Mosadeh from power in Iran and install the Shah as a U.S. puppet.

We not only supported Saddam Hussein against Iran, we also supported Osama bin Laden in the 1980s—aggravating the situation in the Middle East and causing unintended consequences. With CIA assistance, we helped develop the educational program to radicalize Islamic youth in many Arab nations, especially in Saudi Arabia to fight the Soviets. We even provided a nuclear reactor to Iran in 1967—which today leads us to threaten another war. All of this has come back to haunt us. Meddling in the affairs of others has consequences.

Finally, after years of plotting and maneuvering, the neoconservative plan to invade Iraq came before the U.S. House in October 2002 to be rubber-stamped. Though the plan was hatched years before, and the official policy of the United States government was to remove Saddam Hussein ever since 1998, various events delayed the vote until this time. By October the vote was deemed urgent, so as to embarrass anyone who opposed it. This would make them politically vulnerable in the November election. The ploy worked. The resolution passed easily, and it served the interests of proponents of war in the November election.

The resolution, HJ RES 114, explicitly cited the Iraqi Liberation Act of 1998 as one of the reasons we had to go to war. The authorization granted the president to use force against Iraq cited two precise reasons:
1. "To defend the national security of the U.S. against the continuing threat posed by Iraq and"
2. "Enforce all relevant United Nations Council resolutions regarding Iraq."

Many other reasons were given to stir the emotions of the American public and the U.S. Congress, reasons that were grossly misleading and found not to be true. The pretense of a legal justification was a sham.

The fact that Congress is not permitted under the Constitution to transfer the war power to a president was ignored. Only Congress can declare war, if we were inclined to follow the rule of law. To add insult to injury, HJ RES 114 cited United Nations resolutions as justifications for the war. **Ignoring the Constitution, while using the UN to justify the war, showed callous disregard for the restraints carefully written in the**

331

Constitution. The authors deliberately wanted to make war difficult to enter without legislative debate, and they purposely kept the responsibility out of the hands of the executive branch. Surely they never dreamed an international government would have influence over our foreign policy or tell us when we should enter into armed conflict.

The legal maneuvering to permit this war was tragic to watch, but the notion that Saddam Hussein—a third world punk without an air force, navy, and hardly an army or any anti-aircraft weaponry—was an outright threat to the United States six thousand miles away, tells you how hysterical fear can be used to pursue a policy of needless war for quite different reasons.

Today, though, all the old reasons for going to war have been discredited, and are no longer used to justify continuing the war. Now we are told we must "complete the mission," and yet no one seems to know exactly what the mission is or when it can be achieved. By contrast, when war is properly declared against a country we can expect an all-out effort until the country surrenders. Without a declaration of war as the Constitution requires, it's left to the president to decide when to start the war and when the war is over. We had sad experiences with this process in Korea, and especially in Vietnam.

Pursuing this war merely to save face, or claim it's a way to honor those who already have died or been wounded, is hardly a reason that more people should die. We're told that we can't leave until we have a democratic Iraq. But what if Iraq votes to have a Shiite theocracy, which it looks like the majority wants as their form of government—and women, Christians, and Sunnis are made second-class citizens? It's a preposterous notion and it points out the severe shortcomings of a democracy where a majority rules and minorities suffer.

Thankfully, our Founding Fathers understood the great dangers of a democracy. They insisted on a constitutional Republic with a weak central government and an executive branch beholden to the legislative branch in foreign affairs. The sooner we realize we can't afford this war the better. We've gotten ourselves into a civil war within the Islamic community.

But could it be, as it had been for over a hundred years prior to our invasion, that oil really is the driving issue behind a foreign presence in the Middle East? It's rather ironic that the consequence of our intervention has been skyrocketing oil prices, with Iraqi oil production still significantly below pre-war levels.

If democracy is not all it's cracked up to be, and a war for oil is blatantly immoral and unproductive, the question still remains—why do

332

we fight? More precisely, why should we fight? When is enough killing enough? Why does man so casually accept war, which brings so much suffering to so many, when so little is achieved? Why do those who suffer and die so willingly accept the excuses for the wars that need not be fought? Why do so many defer to those who are enthused about war, and who claim it's a solution to a problem, without asking them why they themselves do not fight? It's always other men and other men's children who must sacrifice life and limb for the reasons that make no sense, reasons that are said to be our patriotic duty to fight and die for. How many useless wars have been fought for lies that deserved no hearing? When will it all end?

WHY WE SHOULD NOT FIGHT

Since no logical answers can be given for why we fight, it might be better to talk about why we should not fight. A case can be made that if this war does not end soon it will spread and engulf the entire region. We've already been warned that war against Iran is an option that remains on the table for reasons no more reliable than those given for the pre-emptive strike against Iraq. Let me give you a few reasons why this war in Iraq should not be fought.

It is not in our national interest. **Pursuing this war endangers our security, increases the chances of a domestic terrorist attack, weakens our defenses, and motivates our enemies to join together in opposition to our domineering presence around the world.** Does anyone believe that Russia, China, and Iran will give us free reign over the entire Middle East and its oil? Tragically, we're setting the stage for a much bigger conflict. It's possible that this war could evolve into something much worse than Vietnam.

This war has never been declared. It's not a constitutional war, and without a proper beginning there can be no proper ending. The vagueness instills doubts in all Americans, both supporters and non-supporters, as to what will be accomplished. Supporters of the war want total victory, which is not achievable with a vague mission. Now the majority of Americans are demanding an end to this dragged-out war that many fear will spread before it's over.

It's virtually impossible to beat a determined guerrilla resistance to a foreign occupying force. After 30 years, the Vietnam guerillas, following unbelievable suffering, succeeded in forcing all foreign troops from their homeland. History shows that Iraqi Muslims have always been determined to resist any foreign power on their soil. We ignored that history and learned nothing from Vietnam. How many lives, theirs and ours, are worth losing to prove the tenacity of guerilla fighters supported by a large number of local citizens?

Those who argue that it's legitimate to protect "our oil" someday must realize that it's not our oil, no matter how strong and sophisticated our military is. We know the war so far has played havoc with oil prices, and the market continues to discount problems in the region for years to come. No end is in sight regarding the uncertainty of Middle East oil production caused by this conflict.

So far our policies inadvertently have encouraged the development of an Islamic state, with Iranian-allied Shiites in charge. This has led to Iranian support for the insurgents, and has placed Iran in a position of becoming the true victor in this war as its alliance with Iraq grows. This could place Iran and its allies in the enviable position of becoming the oil powerhouse in the region, if not the world, once it has control over the oil fields near Basra.

This unintended alliance with Iran, plus the benefit to Osama bin Laden's recruiting efforts, will in the end increase the danger to Israel by rallying the Arab and Muslim people against us.

One of the original stated justifications for the war has been accomplished. Since 1998 the stated policy of the United States government was to bring about regime change and get rid of Saddam Hussein. This has been done, but instead of peace and stability we have sown the seeds of chaos. Nevertheless, the goal of removing Saddam Hussein has been achieved and is a reason to stop the fighting.

There were no weapons of mass destruction, no biological or chemical or nuclear weapons, so we can be assured the Iraqis pose no threat to anyone, certainly not to the United States.

No evidence existed to show an alliance between Iraq and al Qaeda before the war, and ironically our presence there is now encouraging al Qaeda and Osama bin Laden to move in to fill the vacuum we created. The only relationship between Iraq and 9/11 is that our policy in the Middle East continues to increase the likelihood of another terrorist attack on our homeland.

We should not fight because it's simply not worth it. What are we going to get for nearly 2,000 soldier deaths and 20 thousand severe casualties? Was the $350 billion worth it? This is a cost that will be passed on to future generations through an expanded national debt. I'll bet most

Americans can think of a lot better ways to have spent this money. Today's program of guns and butter will be more damaging to our economy than a similar program was in the 1960s, which gave us the stagflation of the 1970s. The economic imbalances today are much greater than they were in those decades.

Eventually, we will come to realize that the Wilsonian idealism of using America's resources to promote democracy around the world through force is a seriously flawed policy. Wilson pretended to be spreading democracy worldwide, and yet women in the U.S. at that time were not allowed to vote. Democracy, where the majority dictates the rules, cannot protect minorities and individual rights. And in addition, using force to impose our will on others almost always backfires. There's no reason that our efforts in the 21st Century to impose a Western-style government in Iraq will be any more successful than the British were after World War I. This especially can't work if democracy is only an excuse for our occupation and the real reasons are left unrecognized.

It boils down to the fact that we don't really have any sound reasons for continuing this fight. The original reasons for the war never existed, and the new reasons aren't credible. We hear only that we must carry on so those who have already suffered death and injury didn't do so in vain. If the original reasons for starting the war were false, simply continuing in the name of those fallen makes no sense. More loss of life can never justify earlier loss of life if they died for false reasons. This being the case, it's time to reassess the policies that have gotten us into this mess.

WHAT DOES ALL THIS MEAN?

The mess we face in the Middle East and Afghanistan, and the threat of terrorism within our own borders, are not a result of the policies of this administration alone. Problems have been building for many years, and have only gotten much worse with our most recent policy of forcibly imposing regime change in Iraq. We must recognize that the stalemate in Korea, the loss in Vietnam, and the quagmire in Iraq and Afghanistan all result from the same flawed foreign policy of interventionism that our government has pursued for over 100 years. It would be overly simplistic to say the current administration alone is responsible for the mess in Iraq.

By rejecting the advice of the Founders and our early presidents, our leaders have drifted away from the admonitions against entangling alliances and nation building. Policing the world is not our calling or our mandate.

Besides, the Constitution doesn't permit it. Undeclared wars have not enhanced our national security.

The consensus on foreign interventionism has been pervasive. Both major parties have come to accept our role as the world's policeman, despite periodic campaign rhetoric stating otherwise. The media in particular, especially in the early stages, propagandize in favor of war. It's only when the costs become prohibitive and the war loses popular support that the media criticize the effort.

It isn't only our presidents that deserve the blame when they overstep their authority and lead the country into inappropriate wars. Congress deserves equally severe criticism for acquiescing to the demands of the executive to go needlessly to war. It has been known throughout history that kings, dictators, and the executive branch of governments are always overly eager to go to war. This is precisely why our Founders tried desperately to keep decisions about going to war in the hands of the legislature. But this process has failed us for the last 65 years. Congress routinely has rubber stamped the plans of our presidents and even the United Nations to enter into war through the back door.

Congress at any time can prevent or stop all undue foreign entanglements pursued by the executive branch merely by refusing to finance them. The current Iraq war, now going on for 15 years, spans the administration of three presidents and many congresses controlled by both parties. This makes Congress every bit as responsible for the current quagmire as the president. But the real problem is the acceptance by our country as a whole of the principle of meddling in the internal affairs of other nations when unrelated to our national security. Intervention, no matter how well intended, inevitably boomerangs and comes back to haunt us. Minding our own business is not only economical; it's the only policy that serves our national security interests and the cause of peace.

The neoconservatives who want to remake the entire Middle East are not interested in the pertinent history of this region. Creating an artificial Iraq after World War I as a unified country was like mixing water and oil. It has only led to frustration, anger, and hostilities—with the resulting instability creating conditions ripe for dictatorships. The occupying forces will not permit any of the three regions of Iraq to govern themselves. This is strictly motivated by a desire to exert control over the oil. Self-determination and independence for each region, or even a true republican form of government with a minimalist central authority is never considered—yet it is the only answer to the difficult political problems this area faces.

The relative and accidental independence of the Kurds and the Shiites in the 1990s served those regions well, and no suicide terrorism existed during that decade.

The claim that our immediate withdrawal from Iraq would cause chaos is not proven. It didn't happen in Vietnam or even Somalia. Even today, the militias of the Kurds and the Shiites may well be able to maintain order in their regions much better than we can currently. Certainly the Sunnis can take care of themselves, and it might be in their best interests for all three groups not to fight each other when we leave. One thing for sure: if we left no more young Americans would have to die for an indefinable cause.

Instead, we have been forcing on the people of Iraq a type of democracy that, if implemented, will mean an Islamic state under Sharia law. Already we read stories of barbers no longer being safe shaving beards; Christians are threatened and forced to leave the country; and burqas are returning out of fear. Unemployment is over 50%, and oil production is still significantly below pre-war levels. These results are not worth fighting and dying for.

In this war, like all others, the propagandists and promoters themselves don't fight, nor do their children. It's always worth the effort to wage war when others must suffer and die. Many of those who today pump the nation up with war fever were nowhere to be found when their numbers were called in the 1960s—when previous presidents and Congresses thought so little about sending young men off to war. Then it was in their best interests to find more important things to do— despite the so-called equalizing draft.

The inability of taxpayers to fund both guns and butter has not deterred those who smell the glory of war. Notoriously, great nations fall once their appetite for foreign domination outstrips their citizens' ability or willingness to pay. We tried the "guns and butter" approach in the 1960s with bad results, and the same will happen again as a consequence of the current political decision not to cut back on any expenditure, domestic or foreign. Veto nothing is current policy! Tax, borrow, and print to pay the bills is today's conventional wisdom. The problem is that all the bills eventually must be paid. There's no free lunch, and no free war. The economic consequences of such a policy are well known and documented. Excessive spending leads to excessive deficits, higher taxes, and more borrowing and inflation—which spell economic problems that always clobber the middle class and the poor.

Already the suffering has begun. A lackluster recovery, low-paying

337

jobs, outsourcing, and social unrest already are apparent. This economic price we pay, along with the human suffering, is an extravagant price for a war that was started with false information and now is prolonged for reasons unrelated to our national security.

This policy has led to excessive spending overseas and neglect at home. It invites enemies to attack us, and drains the resources needed to defend our homeland and care for our own people. We are obligated to learn something from the tragedy of Katrina about the misallocation of funds away from our infrastructure to the rebuilding of Iraq after first destroying it. If ever there was a time for us to reassess our policy of foreign interventionism, it is today. It's time to look inward and attend to the constitutional needs of our people, and forget about the grandiose schemes to remake the world in our image through the use of force. These efforts not only are doomed to fail, as they have for the past one hundred years, but they invite economic and strategic military problems that are harmful to our national security interests.

We've been told that we must fight to protect our freedoms here at home. These reasons are given to make the sacrifices more tolerable and noble. Without an honorable cause, the suffering becomes intolerable. Hiding from the truth, though, in the end is no panacea for a war that promises no peace.

The most important misjudgment regarding Iraq that must be dealt with is the charge that Muslim terrorists attack us out of envy for our freedoms, our prosperity, and our way of life. There is no evidence this is the case. On the contrary, those who have extensively researched this issue conclude that the #1 reason suicide terrorists attack anywhere in the world is because their land is occupied by a foreign military power. Pretending otherwise and constantly expanding our military presence in more Arab and Muslim countries, as we have since 1990, has only increased the danger of more attacks on our soil, as well as in those countries that have allied themselves with us. If we deny this truth we do so at our own peril.

It's not unusual for the war crusaders to condemn those who speak the truth in an effort to end an unnecessary war. They claim those who want honest reasons for the enormous sacrifice are unpatriotic and un-American, but these charges only serve to exacerbate the social unrest. Any criticism of policy, no matter how flawed the policy, is said to be motivated by a lack of support for the troops. Yet it is preposterous to suggest that a policy that would have spared the lives of 1,900 servicemen and women lacks concern for the well being of our troops. The absence of good reasoning to pursue this war prompts the supporters of the war to demonize the skeptics and critics. They have no other defense.

Those who want to continue this war accuse those who lost loved ones in Iraq, and oppose the war, of using the dead for personal political gain. But what do the war proponents do when they claim the reason we must fight on is to honor the sacrifice of the military personnel we lost by completing the mission? The big difference is that one group argues for saving lives, while the other justifies more killing. And by that logic, the additional deaths will require even more killing to make sure they too have not died in vain. Therefore, the greater number who have died, the greater is the motivation to complete the mission. This defies logic. This argument to persevere has been used throughout history to continue wars that could and should have ended much sooner. This was true for World War I and Vietnam.

A sad realism struck me recently reading how our Marines in Afghanistan must now rely on donkey transportation in their efforts at nation building and military occupation. Evidently the Taliban is alive and well, as Osama bin Laden remains in this region. But doesn't this tell us something about our naïve assumption that our economic advantages and technical knowledge can subdue and control anybody? We're traversing Afghan mountains on donkeys, and losing lives daily in Baghdad with homemade primitive bombs. Our power and dominance clearly are limited by the determination of those who see us as occupiers, proving that just more money and sophisticated weapons won't bring us victory. Sophisticated weapons and the use of unlimited military power is no substitute for diplomacy designed to promote peace while reserving force only for defending our national interests.

Changing our policy of meddling in the affairs of others won't come quickly or easily. But a few signals to indicate a change in our attitude would go a long way to bringing peace to a troubled land.

1. We must soon (and Congress can do this through the budget process) stop the construction of all permanent bases in Iraq and any other Muslim country in the region. Think of how we would react if the Chinese had the military edge on us and laid claims to the Gulf of Mexico, building bases within the U.S. in order to promote their superior way of life. Isn't it ironic that we close down bases here at home while building new ones overseas? Domestic bases might well promote security, while bases in Muslim nations only elicit more hatred toward us.

2. The plans for the biggest U.S. embassy in the world, costing nearly

$1 billion, must be canceled. This structure in Baghdad sends a message, like the military bases being built, that we expect to be in Iraq and running Iraq for a long time to come.

3. All military forces, especially on the Arabian Peninsula, must be moved offshore at the earliest time possible. All responsibility for security and control of the oil must be transferred to the Iraqis from the United States as soon as possible, within months not years.

The time will come when our policies dealing with foreign affairs will change for the better. But that will be because we can no longer afford the extravagance of war. This will occur when the American people realize that war causes too much suffering here at home, and the benefits of peace again become attractive to us all. Part of this recognition will involve a big drop in the value of the dollar, higher interest rates, and rampant price inflation.

Though these problems are serious and threaten our freedoms and way of life, there's every reason to work for the traditional constitutional foreign policy that promotes peace over war, while not being tempted to mold the world in our image through force. We should not forget that what we did not achieve by military force in Vietnam was essentially achieved with the peace that came from our military failure and withdrawal of our armed forces. Today, through trade and peace, U.S. investment and economic cooperation have Westernized Vietnam far more than our military efforts.

We must remember initiating force to impose our will on others negates all the goodness for which we profess to stand. We cannot be fighting to secure our freedom if we impose laws like the Patriot Act and a national ID card on the American people.

Unfortunately, we have lost faith and confidence in the system of government with which we have been blessed. Today too many Americans support, at least in the early stages, the use of force to spread our message of hope and freedom. They too often are confused by the rhetoric that our armies are needed to spread American goodness. Using force injudiciously, instead of spreading the worthy message of American freedom through peaceful means, antagonizes our enemies, alienates our allies, and threatens personal liberties here at home while burdening our economy.

If confidence can be restored in our American traditions of peace and trade, our influence throughout the world would be enhanced just as it was once we rejected the military approach in Vietnam.

This change in policy can come easily once the people of this country decide that there is a better way to conduct ourselves throughout the world. Whenever the people turn against war as a tool to promote certain beliefs, the war ceases. That's what we need today. Then we can get down to the business of setting an example of how peace and freedom bring prosperity in an atmosphere that allows for excellence and virtue to thrive.

A powerful bureaucratic military state negates all efforts to preserve these conditions that have served America so well up until recent times. That is not what the American dream is all about. Without a change in attitude, the American dream dies: a simple change that restates the principles of liberty enshrined in our Constitution will serve us well in solving all the problems we face. The American people are up to the task; I hope Congress is as well. ■

"War prosperity is like the prosperity that an earthquake or a plague brings."—Ludwig von Mises

CHAPTER 17

Our adversaries perceive the motivations behind Wilsonianism much differently than do many in this country. We would do well to be aware of this fact.

March 28, 2006
MAKING THE WORLD SAFE FOR CHRISTIANITY
HON. RON PAUL of TEXAS
IN THE HOUSE OF REPRESENTATIVES

The top neo-con of the 20th Century was Woodrow Wilson. His supposed idealism, symbolized in the slogan "Make the world safe for democracy," resulted in untold destruction and death across the world for many decades. His deceit and manipulation of the pre-war intelligence from Europe dragged America into an unnecessary conflict that cost the world and us dearly. Without the disastrous Versailles Treaty, World War II could have been averted—and the rise to power of Communists around the world might have been halted.

We seem to never learn from our past mistakes. Today's neo-cons are as idealistically misled and aggressive in remaking the Middle East as the Wilsonian do-gooders. Even given the horrendous costs of the Iraq War and the unintended consequences that plague us today, the neo-cons are eager to expand their regime change policy to Iran by force.

The obvious shortcomings of our regime change and occupation of Afghanistan are now readily apparent. The Taliban was ousted from power, but they have regrouped and threaten the delicate stability that now exists in that country. Opium drug production is once again a major operation, with drugs lords controlling a huge area of the country outside Kabul. And now the real nature of the government we created has been revealed in the case of Abdul Rahman, the Muslim who faced a possible death sentence from the Karzai administration for converting to Christianity. Even now that Mr. Rahman is free due to Western pressure, his life remains in danger.

Our bombs and guns haven't changed the fact that the new puppet Afghan government still follows Sharia law. The same loyalty to Sharia exists in Iraq, where we're trying so hard to stabilize things. And all this is done in the name of spreading democracy.

The sad fact is that even under the despicable rule of Saddam Hussein, Christians were safer in Iraq than they are today. Saddam Hussein's foreign minister was a practicing Christian. Today thousands of Christians have fled Iraq following our occupation to countries like Jordan and Syria. Those Christians who have remained in Iraq fear for their lives every day. That should tell us something about the shortcomings of a policy that presumes to make the world safe for democracy.

The Muslim world is not fooled by our talk about spreading democracy and values. The evidence is too overwhelming that we do not hesitate to support dictators and install puppet governments when it serves our interests. When democratic elections result in the elevation of a leader or party not to our liking, we do not hesitate for a minute to undermine that government. This hypocrisy is rarely recognized by the American people. It's much more comfortable to believe in slogans, to believe that we're defending our goodness and spreading true liberty. We accept this and believe strongly in the cause, strongly enough to sacrifice many of our sons and daughters, and stupendous amounts of money, to spread our ideals through force.

Pointing out the lack of success is taboo. It seems of little concern to many Members of Congress that we lack both the moral right and constitutional authority to impose our will on other nations.

The toughest task is analyzing what we do from their perspective. We should try harder to place ourselves in the shoes of those who live in the Arab countries where our efforts currently are concentrated. We are outraged by a Muslim country that would even consider the death penalty for a Christian convert. But many Muslims see all that we do as a reflection of Western Christianity, which to them includes Europe and America. They see everything in terms of religion.

When our bombs and sanctions kill hundreds of thousands of their citizens, they see it as an attack on their religion by Christians. To them our actions represent a crusade to change their culture and their political systems. They do not see us as having noble intentions. Cynicism and realism tell them we're involved in the Middle East to secure the oil we need.

Our occupation and influence in the holy lands of the Middle East will always be suspect. This includes all the countries of the Arabian Peninsula, Iran, Iraq, and Afghanistan. Naively believing otherwise will guarantee continuing hostilities in Iraq. Our meddling will remain an incitement for radicals to strike us here at home in future terrorist attacks. All the intelligence gathering in the world will serve little purpose if we don't come to understand exactly why they hate us—despite the good intentions that many Americans hold dear. ■

The final two speeches here, given last year, deal with Iran. With our efforts in Iraq going poorly, some wish to distract attention by "putting another oar in the water." To open another front could be a disaster not just for our relations abroad but for our brave service members.

April 5, 2006
IRAN: THE NEXT NECON TARGET
HON. RON PAUL of TEXAS
IN THE HOUSE OF REPRESENTATIVES

It's been three years since the U.S. launched its war against Saddam Hussein and his weapons of mass destruction. Of course now almost everybody knows there were no WMDs, and Saddam Hussein posed no threat to the United States. Though some of our soldiers serving in Iraq still believe they are there because Saddam Hussein was involved in 9/11, even the administration now acknowledges there was no connection. Indeed, no one can be absolutely certain why we invaded Iraq. The current excuse, also given for staying in Iraq, is to make it a democratic state, friendly to the United States. There are now fewer denials that securing oil supplies played a significant role in our decision to go into Iraq and stay there. That certainly would explain why U.S. taxpayers are paying such a price to build and maintain numerous huge, permanent military bases in Iraq. They're also funding a new billion-dollar embassy—the largest in the world.

The significant question we must ask ourselves is: What have we learned from three years in Iraq? With plans now being laid for regime change in Iran, it appears we have learned absolutely nothing. There still are plenty of administration officials who daily paint a rosy picture of the Iraq we have created. But I wonder: If the past three years were nothing more than a bad dream, and our nation suddenly awakened, how many would, for national security reasons, urge the same invasion? Would we instead give a gigantic sigh of relief that it was only a bad dream, that we need not relive the three-year nightmare of death, destruction, chaos and stupendous consumption of tax dollars. Conceivably we would still see oil prices under $30 a barrel, and most importantly, 20,000 severe U.S. causalities would not have occurred. My guess is that 99% of all Americans would be thankful it was only a bad dream, and would never support the invasion knowing what we know today.

Even with the horrible results of the past three years, Congress is abuzz with plans to change the Iranian government. There is little resistance to the rising clamor for "democratizing" Iran, even though their current president, Mahmoud Almadinejad, is an elected leader. Though Iran is hardly a perfect democracy, its system is far superior to most of our Arab allies about which we never complain. Already the coordinating propaganda has galvanized the American people against Iran for the supposed threat it poses to us with weapons of mass destruction that are no more present than those Saddam Hussein was alleged to have had. **It's amazing how soon after being thoroughly discredited over the charges levied against Saddam Hussein the neo-cons are willing to use the same arguments against Iran.** It's frightening to see how easily Congress, the media, and the people accept many of the same arguments against Iran that were used to justify an invasion of Iraq.

Since 2001 we have spent over $300 billion, and occupied two Muslim nations—Afghanistan and Iraq. We're poorer but certainly not safer for it. We invaded Afghanistan to get Osama bin Laden, the ring leader behind 9/11. This effort has been virtually abandoned. Even though the Taliban was removed from power in Afghanistan, most of the country is now occupied and controlled by warlords who manage a drug trade bigger than ever before. Removing the Taliban from power in Afghanistan actually served the interests of Iran, the Taliban's arch enemy, more than our own.

The longtime neo-con goal to remake Iraq prompted us to abandon the search for Osama bin Laden. The invasion of Iraq in 2003 was hyped as a noble mission, justified by misrepresentations of intelligence concerning Saddam Hussein and his ability to attack his neighbors and us. This failed policy has created the current chaos in Iraq—chaos that many describe as a civil war. Saddam Hussein is out of power and most people are pleased. Yet some Iraqis, who dream of stability, long for his authoritarian rule. But once again, Saddam Hussein's removal benefited the Iranians, who consider Saddam Hussein an arch enemy.

Our obsession with democracy—which is clearly conditional, when one looks at our response to the recent Palestinian elections—will allow the majority Shia to claim leadership title if Iraq's election actually leads to an organized government. This delights the Iranians, who are close allies of the Iraqi Shia.

Talk about unintended consequences! This war has produced chaos, civil war, death and destruction, and huge financial costs. It has eliminated two of Iran's worst enemies and placed power in Iraq with Iran's best friends. Even this apparent failure of policy does nothing to restrain the current march toward a similar confrontation with Iran. What will it take for us to learn from our failures?

Common sense tells us the war in Iraq soon will spread to Iran. Fear of imaginary nuclear weapons or an incident involving Iran—whether planned or accidental—will rally the support needed for us to move on Muslim country #3. All the past failures and unintended consequences will be forgotten.

Even with deteriorating support for the Iraq war, new information, well planned propaganda, or a major incident will override the skepticism and heartache of our frustrating fight. **Vocal opponents of an attack on Iran again will be labeled unpatriotic, unsupportive of the troops, and sympathetic to Iran's radicals.**

Instead of capitulating to these charges, we should point out that those who maneuver us into war do so with little concern for our young people serving in the military, and theoretically think little of their own children if they have any. It's hard to conceive that political supporters of the war would consciously claim that a pre-emptive war for regime change, where young people are sacrificed, is only worth it if the deaths and injuries are limited to other people's children. This, I'm sure, would be denied—which means their own children are technically available for this sacrifice that is so often praised and glorified for the benefit of the families who have lost so much. If so, they should think more of their own children. If this is not so, and their children are not available for such sacrifice, the hypocrisy is apparent. Remember, most neo-con planners fall into the category of chicken hawks.

For the past three years, it's been inferred that if one is not in support of the current policy, one is against the troops and supports the enemy. Lack of support for the war in Iraq was said to be supportive of Saddam Hussein and his evil policies. This is an insulting and preposterous argument. Those who argued for the containment of the Soviets were never deemed sympathetic to Stalin or Khrushchev. Lack of support for the Iraq war should never be used as an argument that one was sympathetic to Saddam Hussein. Containment and diplomacy are far superior to confronting a potential enemy, and are less costly and far less dangerous—especially when there's no evidence that our national security is being threatened.

Although a large percentage of the public now rejects the various arguments for the Iraq war, three years ago they were easily persuaded by the politicians and media to fully support the invasion. Now, after three years of terrible pain for so many, even the troops are awakening from their slumber and sensing the fruitlessness of our failing effort. Seventy-two percent of our troops now serving in Iraq say it's time to come home, yet the majority still cling to the propaganda that we're there because of 9/11 attacks, something even the administration has ceased to claim. Propaganda is pushed on our troops to exploit their need to believe in a cause that's worth the risk to life and limb.

I smell an expanded war in the Middle East, and pray that I'm wrong. I sense that circumstances will arise that demand support, regardless of the danger and cost. Any lack of support, once again, will be painted as being soft on terrorism and al Qaeda. We will be told we must support Israel, support patriotism, support the troops, and defend freedom. The public too often only smells the stench of war after the killing starts. Public objection comes later on, but eventually it helps to stop the war. I worry that, before we can finish the war we're in and extricate ourselves, the patriotic fervor for expanding into Iran will drown out the cries of, "enough already!"

The agitation and congressional resolutions painting Iran as an enemy about to attack us have already begun. It's too bad we can't learn from our mistakes.

This time there will be a greater pretense of an international effort

348

sanctioned by the UN before the bombs are dropped. But even without support from the international community, we should expect the plan for regime change to continue. We have been forewarned that "all options" remain on the table. And there's little reason to expect much resistance from Congress. So far there's less resistance expressed in Congress for taking on Iran than there was prior to going into Iraq. It's astonishing that after three years of bad results and tremendous expense, there's little indication we will reconsider our traditional non-interventionist foreign policy. Unfortunately, regime change, nation building, policing the world, and protecting "our oil" still constitute an acceptable policy by the leaders of both major parties.

It's already assumed by many in Washington I talk to that Iran is dead serious about obtaining a nuclear weapon, and is a much more formidable opponent than Iraq. Besides, Mahmoud Almadinjad threatened to destroy Israel and that cannot stand. Washington sees Iran as a greater threat than Iraq ever was, a threat that cannot be ignored.

Iran's history is being ignored, just as we ignored Iraq's history. This ignorance or deliberate misrepresentation of our recent relationship to Iraq and Iran is required to generate the fervor needed to attack once again a country that poses no threat to us. Our policies toward Iran have been more provocative than toward Iraq. Yes, President Bush labeled Iran part of the axis of evil and unnecessarily provoked their anger at us. But our mistakes with Iran started a long time before this president took office.

In 1953 our CIA, with help of the British, participated in overthrowing the democratic elected leader, Mohamed Mossedech. We placed the Shah in power. He ruled ruthlessly but protected our oil interests, and for that we protected him—that is until 1979. We even provided him with Iran's first nuclear reactor. Evidently we didn't buy the argument that his oil supplies precluded a need for civilian nuclear energy. From 1953 to 1979, his authoritarian rule served to incite a radical Muslim opposition led by the Ayatollah Khomeini, who overthrew the Shah and took our hostages in 1979. This blowback event was slow in coming, but Muslims have long memories. The hostage crisis and overthrow of the Shah by the Ayatollah was a major victory for the radical Islamists. Most Americans either never knew about or easily forgot our unwise meddling in the internal affairs of Iran in 1953.

During the 1980s we further antagonized Iran by supporting the Iraqis in their invasion of Iran. This made our relationship with Iran worse, while sending a message to Saddam Hussein that invading a neighboring country is not all that bad. When Hussein got the message from our State Department that his plan to invade Kuwait was not of much concern to the United States he immediately proceeded to do so. We, in a way, encouraged him to do it almost like we encouraged him to go into Iran. Of course this time our reaction was quite different, and all of a sudden our friendly ally Saddam Hussein became our arch enemy. The American people may forget this flip-flop, but those who suffered from it never forget. And the Iranians remember well our meddling in their affairs. Labeling the Iranians part of the axis of evil further alienated them and contributed to the animosity directed toward us.

For whatever reasons the neoconservatives might give, they are bound and determined to confront the Iranian government and demand changes in its leadership. This policy will further spread our military presence and undermine our security. The sad truth is that the supposed dangers posed by Iran are no more real than those claimed about Iraq. The charges made against Iran are unsubstantiated, and amazingly sound very similar to the false charges made against Iraq. One would think promoters of the war against Iraq would be a little bit more reluctant to use the same arguments to stir up hatred toward Iran. The American people and Congress should be more cautious in accepting these charges at face value. Yet it seems the propaganda is working, since few in Washington object as Congress passes resolutions condemning Iran and asking for UN sanctions against her.

There is no evidence of a threat to us by Iran, and no reason to plan and initiate a confrontation with her. There are many reasons not to do so, however.

Iran does not have a nuclear weapon, and there's no evidence that she is working on one—only conjecture.

If Iran had a nuclear weapon, why would this be different from Pakistan, India, and North Korea having one? Why does Iran have less right to a defensive weapon than these other countries?

If Iran had a nuclear weapon, the odds of her initiating an attack against anybody—which would guarantee her own annihilation—are zero. And the same goes for the possibility she would place weapons in the hands of a non-state terrorist group.

Pakistan has spread nuclear technology throughout the world, in particular to the North Koreans. They flaunt international restrictions on nuclear weapons. But we reward them, just as we reward India.

We needlessly and foolishly threaten Iran, even though they have no nuclear weapons. But listen to what a leading Israeli historian, Martin Van Creveld, had to say about this: "Obviously, we don't want Iran to have a nuclear weapon, and I don't know if they're developing them, but if they're not developing them, they're crazy."

There's been a lot of misinformation regarding Iran's nuclear program. This distortion of the truth has been used to pump up emotions in Congress to pass resolutions condemning her and promoting UN sanctions.

IAEA Director General Mohamed El Baradi has never reported any evidence of "undeclared" sources or special nuclear material in Iran, or any diversion of nuclear material.

We demand that Iran prove it is not in violation of nuclear agreements, which is asking them impossibly to prove a negative. El Baradi states Iran is in compliance with the nuclear NPT required IAEA safeguard agreement.

We forget that the weapons we feared Saddam Hussein had were supplied to him by the U.S., and we refused to believe UN inspectors and the CIA that he no longer had them.

Likewise, Iran received her first nuclear reactor from us. Now we're hysterically wondering if someday she might decide to build a bomb in self interest.

Anti-Iran voices, beating the drums of confrontation, distort the agreement made in Paris and the desire of Iran to restart the enrichment process. Their suspension of the enrichment process was voluntary, and not a legal obligation. Iran has an absolute right under the NPT to develop and use nuclear power for peaceful purposes, and this is now said to be an egregious violation of the NPT. It's the U.S. and her allies that are distorting and violating the NPT. Likewise our provision of nuclear materials to India is a clear violation of the NPT.

The demand for UN sanctions is now being strongly encouraged by Congress. The "Iran Freedom Support Act," HR 282, passed in the International Relations Committee; and recently the House passed H Con Res 341, which inaccurately condemned Iran for violating its international nuclear non-proliferation obligations. At present, the likelihood of reason prevailing in Congress is minimal. Let there be no doubt: **The neoconservative warriors are still in charge, and are conditioning Congress, the media, and the American people for a pre-emptive attack on Iran.** Never mind that Afghanistan has unraveled and Iraq is in civil war. Serious plans are being laid for the next distraction that will further spread this war in the Middle East. The unintended consequences of this effort surely will be worse than any of the complications experienced in the three-year occupation of Iraq.

Our offer of political and financial assistance to foreign and domestic individuals who support the overthrow of the current Iranian government is fraught with danger and saturated with arrogance. Imagine how American citizens would respond if China supported similar efforts here in the United States to bring about regime change! How many of us would remain complacent if someone like Timothy McVeigh had been financed by a foreign power? Is it any wonder the Iranian people resent us and the attitude of our leaders? Even though El Baradi and his IAEA investigations have found no violations of the NPT-required IAEA safeguards agreement, the Iran Freedom Support Act still demands that Iran prove they have no nuclear weapons—refusing to acknowledge that proving a negative is impossible.

Let there be no doubt—although the words "regime change" are not found in the bill—that's precisely what they are talking about. Neoconservative Michael Ledeen, one of the architects of the Iraq fiasco, testifying before the International Relations Committee in favor of the IFSA, stated it plainly:

I know some Members would prefer to dance around the explicit declaration of regime change as the policy of this country, but anyone looking closely at the language and context of the IFSA and its close relative in the Senate, can clearly see that this is in fact the essence of the matter. You can't have freedom in Iran without bringing down the Mullahs.

Sanctions, along with financial and political support to persons and groups dedicated to the overthrow of the Iranian government, are acts of war. Once again we're unilaterally declaring a pre-emptive war against a country and a people that have not harmed us and who do not have the capacity to do so. Don't expect Congress to seriously debate a declaration of war resolution. For the past 56 years, Congress has transferred to the executive branch the power to go to war as it pleases, regardless of the tragic results and costs.

Secretary of State Rice recently signaled a sharp shift towards confrontation in Iran policy as she insisted on $75 million to finance propaganda, through TV and radio broadcasts into Iran. She expressed this need because of the so-called "aggressive" policies of the Iranian government. We're seven thousand miles from home, telling the Iraqis and the Iranians what kind of government they will have, backed up by the use of our military force, and we call them the aggressors. We fail to realize the Iranian people, for whatever faults they may have, have not in modern times aggressed against any neighbor. This provocation is so unnecessary, costly, and dangerous.

Just as the invasion of Iraq inadvertently served the interests of the Iranians, military confrontation with Iran will have unintended consequences. The successful alliance engendered between the Iranians and the Iraqi majority Shia will prove a formidable opponent for us in Iraq as that civil war spreads. Shipping in the Persian Gulf through the Straits of Hormuz may well be disrupted by the Iranians in retaliation for any military confrontation. Since Iran would be incapable of defending herself by conventional means, it seems logical that some might resort to a terrorist attack on us. They will not passively lie down, nor can they be destroyed easily.

One of the reasons given for going into Iraq was to secure "our" oil supply. This backfired badly: production in Iraq is down 50%, and world oil prices have more than doubled to $60 per barrel. Meddling with Iran could easily have a similar result. We could see oil over $120 a barrel and, and $6 gas at the pump. The obsession the Neo-cons have with remaking the Middle East is hard to understand. One thing that is easy to understand is that none of those who planned these wars expect to fight in them, nor do they expect their children to die in some IED explosion.

Exactly when an attack will occur is not known, but we have been forewarned more than once that all options remain on the table. The sequence of events now occurring (with regards to Iran) are eerily reminiscent of the hype prior to our pre-emptive strike against Iraq. We should remember the saying: "Fool me once shame on you, fool me twice, shame on me." It looks to me like the Congress and the country are open to being fooled once again.

Interestingly, **many early supporters of the Iraq war are now highly critical of the president, having been misled as to reasons for the invasion and occupation. But these same people are only too eager to accept the same flawed arguments for our need to undermine the Iranian government.**

The president's 2006 National Security Strategy, just released, is every bit as frightening as the one released in 2002 endorsing pre-emptive war. In it he claims: "We face no greater challenge from a single country than from Iran." He claims the Iranians have for 20 years hidden key nuclear activities—though the IAEA makes no such assumptions nor has the Security Council in these 20 years ever sanctioned Iran. The clincher in the National Security Strategy document is if diplomatic efforts fail, confrontation will follow. The problem is the diplomatic effort—if one wants to use that term—is designed to fail by demanding the Iranians prove an unproveable negative. The West—led by the U.S.—is in greater violation by demanding Iran not pursue any nuclear technology, even peaceful, that the NPT guarantees is their right.

The president states: Iran's "desire to have a nuclear weapon is unacceptable." A "desire" is purely subjective, and cannot be substantiated nor disproved. Therefore all that is necessary to justify an attack is if Iran fails to prove it doesn't have a "desire" to be like the United States, China, Russia, Britain, France, Pakistan, India, and Israel—whose nuclear missiles surround Iran. Logic like this to justify a new war, without the least consideration for a congressional declaration of war, is indeed frightening.

Common sense tells us Congress, especially given the civil war in Iraq and the mess in Afghanistan, should move with great caution in condoning a military confrontation with Iran.

CAUSE FOR CONCERN

Most Americans are uninterested in foreign affairs until we get mired down in a war that costs too much, last too long and kills too many U.S. troops. Getting out of a lengthy war is difficult, as I remember all too well with Vietnam while serving in the U.S. Air Force from 1963 to 1968. Getting into war is much easier. Unfortunately the legislative branch of our government too often defers to the executive branch, and offers little resistance to war plans even with no significant threat to our security. The need to go to war is always couched in patriotic terms and falsehoods regarding an imaginary eminent danger. Not supporting the effort is painted as unpatriotic and wimpish against some evil that's about to engulf us. The real reason for our militarism is rarely revealed and hidden from the public. Even Congress is deceived into supporting adventurism they would not accept if fully informed.

If we accepted the traditional American and constitutional foreign policy of non-intervention across the board, there would be no temptation to go along with these unnecessary military operations. A foreign policy of intervention invites all kinds of excuses for spreading ourselves around the world. The debate shifts from non-intervention versus interventionism, to where and for what particular reason we should involve ourselves. Most of the time, it's for less than honorable reasons. Even when cloaked in honorable slogans—like making the world safe for democracy—the unintended consequences and the ultimate costs cancel out the good intentions.

One of the greatest losses suffered these past 60 years from interventionism becoming an acceptable policy of both major parties is respect for the Constitution. Congress flatly has reneged on its huge responsibility to declare war. Going to war was never meant to be an executive decision, used indiscriminately with no resistance from Congress. The strongest attempt by Congress in the past 60 years to properly exert itself over foreign policy was the passage of the Foley Amendment, demanding no assistance be given to the Nicaraguan Contras. Even this explicit prohibition was flaunted by an earlier administration.

Arguing over the relative merits of each intervention is not a true debate, because it assumes that intervention per se is both moral and constitutional. Arguing for a Granada-type intervention because of its "success," and against the Iraq war because of its failure and cost, is not enough. We must once again understand the wisdom of rejecting entangling alliances and rejecting nation building. We must stop trying to police the world and instead embrace non-interventionism as the proper, moral, and constitutional foreign policy.

The best reason to oppose interventionism is that people die, needlessly, on both sides. We have suffered over 20,000 American casualties in Iraq already, and Iraq civilian deaths probably number over 100,000 by all reasonable accounts. The next best reason is that the rule of law is undermined, especially when military interventions are carried out without a declaration of war. Whenever a war is ongoing, civil liberties are under attack at home. The current war in Iraq and the misnamed war on terror have created an environment here at home that affords little constitutional protection of our citizen's rights. Extreme nationalism is common during wars. Signs of this are now apparent.

Prolonged wars, as this one has become, have profound consequences. No matter how much positive spin is put on it, war never makes a society wealthier. World War II was not a solution to the Depression as many claim. If a billion dollars is spent on weapons of war, the GDP records positive growth in that amount. But the expenditure is consumed by destruction of the weapons or bombs it bought, and the real economy is denied $1 billion to produce products that would have raised someone's standard of living.

Excessive spending to finance the war causes deficits to explode. There are never enough tax dollars available to pay the bills, and since there are not enough willing lenders and dollars available, the Federal Reserve must create enough new money and credit for buying Treasury Bills to prevent interest rates from rising too rapidly. Rising rates would tip off everyone that there are not enough savings or taxes to finance the war. This willingness to print whatever amount of money the government needs to pursue the war is literally inflation. Without a fiat monetary system, wars would be very difficult to finance, since the people would never tolerate the taxes required to pay for it. Inflation of the money supply delays and hides the real cost of war. The result of the excessive creation of new money leads to the higher cost of living everyone decries and the Fed denies. Since taxes are not levied, the increase in prices that results from printing too much money is technically the tax required to pay for the war.

The tragedy is that the inflation tax is borne more by the poor and the middle class than the rich. Meanwhile, the well-connected rich, the politicians, the bureaucrats, the bankers, the military industrialists, and the international corporations reap the benefits of war profits.

A sound economic process is disrupted with a war economy and monetary inflation. Strong voices emerge blaming the wrong policies for our problems, prompting an outcry for protectionist legislation. It's always easier to blame foreign producers and savers for our inflation, lack of savings, excess debt, and loss of industrial jobs. Protectionist measures only make economic conditions worse. Inevitably these conditions, if not corrected, lead to a lower standard of living for most of our citizens.

Careless military intervention is also bad for the civil disturbance that results. The chaos in the streets of America in the 1960s while the Vietnam War raged, aggravated by the draft, was an example of domestic strife caused by an ill-advised unconstitutional war that could not be won. The early signs of civil discord are now present. Hopefully we can extricate ourselves from Iraq and avoid a conflict in Iran before our streets explode as they did in the 60s.

In a way, it's amazing there's not a lot more outrage expressed by the American people. There's plenty of complaining but no outrage over policies that are not part of our American tradition. War based on false pretenses, 20,000 American casualties, torture policies, thousands jailed without due process, illegal surveillance of citizens, and unwarranted searches, yet no outrage. When the issues come before Congress, executive authority is maintained or even strengthened while real oversight is ignored.

Though many Americans are starting to feel the economic pain of paying for this war through inflation, the real pain has not yet arrived. We generally remain fat and happy, with a system of money and borrowing that postpones the day of reckoning. Foreigners, in particular the Chinese and Japanese, gladly participate in the charade. We print the money and they take it—as do the OPEC nations—and provide us with consumer goods and oil. Then they loan the money back to us at low interest rates, which we use to finance the war and our housing bubble and excessive consumption. This recycling and perpetual borrowing of inflated dollars allows us to avoid the pain of high taxes to pay for our war and welfare spending. It's fine until the music stops and the real costs are realized, with much higher interest rates and significant price inflation. That's when outrage will be heard, and the people will realize we can't afford the "humanitarianism" of the Neoconservatives.

The notion that our economic problems are principally due to the Chinese is nonsense. If the protectionists were to have their way, the problem of financing the war would become readily apparent and have immediate ramifications—none good. Today's economic problems, caused largely by our funny money system, won't be solved by altering exchange rates to favor us in the short run, or by imposing high tariffs. Only sound money with real value will solve the problems of competing currency devaluations and protectionist measures.

Economic interests almost always are major reasons for wars being fought. Noble and patriotic causes are easier to sell to a public who must pay and provide cannon fodder to defend the financial interests of a privileged class.

The fact that Saddam Hussein demanded Euros for oil in an attempt to undermine the U.S. dollar is believed by many to be one of the ulterior motives for our invasion and occupation of Iraq. Similarly, the Iranian oil purse now about to open may be seen as a threat to those who depend on maintaining the current monetary system with the dollar as the world's reserve currency.

The theory and significance of "peak oil" is believed to be an additional motivating factor for the U.S. and Great Britain wanting to maintain firm control over the oil supplies in the Middle East. The two nations have been protecting "our" oil interests in the Middle East for nearly a hundred years. With diminishing supplies and expanding demands, the incentive to maintain a military presence in the Middle East is quite strong. Fear of China and Russia moving into this region to assume more control alarms those who don't understand how a free market can develop substitutes to replace diminishing resources. Supporters of the military effort to maintain control over large regions of the world to protect oil fail to count the real costs once the DOD budget is factored in. Remember, invading Iraq was costly and oil prices doubled. Confrontation in Iran may evolve differently, but we can be sure it will be costly and oil prices will rise.

There are long-term consequences or blowback from our militant policy of intervention around the world. They are unpredictable as to time and place. 9/11 was a consequence of our military presence on Muslim holy lands; the Ayatollah Khomeini's success in taking over the Iranian government in 1979 was a consequence of our CIA overthrowing Mossadech in 1953. These connections are rarely recognized by the American people and never acknowledged by our government. We never seem to learn how dangerous interventionism is to us and to our security.

There are some who may not agree strongly with any of my arguments, and instead believe the propaganda: Iran and her president, Mahmoud Ahmadinejad, are thoroughly irresponsible and have threatened to destroy Israel. So all measures must be taken to prevent Iran from getting nukes— thus the campaign to intimidate and confront Iran.

First, Iran doesn't have a nuke and is nowhere close to getting one, according to the CIA. If they did have one, using it would guarantee almost instantaneous annihilation by Israel and the United States. **Hysterical fear of Iran is way out of proportion to reality. With a policy of containment, we stood down and won the Cold War against the Soviets and their 30,000 nuclear weapons and missiles.** If you're looking for a real kook with a bomb to worry about, North Korea would be high on the list. Yet we negotiate with Kim Jong il. Pakistan has nukes and was a close ally of the Taliban up until 9/11. Pakistan was never inspected by the IAEA as to their military capability. Yet we not only talk to her, we provide economic assistance—though someday Musharraf may well be overthrown and a pro-al Qaeda government put in place. We have been nearly obsessed with talking about regime change in Iran, while ignoring Pakistan and North Korea. It makes no sense and it's a very costly and dangerous policy.

The conclusion we should derive from this is simple: It's in our best interest to pursue a foreign policy of non-intervention. A strict interpretation of the Constitution mandates it. The moral imperative of not imposing our will on others, no matter how well intentioned, is a powerful argument for minding our own business. The principle of self-determination should be respected. Strict non-intervention removes the incentives for foreign

358

powers and corporate interests to influence our policies overseas. We can't afford the cost that intervention requires, whether through higher taxes or inflation. If the moral arguments against intervention don't suffice for some, the practical arguments should.

Intervention just doesn't work. It backfires and ultimately hurts American citizens both at home and abroad. Spreading ourselves too thin around the world actually diminishes our national security through a weakened military. As the superpower of the world, a constant interventionist policy is perceived as arrogant, and greatly undermines our ability to use diplomacy in a positive manner.

Conservatives, libertarians, constitutionalists, and many of today's liberals all have, at one time or another, endorsed a less interventionist foreign policy. There's no reason a coalition of these groups might not once again present the case for a pro-American, non-militant, non-interventionist foreign policy dealing with all nations. A policy of trade and peace, and a willingness to use diplomacy, is far superior to the foreign policy that has evolved over the past 60 years.

It's time for a change. ■

June 20, 2006
DIALOGUE IS KEY TO DEALING WITH IRAN
HON. RON PAUL of TEXAS
IN THE HOUSE OF REPRESENTATIVES

I am encouraged by recent news that the Administration has offered to put an end to our 26-year-old policy of refusing to speak with the Iranians.

While this is a positive move, I am still concerned about the pre-conditions set by the administration before it will agree to begin talks. Unfortunately, the main U.S. pre-condition is that the Iranians abandon their uranium enrichment program. But this is exactly what the negotiations are meant to discuss! How can a meaningful dialogue take place when one side demands that the other side abandon its position before talks can begin? Is this offer designed to fail so as to clear the way for military action while being able to claim that diplomacy was attempted? If the administration wishes to avoid this perception, it would be wiser to abandon pre-conditions and simply agree to talk to Iran.

By demanding that Iran give up its uranium enrichment program, the United States is unilaterally changing the terms of the Nuclear Non-

Proliferation treaty. **We must remember that Iran has never been found in violation of the Non-Proliferation Treaty. UN inspectors have been in Iran for years, and International Atomic Energy Agency Director El Baradei has repeatedly reported that he can find no indication of diversion of source or special nuclear materials to a military purpose.**

As a signatory of the Non-Proliferation Treaty, Iran has, according to the Treaty, the "inalienable right" to the "development research, production and use of nuclear energy for peaceful purposes without discrimination." Yet the United States is demanding that Iran give up that right even though, after years of monitoring, Iran has never been found to have diverted nuclear material from peaceful to military use.

As my colleagues are well aware, I am strongly opposed to the United Nations and our participation in that organization. In every Congress, I introduce a bill to get us out of the UN. But I also recognize problems with our demanding to have it both ways. On one hand, we pretend to abide by the UN and international law, such as when Congress cited the UN in its resolution authorizing the president to initiate war with Iraq. On the other hand, we feel free to completely ignore the terms of treaties—and even unilaterally demand a change in the terms of treaties—without hesitation. This leads to an increasing perception around the world that we are no longer an honest broker—that we are not to be trusted. Is this the message we really want to send at this critical time?

Some may argue that it does not matter whether the U.S. operates under double standards. We are the lone super-power and can do as we wish, they argue. But this is a problem of the rule of law. Are we a nation that respects the rule of law? **What example does it set for the rest of the world—including rising powers like China and Russia—when we change the rules of the game whenever we see fit?** Won't this come back to haunt us?

We need to remember that decision-making power under Iran's government is not all concentrated in the president. We are all familiar with the inflammatory rhetoric of President Ahmadinejad, but there are other governmental bodies in Iran that are more moderate and eager for dialogue. We have already spent hundreds of billions of dollars on a war in the Middle East. We cannot afford to continue on the path of conflict over dialogue and peaceful resolution. Unnecessarily threatening Iran is not in the U.S. interest and is not in the interest of world peace. ■

SUMMARY

A Foreign Policy for a Constitutional Republic
The Shortcomings of Foreign Interventionism

A policy of foreign intervention has numerous shortcomings. A casual look at the results of interventionist policies, both throughout history and in our American experience over the past hundred years, should convince a thoughtful person that the Founders' policy of nonintervention makes a great deal of sense. There are several reasons, of course, that nations cling to a policy of foreign entanglements. Political power is an aphrodisiac for most politicians, and too many of those with power develop grandiose dreams of world conquest. In the United States, private financial interests frequently benefit from foreign meddling, and foreign nationalistic interests also influence our policies and relationships in world affairs.

Another reason people succumb to dangerous policies of war and conquest relates to the false sense of patriotism promoted by our politicians. Most Americans do not want to appear weak; they enjoy expressions of strength and bravado. They fail to understand that self-confidence and true strength of conviction place restraints on the use of force, that peaceful solutions to problems require greater wisdom than unprovoked force.

Thus the missionary zeal to spread American goodness, always promoted as altruism by neoconservatives, gains public support. Military adventurism seems justified to many, especially before the costs, the failures, and the deaths are widely recognized.

The unintended consequences of foreign intervention often are delayed for years, obscuring the direct cause/effect relationship between certain

361

events. For instance, our unnecessary entrance into World War I was a principal cause of World War II and the subsequent Cold War. The CIA's removal of democratically elected President Mohammed Mossadegh in 1953 significantly contributed to the rise of the Iranian Islamic state.

Fear, usually orchestrated by government, is a powerful catalyst. Fear makes the people demand protection from every sinister evil lurking around the corner that's about to attack us. The embodiment of evil may well be a single demented individual, halfway around the world. Though incapable of attacking anyone, such an individual stirs up irrational fears and encourages policies that over time are not in our best interest.

When the people of a nation are fearful and insecure, it allows bullies in government to throw their weight around with promises of safety. Confidence and true strength, by contrast, encourage humility. Americans should never lack confidence and feel insecure, since we can resort, if needed, to a large stockpile of weapons to protect us from any outside conventional military threat. What we need is more confidence in ourselves, and a stronger belief in our traditions, so that we never are tempted to initiate force to make others live as we do. If we truly have an economic and political message worth emulating, our only responsibility is to set a standard that others will want to follow.

The notion that terrorists attack us because of our freedom and prosperity, and not for our actions abroad, is grossly wrong. If the American people continue to accept the argument that we are threatened because of our freedoms, rather than because American troops are stationed in many places where they are deeply resented, our problems can only get worse. This point is of profound importance, because the philosophy of foreign intervention must be challenged at its core if we truly are interested in peace and prosperity.

The success of government propagandists promoting war is nothing new. The public is too easily led to support war based on concocted fear. Getting into a war is a lot easier than getting out. It is not in the nature of government to admit mistakes and confess that any war, no matter how disastrous, should be ended.

The most succinct statement about how governments get their people to support war came from Hermann Goering at the Nuremberg trials after World War II:

> Why of course the people don't want war. Why should some poor slob on a farm want to risk his life in a war when the best he can get out of it is to come back to his farm in one

piece? Naturally, the common people don't want war, neither in Russia, nor in England, nor for that matter in Germany. That is understood. But, after all, it is the leaders of the country who determine the policy and it is always a simple matter to drag the people along, whether it is a democracy, or a fascist dictatorship, or a parliament, or a communist dictatorship. Voice or no voice, the people can always be brought to the bidding of the leaders. All you have to do is tell them they are being attacked, and denounce the peacemakers for lack of patriotism and exposing the country to danger. It works the same in any country.

It is rather frightening that a convicted Nazi war criminal latched on to an eternal truth!

The famous Christmas truce story from World War I is both heartbreaking and illustrative. On Christmas Eve, and for a few days following, soldiers on both sides spontaneously suspended fighting at the front, exchanged gifts, and sang Christmas carols in a true display of Christmas spirit. The thuggish governments on both sides soon demanded a resumption of the insanity later called the "war to end all wars." Instead, WWI war ushered in the bloodiest of all centuries—a century that saw the deaths of over one hundred million people, mostly non-combatants.

How much longer must the world tolerate the insanity of senseless wars, forced on the people by their various governments appealing to false patriotism, before the true nature of state war propaganda is exposed once and for all?

It should be harder to promote war, especially when there are so many regrets in the end. In the last 60 years, the American people have had little say over decisions to wage war. We have allowed a succession of presidents and the United Nations to decide when and if we go to war, without an express congressional declaration as the Constitution mandates.

Since 1945, our country has been involved in over 70 active or covert foreign engagements. On numerous occasions we have provided weapons and funds to both sides in a conflict. It is not unusual for our so-called allies to turn on us and use these weapons against American troops. In recent decades we have been both allies and enemies of Saddam Hussein, Osama bin Laden, and the Islamists in Iran. And where has it gotten us?

The endless costs resulting from our foolish policies, in human lives, injuries, tax dollars, inflation, and deficits, will burden generations to come.

For civilization to advance, we must reduce the number of wars fought.

Two conditions must be met if we hope to achieve this.

First, all military (and covert paramilitary) personnel worldwide must refuse to initiate offensive wars beyond their borders. This must become a matter of personal honor for every individual. Switzerland is an example of a nation that stands strongly prepared to defend herself, yet refuses to send troops abroad looking for trouble.

Second, the true nature of war must be laid bare, and the glorification must end. Instead of promoting war heroes with parades and medals for wars not fought in the true defense of our country, we should more honestly contemplate the real results of war: death, destruction, horrible wounds, civilian casualties, economic costs, and the loss of liberty at home.

The neoconservative belief that war is inherently patriotic, beneficial, manly, and necessary for human progress must be debunked. These war promoters never send themselves or their own children off to fight. Their hero, Machiavelli, must be buried once and for all.

Some believe economic sanctions and blockades are acceptable alternatives to invasion and occupation. But these too are acts of war, and those on the receiving end rarely capitulate to the pressure. More likely they remain bitter enemies, and resort to terrorism when unable to confront us in a conventional military fashion. We already have been forewarned by the Iranians, and we should not ignore it.

Inflation, sanctions, and military threats all distort international trade and hurt average people in all countries involved, while usually not really hurting the targeted dictators themselves. Our bellicose approach encourages protectionism, authoritarianism, militant nationalism, and go-it-alone isolationism. Our government preaches free trade and commerce, yet condemns those who want any restraints on the use of our military worldwide. We refuse to see how isolated we have become. Our loyal allies are few, and while the UN does our bidding only when we buy the votes we need, our enemies multiply. A billion Muslims around the world now see the U.S. as a pariah.

Our policies breed profiteering and corruption. The military-industrial complex expands; tens of billions of dollars disappear into the black hole of our failed policies in the Persian Gulf. And essentially nothing is done about it.

Our military is more often used to protect private capital overseas, such as oil and natural resources, than it is to protect our own borders. Protecting ourselves from real outside threats is no longer the focus of defense policy, as globalists become more influential inside and outside our government.

The weapons industry never actually advocates killing to enhance its profits, but a policy of endless war and eternal enemies benefits it greatly. Some advocate Cold War strategies, like those used against the Soviets, against the unnamed "terrorists." It's good for business!

Many neoconservatives are not bashful about this:

Thus, paradoxically, peace increases our peril, by making discipline less urgent, encouraging some of our worst instincts, and depriving us of some of our best leaders. The great Prussian general Helmuth von Moltke knew whereof he spoke when he wrote a friend, 'Everlasting peace is a dream, not even a pleasant one; war is a necessary part of God's arrangement of the world...Without war the world would deteriorate into materialism.' As usual, Machiavelli dots his i's and crosses the t's: it's not just that peace undermines discipline and thereby gives the destructive vices greater sway. If we actually achieved peace, 'Indolence would either make (the state) effeminate or shatter her unity; and two things together, or each by itself, would be the cause of her ruin...' This is Machiavelli's variation on a theme by Mitterrand: the absence of movement is the beginning of defeat. (Michael Ledeen; *"Machiavelli on Modern Leadership"*)

Those like Ledeen who approvingly believe in "perpetual struggle" generally are globalists, uninterested in national sovereignty and borders. True national defense is of little concern to them. That's why military bases are closed in the United States regardless of their strategic value, while several new bases are built in the Persian Gulf, even though they provoke our enemies to declare jihad against us. The new Cold War justifies everything.

War, and the threat of war, are big government's best friend. Liberals support big government social programs, and conservatives support big government war policies, thus satisfying two major special interest groups. And when push comes to shove, the two groups cooperate and support big government across the board—always at the expense of personal liberty. Both sides pay lip service to freedom, but neither stands against the welfare/warfare state and its promises of unlimited entitlements and endless war.

In the post 9/11 atmosphere, there is no resistance to any military expenditure. The climate of fear stirred by false patriotism grants more and more unchecked power to the executive branch. The Supreme Court has little power to resist. Both political parties in Congress have participated in creating this new America, with warrantless searches, perpetual surveillance, national ID cards, secret prisons, the possible denial of habeas corpus, and even torture.

Institutionalizing the principle of preemptive war surely will be one of the gravest mistakes made in this new century. A secret war or CIA coup, although bad, is nothing compared to an openly declared policy (established for very questionable reasons) that we now have a moral right and duty to start wars of our bidding. We have crossed the Rubicon. Unless we reverse the policy of preemptive war and fully reinstate habeas corpus, the American republic will remain a dead letter.

This attitude of moral superiority, which to many justifies the initiation of force, makes it virtually impossible for us to understand how our efforts will be received. We have no desire to understand or empathize with the people we propose to democratize. The hundreds of thousands who die become mere collateral damage. Our hatred is driven by artificially generated fear. The propaganda of the neoconservatives and the Christian Zionists makes every citizen of Iraq, no matter how innocent, a potentially hated enemy combatant. No sympathy is expressed even for the hundreds of thousands of Iraqi Christians forced to flee to Syria to escape the chaos. Christian leaders who promote this war seem callous and cruel as they anticipate and welcome the coming of Armageddon.

Intervention creates endless commitments and ongoing unintended consequences. Treaties, and membership in international bodies like the UN, obligate our military and even future generations to fight wars without the slightest involvement by Congress.

Secretary of State Rice, on a recent trip to the Far East, reassured the nation of Japan that the U.S. will defend her if ever attacked. Nobody asked where she got the authority to make this commitment requiring the blood of future generations. Likewise, all recent presidents have reiterated our obligation to bleed for Israel, no matter what, without the slightest hint that Congress is responsible for making such a serious decision. How can one generation of Americans commit another generation to such an overwhelming commitment with absolutely no debate? We obligate ourselves to future wars without reservation, as we have done in South Korea. Our troops are exposed to a possible nuclear attack by North Korea, even against the will of the majority of South Koreans.

Our commitments seem endless. It's estimated we have over 700 bases around the world, in 130 different countries. This expansive military network developed over many decades, accelerating recently due to the vacuum left by the demise of the Soviet empire.

In October 2006, President Bush let it be known there will be no letting up. We will assert our jurisdiction not only worldwide, but in space as well. The president declared, by Executive Order, that the U.S. will determine which countries have access to space. He, by himself, has announced that outer space will be militarized and controlled by the United States.

A hegemonic world power is one thing; the sole power to control outer space is quite another. Funding an empire both worldwide and in outer space is not a simple matter. We mock Kim Jong il for impoverishing millions of his own people to glorify his elite military forces. But in a subtle way that is exactly what is happening here, only at a different level and pace.

Wealth is transferred from the poor to the politically connected rich (including defense contractors) through the inflationary process. The pseudo-strength of the dollar allows endless money creation to pay the bills to police the world. In a country like North Korea, there is direct confiscation from the poor to support the military. In the U.S. it's indirect but insidious. The slow process manifests in the steady decline of living standards through inflation for the poor, the middle class, and the elderly on fixed incomes.

The grandiose and unrealistic plans for policing the world and outer space eventually will collide with limits imposed by reality. These limits will not be established by the arrival of wise and frugal congressmen to Washington. No, the limits of our policies will be exposed by military failures; the loss of political support from the people; and a worldwide rejection of the over-inflated U.S. dollars used to pay our bills. The cost of runaway military spending essentially brought down the Soviet Union, and soon likely will bring down North Korea. We are blindly doing the same thing to ourselves.

It is time for us to reassess our endless commitments, made within the framework of an interventionist foreign policy fraught with foreign entanglements. The results of this policy over the last one hundred years should motivate all Americans to demand a change, but it looks like only a financial crisis will compel us to change our ways.

That the Constitution grants no authority for our government to police the world and engage in grandiose nation-building schemes should have

367

prevented us from embarking on such a dangerous course long ago. In the years following WWII, Congress wrongly ceded responsibility over if and when we go to war to the executive branch. And there's no evidence in Washington that this will be reversed.

The Founders made a serious attempt to limit presidential authority over war powers, but tragically the restraints placed on the executive have failed. This has contributed greatly to the expansion of the state, the diminution of our liberties, and the destruction of our republican form of government.

The lack of congressional restraint on the executive branch has allowed insecure and weak leaders to compensate with bellicosity and aggression to exert influence around the world. They have succumbed to the temptation of the corrupting influence of power. For too many politicians, being a bully with weapons equals strong and positive political leadership. They deliberately pursue an aggressive military policy, not to defend our national security, but to assuage their sense of inadequacy. The tragic irony is that bombast and warmongering are precisely the cause of our current vulnerability to foreign terrorist attacks.

We should consider what a foreign policy of nonintervention looks like, one compatible with a constitutional republic.

First - It would be based on an international "golden rule." The basic principle would be: never initiate an attack on another country! There are a few extreme exceptions to this when a very clear and present danger is obvious, just as the president has the authority to respond to an actual attack without explicit congressional approval. We must remember, however, that this has never happened in all our history. A president under extreme conditions can always act to defend the country, and then as soon as possible go to Congress for a declaration of war.

The important point is that our presidents should have no authority to initiate preemptive war by Executive Order or with a UN resolution.

Second - Under a republican form of government, our officials should recognize the inherent right of self-determination in other nations. This encourages smaller government, ethnic choices, and cultural preferences. This principle was successful in the countries that gained independence from the Soviets in eastern Europe and in central Asia after the Cold War ended.

This principle rejects the notion that outsiders should set boundaries while ignoring the choices of local populations. The artificial nature of national boundaries in the Middle East and the Persian Gulf, established following World War I and World War II, has been the source of much fighting and dying over the decades. An artificial boundary in Korea has maintained a state of perpetual war between North and South for 50 years, with us standing between them. The absence of such an arbitrary division since 1975 has unified Vietnam, which now is more Westernized than ever. What could not be achieved with war has been achieved by diplomacy, time, and a willingness to trade and talk with the people of Vietnam.

We often fail to put ourselves in the place of those nations in which we intervene. Suppose we had a border dispute between Mexico and the United States. How many Americans would be happy for the Chinese or the Russians to dictate a resolution of the conflict? Obviously none! Yet this is exactly what we keep doing worldwide, with miserable results.

Third - A policy of strategic independence is far better than international entanglements. UN mandates, backed by American troops and money, ironically lead to neo-isolationism. Those who advocate the traditional American (and constitutional) policy of nonintervention are ridiculed as "isolationists" by the authoritarians who want the U.S. to decide all disputes. Yet it's their interventionist policies, especially in the last six years, which have isolated us, reduced our allies, and increased our enemies. We are more ostracized and isolated in the world than ever before.

A republic that remains neutral and noninterventionist in foreign affairs would not dispense foreign aid. It would energetically seek diplomatic solutions to international disputes. No direct subsidies would be given to other governments, politicians, or factions involved in internal disputes abroad, and there would be no subsidized loans. There would be no sanctions or blockades placed on other countries, unless war was declared. There would be no threats or intimidation in order to have our way in foreign affairs. There would be no treaties promising to commit later generations to war. There would be no covert or open CIA coups to overthrow particular governments.

In contrast, a policy of strategic independence would encourage true free trade and friendship with all nations. Our military would be used for true national defense. Not only would this policy generate fewer enemies, it would cost far less. Foreign meddling actually undermines true national defense. Today our borders are neglected, our military is demoralized, our military equipment is in terrible condition, and we're threatened with a draft to maintain troop levels. We do not provide adequate care for our injured and sick military veterans. Already over 150,000 veterans from the current Iraq war receive disability benefits. Soon the expense of this policy will overwhelm us. Columbia University Professor Joseph Stiglitz recently revised his estimate upward regarding the total cost of this war: two trillion dollars! And yet the neoconservatives agitate for taking on Iran, Syria, and North Korea.

The more the world accepts the right of people to own property, and understands that all voluntary economic and social contracts should be respected, the better the chance for world peace and prosperity. But these principles cannot be forced on others. Using force only builds resistance to the true principles of liberty that made American great. Using force contradicts the moral foundation of a free society. The harder we try to force others to accept our principles, the more it undermines liberty here at home. We should work to make sure the steady erosion of our liberties here at home, both economic and personal, does not continue. We should not pretend or expect that we can force others to accept our way of life, when we so desperately need to clean our own house.

The reform of monetary policy is absolutely necessary for freedom and prosperity. Many economic distortions and political imbalances result from a world filled with paper money, where governments maintain the monopoly right to counterfeit at will. Just as our interventionist foreign policy will end out of necessity, so too will the fiat dollar system.

In Washington, most politicians line up with their party leaders on the issue of war. It's strictly a partisan issue for many. Republican congressional leaders strongly opposed Clinton's illegal involvement in the Balkans war. Most Democrats adamantly supported Clinton.

Tom DeLay, who later championed Bush's war in the Persian Gulf, said this when Clinton attacked Serbia: "Many who argue we can't pull out say we should stay to save face. If for no other reason I would like to ask these people, was it worth it to stay in Vietnam to save face? President Clinton has never explained to the American people why he was involving the U.S. military in a civil war in a sovereign nation." He never asked the same questions of Mr. Bush.

Unfortunately, Congress is too willing to support the executive branch once we get involved in illegal wars. The Democrats have offered only feeble resistance to the Iraq War, while Republicans in the House and Senate have been enthusiastic cheerleaders—even though they eloquently argued against Clinton's war in Yugoslavia.

Overall, both parties are very supportive of the neoconservative policy of preemption that has proven so unsuccessful in Iraq. Soon this may escalate with an attack on Iran.

More than fifty years ago we had a great Republican leader from the old school of conservatism. Senator Robert Taft spoke out forcefully for a sensible, noninterventionist foreign policy, and warned us against initiating war against a perceived enemy:

> *There are a good many Americans who talk about an American century in which America will dominate the world. They rightly point out that the United States is so powerful today that we should assume a moral leadership in the world...The trouble with those who advocate this policy is that they really do not confine themselves to moral leadership...In their hearts they want to force on these foreign peoples through the use of American money and even, perhaps, American arms, the policies which moral leadership is able to advance only through the sound strength of its principles and the force of its persuasion. I do not think this moral leadership ideal justifies our engaging in any preventive war...I do not believe any policy which has behind it the threat of military force is justified as part of the basic foreign policy of the United States except to defend the liberty of our own people.* (Senator Robert A. Taft, *A Foreign Policy for Americans,* 1951.)

It's rather sad that these sentiments expressed by a conservative Republican have been forgotten. For most of the 20th century Democratic politicians involved us in foreign wars, leaving Republicans to pick up the pieces and benefit politically. Yet now the Republican Party clearly is perceived as the more militantly aggressive party. This statement from Senator Taft should refresh our memories regarding the traditional and proper conservative view that is cautious toward war, counsels nonintervention, and champions liberty. No politician should be rejected for advocating diplomacy and trade over preemptive war. Trade and open diplomatic relations surely are the best way to achieve peace and prosperity for the maximum number of people around the world. All nations, including republics like ours, should be prepared to fight when they must. Proper and sensible policies among nations could make wars very rare, however. A policy of nonintervention would make America stronger, wealthier, more influential, and a respected beacon of liberty.

Other books by Ron Paul

The Case for Gold
Gold, Peace, and Prosperity
Ten Myths About Paper Money
Challenge to Liberty
Freedom Under Siege
Mises and Austrian Economics—a Personal View

To order additional copies of this book or other materials from Congressman Ron Paul and the FREE foundation, including his monthly newsletter the *Freedom Report*, please contact us at:

FREE
P.O. Box 1776
Lake Jackson, Texas 77566
979-265-3034
www.FREE-NEFL.com